DIFFERENTIAL PSYCHOLOGY

Individual and Group Differences in Behavior

BY

ANNE ANASTASI

Chairman, Department of Psychology,
Queens College, New York

THE MACMILLAN COMPANY   NEW YORK

Published May, 1937. Reprinted January, 1939;
May, 1940.

SET UP AND ELECTROTYPED BY T. MOREY & SON

· PRINTED IN THE UNITED STATES OF AMERICA ·

PREFACE

The present book was written with three major aims in mind. In the first place, differential psychology is here presented, not as a separate field of psychology, but as one approach to the understanding of behavior. Its fundamental problems are no different from those of general psychology. It is apparent that if we can explain satisfactorily why individuals react differently from each other, we shall understand why each individual reacts as he does. The data of differential psychology should help to clarify the fundamental mechanisms of behavior in general. It is from this point of view that the problems of individual and group differences are surveyed in the present text.

A second aim of the book has been to coördinate the various topics which have heretofore been loosely joined together under the caption of "individual differences." With the rapid increase in material on any one of these topics, there has appeared a tendency to regard each segment as an independent field of investigation. The mutual interrelation of the various problems has become obscured by the accumulation of data at a more rapid rate than it could comfortably be assimilated. It is an undoubted fact that the various branches of differential psychology have undergone a phenomenal development during the past two decades. This has resulted in an increasing specialization of interest among research workers and a frequent disregard of the broader implications of the data. Many apparently unrelated aspects of differential psychology can profitably be considered together.

··

Thus the data on such questions as familial resemblance, the relationship between mental and physical traits, the growth of abilities, and the organization of mental traits can be shown to have a mutual bearing upon each other. The writer has endeavored to bear constantly in mind the interrelationships among different types of investigations and has attempted to present a systematic organization and integration of the material.

Finally, it has been our aim to report the major data and conclusions of differential psychology in a form suitable for the college student. The present book has, in fact, grown out of a course in differential psychology which the writer has taught at Barnard College since 1930. Much of the material of differential psychology has heretofore been available only in journal articles and highly technical books. Consequently, certain topics have been customarily omitted or touched upon lightly in discussions of individual differences, being considered too "difficult" for the elementary student. Mental organization is a good example of such a topic, although by no means the only one. Even the more advanced student of psychology who has specialized in other phases of the subject often finds it impossible to keep informed on current developments in certain branches of differential psychology. The writer believes that a non-technical and easily comprehensible presentation of such material is both feasible and desirable. An understanding of the basic concepts and major findings of any problem need not be limited to those who have mastered its specialized methodologies.

The present book could serve either as a text in special courses on differential psychology and "individual differences" or as a supplementary text in such courses as general, applied, or educational psychology, and mental testing. It also provides relevant material for courses in social psychology.

There is at present a growing interest in the origin of psychological differences among individuals and especially among groups. Many of the problems of differential psychology have become the subject of frequent popular discussion and controversy. Thus the subject matter of this branch of psychology should prove intrinsically valuable. Moreover, as has already been pointed out, familiarity with the main principles of individual variation will strengthen the student's understanding of general psychology. Lastly, the analysis of the problems and difficulties encountered in the investigation of individual differences should foster a critical attitude towards all data on these questions. Throughout the present book, special emphasis has been placed upon the examination of common sources of errors and pitfalls in the interpretation of obtained facts. We have thus hoped to provide the student with certain tools whereby he may evaluate for himself a set of data with which he is confronted. It seemed to the writer that this was more valuable than a mere compendium of facts. The development of critical ability and of a dispassionate and objective attitude towards human behavior is an urgent need in a world of rapidly changing values.

The writer is indebted to Prof. H. L. Hollingworth of Barnard College for a critical reading of the manuscript and for many stimulating comments. She wishes to acknowledge the invaluable assistance of Dr. J. P. Foley, Jr., of The George Washington University for an intensive reading of the entire manuscript in its early stages and for countless specific suggestions. Grateful acknowledgment is also made to the many authors whose works have been quoted in this book and especially to those who have made accessible to the writer unpublished data from their investigations. Finally, thanks are extended to the various publishers who have generously granted permission for the reproduction of figures and quotations from their publications. In all of these cases, specific acknowledgment has been made in the appropriate places.

ANNE ANASTASI

BARNARD COLLEGE
COLUMBIA UNIVERSITY
April, 1937

TABLE OF CONTENTS

INTRODUCTION

No topic has greater significance for the organization of life among human beings than that of the nature and basis of the individual differences among those human beings. Except for individual differences among us there would be no such distinctions as right and wrong; just and unjust; health and illness. There would be no laws, no courts, no systems of ethics; no politics and no need of government. Individual differences are responsible for such institutions as education, for such episodes as wars, and probably, if the truth were known, for culture, for science, for the church, and for nearly everything else that is characteristically human.

Another striking fact is the way in which activities and institutions, springing from human individual differences, become in turn responsible for further differentiation and variation. There can be no doubt that human diversity in some characteristics is biological in origin, and that to some extent we are different one from another because of the different stocks from which we spring and because of the multitudinous influences that make variation intrinsic to all living things. It is still true that "Men do not gather grapes of thorns nor figs of thistles."

It is equally true that much of human diversity, especially in the more subtle psychological traits, is a reflection of the incidence of differential environmental effects. Theories of the basis of individual differences themselves exhibit variation. They range from a dogmatic hereditarianism, with a somewhat aristocratic air of determinism, through sane and balanced recognitions of

PART I
FUNDAMENTAL PRINCIPLES OF INDIVIDUAL VARIATION

CHAPTER I

HISTORICAL INTRODUCTION

Man has always been aware of differences among his fellow-beings. He has, to be sure, entertained various theories, beliefs, or superstitions regarding the causes of such differences, and has interpreted them differently according to his own traditional background, but he has at all times accepted the fact of their existence. Among primitive peoples, unusual deviations in behavior are clearly recognized. Thus many primitive groups acknowledge exceptional artistic talent among their members and encourage the development of specialized artists. The presence of hysterical or epileptoid symptoms, paranoid trends, and similar peculiarities of behavior has frequently been regarded as an index of religious or magical powers and has been treated accordingly. The history of religion is replete with such instances. At any level of cultural development, specialization of labor itself implies a tacit assumption of differences among people.

Nor is this response to individual differences limited to the human species. Instances from infrahuman behavior can readily be found. The acceptance of certain individuals as "leaders" by herds of elephants, buffaloes, and similar gregarious animals has been widely discussed in the literature both of fact and of fiction. In communities of baboons, a certain member is posted as "sentinel" to watch for the approach of danger and warn the others by conventional cries. The frequently described "hacking" or hen-pecking behavior of chickens is another case in point. A definite relationship of social domination is

3

often displayed by chickens in the barnyard, this fighting or "hacking" behavior usually centering about the acquisition of food. In such cases, A will attack B, although the reverse will not occur. Violent conflicts often ensue when the authority of the chief "hacker" in the group is disputed. These and many other examples all serve to suggest a widespread differential response to individuals within a group.

The objective and quantitative investigation of individual differences in behavior phenomena is the domain of differential psychology. What is the nature and extent of such differences? What can be discovered as to their causes? How are the differences affected by training, growth, physical conditions? In what manner are the differences in various traits related to one another, or organized? These are some of the fundamental questions raised by differential psychology and will be treated in Part I of the present book.

Differential psychology is also concerned with an analysis of the nature and characteristics of major traditional groupings, such as the subnormal and the genius, the sexes, and racial, national, and cultural divisions. This furnishes the subject-matter of Part II. The study of such group differences serves a threefold purpose. In the first place, one cannot ignore the fact that such groupings are being made in the practical realm of everyday life. These distinctions cannot be swept away casually on the grounds that, perhaps, the study of individual differences reveals no need for them or for any sharp divisions into clear-cut categories. Certain groups are recognized and responded to as distinctive in our present-day society. For a purely practical reason, therefore, these groups must be investigated, in the hope that the specific findings may throw some light upon their nature and possibly further a more intelligent practical understanding of them.

Secondly, the comparative investigation of different groups should help to clarify the fundamental problems of individual differences in general. In such groups we can see the principles of individual differences in operation and can note their effects. Group differences in behavior, when considered in conjunction with other concomitant differences among the groups, furnish an excellent available means of analyzing the causes of variability.

Thirdly, the comparison of a psychological phenomenon as it occurs in different groups may contribute towards a clearer understanding of the phenomenon itself. The findings of general psychology, when tested in widely varying groups, are sometimes found to be not so general as was supposed. To study a phenomenon in all its varied manifestations is to have a better grasp of its essential nature.

Notwithstanding the early and widespread recognition of individual differences in the practical adjustments of everyday life, the systematic investigation of such differences is a relatively recent development in psychology. A brief historical survey of theories as well as investigations in the field of differential psychology will be given.

INDIVIDUAL DIFFERENCES IN PRE-EXPERIMENTAL PSYCHOLOGICAL THEORY

One of the earliest instances of explicit recognition of individual differences is to be found in the *Republic* of Plato. A fundamental aim of Plato's ideal state is, in fact, the assignment of individuals to the special tasks for which they are suited. In Book II of the *Republic* appears the following statement: "Really, I said, it is not improbable; for I recollect myself, after your answer, that, in the first place, no two persons are born exactly alike, but each differs from each in natural endowments, one being suited for one occupation and another for another" (21, p. 60).[1] Plato proposes a series of "actions to perform" for use as tests of military aptitude on those who are to be the soldiers of his ideal state. These actions are designed to sample the various traits considered essential to military prowess, and represent the first systematic description of an aptitude test on record.

Nor did the versatile genius of Aristotle overlook individual variation. He discusses at some length group differences, including species, racial, social, and sex differences in mental and moral traits. In many of his works there is also an implicit assumption of individual differences, although it is interesting to note that Aristotle does not offer any extensive treatment of these differences as such. One gets the impression that he regards the existence of individual variation as too obvious to need special mention. That he attributes such differences at least in part to innate factors seems to be indicated by a number of statements such as the following:

> Perhaps, then, some one may say, "Since it is in my power to be just and good, if I wish I shall be the best of all men." This, of course, is not possible. . . . For he who wills to be best will not be so, unless Nature also be presupposed (1, *Magna Moralia*, 1187ᵇ).

Throughout the several *Ethics* of Aristotle, there appear passages which imply individual variation. The following statement, for example, leaves little doubt regarding Aristotle's position on this point.

> After these distinctions we must notice that in everything continuous and divisible there is excess, deficiency, and the

---

[1] The numbers in parentheses refer to the numbered References at the end of the chapter.

mean, and these in relation to one another or in relation to us, e.g., in the gymnastic or medical arts, and in those of building and navigation, and in any sort of action, alike scientific and non-scientific, skilled and unskilled. For motion is continuous, and action is motion (1, *Ethica Eudemia*, 1220[b]).

Aristotle then proceeds to describe the characteristics of men possessing an excess or a deficient amount of various traits such as irascibility, audacity, shamelessness, and others.

In the Scholasticism of the Middle Ages, individual differences were completely neglected. The individual as such had no part in the doctrines and generalizations of the Schoolmen. Rationalistic methods persisted even longer in the study of mental life than in other disciplines, where empiricism was gradually making itself felt. The keen observation of the ancients which had led to the discovery of many facts about human traits and behavior was now subordinated to religious speculation. The logical techniques of the Greeks were being employed primarily to build elaborate justifications for current theological dogmas. The spread of Christianity itself, with its emphasis upon otherworldliness and spiritual equality, was also doubtlessly influential in turning attention away from the individual.

The many varieties of Associationism which flourished from the seventeenth to the nineteenth centuries likewise took little heed of individual differences. It was with the elaborate mechanics whereby ideas become associated, giving rise to complex mental processes, that the associationists were primarily concerned. Their statements were general principles with no allowance for individual variation. Bain, the last of the so-called pure associationists, does, however, give some attention to individual differences in his writings. The following passage is taken from his book on *The Senses and the Intellect* (1855). "There is a natural force of adhesiveness, specific to each constitution, and distinguishing one individual from another. This property, like almost every other assignable property of human nature, I consider to be unequally distributed" (2, p. 237).

A simultaneous development in educational theory should probably be included at this point. In the writings and practices of a group of "naturalist" educators of the late eighteenth and early nineteenth centuries, including Rousseau, Pestalozzi, Herbart, and Froebel, there is found a definite shift of interest to the individual child (cf. 16). Educational policies and methods were to be determined, not by external criteria, but by direct observation of the child and his capacities. The emphasis still seemed to be, however, on the observation of the individual as representative of individuals in general, rather than as distinct from other individuals. Although statements can be found in the writings of these educators to the effect that individuals differ and that their education should be adapted to these differences, still the emphasis is laid more heavily upon free, "natural" education in contrast to externally and arbitrarily imposed procedures, rather than upon individual differences themselves. The term "individual" is often used to mean simply "human nature."

Finally, mention may be made of the various treatises on race and racial psychology which appeared in the late eighteenth and early nineteenth centuries. Discussions of race differences are to be found in the works of such writers as Buffon, Herder, and de Gobineau, the last having been especially influential in determining subsequent popular beliefs about race.

The Personal Equation in Astronomy

Curiously enough, the first systematic measurements of individual differences were undertaken not in psychology but in the old and time-honored science of astronomy. In 1796, Maskelyne, the astronomer royal at the Greenwich Observatory, dismissed Kinnebrook, his assistant, because the latter observed the times of stellar transits nearly a second later than he did. The method employed at the time to make such observations was the "eye and ear" method. This method involved not only coördination of visual and auditory impressions, but also rather complex spatial judgments. The observer noted the time to a second on the clock, then began to count seconds with the heard beats of the clock, at the same time watching the star as it crossed the field of the telescope. He noted the position of the star at the last beat of the clock just before it reached the "critical" line in the field; then, similarly, he noted its position with the first beat immediately after it had crossed that line. From these observations, an estimate was made in tenths of a second of the exact time when the star crossed the critical line. This was the accepted procedure and was regarded as accurate to one- or two-tenths of a second.

In 1816, Bessel, astronomer at Königsberg, read of the Kinnebrook incident in a history of the Greenwich Astronomical Observatory. As a result, he became interested in measuring what came to be known as the "personal equation" of different observers. Originally, the personal equation referred to the difference in seconds between the estimates of two observers. Bessel collected and published data on several trained observers, and pointed out not only the presence of such a personal equation or error when comparing any two observers, but also the variability in the equation from time to time. This represents the first published record of quantitative data on individual differences.

Many astronomers followed up Bessel's measurements. In the latter half of the nineteenth century, with the introduction of chronographs and chronoscopes, it became possible to measure the personal equation of a given observer without reference to any other observer. The attempt was made to reduce all observations to their objectively correct values without reference to a system of time based upon one observer as a standard. Astronomers also undertook an analysis of the various conditions which affected the size of the personal equation. It was this latter problem, rather than the measurement of individual differences, which was taken up by the early experimental psychologists in their studies of "reaction time."

THE RISE OF EXPERIMENTAL PSYCHOLOGY

During the latter half of the nineteenth century, psychology began to venture away from its armchair and enter the laboratory. Most of the early experimental psychologists were physiologists whose experiments gradually came to take on a psychological tinge. As a result, both the viewpoints and the methods of physiology were frequently carried over directly into the infant science of psychology. In 1879, Wilhelm Wundt established the first laboratory of experimental psychology at Leipzig. Experiments of a psychological nature had been performed previously by Weber, Fechner, Helmholtz, and others, but Wundt's laboratory was the first to be devoted exclusively to psychology and to offer facilities for training students in the methods of the new science. Students from many parts of the world were attracted to Wundt's laboratory, and upon their return founded laboratories in their own countries.

The problems investigated in these early laboratories testify to the close kinship of experimental psychology with physiology. The psychology of visual and auditory sensation, reaction time, psychophysics, and association constituted nearly the entire field of experimentation. It was characteristic of the early experimental psychologists either to ignore individual differences or to regard them in the nature of experimental "errors." The greater the individual variation in a phenomenon, the less accurate would be the general laws discovered in regard to it. Thus the extent of individual differences represented the "probable error" to be expected in the operation of the general laws whose formulation was the only aim of the experimental psychology of this period.

It is apparent that the rise of experimental psychology shifted the emphasis away from the study of individual differences rather than towards it. Its one contribution to the development of a differential psychology is to be found in its demonstration that psychological phenomena are amenable to objective and even quantitative investigation, that psychological theories can be tested by actual data, that psychology, in short, could become an empirical science. Such a step was required before theories about the individual could be replaced by studies on individual differences.

GALTON AND THE BIOLOGICAL INFLUENCE

With the spread of Darwinism in the late nineteenth century, psychology became consistently more biological in its approach. One of the most widely known of Darwin's followers was Sir Francis Galton, who first attempted to apply the evolutionary principles of variation, selection, and adaptation to the study of human individuals. Galton's scientific pursuits were many and varied, but they

were unified by an underlying interest in the study of
heredity. The science of Eugenics, whose aim is the
control and direction of human evolution, was originated
by Galton. In 1869, he published a book entitled *Hereditary Genius*, in which, by the application of the now
well-known family history method, he tried to demonstrate the inheritance of specific talents in various fields
of work. In connection with the study of human inheritance, it soon became apparent that related and unrelated
individuals must be measured, objectively and in large
numbers, in order to discover the degrees of resemblance
among them. For this purpose, Galton devised numerous
tests and measures and in 1882 established his famous
anthropometric laboratory at South Kensington Museum
in London. There, for the payment of a small fee, individuals could be tested in sensory discrimination, motor
capacities, and other simple processes.

Through the measurement of sensory processes, Galton
hoped to arrive at an estimate of the subject's intellectual
level. In the *Inquiries into Human Faculty*, a collection
of miscellaneous essays published in 1883, he wrote: "The
only information that reaches us concerning outward
events appears to pass through the avenue of our senses;
and the more perceptive the senses are of difference, the
larger is the field upon which our judgment and intelligence
can act" (9, p. 27). And again, on the basis of findings
on the inferior sensitivity of idiots, he observes that this
sensory discriminative capacity "would on the whole be
highest among the intellectually ablest" (9, p. 29). For
this reason, measures of sensory capacity, such as vision
and hearing, constituted a relatively large portion of the
tests which Galton constructed and employed. Among
these tests may be mentioned the Galton bar for visual
discrimination of length, the Galton whistle for the de-

termination of the highest audible pitch, kinæsthetic discrimination tests based on the arrangement of a series of weights, as well as tests of strength of movement, speed of simple reactions, and many others of a similar nature.

Galton also initiated the use of "free association" tests, a technique which was subsequently adopted and followed up by Wundt. Galton's study of mental imagery is well known and represents the first extensive psychological use of questionnaire methods. In this questionnaire, the subject was directed "to think of some definite object—suppose it is your breakfast table as you sat down to it this morning—and consider carefully the picture that rises before your mind's eye" (9, p. 84). They were then to describe the picture with reference to illumination, definition, and coloring. Wide individual and group differences were revealed by this analysis of imagery.

A further and very significant contribution of Galton to differential psychology was his development of statistical methods for the analysis of the data of individual differences. Formerly, statistics had been chiefly the tool of the trained mathematician and the professional gambler. Statistical techniques were not available in a form which would enable the mathematically untrained worker in the biological sciences to employ them. Galton realized the need for such techniques and developed many of the statistical procedures in current use today. This phase of his work has been extended and increased in scope by many eminent students, chief among whom is Karl Pearson, who succeeded Galton as director of the anthropometric laboratory in 1911.

Early Experimentation with Tests

The term "mental test" was first employed in 1890 by Cattell, in an article entitled *Mental Tests and Measure-*

ments (6). James McKeen Cattell was an American student of Wundt. In 1888, having obtained his doctorate at Leipzig, he returned to this country, where he was instrumental both in the spread of experimental psychology and in the development of mental testing. He was influenced by Galton's work in test construction and statistics. In Cattell, we find a convergence of two contemporary movements in psychology, the rise of the experimental method and the measurement of individual differences. It was characteristic of all of the early American mental tests that they developed in the psychological laboratory and partook of the nature of the experimental psychology of the time. This was not true of many of the tests developed in other countries.

In addition to his experiments on reaction time, attention span, controlled association, reading, psychophysics, and similar problems, Cattell constructed a series of tests which were administered for many years to freshmen and seniors at Columbia College. This series included the following tests: [1] (1) strength of grip; (2) rate of arm movement; (3) two-point threshold on the back of the hand; (4) amount of pressure required to produce pain on the forehead; (5) least noticeable difference in weights; (6) reaction time to sound; (7) speed of color naming; (8) bisection of a 50-cm. line; (9) reproduction of a 10-second time interval; (10) auditory memory span for letters. This list is reproduced in full since it is typical of the various test series which appeared at the time.

In 1891, Münsterberg (17) described a series of tests which he had employed on schoolchildren. Tests of reading, controlled association of various sorts, judgment, memory, and other simple mental processes were included. At the 1893 Columbian Exposition at Chicago, Jastrow

[1] For a fuller description, cf. Cattell and Farrand (7).

administered a series of sensory, motor, and simple perceptual tests to all persons interested. Norms of physical growth and mental development were presented with the tests (cf. 20).

What is probably the first attempt to evaluate test scores in terms of an independent criterion is to be found in the study by Bolton (4) reported in 1892. Bolton analyzed data collected by Boas on about 1500 school-children. The children's memory spans were compared with their teachers' estimates of "intellectual acuteness," very little correspondence being found. Gilbert (10), in 1893, compared teachers' estimates of "general ability" on some 1200 children with their scores on eight tests of sensory and motor functions, reaction time, sensory memory, and suggestibility. Three years later, Gilbert (11) described some additional tests and reported the results obtained with them on several hundred children. The data were analyzed in respect to sex differences, intel-. lectual growth, and the relationship of mental and physical development.

In Germany, Oehrn (19), a pupil of Kraepelin, published in 1889 the results of an intensive study of a series of tests on ten subjects. The tests had been rather arbitrarily selected to measure perception, memory, association, and motor functions. In 1895, Kraepelin (15) proposed a set of traits which he regarded as basic in the characterization of any individual. He also devised tests for the measurement of these traits, most of the tests involving simple arithmetic operations. These tests were of rather dubious validity for measuring the traits in question, and in addition they were quite impracticable, some of them requiring several days for their completion. Research on mental tests was also being conducted simultaneously under the direction of the Italian psychologist

Ferrari. In an article appearing in 1896, some of these tests were described (12). They included measures of vasomotor activity, motor strength and skill, range of apprehension, description of pictures, and temporal estimation. Interesting individual differences were reported in many of these tests.

BEGINNINGS OF DIFFERENTIAL PSYCHOLOGY

At the turn of the century, differential psychology had begun to assume very definite shape. In 1895, Binet and Henri published an article entitled *La psychologie individuelle* (3), which represents the first systematic analysis of the aims, scope, and methods of differential psychology. Their opening sentence suggests the status of this branch of psychology at the time. It reads: "We broach here a new subject, difficult and as yet very meagerly explored" (p. 411). Binet and Henri put forth as the two major problems of differential psychology, first, the study of the nature and extent of individual differences in psychological processes; and secondly, the discovery of the interrelationships of mental processes within the individual, so that we may arrive at a classification of traits and determine which are the more basic functions.

In 1900 appeared the first edition of Stern's book on differential psychology, under the title *Über Psychologie der individuellen Differenzen* (25). Part I deals with the nature, problems, and methods of differential psychology. Within the scope of this branch of psychology Stern included differences among individuals as well as among racial and cultural groups, occupational and social levels, and the two sexes. The fundamental problem of differential psychology he characterized as threefold: (1) What is the nature and extent of differences in the psychological life of individuals and groups? (2) What factors determine or affect these differences?—in this connection he mentioned heredity, climate, social or cultural level, training, adaptation, etc. (3) How are the differences manifested? Can they be detected by such indices as handwriting, facial conformation, etc.? Stern also included a discussion of the concepts of psychological type, individuality, and normality and abnormality. Under methods of differential psychology, he gave an evaluation of introspection, objective observation, the use of material from history and poetry, the study of culture, quantitative testing, and experiment. Part II contains a general discussion and certain data on individual differences in various psychological traits, from simple sensory capacities to more complex mental processes and emotional characteristics. Stern's book appeared in a highly revised and enlarged edition in 1911, and again in 1921, under the title of *Differentielle Psychologie in ihren methodischen Grundlagen* (26).

In America, committees were being appointed to investigate testing methods and to sponsor the accumulation of data on individual differences. At its 1895 meeting, the American Psychological Association appointed a committee "to consider the feasibility of coöperation among the various psychological laboratories in the collection of mental and physical statistics" (7, p. 619). In the following year, the American Association for the Advancement of Science established a standing committee to organize an ethnographic survey of the white population in the United States. Cattell, one of the members of this committee, pointed out the importance of including psychological tests in this survey and suggested that its work be coördinated with that proposed by the American Psychological Association (7, pp. 619–620).

The application of the newly devised mental tests to

various groups was also getting under way. R. L. Kelly (13) in 1903 and Norsworthy (18) in 1906 compared normal and feebleminded children on sensori-motor and simple mental tests, and called attention to the continuous gradation in ability which exists between these groups, the feebleminded not constituting a distinct category. In 1903 appeared Thompson's *The Mental Traits of Sex* (28), the result of several years' testing of men and women with a variety of tests. This represents the first comprehensive investigation on sex differences. Tests of sensory acuity, motor capacities, and a few simple mental processes were also being administered for the first time to various racial groups. A few scattered investigations appeared before 1900. In 1904 Woodworth (30) and Bruner (5) tested several primitive groups at the St. Louis Exposition. In the same year appeared Spearman's original article putting forth his Two-Factor theory of mental organization and introducing a statistical technique for investigating the problem. Thus, shortly after the beginning of the century, the foundations had been laid for every branch of differential psychology.

INTELLIGENCE TESTING

The intelligence test is a product of the twentieth century. The early mental tests were predominantly sensori-motor or very simple in nature. This was no doubt a carry-over from the sensationism current in the psychological laboratories of the time. Complex mental processes were believed to be best understood by analyzing them into their elementary components, usually of a sensory nature. Most of the efforts of the early experimentalists were therefore devoted to the study of sensations and simple reactions, and this influence left its mark on the newly developing mental tests.

Binet and Henri, in their 1895 article (3), were the first definitely to point out the need for more complex tests to measure "intelligence." They examined the five most comprehensive current test series, those of Cattell, Münsterberg, Jastrow, Kraepelin, and Gilbert, and found all of them greatly overweighted with sensory tests and lacking in tests of complex processes. From an analysis of the available data, they concluded that individual differences are more marked in complex tasks and that the latter are therefore better suited to the study of such differences. Partly to remedy this deficiency in the current tests, Binet and Henri described ten types of tests which in their opinion would yield the largest and most significant individual differences. The series included tests of memory, mental imagery, imagination, attention, comprehension, suggestibility, æsthetic appreciation, moral feelings, muscular force and force of will, and motor ability and visual discrimination. The entire series, according to the authors, would require only from one to one and one-half hours.

In 1897, Ebbinghaus (8) proposed a theory to the effect that intelligence is the ability to combine or integrate the items of experience, and offered the sentence completion test as a technique for measuring this ability. In this test, the subject is presented with sentences in which certain of the words are missing and he is required to fill in the proper words. In experiments on German schoolchildren, Ebbinghaus had found this test more effective than simpler tests of calculation and memory. The completion test showed the most regular increase in score with age and it was also the only one of the tests employed which differentiated clearly among those pupils within each grade whose scholastic standing was good, average, or poor. Binet's contention for the superiority of the more complex tests in differential psychology was thus corroborated.

Two American studies of this period lent further support to Binet's statements. One of these studies (22) was conducted by Sharp, a student of Titchener, and was designed as a specific investigation of the conclusions of Binet and Henri. A set of tests, modeled largely on those of Binet and Henri, was administered to seven advanced psychology students. The experiment was very intensive and included the repetition of similar tests on different days to determine the consistency of the processes tested. In general, although the need for further controls and refinements was suggested, the tests proved satisfactory and yielded sizable individual differences in spite of the homogeneous and select nature of the group. Sharp concluded: "We concur with Mm. Binet and Henri in believing that individual psychical differences should be sought for in the complex rather than in the elementary processes of mind, and that the test method is the most workable one that has yet been proposed for investigating these processes" (22, p. 390). A few years later, Wissler (29) published the results of his correlation analysis of the data collected in Cattell's laboratory. The correlations showed "little more than a chance relation" among the tests, and also a negligible correspondence with academic grades. Thus the inadequacy of the simple tests originally employed was again indicated.

Against this background of theory and data appeared the first intelligence scale. In 1904 the French Minister of Public Instruction appointed a committee to investigate the causes of retardation among public schoolchildren. Binet was one of the members of this committee. As a direct outgrowth of his work in this connection, Binet published, in collaboration with Simon, the 1905 scale for measuring intelligence. This scale consisted of 30 problems arranged in a rough order of difficulty. In 1908 appeared Binet's first revision of the scale, in which the tests were grouped into age levels and the concept of "mental age" [1] was introduced. The scale was again revised in 1911, the year of Binet's untimely death.[2]

The Binet tests have been translated into more than a dozen languages and their use has spread over every continent. In America, five different revisions have appeared, of which the most widely known are the Stanford-Binet, prepared by Terman and his associates at Stanford University, and the Kuhlman-Binet which extended the scale down to the three-months age level. The intelligence quotient (I.Q.), found by dividing the child's mental age by his chronological age, was first employed in the Stanford-Binet, although its use and advantages had been previously discussed by Stern and others. The development of performance scales for testing the deaf, the illiterate, and the foreign, to whom language tests are inapplicable, may be mentioned as a further development of intelligence testing.

GROUP TESTING

The Binet scale and its revisions are "individual tests" in the sense that only one subject can be tested at a time. Furthermore, owing to the nature of these tests, a highly trained examiner is required to administer them. Testing

---

[1] The child's score on an age scale is expressed as a mental age (M.A.). If, for example, he passes successfully all of the tests assigned to the 10-year level, he has a mental age of 10, regardless of what his chronological age may be.

[2] Attention has recently been called to the fact that as early as 1887 a series of developmental standards and simple tests for judging the mental level of infants during the first three years was worked out by an American physician, Dr. S. E. Chaille. The concept of mental age seems to have been implicit in his treatment of the data, although this term was not employed (cf. Goodenough, F. L., "An Early Intelligence Test," *Child Dev.*, 1934, 5, 13–18).

on a large scale could not be carried on under these conditions. Data on such problems as sex and race differences, for example, which require the investigation of large samples, would be very slow in accumulating.

The advent of the group intelligence scale was probably the chief factor in bringing about the popular mental testing fad. The group test is designed with a view to its general use. It is not only adapted to the simultaneous testing of large groups, but it is also relatively easy to administer and fool-proof in its scoring. The impetus for the development of group tests was given by the pressing need of testing over one and one-half million men in the United States army in 1917. A quick, rough classification in respect to intelligence was necessary for many purposes. Discharge because of serious mental defect, assignment to labor battalions requiring only low-grade work, admittance to officers' training camps, and a number of similar problems required a knowledge of the intellectual level of the soldier.

Accordingly, a committee was appointed by the American Psychological Association to devise a test suited to this purpose. The committee consisted of five psychologists who were specialists in mental testing, and was under the direction of Robert M. Yerkes. All of the available material on mental tests was examined for its suitability to the needs of the army testing program. The greatest assistance was derived from an unpublished group scale which had previously been developed by Otis, and which the latter made available to the government. The final outcome of the research of the army psychologists was the Army Alpha and the Army Beta. The former was the more widely used of the two; the latter is a non-language scale, and was designed for testing illiterates and foreigners unfamiliar with English.

After the close of the World War, group tests were constructed at a rapid rate. Soon special tests were available for elementary schoolchildren as well as kindergarten and pre-school levels, high school and college students, and unselected adults. Mental testing attained heretofore undreamed-of proportions. School teachers were now qualified to administer the newly simplified tests; large-scale school surveys were initiated; college freshmen were tested as part of the routine of admission; the general public became intelligence-test-conscious, and the I.Q. became a byword in everyday conversation.

This sudden popularization and publicity was an unfortunate handicap in the development of a measuring instrument still in its infancy. The intelligence scales were as yet very crude when they were put into the hands of the layman. They were too often accepted as a finished product and an infallible guide. Analysis of results and evaluation of techniques were subordinated to the more alluring occupation of classifying people. Occasionally psychologists themselves were guilty of over-hasty generalization. Data on the various problems of differential psychology were being amassed in a rush. Sweeping conclusions were drawn—and quoted.

THE MEASUREMENT OF PERSONALITY

The extension of testing techniques from sensory and intellectual capacities to emotional and social traits is also a very recent development. An antecedent of current personality testing may be found in Kraepelin's first use of the free association test on pathological cases and on individuals who had been experimentally subjected to various influences such as fatigue, hunger, and drugs. Kraepelin (14) reported that all of these agencies increased the number of superficial associations. In 1894, Sommer

(23) suggested that mental disorders could be differentiated by means of the free association test. The use of this test, for a variety of purposes, has persisted to the present. The most fruitful approach to the measurement of personality traits, however, has proved to be through standardized questionnaire and rating scale methods. These methods were originally developed by Galton, Pearson, and Cattell in a different connection. The first widely employed personality questionnaire was the Woodworth "Personal Data Sheet" (cf. 27, Ch. V), an inventory of neurotic tendencies and emotional maladjustments devised for use on the American soldiers during the World War. This questionnaire was prepared by Woodworth, who was chairman of the Committee on Emotional Fitness appointed by the National Research Council. Although the armistice came before the final form of the questionnaire could be extensively applied, it was used subsequently in army hospitals and yielded much interesting information.

Several revisions and adaptations of the Woodworth questionnaire have appeared, including forms especially suited for children, and for college students. Tests have also appeared for the measurement of various other social and emotional characteristics, such as introversion-extroversion, ascendance-submission, and self-sufficiency. A fairly recent development is the construction of objective "performance" tests of moral or character traits, such as honesty, coöperation, and self-control. Data on individual and, to a lesser extent, group differences are being steadily accumulated with all of these tests.

Current Trends in Differential Psychology

After about twenty years of phenomenal development in the construction and application of mental tests, psychologists are beginning to turn their attention to a critical analysis of testing techniques themselves. There is apparent a growing tendency to question generalizations, to scrutinize the conditions under which data were obtained, and to evaluate the results in the light of such conditions. A reaction is setting in against the indiscriminate use of mental tests which followed the rise of group testing. In differential psychology, this reaction is manifested in two chief ways. In the first place, increasing stress is being laid upon the influence of environmental conditions in determining or modifying the individual's characteristics. In the second place, the measurement of "general intelligence" is losing its prominence as the goal of testing. Individual as well as group differences are being sought in narrower and more clearly definable traits.

The original aim of the mental testers was the measurement of the individual's "capacities" or potentialities of intellectual development, as distinguished from his present skills and information. The measurement of the latter would have been a relatively simple task. If we wish to ascertain whether an individual is proficient in many languages, for example, we need only examine his knowledge of all languages with which he claims familiarity. But if we want to know whether this individual can learn languages easily, whether it would be worth while to teach him, or to advise him to enter a vocation which demands a mastery of several languages, then we are faced with a much more difficult problem. This was the type of problem with which the mental tester tried to cope.

If one is to determine what the individual *can* do rather than what he has already accomplished, it was argued, it is necessary in some way to "rule out" differences in the previous experience or training of the subjects. This was attempted either by presenting material which was equally unfamiliar to all, or by the reverse procedure of utilizing only material common to everyone's experience. Frequently, the two methods were combined, as in the use of familiar material in a novel and unusual manner. Such a procedure is a practicable one and will yield useful information, provided its limitations and assumptions are kept clearly in view. In respect to the use of familiar material, it becomes necessary to ascertain that the material is actually familiar, in an approximately equal degree, to all of the subjects. A test is applicable only to individuals similar in their experiential background to the group upon whom it was standardized. *When given to individuals from different national or cultural groups, or from widely differing economic, social, or educational levels, "intelligence tests" do little more than reflect the varied backgrounds of the subjects.* Under such conditions, the tests fail to fulfill the original purpose for which they were constructed. We are here concerned only in presenting this point of view as a recent historical development; further elaboration of its theoretical implications will be found in subsequent chapters.

The current trend toward the development of tests of separate traits and special aptitudes likewise results from a more searching analysis of testing methods. Recent research on the relationships among abilities suggests that important individual differences might be obscured if all abilities are lumped indiscriminately under the inclusive concept of "general intelligence." From the practical standpoint of prediction, tests of special aptitudes are being constructed to fit the needs of particular educational or vocational situations. From the standpoint of theoretical interpretation, investigations on independent traits or unitary abilities are contributing towards a clearer understanding of individual and group differences.

REFERENCES

1. Aristotle. *The Works of Aristotle*, ed. by W. D. Ross. Oxford: Clarendon Press, 1915. Vol. IX, Magna Moralia, Ethica Eudemia, de Virtutibus et Vittis.

2. Bain, Alexander. *The Senses and the Intellect*. London: Parker, 1855. Pp. 614.

3. Binet, A., and Henri, V. "La psychologie individuelle," *Année psychol.*, 1895, 2, 411–463.

4. Bolton, T. L. "The Growth of Memory in Schoolchildren," *Amer. J. Psychol.*, 1891–92, 4, 362–380.

5. Bruner, F. G. "The Hearing of Primitive Peoples," *Arch. Psychol.*, 1908, No. 11. Pp. 113.

6. Cattell, J. McK. "Mental Tests and Measurements," *Mind*, 1890, 15, 373–380.

7. Cattell, J. McK., and Farrand, L. "Physical and Mental Measurements of the Students of Columbia University," *Psychol. Rev.*, 1896, 3, 618–648.

8. Ebbinghaus, H. "Über eine neue Methode zur Prüfung geistiger Fähigkeiten und ihre Anwendung bei Schulkindern," *Zscht. f. angew. Psychol.*, 1897, 13, 401–459.

9. Galton, F. *Inquiries into Human Faculty and Its Development*. London: Macmillan, 1883. Pp. 387.

10. Gilbert, J. A. "Researches on the Mental and Physical Development of School Children," *Stud. Yale Psychol. Lab.*, 1894, 2, 40–100.

11. ——. "Researches upon Children and College Students," *Iowa Univ. Stud. Psychol.*, 1897, 1, 1–39.

12. Guiccardi, G., and Ferrari, G. C. "I testi mentali per l'esame degli alienati," *Riv. sper. di freniatria*, 1896, 22, 297–314.

13. Kelly, R. L. "Psychophysical Tests of Mentally Deficient Children," *Psychol. Rev.*, 1903, 10, 345–372.

14. Kraepelin, E. *Über die Beeinflüssung einfacher psychischer Vorgänge durch einige Arzneimittel*. Jena: Fischer, 1892. Pp. 259.

15. ——. "Der psychologische Versuch in der Psychiatrie," *Psychol. Arbeiten*, 1895, 1, 1–91.

16. Monroe, P. *A Textbook in the History of Education.* N. Y.: Macmillan, 1926. Pp. 759.

17. Münsterberg, H. "Zur Individualpsychologie," *Centralblatt für Nervenheilkunde und Psychiatrie,* 1891, 14, 196–198.

18. Norsworthy, N. "The Psychology of Mentally Deficient Children," *Arch. Psychol.,* 1906, No. 1. Pp. 111.

19. Oehrn, A. *Experimentelle Studien zur Individualpsychologie.* Dorpater Dissertation, 1889 (also publ. in *Psychol. Arbeiten,* 1895, 1, 92–152).

20. Philippe, J. "Jastrow—Exposition d'anthropologie de Chicago—Tests psychologiques, etc.," *Année Psychol.,* 1894, 1, 522–526.

21. Plato. *The Republic of Plato* (transl. by J. L. Davies and D. J. Vaughan). N. Y.: Burt, 19—. Pp. 406.

22. Sharp, S. E. "Individual Psychology: a Study in Psychological Method," *Amer. J. Psychol.,* 1898–99, 10, 329–391.

23. Sommer, R. *Diagnostik der Geisteskrankheiten für praktische Ärzte und Studierende.* Wien und Leipzig: Urban und Schwarzenberg, 1894. Pp. 302.

24. Spearman, C. " 'General Intelligence' Objectively Determined and Measured," *Amer. J. Psychol.,* 1904, 15, 201–293.

25. Stern, W. *Über Psychologie der individuellen Differenzen (Ideen zur einer "Differenzellen Psychologie").* Leipzig: Barth, 1900. Pp. 146.

26. ——. *Die Differentielle Psychologie in ihren methodischen Grundlagen.* Leipzig: Barth, 1921. Pp. 545.

27. Symonds, P. M. *Diagnosing Personality and Conduct.* N. Y.: Century, 1931. Pp. 602.

28. Thompson, H. B. *The Mental Traits of Sex.* Chicago: Univ. Chicago Press, 1903. Pp. 188.

29. Wissler, C. "The Correlation of Mental and Physical Tests," *Psychol. Mon.,* 1901, 3, No. 16. Pp. 62.

30. Woodworth, R. S. "Race Differences in Mental Traits," *Science,* N. S., 1910, 31, 171–186.

CHAPTER II

NATURE AND EXTENT OF INDIVIDUAL DIFFERENCES

Individual differences are quantitative rather than qualitative. Popular opinion frequently classifies people in reference to the possession or non-possession of certain traits. Thus one individual is said to have a talent for music, another for painting, a third for mathematics, a fourth for organizing people. Such a characterization, however, results from purely practical considerations. In order to choose music as a vocation, or even as a serious avocation, for example, an individual must have a certain minimum of musical talent; if his degree of musical ability falls below that minimum, he is not regarded as "a musical person." Furthermore, if such an individual has more outstanding ability along some other line, he will be classified in respect to the latter trait and not on the basis of his musical aptitude. Qualitative distinctions of this sort are made in practice and are based on arbitrary or socially determined criteria and limits. Actually, however, every individual can be described in terms of the same traits.

There are no "alternative" psychological traits, in the sense that one trait serves as a substitute for the other. No traits are mutually exclusive. It might be argued, however, that there are certain characteristics which a person may either have or not have, and that in this respect we may speak of qualitative differences. The classical examples are loss of sensation, such as blindness or deafness. Here, it would seem, are traits characterized by presence or absence: a person can see or he cannot see, he can hear or not hear. This, too, turns out to be a purely conventional and practical distinction. Anyone who has visited an institution for the blind knows that there are many degrees of blindness, and that not all those classified as blind are totally blind. The everyday working definition of blindness is any *degree* of visual deficiency too serious to permit normal activity. The same is obviously true of deafness and any other sensory disorder. Between the empirically established "normal" vision or hearing and what is classed as blindness or deafness there is to be found a continuous gradation of minor deficiencies. It should be added that the existence of a trait in zero degree, as in total blindness, is not inconsistent with the quantitative view of individual differences. The latter implies only that there be intermediate degrees rather than simple presence or absence.

The Distribution of Individual Differences

Since individual differences have been found to be quantitative, we may now ask how the varying degrees of each trait are distributed among people. Are individuals scattered uniformly over the entire range or do they cluster at one or more points? What are the relative frequencies with which different degrees of a trait occur? These questions can best be answered by an examination of frequency distributions and frequency graphs.

Like all statistical devices, the frequency distribution is a means of summarizing and organizing quantitative data in order to facilitate its treatment and reveal significant trends. Scores on a test, or any other set of measures, are grouped into class-intervals, and the number of cases falling within each interval is tabulated. An example of a frequency distribution is given in Table I.

This shows the scores of 1000 college students on a simple learning test. The scores range from 8 to 52 and have been grouped into class-intervals of four points. The advantages of such a table over a list of 1000 individual scores are obvious.

The facts brought out by a frequency distribution can be made more vivid if presented pictorially by means of a frequency graph. In Figure 1 are shown the data of Table I in graphic form. The base line or horizontal axis represents the scores; the vertical axis shows the frequency or number of cases falling within each class-

TABLE I

FREQUENCY DISTRIBUTION OF SCORES OF 1000 COLLEGE STUDENTS ON A SIMPLE LEARNING TEST

(After Anastasi, 2, p. 34)

Class-Interval	Frequency
52–55	1
48–51	1
44–47	20
40–43	73
36–39	156
32–35	328
28–31	244
24–27	136
20–23	28
16–19	8
12–15	3
8–11	2
	N = 1000

interval. The graph has been plotted in two ways, both being about equally common. One graph is a *frequency polygon*, in which the number of individuals within each interval is indicated by a point, centrally located in respect to the class-interval; the successive points are then joined by straight lines. The other is obtained by

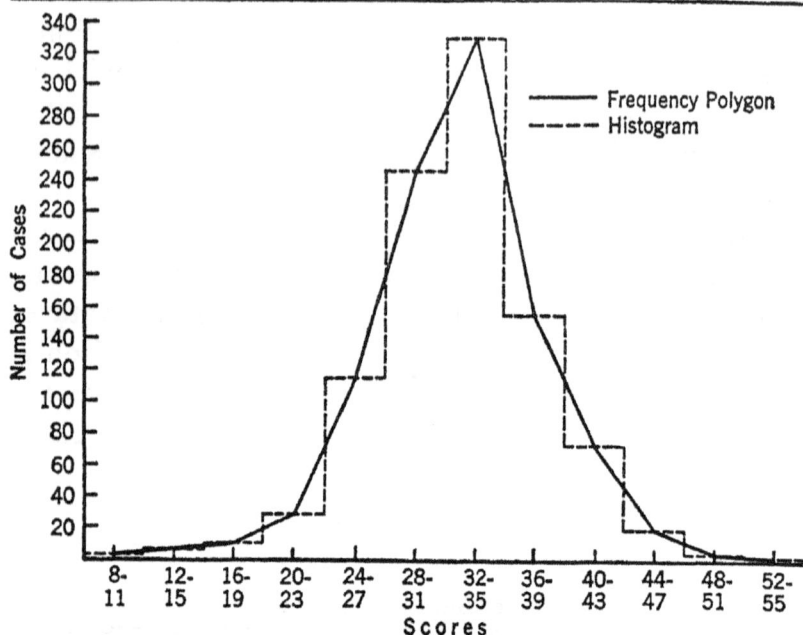

FIG. 1. DISTRIBUTION CURVES: FREQUENCY POLYGON AND HISTOGRAM.
(Data from Table I.)

erecting a column or rectangle over each class-interval, the height of the column depending upon the number of cases in that interval. This type of graph is known as a *histogram*.

THE NORMAL CURVE

The reader will already have noticed certain characteristics of the distribution presented in Table I and Figure 1. The majority of cases cluster in the center of the range and as the extremes are approached there is a gradual and continuous tapering off. The curve shows no gaps or breaks; no clearly separated classes can be discerned. The curve is also bilaterally symmetrical, that is, if it should be divided by a vertical line through the center, the two halves so obtained would be nearly identical. This distribution curve resembles the bell-shaped "normal curve," the type most commonly found in the measurement of individual differences. The theoretically determined, ideal normal curve will be found in Figure 2.

The concept of the normal curve is an old one in statistics. It first became prominent as the *normal probability curve.* The probability of the occurrence of an event is

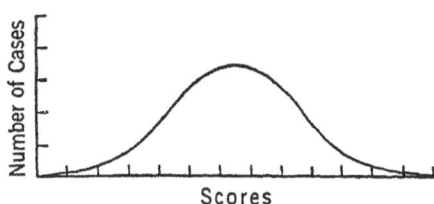

FIG. 2. THEORETICAL NORMAL CURVE.

the expected relative frequency of occurrence of the given event in a very large, or infinite, number of observations. This probability is represented by a ratio or fraction, the numerator of which is the expected outcome, and the denominator the total possible outcomes. Thus the probability or chances that when two coins are tossed only heads will come up is $\frac{1}{4}$, or one out of four possible occurrences; the probability of one head and one tail is $\frac{1}{2}$; and that of two tails, $\frac{1}{4}$. If the number of coins is increased, say to 100, so that the number of possible occurrences or combinations becomes very large, we can still determine mathematically the chances of any one combination, such as all heads or twenty heads and eighty tails, occurring. These probabilities, or expected frequencies of occurrence, can be plotted graphically by the same method outlined above for plotting scores. The curve obtained when the number of coins is very large will be the bell-shaped normal probability curve. In Figure 3 are shown the theoretical and obtained frequencies for 12 dice thrown 4096 times. In each throw, the number of dice showing a 4, 5, or 6 spot uppermost was determined. This number could, of course, vary from zero to 12, the total number of dice thrown. The graph shows the relative frequency

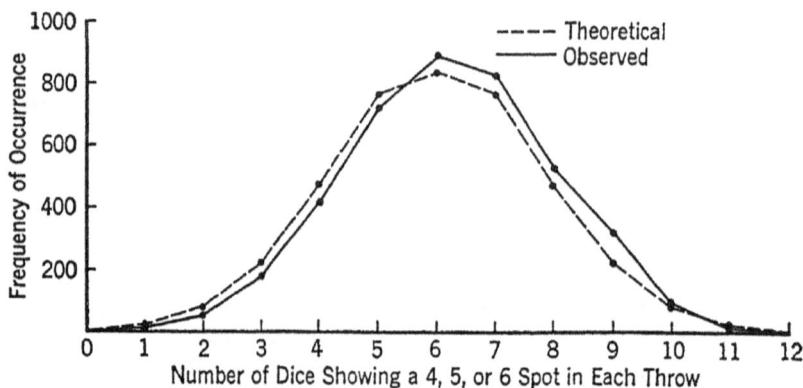

FIG. 3. THEORETICAL AND OBSERVED DISTRIBUTIONS OF RESULTS
IN 4096 THROWS OF 12 DICE. (After Yule, 21, p. 258.)

of each combination in the total 4096 throws. It will be
noted that there is a very close agreement between the
theoretical and obtained curves.

The results obtained by tossing coins or throwing dice
are said to depend upon "chance." By this is meant that
the outcome is determined by a large number of similar,
equal, and independent factors. The height from which
a coin or die is thrown, its weight and size, the twist of
the hand employed, and many similar conditions determine which particular face will fall uppermost. Likewise,
a person's height, or weight, or performance on an intelligence test can be regarded as depending upon a variety
of independent factors, each having about equal influence
upon the result. Thus it has been suggested that the
operation of chance is responsible for the distribution of
human traits according to the normal frequency curve.

The normal curve also appears in a different situation
as the *curve of error*. When repeated measurements are
made, the results will not be identical on successive occasions. These errors are present to a greater or lesser degree
in all types of measurement. The length of a table as
measured by a meterstick, the speed of a simple move-

ment, or the æsthetic appeal of a work of art will not remain the same on repeated observations. If a very large number of observations of the same object or phenomenon are made, and the results found on successive occasions are plotted in a frequency graph, a normal curve will be obtained. The errors of observation or measurement which produce the variation are themselves the result of chance factors, and hence the curve of error, like the distribution curve, will coincide with the normal probability curve.

Other Types of Distribution Curves and What They Mean

The implications of the normal distribution curve for a psychology of individual differences can be realized more vividly by contrasting this form of distribution with other possible types. The distributions chosen in particular for this comparison are those implied by certain common theories and beliefs in regard to individual differences. They are also occasionally found with actual test results because of the use of faulty techniques.

A *skewed distribution* is one in which the peak or "mode" of the curve is displaced to either side of the center. Such a distribution lacks the bilateral symmetry of the normal curve. In Figure 4 will be found an illustration of a skewed curve, with piling up of scores at the

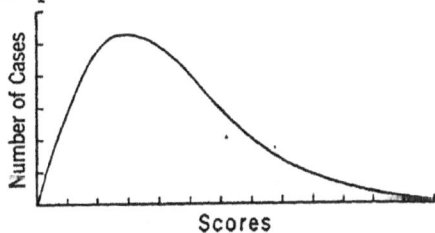

Fig. 4. A Skewed Distribution.

upper end of the distribution. Such a distribution is implicit in the popular conception of many character traits. Thus the majority of people are considered "honest" and are piled up at one extreme of the scale; from this point, the number of cases is believed to decrease steadily as the opposite extreme is approached. As will be shown in the following section, this type of distribution is not ordinarily found when objective measures or tests of character traits are used.

A skewed distribution may, however, be obtained with any test employed on a group to which it is not suited. If the National Intelligence Test, which is adapted to grades 3 to 8, were administered to a college class, the large majority of subjects would score very near the maximum, and the number of cases would decrease rapidly towards the lower scores. Similarly, if one of the many tests constructed for use on college freshmen were given to elementary schoolchildren, there would be a marked piling of scores near the zero end of the scale, and the distribution would be equally asymmetrical. Obviously these data could not be taken to mean that intelligence is not normally distributed among schoolchildren or college students. Such skewed distributions result from the fact that the difficulty range of the test does not extend far enough in the upper or lower direction. In the one case, all of those subjects who have more than a certain minimum of the ability tested will make a perfect or nearly perfect score, whereas if the test had included more difficult items, these subjects would have scattered over a wide range. The same holds true for zero or very low scores when the test is too difficult for the group. In choosing a test for a given group, care must be taken to insure that the subjects have sufficient leeway at both ends of the scale. The highest and lowest scores obtained should be a considerable distance from zero and perfect scores, respectively.

Skewness may also result from the inclusion within a single distribution of two normally distributed groups which differ pronouncedly in both average and variability. This effect is illustrated in Figure 5. On Graph A are

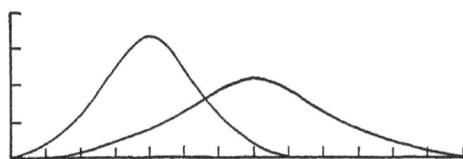

A. Two groups Plotted Separately

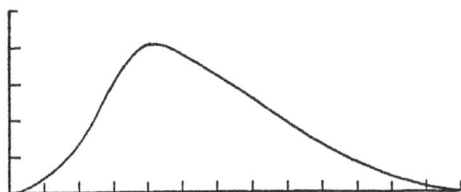

B. Two Groups Combined

FIG. 5. SKEWNESS RESULTING FROM THE COMBINATION OF GROUPS WITH DIFFERENT MEANS AND VARIABILITIES.

given the separate distribution curves of the two groups, one of which has a lower average as well as a narrower scatter of scores than the other. Graph B shows the definitely skewed curve which is obtained when both groups are combined and plotted as one distribution.

A type of distribution not so frequently found as the skewed curve but nevertheless assumed in certain common practices is the *rectangular distribution* illustrated in Figure 6. If individual differences were distributed in this manner, it would mean that there were as many geniuses and idiots as mediocre people, as many men whose height is 6 feet 6 inches as those whose height is 5 feet 8 inches. It is

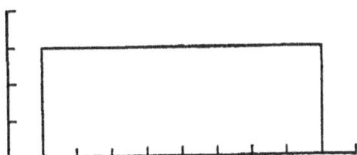

FIG. 6. A RECTANGULAR DISTRIBUTION.

interesting to speculate on the effect which such a situation would have on our sense of values. Our thinking is so permeated with the knowledge that extreme degrees of a trait are relatively infrequent, that it is difficult even to conceive of a world in which extremity did not imply rarity.

In spite of this fact, the assumption of a rectangular distribution is sometimes made in the interpretation of percentile scores. In the percentile system of scoring, the subject's standing on any test is expressed in terms of the percentage of people in a given group whose scores he equals or excels. If an individual, for example, answers ten questions correctly on a test, and if 50% of the group complete ten questions or less on the same test, then the individual falls just midway in the group and is given a percentile rating of 50. When comparing individuals who receive, let us say, percentile scores of 90, 80, 60, and 50, we must bear in mind that the difference in ability between the first two cases is greater than that between the last two, although in both pairs the difference is 10 percentile points. In order to include 10% of the cases between the 90th and 80th persons, we must cover a much longer distance on the base line of the normal curve than is necessary in going from the 50th to the 60th percentiles. This results from the greater clustering of individuals near the center of the curve, and the relatively small number of cases at the extremes. Only if the distribution were rectangular would successive percentile scores represent equal units of ability. This does not mean that percentile scores are of no value. Like "mental ages," they furnish a simple and vivid means of expressing the subject's standing on a test. Such devices do not, however, furnish an equal unit scale of ability.

Lastly, special mention should be made of the *multi-modal distribution* because of the prominent part it plays in current "type theories." A multi-modal curve is one having more than one mode or peak. Instead of a single clustering of individuals in the center as in the normal curve, or at either extreme as in a skewed curve, the clustering occurs at several points. The peaks may be equally large, or there may be a major peak and one or more minor ones. The most popular variety seems to be the bi-modal curve, with two approximately equal peaks. All of the common schemes of classification which place individuals into distinct categories presuppose some form of multi-modal distribution. The division of men into the genius, the normal, and the feebleminded, the sane and the insane, the sociable and the unsociable, all rest upon a tacit assumption that "most people" can be classified clearly into one of these groups, with possibly a few intermediate doubtful cases. It is interesting to note that these distinctions are much less common in the realm of physical traits, where continuity of variation is more apparent to the naked eye.

A multi-modal curve can be obtained in any trait through the arbitrary selection of cases. If the sampling tested is not chosen at random from the general population, but consists of individuals selected from widely differing levels and arbitrarily combined into a single group, a multi-modal distribution will result. A group consisting of five-year-olds and ten-year-olds, for example, would present a definitely bi-modal distribution in intelligence test scores, as well as in height, weight, and many other characteristics. Were the intervening age groups from six to nine to be included in this sampling, the distribution would take on the appearance of the normal bell-shaped curve.

The production of a bi-modal distribution by combining two curves of widely separated groups is illustrated in Figure 7. It will be noted that the overlapping between the two groups is very slight. When the overlapping is large, as in the case of adjacent age groups, the resulting

combined curve will be normal and uni-modal. An example of a bi-modal curve plotted with actual scores is
presented in Figure 8. The two distributions which are
combined in this curve consist of the Army Alpha scores
obtained by two groups in the United States army. The
lower group includes 2773 native-born white soldiers who
had reached no higher than the fourth elementary grade

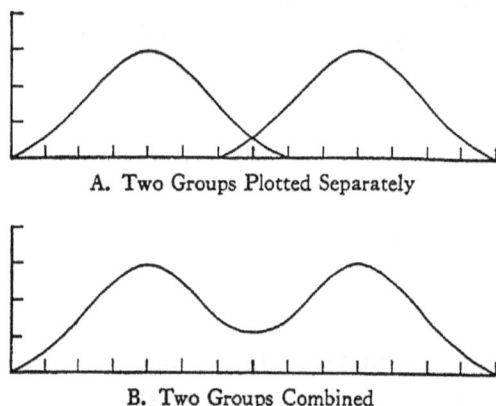

A. Two Groups Plotted Separately

B. Two Groups Combined

Fig. 7. Bi-modality Resulting from the Combination of Two
Groups with Widely Varying Means.

when they left school; the upper group consists of 3954 of
ficers who had had four years of college work. The
combined curve exhibits the definite bi-modality which
would be expected.

We have seen that various types of distributions other
than the normal curve are frequently implied in current
popular conceptions, and are occasionally found because
of faulty techniques or inadequate data. It now remains
to examine some typical findings on trait distributions
obtained under conditions relatively free from the errors
described. A few last words of caution should, however,
be added. In the first place, an unlimited number of
irregularities and variations in distribution curves may
occur through the use of small groups. Curves plotted

with a small number of cases present an uneven, jagged appearance since individual exceptions loom relatively large.   For this reason, only curves obtained on fairly large groups will be considered in the following section.

A second point to bear in mind relates to the concept of a mathematically perfect normal curve as contrasted

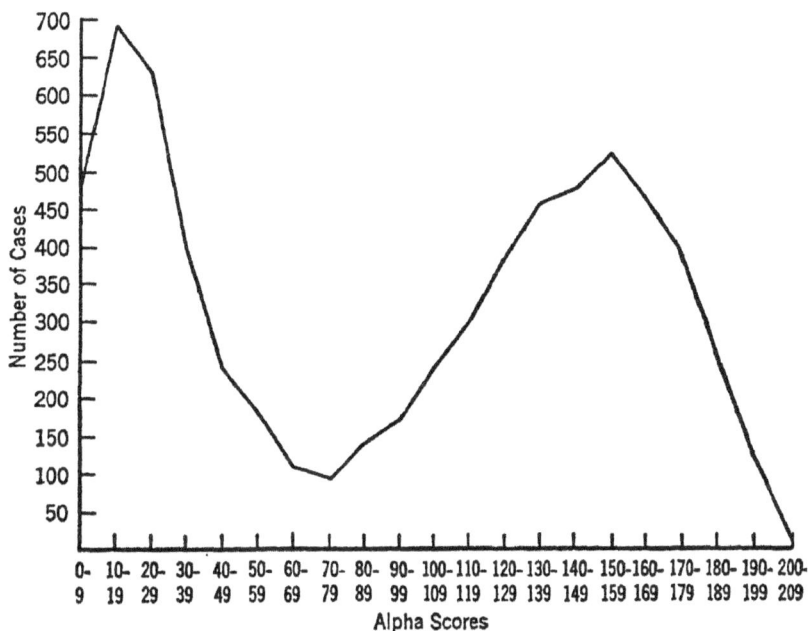

Fig. 8.   A Bi-modal Distribution Obtained by Combining Extreme Groups: Alpha Scores of 2773 Soldiers with 4th Grade Education and 3954 Officers with 4 Years of College. (Data from Yerkes, 20, pp. 773, 777.)

to the more or less rough approximations obtained with actual data.   In several instances, especially when the groups were very large, the characteristics of the distribution curves were investigated mathematically and found to fall within the expected limits of normality.   In many other instances, however, where such mathematical tests have not been employed, or where the curve has been found to deviate significantly in some one respect from the mathematically normal curve, we still speak of "normal distribution." In these cases, what is meant is that the distribution resembles the normal curve more closely than it does, let us say, a skewed, rectangular, or multimodal curve. It exhibits the general characteristics of clustering near the center with a gradual and continuous sloping toward the extremes. For a general picture of the distribution of a trait, such knowledge is sufficient. Only when certain statistical techniques which assume a normal curve are to be applied to the data, is it necessary to stress the requirement of mathematically established normality.

Some Typical Distributions

In Figures 9 to 22 will be found examples of distribution curves obtained for a wide variety of traits. Only distributions based on large samplings have been included. The two smallest groups, comprising 200 and 400 cases, respectively, are taken from the field of personality testing. In this there is little from which to choose, since unfortunately very few frequency tables for personality tests are available.

An example of the distribution of a purely structural trait is furnished in Figure 9, which shows the height in inches of 6194 English-born men. It will be seen that the graph approximates the mathematical normal curve to a remarkably close degree. Figure 10 presents the frequency curve of a more functional, physiological trait, vital capacity. This is the total volume of air, measured in cubic centimeters, that can be expelled from the lungs after a maximal inspiration. The measurements from which the curve is plotted were made on 1633 male students at the University of Minnesota. The general correspondence to the normal curve is again apparent.

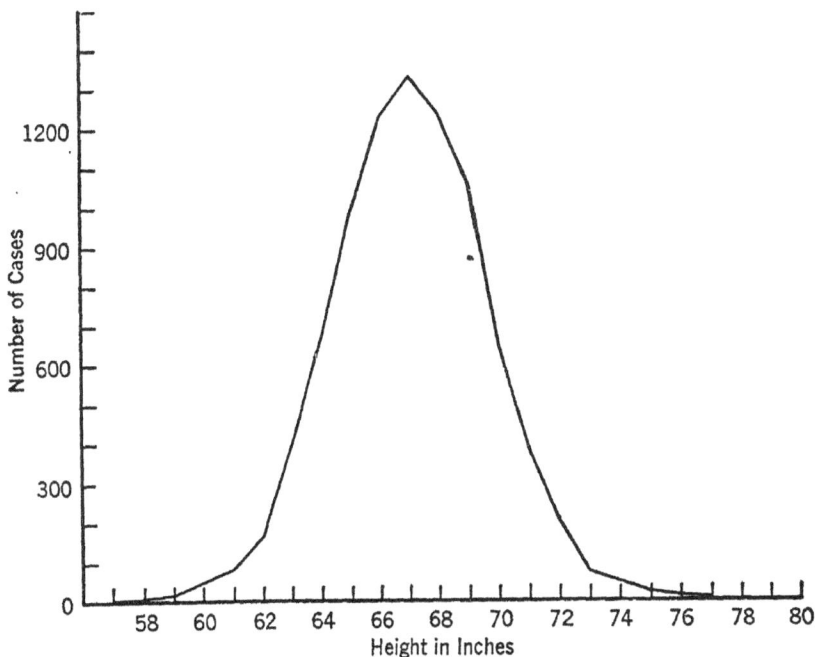

FIG. 9. DISTRIBUTION OF HEIGHT FOR 8585 ADULT ENGLISH-BORN MEN.
(After Yule, 21, p. 89.)

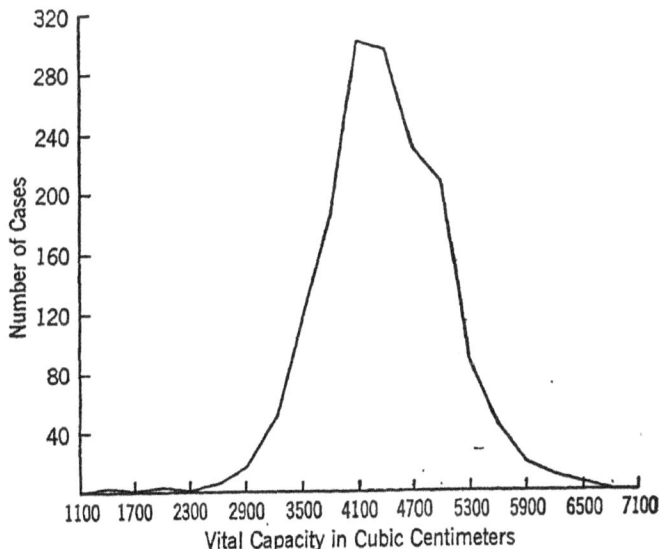

FIG. 10. VITAL CAPACITY OF 1633 MALE COLLEGE STUDENTS.
(After Jackson, 5, p. 94.)

The two graphs reproduced in Figures 11 and 12 represent the distribution of performance on relatively simple sensori-motor and mental tests. Reference may also be made in this connection to the data reported previously in Table I and Figure 1. All three sets of measures were

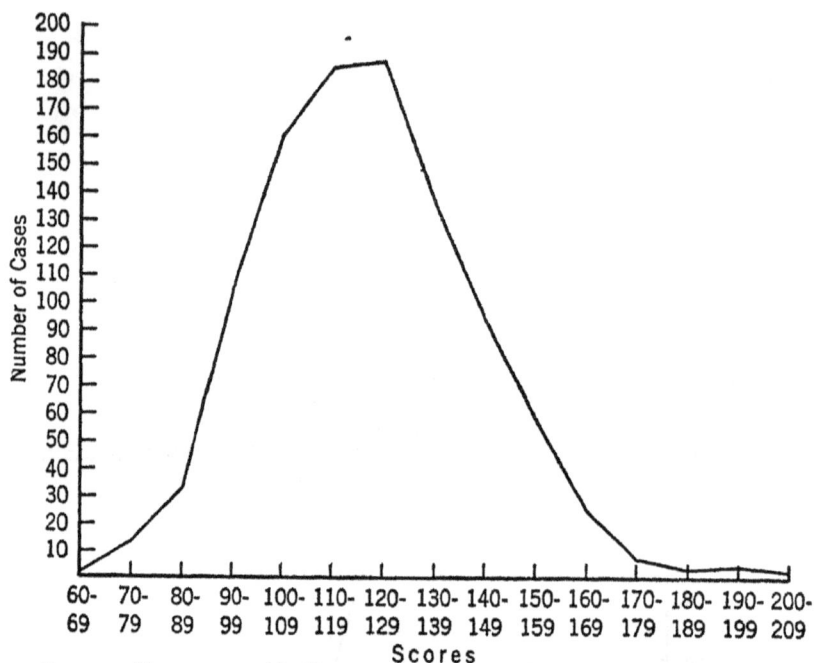

FIG. 11. NUMBER OF A's CANCELLED IN ONE MINUTE BY 1000 COLLEGE STUDENTS. (After Anastasi, 2, p. 32.)

obtained on the same group of 1000 college students. The tests whose distributions have been reproduced include cancellation, Pyle symbol-digit, and a nonsense-syllable vocabulary test. In the first, the score is the total number of A's in a page of pied type cancelled in one minute. This is generally regarded as a simple test of attention and perception, although speed and control of movement are also involved. The symbol-digit test is a simple learning test of the code substitution variety. The vocabulary test is a more difficult learning test, also employing a code, which in this case consists of paired nonsense syllables. The distributions of all three tests

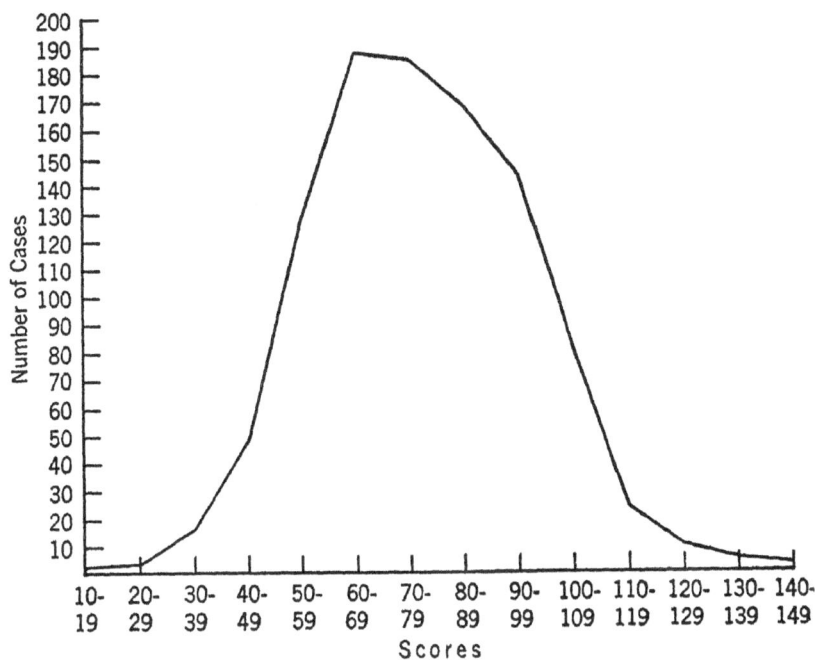

FIG. 12. SCORES OF 1000 COLLEGE STUDENTS ON THE PYLE SYMBOL-DIGIT TEST.
(After Anastasi, 2, p. 34.)

fall within the expected values of the theoretical normal curve.[1]

Typical results obtained with intelligence tests on large samplings are presented in Figures 13 to 16. Figure 13 gives the intelligence ratings on the "combined scale" obtained by 93,965 soldiers in the United States army during the World War. This group constituted a random sampling of the white draft, both native and foreign-born. The "combined scale" ratings are based on Army Alpha, Army Beta, Stanford-Binet, and performance scale

---

[1] Mathematical tests of normality were applied to these curves (cf. Anastasi, 2).

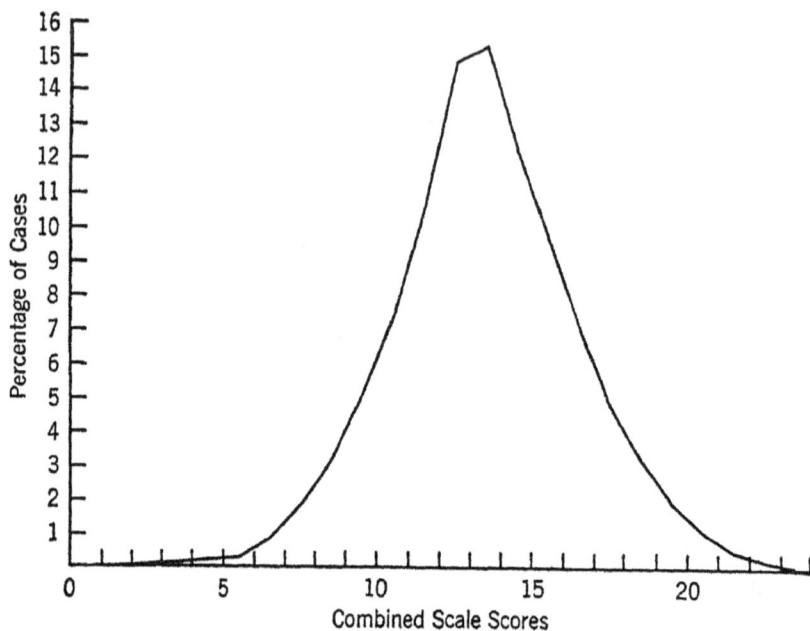

Fig. 13. Distribution of White Draft on the Combined Scale (N = 93,965). (Data from Yerkes, 20, p. 654.)

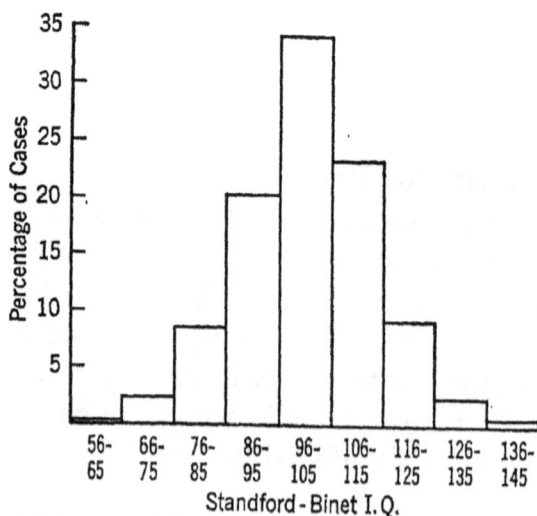

Fig. 14. I.Q.'s of 905 Unselected Children, 5-14 Years of Age. (After Terman, 14, p. 66.)

examinations, the scores on all tests having been reduced to comparable terms and expressed on a single scale ranging from 0 to 25 points. Since all the recruits were unable to take the same test, it was necessary to combine scores in this manner.

In Figure 14 will be found the distribution of Stanford-Binet I.Q.'s of 905 unselected schoolchildren, ranging in age from 5 to 14. The percentages of children whose I.Q.'s fell within each class-interval are given below the graph. Figure 15 shows the percentage distribution of scores made by 5952 sixth-grade schoolchildren on the Otis Advanced Examination. This is a widely used group test of general intelligence. Finally, in Figure 16 can be seen a composite curve for college freshmen, obtained by combining the results of eleven different intelligence examinations administered to groups of 623 to 5495 freshmen in various American colleges. The theoretical normal curve is shown in broken line on the same graph.

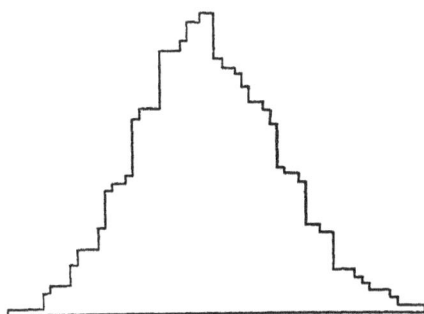

FIG. 15.   PERCENTAGE DISTRIBUTION OF SIXTH GRADE SCORES IN THE OTIS ADVANCED EXAMINATION (N = 5952). (After Thorndike, 15, p. 523.)

In the measurement of personality and character traits, testing techniques are still in a relatively crude and undeveloped stage. Many sources of error remain, so that one should scarcely expect to find perfect specimens of the normal distribution curve. Despite a more jagged appearance and many minor irregularities, however, the available distribution curves exhibit quite generally the fundamental characteristics of the normal curve. Inspection of Figures 17 to 22 will make this apparent.

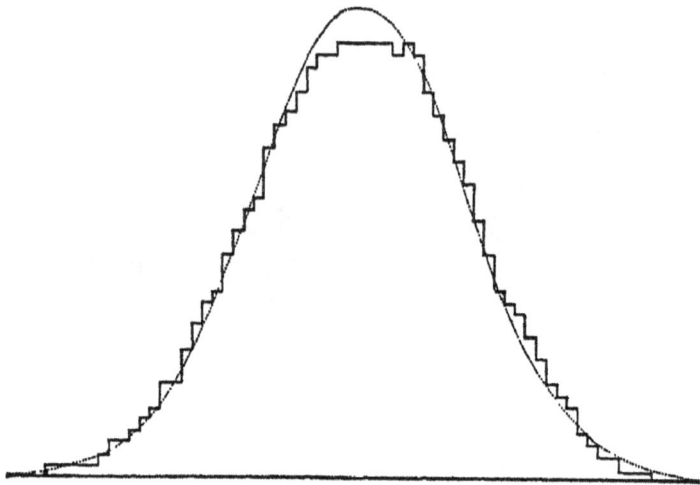

FIG. 16. COMPOSITE CURVE FOR COLLEGE FRESHMEN, DERIVED FROM ELEVEN INTELLIGENCE TEST CURVES. THE BROKEN LINE INDICATES THE THEORETICAL NORMAL CURVE. (After Thorndike, 15, p. 545.)

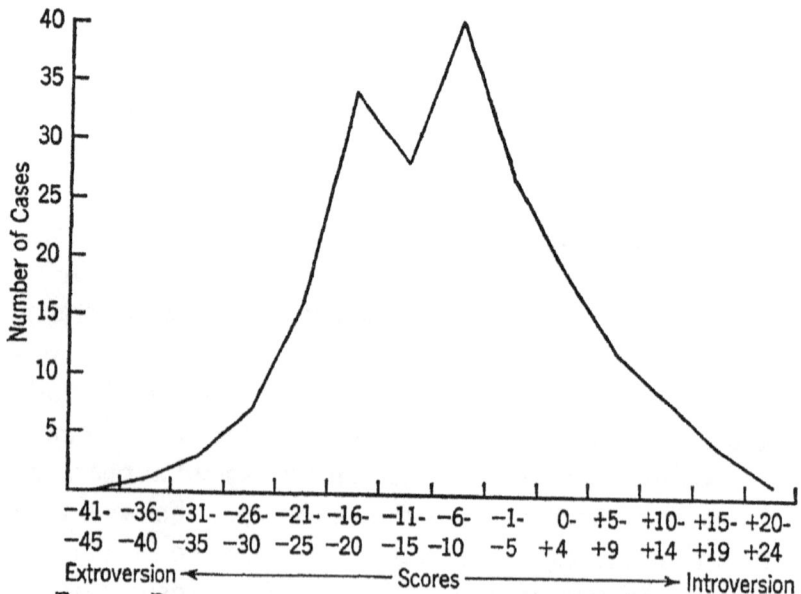

FIG. 17. DISTRIBUTION OF INTROVERSION-EXTROVERSION SCORES OF 200 COLLEGE STUDENTS. (Data from Heidbreder, 9, p. 124.)

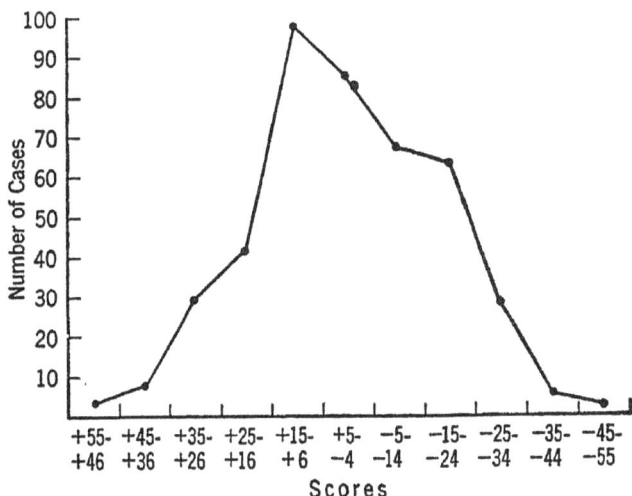

FIG. 18. SCORES OF 400 COLLEGE MEN ON THE ALLPORT ASCENDANCE-SUBMISSION TEST. (After Allport, 1, p. 129.)

Figure 17 gives the distribution of total introversion-extroversion scores on a self-rating questionnaire administered to 200 college students. The positive scores correspond to the introvert end of the scale, the negative scores to the extrovert end. It will be readily seen that individuals do not cluster at opposite ends of the scale, as a clear-cut division into introverts and extroverts would imply. The greatest clustering occurs in the center, with a gradual dropping off as the extremes are approached. Figure 18, giving the distribution

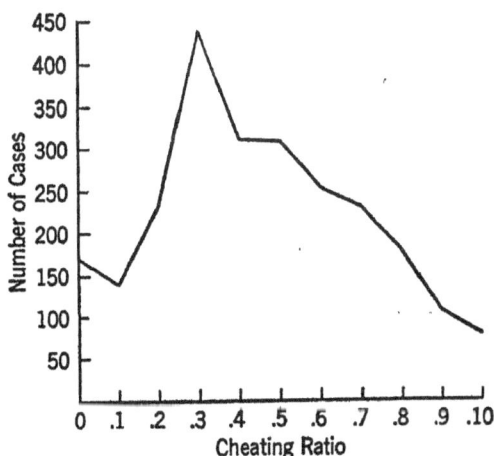

FIG. 19. DISTRIBUTION OF "CHEATING RATIOS" OF 2443 SCHOOLCHILDREN. (Data from Hartshorne and May, 6, p. 220.)

of 400 male college students on a test of ascendance-submission, exhibits the same general form.

Figures 19 to 22 are plotted with data taken from the studies of May and Hartshorne (6, 7, 8) on the measurement of character in schoolchildren. Figure 19 gives the distribution of "cheating ratios" for 2443 children. The cheating ratio indicates the number of times each child cheated relative to the number of opportunities offered. The obtained curve does not admit of a clear-cut division into "honest" and "dishonest," or those who cheat and those who do not. A slight skewness is exhibited, with a tendency for scores to pile up at

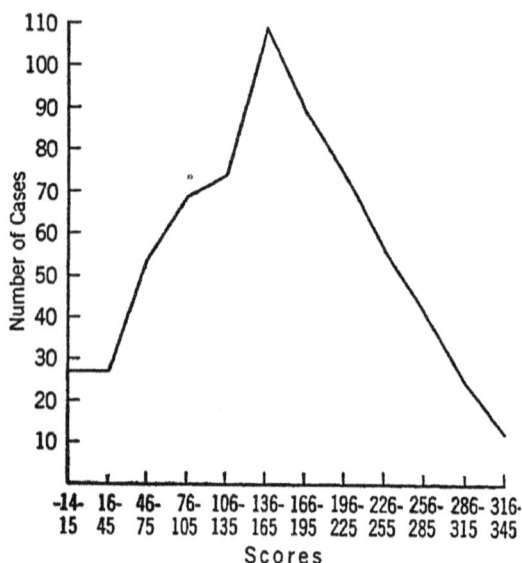

Fig. 20. Distribution of Persistence Scores among 656 Schoolchildren. (Unpubl. data from investigation of Hartshorne, May, and Maller, 7.)

the "honest" end, but this may be caused by a limitation in the scale. The tests probably presented an insufficient number of situations in which cheating was made very easy or involved a relatively minor "moral issue." This would cut the scale short at the lower end and produce an excess of zero or very low cheating scores. The distribution of combined scores on several tests of service or coöperativeness, presented in Figure 20, exhibits a very close resemblance to the normal curve. The same general features also characterize the distributions in Figures 21 and 22. The former gives the combined scores on several persistence

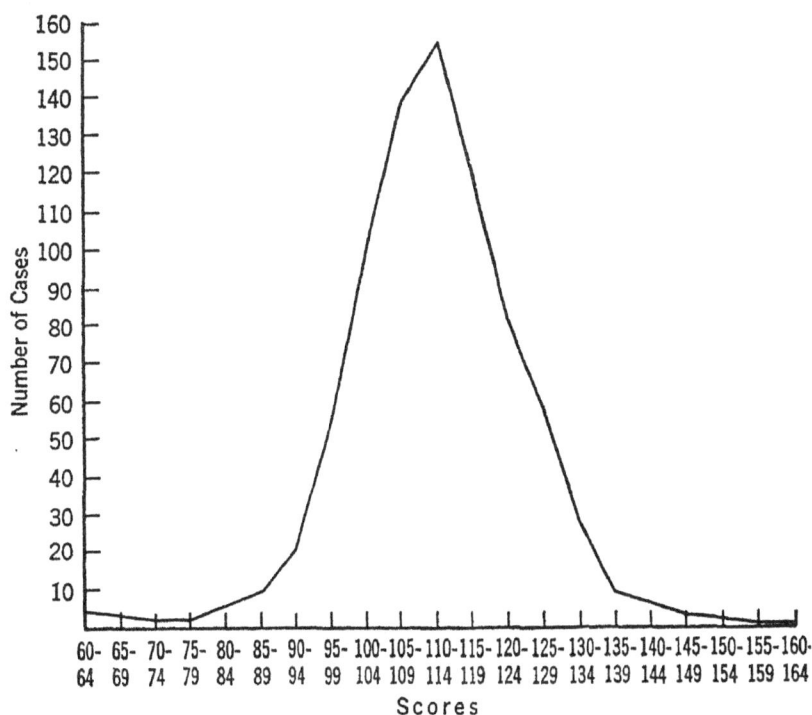

FIG. 21. DISTRIBUTION OF COÖPERATIVENESS AMONG 801 SCHOOLCHILDREN.
(Unpubl. data from investigation of Hartshorne, May, and Maller, 7.)

tests; the latter is based on the results of a question-naire of moral knowledge, designed to measure "good citizenship."

EXTENT OF VARIABILITY IN DIFFERENT TRAITS

One is tempted to compare the distributions of different traits in the effort to discover the relative variability of such traits. Do individuals differ more in physical or in mental traits? Are they more alike in intellectual or in emotional characteristics? These and many similar questions have been raised repeatedly and answers have occasionally been offered.[1] It is probably correct to state

---

. [1] Cf., for example, the interesting although rather futile discussion by Wechsler (19).

as a general principle that individual differences will be larger in the more complex than in the simpler traits. Any characteristic which depends upon the simultaneous variation of a large number of factors will exhibit more

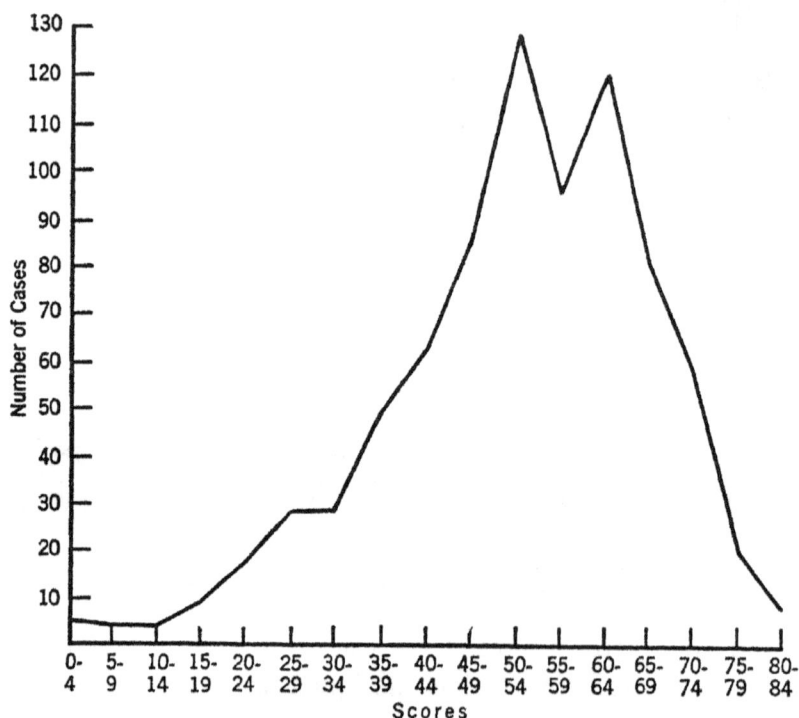

FIG. 22. SCORES OF 801 SCHOOLCHILDREN ON A TEST OF GOOD CITIZENSHIP.
(Unpubl. data from Hartshorne, May, and Shuttleworth, 8.)

marked differences than one which is determined by relatively few factors. An illustration from coin tossing will again prove serviceable. If two coins are employed, the number of possible combinations which may result is only four; if, however, the number of coins is increased to ten, the possible variations, or patterns of head-and-tail combinations, total 1024. A complex trait is one which is determined by a large number of factors or conditions, and hence it will be expected to exhibit a greater range of variation.

Apart from this rather obvious generalization, little can be said about the extent of individual variation in different traits. Upon close analysis, in fact, the question of the extent of variability itself appears to be ambiguous and quite meaningless. The first problem which confronts one when trying to compare human variability in separate traits is that of the measuring rod employed for the different traits, or the units in which the measurements are reported. That the particular scale employed affects the amount of variability found is easily demonstrated. If the height of buildings in one city is measured in feet and in another city in yards, the buildings in the former city will seem to vary among themselves three times as much as in the latter, even though the actual range in height may be identical in the two cities. Fortunately, feet can be translated into yards and vice versa. But this cannot be done with the units of psychological tests. The number of problems correctly solved on an arithmetic test cannot be transmuted into the same kind of units as neurotic symptoms checked on an emotional adjustment questionnaire. The only solution offered for this difficulty is the use of measures of relative variability.

All indices of relative variability are ratios. One such measure, the coefficient of variation, is found by dividing the standard deviation [1] by the average of the distribution. Thus variability is expressed in relation to the average, the difference in units from one test to the other being automatically ruled out. For the same purpose, the ratio between the highest and lowest scores or the tenth highest and tenth lowest, or any other similar combination, is

[1] The standard deviation is a statistical measure of the extent of variability within a group. It is found by subtracting each score from the average, squaring the differences, and then finding the square root of the average of these squares.

$$S.D. = \sqrt{\frac{\Sigma d^2}{N}}.$$

frequently computed. Although in current use, all such measures are open to a serious objection. The difficulty arises from the fact that psychological scales do not measure the individual from a true zero of ability as a base. Thus a zero score on Army Alpha does not mean zero intelligence, as was demonstrated when soldiers who had failed to make any score on the Alpha were given the Beta or the Stanford-Binet examinations. The Army Alpha begins at an arbitrary level of ability which is higher than that reached by some individuals; anyone falling below that level will receive a zero score.

The custom of measuring from "absolute zero" in our physical scales is so general that it is difficult to conceive of the effects of using a scale that begins at an arbitrary zero point. Think of a measuring stick on which height is measured, not from absolute zero or no height at all, but from some arbitrary point such as two feet. The following diagram illustrates the situation. Any object

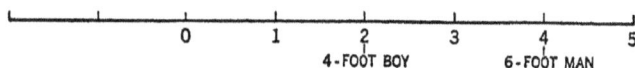

```
 |____|____|____|____|____|____|____|
      0    1    2    3    4    5
               4-FOOT BOY    6-FOOT MAN
```

two feet or less in height would register zero on this scale. If such a scale were to be employed only to measure the heights of individuals over five years of age, the arbitrary limit would perhaps not appear so absurd, since no one would be under two feet tall. This is in fact what has occurred in the construction of psychological tests. Since the Army Alpha, for example, was designed for adult men, it would have been wasteful and, from a practical standpoint impossible, to extend it down to the intellectual level of a newborn child. To return to our yardstick with an arbitrary zero point at two feet, let us suppose that it has been used to measure the heights of a six-foot man and a four-foot boy. The man will measure four feet and the boy two feet, as has been indicated on the diagram. For many purposes, no error has been introduced in the data by the use of the artificial zero point. On any scale, the man is two feet taller than the boy. If, however, we express their respective heights as a ratio, we reach the conclusion that the man is twice as tall as the boy ($\frac{4}{2}$). This is not true of their actual heights from absolute zero, the man being only $1\frac{1}{2}$ times as tall as the boy ($\frac{6}{4}$). The subtraction of a constant, two feet, from both heights has yielded a false ratio.

Such is the effect of an arbitrary zero point on any value which involves the *division* of one measure by another. For this reason, ratio or other relative measures cannot be employed with the large majority of psychological tests which are not scaled from absolute zero.[1] Such measures would hold true only for the specific tests in the form in which they were employed; the addition or removal of a few easy items at the lower end of the scale would completely alter the relative variabilities. Obviously the values thus computed could not be regarded as very meaningful. We arrive at the conclusion, then, that *with available psychological tests it is impossible to compare variability from one trait to another.*

Other difficulties also appear as the problem is inspected more closely. Does the question of the extent of variability refer to the whole human race? Which individuals, if any, shall be omitted in order to arrive at an estimate of human variability? Shall those who are regarded as definitely pathological and represent very extreme deviations be excluded? If so, where should the line be drawn between a typical human group and an abnormal deviant?

---

[1] The only important exception to date is the CAVD Intelligence Examination, prepared by the Institute of Educational Research at Teachers' College, Columbia University (cf. Thorndike, 15).

It seems reasonable, for example, to exclude from an estimate of the range of human variation in speed of movement one who has suffered an injury which renders his movements slow and halting. It is but a short step from this procedure to that which would exclude those incapacitated through disease. How, then, would this criterion operate in the case of a feebleminded person in whom no physical defect can be discovered? How far shall this process of eliminating extreme cases be carried?

A further question relates to the factors which are to be held constant in measuring the variability of any one trait. How homogeneous should the group be? The inclusion of children of different age levels would certainly increase the extent of variation in most traits. If only the range of individual differences within a fairly homogeneous population is desired, the difficulty of defining the required degree of homogeneity is encountered. Many traits are influenced by the social and economic level in which the individual finds himself. Should conditions of this sort also be held constant? Should differences in speed of performance be ruled out when determining variability in "intelligence"? Such questions could be raised *ad infinitum* unless an arbitrary limit is set up and adhered to consistently for the purposes of some one particular investigation.

We may conclude from this analysis that the question of the extent of individual differences in different traits cannot be answered unless put in very specific terms. The population must be defined in detail within each investigation and the nature of the trait measured must be made clear, especially by indicating which conditions are to be held constant and which will be allowed to vary. Obviously all conditions which affect a given trait cannot be held constant; otherwise variation would disappear.

It should be added that at the present stage in the development of mental testing, owing to the use of incomparable units and arbitrary zero points, the question cannot be answered at all, in any form.

INDIVIDUAL DIFFERENCES IN INFRAHUMAN GROUPS

Individual differences are not to be regarded as characteristically human. Variation is a universal phenomenon throughout the organic scale. "All cats look grey at night," but upon closer inspection each becomes an individual in his own right. Cursory or inadequate observation often creates an impression of similarity or even identity among members of a group while the differences pass unnoticed. For this reason, only the very exceptional deviations among animals have attracted attention in the past, all other members of the species having been implicitly relegated to the limbo of "normality."

Several cases of exceptionally "gifted" animals [1] have been described by their trainers or by observers, the remarkable feats of the animals having aroused the wonder and admiration of spectators. Among the most famous examples is Clever Hans, a stallion purchased in 1900 by a Mr. Van Osten of Berlin and subsequently trained by him. The horse was first taught a conventional alphabet in which each letter was represented by a certain combination of taps with the forefoot. Digits were indicated by the appropriate number of taps. By this system, the horse learned to "count" objects presented to him and also to perform all forms of simple arithmetic operations. He could handle fractions, first changing them into decimals. He was able to give the correct answer to such a problem as the following: "I have a number in mind; I subtract 9 and have 3 as a remainder; what is

[1] For a fuller discussion see Watson (18, Ch. IX) and Tinklepaugh (16).

the number?" He seemed to read German readily, and if presented with a series of cards containing written words, he would step up and point with his nose to any words required of him. He answered simple questions put to him orally, tapping out each letter of the answer in his conventional alphabet. He could give the date of any day one might mention, would tell time to the minute, and was able to analyze a discordant clang, telling his observers which note should be changed.

Most of these feats are not, to be sure, as remarkable as they appear at first glance. Thus, it was found that Clever Hans was unable to respond correctly to a problem if no one present knew the answer. Likewise, when the observers were concealed, the horse failed. The unusual achievements of Clever Hans and of many other performing animals result not from an understanding of arithmetic or an ability to read but from an exceptionally keen observation of slight cues given by the observers. The trainer, or other persons present, will make some slight gesture, such as lifting the head a few millimeters, as soon as the animal has tapped the correct number of times. Such cues, it may be added, are usually given unintentionally and unconsciously. They may be too slight to attract the attention of spectators, but an observant animal will learn to respond to them. Although destroying some of the glamor which such feats have had for the public, this explanation does not imply that the task of learning to observe and respond to the proper cues is an easy one which any animal could accomplish.

There remain, furthermore, the cases of animals who have been shown genuinely to respond to a wide variety of verbal commands in the absence of any other cues, or who have learned intricate combinations of movements, or have in many other ways proved their ability to react to very complex situations. Performing dogs, such as "Fellow" who could respond to approximately 400 words and execute the same commands even when worded differently, have been repeatedly exhibited. Dogs who lead the blind show a remarkably keen adjustment of their responses to the changing demands of the situation. Chimpanzees have been taught a wide variety of acts such as skating, riding a bicycle, eating with knife and fork, unlocking doors. The performances of circus animals, and especially "musical" sea lions, are well known. The observation of such animals, even when stripped of popular overstatement, still yields instances of marked individual differences.

Nor is the evidence for individual variation among infrahuman animals confined to the study of unusual cases. Every laboratory investigation employing more than one subject has revealed individual differences.[1] Animal psychologists have not as a rule been concerned with the measurement of variability, so that the data on this problem are usually mentioned only incidentally and frequently are not given in quantitative form. Whenever such data are reported, however, the range of performance in a randomly selected group is surprisingly large. Wide individual variation has been found in every phase of behavior investigated, such as the amount of general spontaneous activity, the relative strength of motives, speed of movement, quickness of learning simple tasks, and behavior in more complex problem-solving situations. Some typical quantitative results on learning behavior have been brought together in Table II. The average, range, and standard deviation for each set of data have been given whenever available.

[1] Cf., for example, the discussion of this problem from various angles by Tryon (17).

The first set of data are taken from experiments on conditioning. Two stimuli, such as a flash of light and an electric shock to the foot, are presented together. After a number of combined repetitions of these stimuli, the withdrawal response becomes conditioned to the light, i.e., the animal will withdraw its foot upon appearance of the light alone, without the presence of the electric shock. It is customary in such an experiment to refer to the original stimulus (in this case, the shock) as the conditioning stimulus, and to the other as the conditioned stimulus. The general nature of the conditioning and conditioned stimuli employed in each experiment has been indicated in Table II, together with the type and number of animals investigated. It will be noted that the number of combined repetitions of the two stimuli required to establish the conditioned reaction differs widely from individual to individual within each group.

The second set of data are taken from a series of learning projects conducted at the Columbia University laboratory of comparative psychology. Small samplings of guinea pigs, albino rats, common short-haired cats, and monkeys of two species were tested with the same type of "problem box" in which a series of steps of increasing complexity is presented to the animal. The box consists essentially of an outer and an inner cage, the latter containing the incentive which the animal obtains at the completion of each successful trial. In the outer cage are three plates to be depressed in a given order by the animal before the door to the incentive compartment is opened. In Table II, only the number of trials required to learn step I are reproduced, since this is the only step learned by all of the groups. The problem in step I consists simply in stepping on the first plate to the right as the animal en-

TABLE II

Some Typical Data on Individual Differences in Infrahuman Organisms

Conditioning Experiments *

Organism	No. of Subjects	Conditioning Stimulus	Conditioned Stimulus	Combinations for Conditioning		
				Average	Range	S.D.
Protozoa	82	Tactile	Light	138.5	79–284	24.6
Crustacea	14	Tactile	Light	503.	34–1112	
Fish	59	Food	Sounds	12.7	3–35	7.7
Pigeons	13	Shock; Food	Lights; Sounds; Rotation		30–40	
Sheep	11 (estimated)	Shock	Sounds; Tactile		3–17	

Problem Box †

Organism	No. of Subjects	No. Learning Step I	Trials to Learn Step I			Range in Steps Learned
			Average	Range	S.D.	
Guinea pigs	30	16	185.50	53–407	176.28	0–1
Albino rats	35	24	221.04	30–453	125.26	0–2
Cats	62	62	46.69 ‡	9–136	25.28	3–7
Monkeys (Rhesus)	17	17	162.47	19–310	94.36	2–22
Monkeys (Cebus)	6	6	137.17	42–327	108.41	5–15

Maze-Learning §

Organism	Type of Maze	No. of Cases	No. of Trials to Learn		
			Average	Range	S.D.
Albino rats	8 cul-de-sac elevated skeleton maze	186	32.75		16.59
Albino rats	Equal-unit maze	40	6.40		2.99

* From Razran (13), pp. 308–309.
† From Fjeld (4), p. 528, and Koch (11), pp. 186, 208.
‡ Cf. footnote on p. 62.
§ From Corey (3), p. 256, and Jackson (10), p. 27.

61

ters.[1] The other steps involved stepping on plates 1 and 2; 1, 2, and 3; 1, 2, 3, and back to 2; 1, 2, 3, 2, 1; and so on to other combinations. Although these studies were conducted mainly to determine the highest number of steps which any animal within a given species could master, the data yield striking evidence of individual differences within each species. Not only the number of trials required to learn each step, but also the number of steps which could be learned, differed from individual to individual. Thus in the group of guinea pigs, some were unable to learn even step I, while others succeeded; among the rats, some learned two steps, some one, and a few none; among the cats, the range is from 3 to 7 steps; among the rhesus monkeys 2 to 22, and among the cebus 5 to 15. Thus the individual variation was so large that an individual could easily be found in a "higher" species who was unable to learn as much as a given individual in a "lower" species.

In the third section of Table II are presented some typical data on maze learning among albino rats. The individual differences are again marked, as is indicated by the standard deviations of the number of trials required to master the correct path in each maze. Thus it is apparent that close observation and measurement of animal behavior reveal fully as wide an individual variation as the studies on human subjects.

An interesting example of the normal distribution curve in a functional trait in animals is to be found in the photograph and accompanying curve reproduced in Figure 23. The photograph shows horses on the race track just before the finish. The relative position of the horses

[1] In the study on cats, the problem set in step I was simpler, the animal being allowed to step on *any one* of the three plates. The data on this group are therefore not directly comparable to those on the other species.

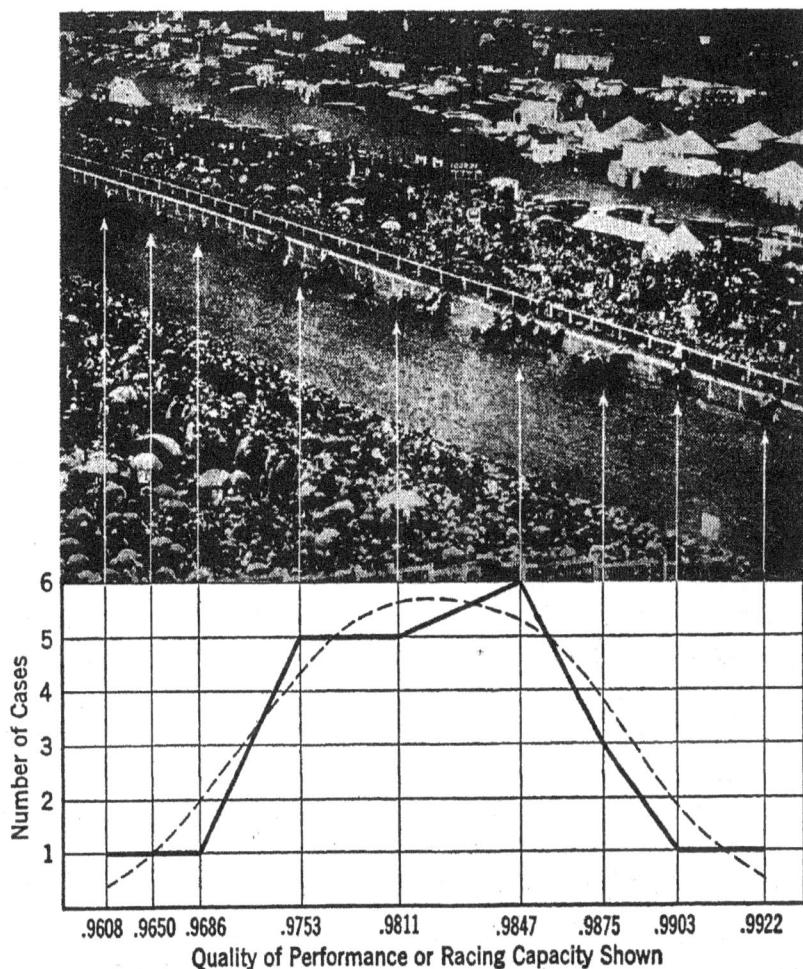

FIG. 23. A NORMAL DISTRIBUTION CURVE OF RACING CAPACITY SHOWING THE FIELD OF 24 HORSES "NEARING THE LINE" IN THE DERBY STAKES AT EPSOM DOWNS, JUNE 5, 1929. (After Laughlin, 12, p. 215.)

furnishes a vivid demonstration of the normal distribution of racing performance. A few are in the lead, an equally small number lag behind, and the majority are scattered in intermediate positions. The graph is a frequency curve of the "racing capacity" of the same horses, computed by a standardized formula.

REFERENCES

1. Allport, G. W. "A Test for Ascendance-Submission," *J. Abn. and Soc. Psychol.*, 1928–29, 23, 118–136.

2. Anastasi, A. "Practice and Variability," *Psychol. Mon.*, 1934, 45, No. 5. Pp. 55.

3. Corey, S. M. "An Experimental Study of Retention in the White Rat," *J. Exp. Psychol.*, 1931, 14, 252–259.

4. Fjeld, H. A. "The Limits of Learning Ability in Rhesus Monkeys," *Genet. Psychol. Mon.*, 1934, 15, 369–537.

5. Harris, J. A., Jackson, C. M., Paterson, D. G., and Scammon, R. L. *The Measurement of Man.* Minneapolis: Univ. Minn. Press, 1930. Pp. 215.

6. Hartshorne, H., and May, M. A. *Studies in Deceit.* N. Y.: Macmillan, 1928. Pp. 306.

7. Hartshorne, H., May, M. A., and Maller, J. B. *Studies in Service and Self-Control.* N. Y.: Macmillan, 1929. Pp. 559.

8. Hartshorne, H., May, M. A., and Shuttleworth, F. K. *Studies in the Organization of Character.* N. Y.: Macmillan, 1930. Pp. 503.

9. Heidbreder, E. "Measuring Introversion and Extroversion," *J. Abn. and Soc. Psychol.*, 1926, 21, 120–134.

10. Jackson, T. A. "General Factors in Transfer of Training in the White Rat," *Genet. Psychol. Mon.*, 1932, 11, 1–52.

11. Koch, A. M. "The Limits of Learning Ability in Cebus Monkeys," *Genet. Psychol. Mon.*, 1935, 17, 165–234.

12. Laughlin, H. H. "Racing Capacity in the Thoroughbred Horse," *Sci. Monthly*, 1934, 38, 210–222; 310–321.

13. Razran, G. H. S. "Conditioned Responses in Animals Other than Dogs," *Psychol. Bull.*, 1933, 30, 261–324.

14. Terman, L. M. *The Measurement of Intelligence.* N. Y.: Houghton Mifflin, 1916. Pp. 362.

15. Thorndike, E. L., Bregman, E. O., Cobb, M. V., and Woodyard, Ella. *The Measurement of Intelligence.* N. Y.: Teachers College, Columbia Univ., Bur. Pub., 1926. Pp. 616.

16. Tinklepaugh, O. L. "'Gifted' Animals." Ch. XV in *Com-*

parative Psychology, ed. by Moss, F. A. N. Y.: Prentice-Hall, 1934. Pp. 529.

17. Tryon, R. C. "Individual Differences." Ch. XIII in *Comparative Psychology*, ed. by Moss, F. A. N. Y.: Prentice-Hall, 1934. Pp. 529.

18. Watson, J. B. *Behavior: an Introduction to Comparative Psychology*. N. Y.: Holt, 1929. Pp. 439.

19. Wechsler, David. *The Range of Human Capacities*. Baltimore: Williams and Wilkins, 1935. Pp. 159.

20. Yerkes, R. M., ed. "Psychological Examining in the United States Army," *Memoirs Nat. Acad. Sci.*, 1921, 15. Pp. 890.

21. Yule, G. U. *An Introduction to the Theory of Statistics.* London: Griffin, 1919. Pp. 422.

CHAPTER III
HEREDITY AND ENVIRONMENT

Why do individuals differ from one another? What are the factors which produce variation? These questions have stimulated intense discussion and led to lively controversy. In addition to its fundamental theoretical import, the problem of the causation of individual differences has far-reaching practical significance in many fields. Any procedure involving the control of human development must be based upon an understanding of the factors which influence such development. All educational methods make some assumption regarding the causes of individual differences. Is the main function of education to produce certain desirable traits, or merely to offer opportunities for the development of the child's potentialities? Volumes have been devoted to argumentative and frequently verbose analyses of this question. The empirical accumulation of facts on the causes of individual variation alone can furnish a conclusive answer. The type of educational activities, vocations, and other pursuits traditionally allotted to men and women rests upon certain beliefs regarding the cause of sex differences in psychological traits. Relationships among racial and national groups, and the attitudes of one group towards another, are built up on the basis of theories, either implicitly assumed or overtly stated, regarding the origin of racial and national characteristics. Any caste system implies an hereditary differentiation of people. Such systems, although not formally prescribed, are quite prevalent and operate in the choice of a vocation and similar situations of everyday life. The interpretation of family resemblances, and even in some cases the development of family groupings themselves, rest upon specific underlying hypotheses regarding the causal factors in human resemblance and dissimilarity.

Fundamental Concepts

The causes of individual variation are to be sought in the individual's hereditary background and in the environmental conditions to which he has been exposed. Every trait or behavior manifestation of the individual depends both on his heredity and on his environment. Traits and activities cannot be classified into those which are inherited and those which are acquired. The problem thus resolves itself into a determination of the relative contribution of hereditary and environmental factors in the development of the individual. To what extent can the development of any given characteristic be altered by the control of environmental influences, and to what extent is such modification limited by hereditary conditions? Individual variations found under similar hereditary conditions may be attributed to the operation of different environmental factors. Similarly, when the environments are sufficiently similar, any dissimilarity of behavior may be regarded as indicative of a difference in heredity. We may speak, therefore, of hereditary and environmental determiners or factors in the development of a given characteristic, although such a dichotomy cannot be applied to traits.

How does heredity operate in the development of the individual? The understanding of the mechanism of heredity has been greatly furthered by the concept of the gene. The individual begins life at conception with the union of one germ cell from each parent, the ovum of the female and the spermatozoön of the male. Each of these cells contains hundreds of thousands of very minute particles, called genes. A gene is the carrier of a "unit character," i.e., an hereditary factor or influence which always operates as a unit, or in an all-or-none fashion. These unit characters of the geneticists are not to be confused with traits as ordinarily conceived, but are of a much more elementary nature. Thus, even a relatively simple characteristic such as eye color depends upon the combined influence of a very large number of separate genes. Such complex hereditary determination would of course produce varying degrees of a trait, even though the individual genes may be characterized only by presence or absence.

It is obvious that any attempt to identify psychological characteristics, and especially such a manifold and ill-defined phenomenon as "intelligence," with unit characters is entirely inconsistent with the concepts and data of genetics. Nevertheless such an attempt was actually made in the zeal which followed the early spread of mental tests.[1] The experimental location of the specific genes which contribute towards the development of observable traits of the organism is, on the other hand, an extremely difficult task. In recent years rapid strides have been made along these lines by geneticists, as is illustrated by the excellent work of Morgan (18) on the gene "maps" of the fruit fly, *Drosophila melanogaster*. This phase of the geneticist's work is, however, still in its infancy. The data available at present are too meagre to be of any direct assistance in the understanding of complex behavior phenomena.

The hereditary basis of individual differences is to be found in the almost unlimited variety of possible gene

[1] Cf. Goddard (8), especially Chs. VII and VIII.

combinations which presents itself, especially in the case of such a complex organism as man. When male and female germ cells unite at conception, the fertilized ovum contains two sets of genes, one from each parent. These genes combine in a variety of ways in each of the daughter cells, and hence the different germ cells of the resulting organism will not be identical in their gene constitution. The individual offspring of this organism will therefore differ among themselves because they have developed from different germ cells. When we add to this the fact that such offspring result from the union of germ cells from *two* parents, each of whom has germ cells which differ among themselves, the number of possible variations becomes very large. Thus it is small wonder that duplicate individuals are not produced by chance.

The only exception to this individual diversity of gene constitution is that of identical twins, which develop from a single fertilized ovum. Such twins are always of the same sex and identical in appearance. Fraternal twins, on the other hand, do not reveal such close resemblance and may be either of the same or opposite sex. The hereditary similarity of fraternal twins is no greater than that of ordinary siblings,[1] since they result from the simultaneous development of two different cells. Fraternal twins are, however, exposed to the same prenatal environment, which may be an important factor in rendering them similar in their subsequent development.

Certain popular misconceptions regarding the manifestations of heredity should be cleared up at the outset. In the first place, there is a common belief that inheritance is indicated only by resemblance to parents or immediate ancestors. This is shown to be false by a consideration of the mechanism of inheritance. The germ plasm is

[1] *Siblings* is a general term employed to cover both brothers and sisters.

continuous from generation to generation and is not "produced" by the individual parents. The parents simply transmit this germ plasm to the offspring. Hence the individual inherits from all of his direct ancestors, and not only from his parents. Some characteristic which may have been latent for many generations may become dominant because of a particular combination of genes and the result will be an individual very unlike his parents or immediate forbears in some one respect. Instances of this sort are not uncommon in family histories. In such a case, heredity actually serves to make the child unlike his parents.

A further possible source of misunderstanding is to be found in the common habit of speaking about functions and activities as determined by hereditary factors. Heredity can only exert a direct control over the development of structures. Insofar as a given activity involves the presence of certain structures, such as vocal organs, hands, glands, nervous system, the hereditary factors underlying the development of these structures will influence activity. Likewise, the nature and degree of development of organs will affect their functions. But this is only a limiting condition imposed upon the development of a given type of behavior. Hereditary factors may prevent the appearance of a function through the absence of the necessary structures, but the converse does not hold. The presence of such structures does not imply that the particular form of behavior in question will appear.

Another popular notion occasionally met is that whatever is present at birth is inherited and whatever appears subsequently is acquired. As it stands, this statement is inconsistent with the fundamental concept of development as an interaction of hereditary and environmental influences. Even if reworded to eliminate this inconsistency,

however, it is still misleading. Thus it is equally false
to think of the operation of hereditary influences in the
development of any trait as ceasing at birth or, conversely,
to think of environmental influences as beginning to operate at birth. Hereditary factors may influence the development of the individual long after birth, and in fact
throughout the life span. Even the onset of death itself
may be determined partly by hereditary factors, as suggested by the observation that longevity or "long life"
tends to run in families. Hereditary influences may become manifest for the first time at any age. Similarly,
environmental influences begin to operate upon the individual from the moment of conception. The importance
of temperature, chemical, and other types of stimulation
in the prenatal surroundings of the developing embryo is
rapidly coming to be recognized. Birth is not to be regarded as either a beginning or an end in the life of the
organism, but as a relatively minor occurrence in a
developmental continuum which begins at conception and
ends at death.

Prenatal Environment

In general it may be said that the earlier an environmental condition operates in the life of the individual, the
more pronounced will be its effect. After an advanced
state of growth has been reached, the organism becomes
much less modifiable. For this reason, the stimuli to
which the individual is exposed during the embryonic
stage exert a pronounced and lasting influence upon its
future development. Variations in diet and nutrition,
glandular secretion, and other conditions of the mother
which are manifested in the chemical condition of the
blood have a marked effect upon the characteristics of
the embryo. The structural development of the individual

is definitely influenced by such environmental factors. It is also possible that a certain amount of rudimentary learning may occur during prenatal life. The presence of certain reflexes and other simple movements in young embryos has been definitely established. Such responses may early become conditioned in various ways to changes of temperature, pressure, and other stimuli furnished by the intra-uterine environment. The study of prenatal behavior opens interesting possibilities, although so far it offers only very meagre information. In the field of structural development, however, the data are much more conclusive.

Many instances of experimentally induced structural changes in lower animals have been reported from time to time. A very curious transformation can be produced in the axolotl, a large salamander (cf. 14, pp. 117, 124–125). Normally, this animal has prominent external gills, a large tail adapted for swimming, and other characteristics suited for life in the water. If the young axolotl is fed on thyroid, it loses its gills, and its body becomes generally altered so that it is no longer adapted to swimming. The animal then becomes a land salamander, known as Amblystoma, and returns to the water only to lay its eggs.

In the fruit fly, a defective gene causes the animal to produce "reduplicated legs," i.e., certain joints of the legs, or entire legs, are doubled. Although the inheritance of this defective gene has been definitely traced, this characteristic will not appear under certain environmental conditions (12). If animals known to have the defective gene are kept at a sufficiently warm temperature, the additional leg or joint will not develop. Successive generations bred under these conditions will have a normal appearance. If, however, any of their offspring are allowed to develop in colder temperatures, the defect will reappear. This furnishes a definite illustration of the fact that even a clearly demonstrable "inherited defect" is actually only a tendency to develop in a given way under certain environmental conditions.

Experimentally produced "monsters" furnish very striking examples of the influence of prenatal environment (24, Chs. VI and VII). In experiments on fish eggs, "siamese twin" fish have been produced by artificially inhibiting or slowing down the rate of development at an early age through cold, insufficient oxygen, or the application of ultra-violet rays. In some cases, one twin is much smaller than the other and is deformed, the larger twin being a perfectly normal fish. Two-headed monsters have been produced among tadpoles and several species of fish by the application of various chemical or mechanical stimuli. Striking variations in the number and position of the eyes of minnows have likewise been induced. If the eggs of the minnow are allowed to develop in sea water to which has been added an excess of magnesium chloride, peculiar eye conditions will appear in a large majority of the embryos. Instead of the usual two eyes, many will develop a centrally placed "cyclopean" eye, so named after the one-eyed Cyclops of mythology. Others may show a single lateral eye, placed to the right or left of the head. Or the two eyes may be abnormally close together. Other physical or chemical agents may be employed to produce the same anomalies of development. The determining factor in the development of a particular abnormality seems to be the stage at which the agent is introduced, rather than the nature of the specific agent employed. The essential effect is a change in the rate of development, which alters the balance of growth among the different parts of the organism.

Thus we cannot even speak of certain structural characteristics as being "normal" for a given species and fixed by hereditary constitution. If the environment in which the organisms develop were to undergo a change of a more or less permanent nature, a different set of characteristics would come to be considered normal. Similarities of development are attributable to common exposure to an essentially similar environment as much as to the possession of common genes.[1]

EXPERIMENTALLY PRODUCED VARIATIONS IN BEHAVIOR

Numerous experiments have shown the possibility of pronounced alteration in behavior as a result of environmental differences. Animals reared in isolation from other members of the species or from individuals of the opposite sex, or in close association with a human child, have developed curious modifications of behavior. Activities which are commonly assumed to be "unlearned" and fixed by hereditary constitution have proved susceptible to marked change. Universal characteristics in behavior, as in structure, have been shown to result as much from common environments and similar opportunities for learning as from common heredity. A few illustrations of experimental attempts to alter behavior traits will be considered. It is understood, of course, that by alteration is here meant simply the production of behavior different from that which develops in the ordinary environment. There is no implication that one kind of behavior is fundamentally any more "natural" than another.

The songs of different birds, generally considered so characteristic of the species, have been found to contain

---

[1] A very comprehensive survey of data showing the effect of environmental factors upon the development of *stature* and *weight* in the human is to be found in Sanders (21).

much that is learned in their specific manifestations. A group of newly hatched orioles were segregated from all older members of the species and brought up by themselves (22). When the birds reached a certain age, they began to sing. Their song, however, was not the characteristic oriole song, but a new one. When other newly hatched orioles were reared with the group that had grown up in the laboratory, the young birds in turn learned the new song developed by the first group.

Similarly, a sparrow reared in a nest of canaries gradually abandoned his own chirps and began to take over the canary's call note (1). After about a month of association with the canaries, the sparrow began to imitate their song. Although at first very harsh and confused, this song eventually developed into a genuine canary-like performance. These and similar experiments have shown that although birds will develop some sort of song when they reach a certain stage of structural development, the specific nature of the song depends upon environmental factors.

Sexual behavior has also proved to be dependent upon learning in its specific manifestations. Some form of sexual activity will occur at a definite developmental stage, because of the presence of glandular secretions in the blood and other physiological factors. The particular way in which such activity is expressed and the object towards which it is directed, however, will vary according to environmental circumstances. In an experiment on male doves reared in isolation from other members of the species, a number of sexual "abnormalities" were observed (3). The birds would bow and coo to the experimenter as normal birds do to members of their own species. They seemed to pay especial attention to the experimenter's hand with which they came into contact when fed; one bird actually went through the act of copulation while on the hand taking food. Female doves reared in isolation developed similar anomalies of behavior (2). If the experimenter stroked them and preened the feathers of their head and neck, they exhibited characteristic courting behavior. Egg-laying was actually induced in many instances by this method. Experimental "homosexuality" was produced in a large number of cases when two female pigeons were reared together. In such cases, the animals would display the usual courting performance towards each other, egg-laying then following in both.

Equally curious variations of behavior were noted in a young monkey separated from its mother at the age of three days and brought up in isolation from all members of the species during the first 18 months of life (5, 6). The development of sexual behavior in general was markedly delayed. During the period of isolation there was a minimum of the sex behavior ordinarily displayed by monkeys at that age. At the age of 18 months, the period of isolation was discontinued, and the monkey was subsequently brought up with other members of the species. At this time, sex behavior began to appear, but in a very rudimentary form. Attempts at copulation were very crude and trial-and-error was exhibited. Sexual activity was shown indiscriminately towards males and females, as well as towards monkeys of other species, rags and other soft objects, and the experimenter's arm and hand. With continued association with other members of the species, normal sexual activity eventually developed. Other forms of behavior, such as feeding, play-activity, and grooming, were also affected by the prolonged period of isolation.

The recent investigation of Kellogg and Kellogg (16),

in which a young chimpanzee was reared for a short
period in a typically human environment, throws further
light upon the factors affecting behavioral development.
The chimpanzee, a female named "Gua," was isolated
from its mother at the age of 7½ months and brought up
in the company of the investigator's own son, Donald,
then 10 months old. The association was continued for
a period of nine months. The chimpanzee was not treated
as a pet, but as a child, and the two subjects were given
as nearly as possible identical care. Gua was clothed in
the same manner as the child, and showed no difficulty
in keeping on shoes, stockings, and other common articles
of clothing. She slept in a bed with the usual accessories,
such as sheets and blankets. Excellent progress was
made by the chimpanzee in learning to eat with a spoon
and drink out of a glass. She was able to manipulate
pencil and paper and produce simple scribblings. Gua
also learned to respond to oral language, and by the
termination of the experimental period understood over
50 words or simple phrases, such as: "Blow the horn"
(in the car); "Show me your nose"; "Do you want to go
bye-bye?" "Take it out of your mouth." The degree to
which it proved possible to "humanize" the behavior of
this ape is indeed suggestive, especially in view of the
fact that the period of residence in the human environment
was of relatively short duration and did not begin at
birth.

Human Children Reared in Abnormal Environments

What would be the effect of bringing up a human child
in isolation or in exclusive contact with lower animals?
Several cases of children found in such situations are on
record. The child's condition and behavior repertory at
the time of discovery, as well as its subsequent develop-

ment when transferred to a normal environment, furnish interesting material on the heredity-environment question.

The most famous case is probably that of the Wild Boy of Aveyron, as it has come to be known in the psychological literature. In September, 1799, three sportsmen came upon a boy of 11 or 12 in a French forest. The boy was completely naked, unkempt, scarred, unable to talk, and seemed to have been leading a wild, animal-like existence. He was seized by the men as he was climbing a tree to escape their pursuit, and was subsequently brought to civilization. He finally came under the guidance and observation of the French physician, Itard. The very illuminating account which Itard published on his own findings has immortalized the Wild Boy of Aveyron. When found, the boy seems to have been deficient in all forms of behavioral development, including sensory, motor, intellectual, and emotional. This is clearly brought out in the following brief description (13, pp. 5–8).

> His eyes were unsteady, expressionless, wandering vaguely from one object to another without resting on anybody; they were so little experienced in other ways and so little trained by the sense of touch, that they never distinguished an object in relief from one in a picture. His organ of hearing was equally insensible to the loudest noises and to the most touching music. His voice was reduced to a state of complete muteness and only a uniform guttural sound escaped him. His sense of smell was so uncultivated that he was equally indifferent to the odor of perfumes and to the fetid exhalation of the dirt with which his bed was filled. Finally, the organ of touch was restricted to the mechanical function of grasping objects. Proceeding then to the state of the intellectual functions of this child, the author of the report presented him to us as being quite incapable of attention (except for the objects of his needs) and consequently of all those op-

erations of the mind which attention involves. He was destitute of memory, of judgment, of aptitude for imitation, and
was so limited in his ideas, even those relative to his immediate
needs, that he had never yet succeeded in opening a door or
climbing upon a chair to get the food that had been raised
out of reach of his hand. In short, he was destitute of all
means of communication and attached neither expression
nor intention to his gestures or to the movements of his
body. He passed rapidly and without any apparent motive
from apathetic melancholy to the most immoderate peals of
laughter. . . . His locomotion was extraordinary, literally
heavy after he wore shoes, but always remarkable because
of his difficulty in adjusting himself to our sober and measured gait, and because of his constant tendency to trot and
to gallop. He had an obstinate habit of smelling at anything
that was given to him, even the things which we consider
void of smell; his mastication was equally astonishing, executed as it was solely by the sudden action of the incisors,
which because of its similarity to that of certain rodents,
was a sufficient indication that our savage, like these animals,
most commonly lived on vegetable products.

It is interesting to note that the sensory deficiency of
this boy seems to have been quite specific and in many
instances directly traceable to his mode of life. Thus
Itard observed that "the sound of a cracking walnut or
other favorite eatable never failed to make him turn
around . . . nevertheless, this same organ showed itself
insensible to the loudest noises and the explosion of fire-
arms" (13, p. 15). Sexual development showed the same
general undifferentiated type of response observed in the
case of animals reared in isolation. Following the onset
of puberty, periods of vague restlessness and discomfort
as well as occasional fits of sadness or anger were noted,
without, however, the development of specific, normal
sexual activity.

After five years of ingenious, painstaking, and methodical training, Itard abandoned the task, having failed to bring the boy up to normal. This has led many to conclude that the Wild Boy of Aveyron must have been an imbecile from birth, who had been abandoned by his parents because of his mental deficiency. Such a conclusion, however, overlooks several important points. In the first place, marked improvements were effected by the training, even though a normal level was not reached. For example, although the boy could not learn to articulate sounds, he succeeded in learning simple written language, so that he was finally able to reproduce written words from memory and to use them "to express his wants, to solicit the means to satisfy them and to grasp by the same method of expression the needs or the will of others" (13, p. 84). Secondly, had the boy actually been feebleminded, he should very probably have been unable to survive in the very trying circumstances of his primitive environment. Finally, the fact that the training was begun so late in life may furnish an adequate explanation of its lack of success. The environment of early childhood is too important in determining subsequent development.

The more recently discovered "wolf children" of India (23, 15) represent a similar case. In 1921, two girls, aged about two to four and eight to nine, respectively, were found living in a cave with wolves in a sparsely settled region of India. They were taken into a local orphanage where some attempts were made to train them. It proved very difficult, however, to keep the girls in good health, particularly because they could not be induced to eat a normal, varied human diet, but retained the feeding habits they had acquired from association with carnivorous animals. The younger girl, "Amala," died in less than a month; the elder, "Kamala," lived for about eight years. As a result, most of the observations which have been recorded were made on the older child.

Kamala, like her younger companion, showed a great preference for raw meat. Although never known to kill any domestic animal, she was fond of pouncing upon any killed animal which she found. The odor of meat could be detected at a great distance and a keen animal-like sense of smell was generally exhibited. Hearing was also very acute. The eyes are described as possessing a peculiar glare, like the eyes of dogs or cats in the dark. It seemed that Kamala could see much better at night than in the daytime, and she seldom slept after midnight. When dressed, she tore off her clothes. Eating and drinking were accomplished by lowering the mouth into the plate, like a dog. Eventually, however, she was taught to use her hands in eating. Locomotion originally consisted of crawling on all fours. She finally learned to walk erect on two legs, although she was never able to run in this position. She was accustomed to emit a cry or howl in a peculiar voice, neither animal nor human. With prolonged training, she was able to say about forty words and form simple sentences of two or three words, although the original howl was still repeated occasionally.

Mention should also be made of the celebrated and mysterious case of Kaspar Hauser (cf. 26, pp. 290–292), about whom so much has been written. Some accounts suggest that this boy was an heir to some princely house and was put out of the way by political enemies. He was apparently confined from early childhood in a dark cell, not large enough for him to stand upright. No clothing or cover was furnished except a shirt and trousers. When he awoke, he was accustomed to find bread and water, but he never saw the person who brought them and he had no knowledge of the existence of other living creatures besides himself. He was released in 1828, when about 17 years of age. At this time he was first discovered, wandering aimlessly about the streets of Nuremberg. He could not talk, but repeatedly uttered certain phrases meaninglessly. He is reputed to have had a remarkable sense of smell and a surprising ability to see in the dark. His walking resembled the first efforts of a child. After various vicissitudes, his instruction was undertaken by Prof. Daumer. Under the latter's tutelage, Kaspar Hauser made rapid progress, and soon learned to speak. By this means he was able to communicate what he recalled of his life in the cell. As in other cases of children brought into contact with civilization relatively late in life, his education never brought him quite up to normal.

These examples illustrate the close dependence of human development upon the environment in which the subject is reared and the type of stimulation to which he is exposed. If a child is deprived of normal human contacts, his behavior will come to resemble in many ways that of a low-grade idiot. Such a condition has, in fact, been regarded as a sort of environmental feeble-mindedness and has been given the name of *isolation amentia* (cf. 26, pp. 285, 290). When a child is brought up in contact with animals, striking similarity to the behavior of those animals is exhibited, and such behavior proves difficult to eradicate once it has become firmly established. Subsequent educational efforts are inadequate to undo the effects of early nurture. Rousseau's dream of the "noble savage" whose inner nature is allowed to develop, free and unhampered by human interference, proves to be a vain chimera. The situation has been very aptly summarized by Stratton (25, p. 597):

Lack of association with adults during a certain critical period of early childhood, it seems likely, produces in some or all normal children marks like those of congenital defect. The evidence seems against the romantic view that a civilized community is a chief obstacle to the development of personality. On the contrary, the higher forms of personality become possible only in and through such a community. By our biological endowment alone, or by this as developed by maturing and learning in an infrahuman environment, we remain man-beasts. We become human only by active intercourse in a society of those who already have become human.

DIFFERENCES AMONG SOCIAL OR OCCUPATIONAL GROUPS

The environmental variations described in the preceding sections were all of a very drastic nature. It might be objected that such cases tell us little about the ordinary range of individual differences observed in everyday life. Then, too, the examples cited above represent single cases; little is known about the exact antecedents of the children; and the observations were not in most cases very well controlled. It would seem difficult to draw conclusions from such information alone. The facts of human development suggested by these strange cases have, however, been corroborated by data gathered from various other sources. The comparison of children brought up in different social and cultural classes or occupational levels presents in a much milder form the same type of environmental dissimilarity and concomitant behavior variations found in the cases of "wild children." Such investigations have ordinarily dealt with very large groups and have arrived at their results by the use of standardized tests.

Among the most clear-cut findings on the effect of home environment and schooling upon intelligence as measured by current tests are those of Gordon (10) on canal-boat and gypsy children in England. Gordon's report, made in the course of his official duties as Inspector of Schools, is based on the Stanford-Binet I.Q.'s and educational test scores of various groups of children whose schooling is deficient. The canal-boat children were obtained from two special schools maintained for such groups. Their only opportunity to attend school occurs when the canal-boats are tied up for loading or discharging. It has been estimated that the average school attendance of canal-boat children is only 5% of that in ordinary elementary schools. The majority are only able to attend school about once a month for one or two consecutive half-days. Their home surroundings, although satisfactory in respect to conditions of health and cleanliness, are intellectually of a very low order. Many of the adults are themselves illiterate, and each family leads a relatively isolated existence, with a minimum of social intercourse.

The average I.Q. of the entire group of 76 canal-boat children was 69.6. Taken at face value, this would suggest at best a borderline group, with a few distinctly feebleminded individuals. Gordon's analysis of the data, however, brings out very vividly the influence of the restricted social and educational facilities. Thus the correlation between age and I.Q. within the entire group proved to be −.755. This indicates a marked and consistent tendency for the older children to get lower I.Q.'s than the younger. Such a finding is quite contrary to the data on growth of intelligence in the usual child. The discrepancy can only be understood in terms of specific environmental influences. The intellectual environment of the younger canal-boat children is not as far below normal as that of their older brothers and sisters. The younger child in any home is exposed to relatively simple intellectual stimulation; as the child grows older, differences in schooling and in the cultural level of the home become much more apparent.

The high negative correlation with age is corroborated by analysis of individual scores. In 22 cases, two or more children from the same family were tested. With only one or two exceptions, there was found a consistent drop in I.Q. from the youngest to the eldest child within each family. Most of the youngest children had I.Q.'s between 90 and 100, which would place them within the normal group; among the eldest, on the other hand, were several whose I.Q.'s were low enough to make them appear distinctly feebleminded. A further corroborative fact brought out by this analysis is that the mental ages of children within a single family tended to be very similar, even though their chronological ages differed. Such a mental age might well represent the limit of intellectual development which was made possible by the available educational opportunities and the type of home environment furnished within the given family.

Gordon's report on gypsy children lends further support to the interpretations offered above. A total of 82 gypsy children attending four schools were given the Stanford-Binet. The school attendance of gypsy children, although still below normal, is better than that of canal-boat children. Actual records on the group investigated showed that the average school attendance from the age of five to the time of testing was only 34.9% of the total number of possible school days. Living conditions were in general quite crude and primitive. The groups led a nomadic existence, having a fixed home only during a few winter months; it was at this time that the children attended school, although even then attendance was irregular. The gypsy children, however, mixed more frequently with other people and had more social contacts than the canal-boat children.

The average I.Q. of the entire group of 82 gypsy children was 74.5. A significant positive correlation of .368 was found between I.Q. and percentage of school attendance. Those children whose school attendance had been less regular, then, tended on the whole to have lower I.Q.'s. As in the case of the canal-boat children, a significant negative correlation was found between I.Q. and age, in this group the correlation being −.430. Analysis of siblings within each family also showed a consistent decrease in I.Q. with increase in age. It is significant that the chief exceptions to this trend occurred in those families in which there had been a high percentage of school attendance.

The findings of Gordon on both groups seem to point quite irrevocably to factors of home environment and schooling in the development of intelligence as commonly measured. The evidence indicates in many ways that the condition of mental deficiency was not present at the outset. These were not, as might be supposed, select groups, in the sense that the duller persons are by a gradual process attracted into the life of the gypsy caravan or the canal-boat and their offspring will in turn tend to be duller than average. Such an interpretation is inconsistent with many of the facts given above. First, the younger children were on the whole of normal intelligence; secondly, the older the child and the longer the differential effects of inferior home and school conditions had operated, the lower the I.Q.; thirdly, a significant positive correlation was found between regularity of school attendance and I.Q.; fourthly, the gypsy children as a group had higher I.Q.'s and at the same time a much higher percentage of school attendance than the canal-boat children. Nor can the greater school attendance of the former be attributed to more intelligent and progressive parents, since all too frequently the local authorities found it necessary to force the children to attend school during their brief winter periods of stable residence.

Numerous studies have appeared on the relationship of occupational level to intelligence. Large groups of children have been tested and classified according to father's occupation. The latter has been taken as an objective, easily obtained, and fairly reliable index of general cultural level. All of these studies have shown consistent differences in the average intelligence of children in various broad occupational groupings. Such data are not, however, unambiguous. It is difficult to determine, without probing further into the particular circumstances in each case, which is cause and which is effect. Several investigators have argued, for instance, that the intellectual differences found today among occupational groups testify to a gradual hereditary differentiation which has been going on through selection. Thus the higher, more intellectual positions come to be filled by the more intelligent individuals. Since intellectually superior parents tend to have intellectually superior offspring, the children in the higher occupational strata will be more intelligent, on the whole, than those from the semi-skilled or unskilled labor classes. The alternative hypothesis explains the intellectual development of the child in terms of the cultural level in which he is brought up. Thus the child who grows up in the home of a construction laborer does not have the opportunities for intellectual development and consequently will not attain the same mental level as a child of equal initial capacity brought up in the home of an eminent scientist or author. With these alternative interpretations in view, some of the relevant evidence will be examined.

In Great Britain, two extensive surveys were conducted with an intelligence scale of British construction. In one study (4), data were collected on 13,419 children attending elementary and secondary schools in Northumberland. The other study (17) was conducted on 2047 elementary schoolchildren in the Isle of Wight. In both studies, only children between the ages of 11 and 13 were included. The children were classified into a large number of groups on the basis of specific paternal occupation. More general trends are revealed, however, when the occupations are grouped into certain major categories. The average I.Q. as well as the number of children in each category have been reproduced below. The data of the two studies are here reported together (4, p. 195; 17, p. 127).

Category	Northumberland Study		Isle of Wight Study	
	N	Average I.Q.	N	Average I.Q.
A. Professional	137	112.2	8	106.6
B. Managers	92	110.0	21	108.7
C. Higher commercial class	368	109.3	83	103.3
D. Army, navy, police, postmen	129	105.5	141	99.9
E. Shopkeeping class	748	105.0	224	100.7
F. Engineers	571	102.9	111	100.8
G. Foremen	256	102.7	17	103.3
H. Building trades	717	102.0	207	99.1
I. Metal workers, ship-builders	820	100.9	123	99.3
J. Miscellaneous industrial workers	472	100.6	201	99.1
K. Mining and quarrymen	5968	97.6	6	97.9
L. Agriculture, all classes	1128	97.6	277	96.7
M. Low-grade occupations, laborers	1214	96.0	328	96.0
N. Seamen, bargemen, boatmen, etc.			60	97.4

The differences, though small, show a certain degree of consistency. This is particularly apparent if the upper seven categories in the list are compared with the lower eight. The latter are predominantly manual occupations, whereas the former depend primarily upon intellectual, clerical, or executive functions.

In America, similar investigations have been conducted on children of all ages. Goodenough (9) administered the Kuhlman-Binet tests to 380 children between the ages of 18 and 54 months. Paternal occupations were classified into six commonly employed categories. The average I.Q.'s of children within each group are presented below.

Occupational Group	Average I.Q.[1]
I. Professional	125.0
II. Semi-professional (accountants, draftsmen, etc., and managerial)	119.7
III. Clerical and skilled trades	113.4
IV. Semi-skilled trades and minor clerical	108.0
V. Slightly skilled	107.4
VI. Unskilled labor	95.8

Similar data on elementary and high school students are to be found in a study by Haggerty and Nash (11). The Haggerty Delta 2, a common group intelligence test, was administered to children in grades 3 to 8 and high school in rural districts and small towns of New York State. The authors demonstrate that the sampling thus obtained is quite representative of the country at large in respect to occupations. The number of cases and median and range of I.Q. found within each occupational group are given below (11, pp. 569–570). The data for elementary and high school groups have been kept separate.

---

[1] The I.Q.'s obtained by the children on the second administration of the test are given here, as these were shown by Goodenough to be more significant than the I.Q.'s on the first trial.

Occupational Group	Data on 6688 Elementary School Children			Data on 1433 High School Students		
	N	Median I.Q.	Range in I.Q.	N	Median I.Q.	Range in I.Q.
1. Professional	349	116	70–177	201	121	80–167
2. Business and clerical	944	107	54–169	374	112	60–168
3. Skilled	1028	98	54–177	54	111	69–139
4. Semi-skilled	524	95	53–152	267	108	78–149
5. Farmer	3098	91	50–161	48	108	90–159
6. Unskilled	745	89	51–146	489	106	72–155

In two studies, covering both high school and all grades of the elementary school, Pressey (19, 20) attempted to show the dependence of occupational differences in intelligence upon hereditary factors. The children were all taken from a small middle western city with a population of about 12,000 and no foreign element. In the earlier study, all children between the ages of 10 and 14 inclusive were given the Pressey Group Intelligence Test; the total number of cases obtained was 548 and ranged academically from the third grade through the high school. The later study was conducted on 337 children between the ages of 6 and 8 and in grades one to three. The latter group was examined with the Pressey Primer Scale, a non-verbal test. Pressey argued that since, in the first place, the second group consisted of much younger children upon whom differential home environment had had less chance to operate, and since secondly, the test employed was non-verbal, the differences in intelligence test performance between the occupational groups could be attributed chiefly to heredity. If environment had been the major cause, the occupational differences in intelligence found in the first study on older children should either disappear entirely or be greatly minimized in the second study. The percentage of children in each group

whose scores fell above the median for their age is reported
below (20, p. 369; 19, p. 94).

| Occupational Group | Percentage above Age Median (for the Total Group) | |
	Older Group (Ages 10–14)	Younger Group (Ages 6–8)
1. Professional	85	79
2. Executive	68	60
3. Artisan	41	54
4. Laborer	39	38

The findings of these studies are typical of investigations on occupational intelligence. The interpretations
offered by the authors have frequently stressed heredity
as the underlying cause of the existing differences. What
do the data themselves suggest? A number of facts
should be noted before this question is answered. First,
the use of non-verbal tests such as the Kuhlman-Binet
and the Pressey Primer Scale does not in itself rule out
environmental influences. Verbal tests, to be sure, are
more directly affected by specific training than are non-
verbal, but the latter still imply certain stimulating circumstances of which the child in the poorer home may
be deprived. Confidence in the use of paper and pencil,
adaptation to adults outside the family, practice in following directions, familiarity with pictures, and many
similar conditions will influence the child's performance.

Secondly, it is impossible to make a universal statement
that differences resulting from environmental factors increase with age, whereas those owing principally to hereditary factors are manifested from a very early age. This
was found to be the case in the groups of canal-boat and
gipsy children investigated by Gordon. It is not true,
however, of children whose school attendance is normal,
but who may come from inferior homes. In such a group,

we should in fact expect intellectual inferiority to be present at the preschool level, when the child has been exposed only to the inferior home surroundings; as the children grow older and the influence of equal schooling becomes effective, the original differences may actually become reduced. The differences will not disappear, of course, because of the ineradicable nature of early influences. In a group from a small city such as was employed by Pressey, for example, the schooling of all the children was probably very similar and hence there was no increase in intellectual differences with age among the occupational groups. The large amount of overlapping of scores in the various groups is also to be expected from the equalizing influence of universal education. Furthermore, occupational classes are not a sufficient index of general cultural level, and this too may account for the marked overlapping found. From every angle, then, the data seem to be consistent with an environmental interpretation.

No discussion of occupational intelligence is complete without mention of the vast array of data on this subject collected in the course of the army testing. These data have subsequently been worked over to show average and range of scores obtained by men in each of 96 major occupations (cf. 7). The differences in average score are large when extreme groups are compared, but the overlapping of individual scores is pronounced throughout. The influence of specific environmental stimulation is again apparent. Thus the Army Alpha, being predominantly verbal in content, would be expected to place at an advantage those individuals who have been engaged in office work, even if this be of a simple nature. Such has actually been found to be the case. Routine clerical workers, for example, obtained higher average scores (96,

91) than highly skilled mechanics (74, 66). It would seem, then, that investigations of occupational intelligence, whether conducted on adults or children, serve but to illustrate the dependence of intelligence upon the psychological milieu in which the individual develops.

REFERENCES

1. Conradi, E. "Song and Call-Notes of English Sparrows When Reared by Canaries," *Amer. J. Psychol.*, 1905, 16, 190–199.
2. Craig, W. "The Stimulation and Inhibition of Ovulation in Birds and Mammals," *J. An. Beh.*, 1913, 3, 215–221.
3. ——. "Male Doves Reared in Isolation," *J. An. Beh.*, 1914, 4, 121–133.
4. Duff, J. F., and Thomson, G. H. "The Social and Geographical Distribution of Intelligence in Northumberland," *Brit. J. Psychol.*, 1923, 14, 192–198.
5. Foley, J. P., Jr. "First Year Development of a Rhesus Monkey (*Macaca mulatta*) Reared in Isolation," *J. Genet. Psychol.*, 1934, 45, 39–105.
6. ——. "Second Year Development of a Rhesus Monkey (*Macaca mulatta*) Reared in Isolation during the First Eighteen Months," *J. Genet. Psychol.*, 1935, 47, 73–97.
7. Fryer, D. "Occupational Intelligence Standards," *School and Society*, 1922, 16, 273–277.
8. Goddard, H. H. *Feeblemindedness*. N. Y.: Macmillan, 1914. Pp. 599.
9. Goodenough, F. L. "The Relation of the Intelligence of Preschool Children to the Occupation of Their Fathers," *Amer. J. Psychol.*, 1928, 40, 284–294.
10. Gordon, H. *Mental and Scholastic Tests among Retarded Children*. London: Board of Educ., Educ. Pamphlet No. 44, 1923.
11. Haggerty, M. E., and Nash, H. B. "Mental Capacity of Children and Parental Occupation," *J. Educ. Psychol.*, 1924, 15, 559–572.
12. Hoge, M. A. "The Influence of Temperature on the De-

velopment of a Mendelian Character," *J. Exper. Zool.*, 1915, 18, 241–285.

13. Itard, J. M. G. *The Wild Boy of Aveyron* (transl. by G. and M. Humphrey). N. Y.: Century, 1932. Pp. 104.

14. Jennings, H. S. *The Biological Basis of Human Nature.* N. Y.: Norton, 1930. Pp. 384.

15. Kellogg, W. N. "A Further Note on the 'Wolf Children' of India," *Amer. J. Psychol.*, 1934, 46, 149–150.

16. Kellogg, W. N., and L. A. *The Ape and the Child.* N. Y.: Whittlesey House, McGraw-Hill, 1933. Pp. 341.

17. McDonald, H. "The Social Distribution of Intelligence in the Isle of Wight," *Brit. J. Psychol.*, 1925, 16, 123–129.

18. Morgan, T. H., Bridges, C. B., and Sturtevant, A. H. *The Genetics of Drosophila.* Hague: Nijhoff, 1925. Pp. 262.

19. Pressey, L. W. "The Influence of Inadequate Schooling and Poor Environment upon Results with Tests of Intelligence," *J. Appl. Psychol.*, 4, 1920, 91–96.

20. Pressey, S. L., and Ralston, R. "The Relation of Occupation to Intelligence as It Appears in the School Children of a Community," *J. Appl. Psychol.*, 1919, 3, 366–373.

21. Sanders, B. S. *Environment and Growth.* Baltimore: Warwick and York, 1934. Pp. 375.

22. Scott, W. E. D. "Data on Song in Birds," *Science*, 1901, N. S. 14, 522–526.

23. Squires, P. C. "Wolf Children of India," *Amer. J. Psychol.*, 1927, 38, 313–315.

24. Stockard, C. R. *The Physical Basis of Personality.* N. Y.: Norton, 1931. Pp. 320.

25. Stratton, G. M. "Jungle Children," *Psychol. Bull.*, 1934, 31, 596–597.

26. Tredgold, A. F. *Mental Deficiency.* N. Y.: Wood, 1929. Pp. 535.

CHAPTER IV

GENERAL FAMILY RESEMBLANCES

The interpretation of family resemblances is complicated by the fact that close relatives generally live together. The environment of individuals within a single home is certainly more similar than in any other situation outside of an experimental set-up. As a result, the two classes of factors, hereditary and environmental, operate simultaneously to produce greater likeness within the ordinary family than is found among individuals chosen at random. The closer the hereditary relationship, furthermore, the greater the environmental proximity. Thus parents and children, and brothers and sisters usually live in the same home, whereas more distant relatives, such as uncles and nephews, or cousins, come into less frequent contact. Not only are related individuals exposed to common environmental stimulation because of similarity of living conditions, but they also constitute in part each other's environment and are rendered more alike by this mutual interaction. It would seem that family groupings offer an excellent example of the operation of environmental influences in the development of behavioral similarities.

Curiously enough, however, family resemblances are commonly attributed directly to the operation of heredity. The child is described as having his father's business acumen, his aunt's musical talent, "taking after" his grandfather in obstinacy, and perhaps inheriting a keen sense of humor from an Irish grandmother on his father's side! The successful son of an eminent family attributes his accomplishments to the fact that he is well-born. A lecturer's vigor and zeal are explained by his coming from pioneer stock. A boy's ingenuity with mechanical toys is regarded as only natural when one finds that he is descended from a "long line" of boat builders and inventors. Nor is this type of interpretation limited to popular slip-shod thinking and everyday conversation. Many otherwise accurate and well-conducted scientific investigations on family resemblances contain the same logical fallacy.

The two major methods employed in the study of family similarities and differences are family history and correlation. The former method has been applied chiefly by eugenicists. Geneologies are traced and elaborate pedigree charts drawn up for families outstanding either for their deficiencies or for their talents. The correlation studies usually deal with the scores of relatives on standardized tests. Parents and children, siblings, and twins have been compared by this method. The correlation coefficient [1] furnishes a convenient numerical index of the degree of correspondence between the scores of any such groups.

It is of course impossible to determine directly by either of these methods what is the relative contribution of hereditary or environmental factors in producing the obtained similarities. Both methods are at best descriptive and serve only to discover more or less objectively the degree

---

[1] The correlation coefficient (r) is an index of relationship between two sets of measures. It varies from $+1.00$, a perfect positive correlation, through 0, to -1.00, a perfect negative or inverse correlation. A $+1.00$ correlation means that the highest score in the one set of measures is paired off with the highest in the other set, the second highest in the first with the second highest in the second, etc. A -1.00 correlation indicates that the highest score in one group corresponds to the lowest in the other, a similar, perfect reversal occurring throughout the distribution. A zero correlation indicates no relation at all, or the sort of arrangement which would result if the scores in the two sets were to be shuffled and paired off at random.

of familial resemblance existing under present-day conditions of living. Only the experimental approach could yield a conclusive solution to this problem. Thus if a child of known parentage were isolated from its family immediately after birth and brought up under rigidly controlled conditions, many of the questions on heredity and environment might be answered. In such an experiment, it would also be necessary to exert some control over prenatal environment, such as by proper care and diet of the mother. Unfortunately, popular sentiment and social custom have stood in the way of any sufficiently extensive experimentation along these lines. An approximation to this set-up is, however, afforded by the study of foster children. The earlier the child is adopted, the more nearly does this situation resemble the experimental situation described above. An excellent opportunity for the analysis of hereditary and environmental factors is also furnished by identical twins who have been reared apart from an early age, although the number of such cases is necessarily small.

Because of their more direct bearing upon the heredity-environment problem, all studies on *twins* and on *foster children* have been reserved for a detailed treatment in the next chapter. The present chapter will deal exclusively with the more common and general sort of family relationships, including parents and children, siblings, and more remote relatives or ancestors.

THE FAMILIES OF EMINENT MEN

Prompted by his interest in eugenics and the control of human evolution, and by his desire to unearth all possible data bearing on the laws of human inheritance, Sir Francis Galton launched the family-history method on its career. This method was employed by Galton in his extensive investigations on the inheritance of genius, the results of which were brought together in 1869 in a book entitled *Hereditary Genius*. Galton's approach was distinctly hereditarian, as is illustrated by the following summary of the aim of his investigation: "I propose to show in this book that a man's natural abilities are derived by inheritance, under exactly the same limitations as are the form and physical features of the whole organic world" (5, p. 1).

In this investigation, data were collected on 997 eminent men in 300 families. In order to facilitate the tracing of family histories and the location of descendants and other relatives, the study was limited to eminent men who were either English or well-known in England. The information was obtained from biographical collections or through direct inquiry among relatives and acquaintances of the men themselves. Galton defined as follows the degree of eminence necessary for inclusion in his survey: "When I speak of an eminent man, I mean one who has achieved a position that is attained by only 250 persons in each million of men, or by one person in each 4000" (5, p. 9). The classes of men in Galton's survey comprised English judges,[1] statesmen, commanders, literary men, scientists, poets, artists (musicians and painters), and protestant divines, the last including men who had achieved fame through some phase of religious activity, such as theological scholars, administrators, religious leaders, martyrs, preachers.

Within each family, the most eminent man was taken as a point of reference, and all kinships were expressed in relation to him. Following the name of each of these men, Galton appended a list of famous relatives together with the major field in which each had achieved distinction.

---

[1] The only category limited exclusively to England.

Whenever more complete information was available, these data were presented in the form of a family chart, a device which has gained in popularity among present-day eugenicists. As a final summary of his findings, Galton computed the percentage of eminent men in each degree of kinship to the most eminent man of the family, the latter still serving as the point of reference. These percentages are given in Table III for each class of "eminence" separately, as well as for all classes combined. It should be noted that the eminent relatives within any class have not necessarily achieved distinction in that particular class; thus the famous kinsmen of a statesman may in-

TABLE III

PERCENTAGE OF EMINENT RELATIVES OF MEN IN EACH CLASS

(After Galton, 5, p. 308)

Nature of Kinship *	Judges	Statesmen	Commanders	Literary	Scientific	Poets	Artists	Divines	All Classes
Father	26	33	47	48	26	20	32	28	31
Brother	35	39	50	42	47	40	50	36	41
Son	36	49	31	51	60	45	89	40	48
Grandfather	15	28	16	24	14	5	7	20	17
Uncle	18	18	8	24	16	5	14	40	18
Nephew	19	18	35	24	23	50	18	4	22
Grandson	19	10	12	9	14	5	18	16	14
Great-grandfather	2	8	8	3	0	0	0	4	3
Great-uncle	4	5	8	6	5	5	7	4	5
First cousin	11	21	20	18	16	0	1	8	13
Great-nephew	17	5	8	6	16	10	0	0	10
Great-grandson	6	0	0	3	7	0	0	0	3
All more remote	14	37	44	15	23	5	18	16	31

* No female relatives are included in these summary figures, although the names and achievements of such relatives are given in the specific family histories.

clude scientists, artists, divines, etc. The classification is based solely on the field of activity of the "most eminent" man in the family, around whom the data are organized.

These figures suggest quite strongly that eminence tends to run in families. Not only are the percentages much greater than is expected by chance and quite consistent from class to class, but they also show a definite decrease in the frequency of eminent relatives as the degree of relationship becomes more remote. It is quite a different matter, however, to conclude that genius is inherited. Galton, to be sure, recognized the difficulties in the way of such a conclusion and attempted a systematic analysis of them. To the question of whether reputation is a fair test of ability, he answers in the affirmative. He argues that reputation or eminence, as the criterion is employed in his survey, is "the opinion of contemporaries, revised by posterity—the favorable result of a critical analysis of each man's character, by many biographers" (5, p. 33), and hence not an accidental rise to short-lived notoriety. Natural ability he defines quite circularly as "those qualities of intellect and disposition, which urge and qualify a man to perform acts that lead to reputation" (5, p. 33).

Although admitting the influence of training, surroundings, and opportunities, Galton minimizes the part which they play in the attainment of eminence. He constantly holds up to the reader the heroic picture of genius triumphing over obstacles. By definition, genius means to him "a nature which, when left to itself, will, urged by an inherent stimulus, climb the path that leads to eminence, and has strength to reach the summit—one which, if hindered or thwarted, will fret and strive until the hindrance is overcome, and it is again free to follow its labour-loving instinct" (5, pp. 33–34). He concludes that "It is almost a contradiction in terms, to doubt that such men will generally become eminent," and adds that "there is plenty of evidence in this volume to show that few have won high reputations without possessing these peculiar gifts" (5, p. 34). This is true enough, but it remains to be proved that such "gifts" as the impulse to climb, the strength to reach the summit, and the love of labor are themselves independent of environment. Unfortunately, the optimistic picture painted by Galton is not borne out by observations of everyday life; and in the absence of experimental proof, it is impossible to accept Galton's interpretations of his findings.[1]

DEGENERATE FAMILIES

The family history method has also been widely employed in the effort to analyze the causes of intellectual defect, crime, pauperism, and similar conditions. By this method, a number of families have been discovered which present an overwhelming array of socially inadequate persons over several generations. The same general techniques are used in tracing the history of these families as in the study of eminent groups. Living relatives or descendants are visited and observed, residents of the vicinity are interviewed, and certificates of marriage and birth, and similar public records are examined whenever available. These families are usually found in rural districts in many parts of the country, often inhabiting the same crude huts built by their ancestors many generations ago. They frequently interbreed, are quite prolific, and eventually come to constitute their own community, shunned and ridiculed by their neighbors.

The earliest published pedigree of such a "degenerate"

---

[1] Other studies on eminent families will be found in Ch. XIII on *Genius*. Galton's study is here reported only as an illustration of the family history method.

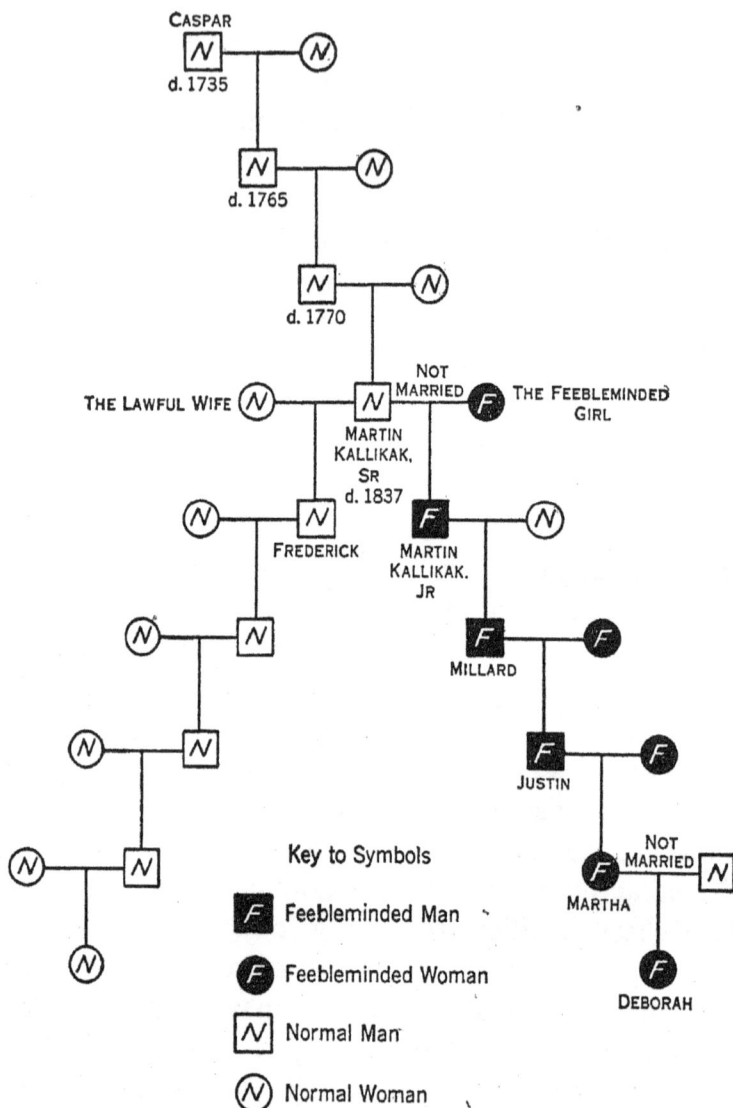

FIG. 24. A PEDIGREE CHART OF THE KALLIKAK FAMILY.
(After Goddard, 7, p. 36.)

dard constantly emphasizes the rôle of heredity. Having laid great stress upon the fact that the two groups were branches of the same family, furnishing, "as it were, a natural experiment with a normal branch with which to compare our defective side," he states that "from this comparison, the conclusion is inevitable that all this degeneracy has come as the result of the defective mentality and bad blood having been brought into the normal family of good blood" (7, pp. 68–69). It seems rather curious that the common descent of the two branches from Martin Kallikak should be regarded as strengthening an hereditary interpretation of the differences between them. The environments of the two groups were not in any way equated by this common ancestry and in fact, it is evident that the members of the two branches were reared under widely differing conditions. Common descent from Martin Kallikak simply made the heredity of the two groups more alike than would be the case in the comparison of two distinct families and thus seems to strengthen an environmental explanation of the differences, if it contributes anything at all.

A more crucial test would have been available if the legitimate offspring of Martin and his well-born wife had been exchanged at birth with those of the feebleminded woman. It would then have been very illuminating to ascertain the relative percentage of feeblemindedness and other defects in the "normal" and "degenerate" stock. The practical obstacles in the way of such a procedure in no way strengthen the validity of conclusions drawn from an inadequately controlled situation.

Many equally "degenerate" families have been subsequently investigated by psychologists, sociologists, or eugenicists. The research staff of the Eugenics Record

Office [1] conducts such surveys as one phase of their regular work. Among the groups they have studied are the Hill Folk, the Nam family, and the W family of Indiana, all presenting the same picture of degeneracy, mental defect, disease, and social incompetence through successive generations. Surveys of eminent families have likewise been sponsored by the Eugenics Record Office. Specific lines of achievement, such as scholarly pursuits or boat designing, have been traced from generation to generation in the attempt to show that such talents are transmitted through heredity. Although offering much interesting material, such studies cannot yield any data on the heredity-environment question; the opportunities for environmental transmission of such family qualities are too obvious to overlook or dismiss.

Parent-Child Resemblance

The use of the correlation technique, although more accurate and quantitative, does not eliminate the essential difficulty inherent in the family history method, namely, the confusion of hereditary and environmental contributions. Pearson (14) was among the first to apply correlation analysis to parent-child resemblances. Continuing a line of research initiated by Galton (6), he collected measures on parents and offspring in physical traits such as stature, arm span, and forearm length. The parent-child correlations in these traits averaged about .52. The similarity of this correlation to those obtained for bodily characteristics of many animal forms led Pearson and others to suggest that this figure indicates the contribution of hereditary factors to the development of physical traits. Family resemblance in

---

[1] Eugenics Record Office, Cold Spring Harbor, Long Island, N. Y. Cf., e.g., references (1) and (4).

such traits is doubtlessly owing in large part to the influence of common heredity, although the rôle of similar environment, especially in the prenatal stage, cannot be ignored.

A crude but frequently quoted early study on parental resemblance in psychological traits is that of Woods (19) on royal families. Because of the large amount of inbreeding among royal houses, such a group seemed to offer an especially good opportunity for the analysis of family likenesses. In addition, genealogies could be traced more easily in royalty, and information regarding the characters and abilities of royal personages was relatively accessible. Each individual investigated was assigned a rating from 1 to 10, representing different degrees of intellect from feeblemindedness to genius. By a similar procedure, each was rated for moral qualities. The ratings were based upon available historical and biographical material and are therefore subject to all the errors inherent in such data, plus a possible error of judgment introduced by Woods' own evaluation of the facts.

In the entire survey, data on several thousand persons from various European royal houses were employed. From the available information, it proved possible to assign ratings on intellectual quality to a total of 671 cases and on moral traits to 608. The correlations between the ratings of offspring and fathers, grandfathers, and great-grandfathers, respectively, are given below.[1]

Relationship	Intellect	Morals
Fathers and offspring	.30	.30
Grandfathers and offspring	.16	.18
Great-grandfathers and offspring	.15	

[1] These correlation coefficients, although utilizing the ratings on the 10-point scale, were computed by means of a four-fold correlation table. All individuals receiving ratings from 1 to 5 were classified as below average, those between 6 and 10 as above average.

That there exists a noticeable correspondence and that this correspondence is stronger the closer the relationship, seems clear from these correlations. Little can be concluded, however, regarding the amount of relationship, since the size of a correlation coefficient is too largely influenced by such errors of measurement as were present in these data.

More recently, scores obtained by parents and children on standardized tests have been correlated. Jones (11) administered intelligence tests to over 300 families in a rural district in New England. In order to minimize the factors of language handicap and differential group traditions, communities were chosen in which the population was composed entirely of native-born stock. All children between the ages of 3 and 14 were given the Stanford-Binet; older offspring and all parents were tested with the Army Alpha. In 105 families, it was possible to test both parents and two or more children. It was upon this sampling, consisting of 210 parents and 317 children, that the parent-child correlations were computed.

The following are some of the correlations [1] reported by Jones.

	Son	Daughter	Son and Daughter
Father	.524	.505	.509
Mother	.544	.557	.548

The correlations of like-sex parent and child, i.e., father and son or mother and daughter, are not significantly higher than those between unlike-sex parent and child.

[1] It is a frequent practice, in studies on parent-child resemblance, to compute a "midparent"-child correlation, in which the average score of the two parents is correlated with the child's score in order to furnish a final summary measure of relationship. Such a correlation is, however, misleading, because in the process of averaging scores a certain amount of individual variation is eliminated and as a result the correlation may be too high.

Thus there seemed to be no basis to the belief that boys tend to resemble more closely their fathers, and girls their mothers in intellectual level. There was, however, a small but consistent tendency for the scores of children of either sex to correlate more highly with the mother's score than with that of the father. This might be attributed to the closer contact which the mother has with the children.

In a similar study by Willoughby (17) eleven tests were administered to about 141 children, 100 mothers, and 90 fathers, all of whom lived in the vicinity of Palo Alto, California. The tests ranged from highly verbal to highly non-verbal, and were selected from various current scales for the measurement of intelligence and scholastic achievement. The average of the parent-child correlations in all of the tests was .35. There was no consistent tendency for the correlations to be higher with either parent. A comparison of the correlations on each test, however, reveals large discrepancies. The average parental correlations [1] on different tests ranged from .17 to .48. When the tests were classified into verbal and non-verbal, the average parental correlation was .39 for the former and .30 for the latter. This difference is also borne out by a comparison of individual tests. Thus the three highest correlations were obtained with relatively abstract tests in which learning and past experience predominate, viz., history-literature information (.48), number-series completion (.42), and analogies (.41); the three yielding the lowest correlations were checking similarities (.17), geometric forms test from Army Beta (.28), and symbol-digit code learning test, also from Army Beta (.30).

The results of Willoughby again suggest the part played

---

[1] Average of the following separate correlations: mother-daughter, mother-son, father-daughter, and father-son.

by environment and stimulation in determining the degree of familial resemblance. Performance on verbal tests is more susceptible to training and home conditions than is performance on the non-verbal, and it is the former which yielded the highest parental correlations. In Willoughby's study, furthermore, the correlations run lower than those of Jones. This, too, would be expected from the nature of the tests, since the latter used only intelligence tests of a highly verbal type. The fact that Jones correlated total scores on composite tests made up of many parts, whereas Willoughby employed scores on single and fairly homogeneous tests, may also account for the higher correlations found by Jones. The more complex the measures correlated, the greater are the chances that they will have common elements and the higher will their intercorrelations tend to be.

Certain tentative conclusions are suggested by an analysis of the data on parental resemblance. In the first place, parents and children exhibit a distinct similarity in physical traits, which may be expressed by a correlation in the neighborhood of .50. Approximately the same degree of correspondence is found on most common intelligence tests of the verbal type. When, however, comparisons are made on more homogeneous tests or on tests which are less susceptible to common home environment, the correlations are much lower. There is a suggestion of a closer resemblance to the mother than to the father in intelligence test performance, although the data on this point are inconclusive.

The Comparison of Siblings

Investigations on the resemblance of siblings have been much more numerous than those on parent-child similarity. As Pearson pointed out, the comparison of siblings, especially when both are in school, does not present the practical difficulties met in the testing or rating of parents. In addition to extensive comparisons of siblings in physical traits such as eye-color, hair-color and curliness, health, and head dimensions, in which about the same degree of relationship was found as in the parent-child studies, Pearson (13) undertook an investigation of sibling resemblances in mental traits. The data of the latter study consisted exclusively of teachers' ratings on schoolchildren. The measures used are necessarily crude and may be biased by the teachers' own reaction to family relationships; thus, two brothers might be rated more nearly alike because the teacher knows that they come from the same family. The correlations are based on large samplings, however, the number of cases varying from 554 to 2152 for different traits. Below are the correlations found by Pearson between pairs of brothers, pairs of sisters, and mixed pairs, consisting of a brother and a sister.

Trait	Brothers	Sisters	Mixed Pairs
Vivacity	.47	.64	.63
Self-assertiveness	.53	.49	.51
Popularity	.50	.56	.48
Conscientiousness	.59	.61	.52
Temper	.51	.43	.49
Ability	.46	.44	.52
Handwriting	.53	.47	.63
Introspection	.59	.47	.44
Average	.52	.57	.49

Pearson himself gives a strongly hereditarian interpretation to these findings, offering the opinion that: "It is the stock itself which makes its home environment, the education is of small service, unless it be applied to an intelligent race of men" (13, p. 159). It is characteristic of many discussions in which the influence of environment is minimized, to cite formal education as the principal environmental force and to overlook the broader and probably more effective aspects of general environment.   Since Pearson found very similar sibling correlations in mental and physical traits, and since he believed the latter could be little influenced by environment, he concluded that the same must be true of mental traits. Such a conclusion does not necessarily follow. It is itself based on the assumption that mental and physical traits are inherited in the same manner and thus involves a circular argument.

Investigations with mental tests have all yielded positive and significant sibling correlations, although the amount of relationship varies with the particular test, the age of the subjects, and other conditions. Gordon (8) found a correlation of .53 between the Stanford-Binet I.Q.'s of 91 pairs of siblings in an orphanage in California. Pintner (15) administered six simple tests to 180 pairs of siblings and computed "mental indices" for each child on the basis of scores on all the tests; the sibling correlation in mental indices was .22. Hart (9) correlated the I.Q.'s of siblings in three groups of schoolchildren, the number of sibling pairs in each group being 252, 147, and 219, respectively. The I.Q.'s were found from scores on Army Alpha, National Intelligence Test, and Stanford-Binet. Correlations of .447, .459, and .399 were obtained in the three groups.

In an extensive investigation of sibling resemblance, Hildreth (10) analyzed the I.Q.'s of three large groups of schoolchildren. The first group consisted of 671 public schoolchildren from 300 families in Oklahoma City; this was a group of average social status. The second group was composed of 523 children attending the Horace Mann School in New York City, the number of families represented totaling 241; the social and cultural level of this

group was definitely superior. The third was a group of
inferior social status obtained from the Hebrew Orphan
Asylum in New York City; it included 346 children in
146 families. The number of siblings within any single
family ranged from two to five. The I.Q.'s were based
on some form of the Binet scales, about 98% of them
having been obtained with the Stanford Revision.

The sibling correlations in each of the three groups,
in the order named above, were .629, .274, and .322,
respectively. The variation from group to group is large,
especially since the same test was employed. The discrepancies probably result chiefly from differences in heterogeneity of the groups. The Horace Mann group, being
the most highly select and homogeneous, gave the lowest
correlation, whereas the Oklahoma group, a more nearly
random sample than either of the other two, yielded the
highest correlation. In general, the wider the range of
individual differences within a group, the higher will be
the correlations.[1]   Hildreth concludes that the sibling
correlation in intelligence would "certainly appear to be
greater than .3 and less than .7" (10, p. 56), and proposes
"heredity rather than environment as the cause of the
resemblance found" (10, p. 60), although admitting that
the data relevant to the latter point are fairly scant.

Thorndike (16) reported a correlation [2] of .60 between
the scores of about 1200 pairs of siblings on the I.E.R.
Tests of Selective and Relational Thinking, Generalization, and Organization.[3]   Since all of the subjects were

[1] For a fuller discussion of the effect of homogeneity of the sampling upon the
size of a correlation coefficient, the reader is referred to Ch. XI.

[2] The value given (.60) was estimated by Thorndike after applying corrections
for selective factors and other conditions.

[3] A series of tests of the type usually found in intelligence scales, including
opposites, analogies, sentence completion, arithmetic reasoning, number series
completion, etc. They have an added advantage in that the scores are expressed
in terms of an equal unit scale.

attending high school, this group is older and more select
than those ordinarily employed in other sibling studies.
In interpreting his findings, Thorndike follows the argument originally proposed by Pearson (cf. above). Thus
he concludes that the difference of .08 between the correlation of .60 on the I.E.R. test and that of .52 established by Pearson (13) for physical resemblances in siblings may be attributed to the equalizing influence of
similar school environment. This would only follow if the
influence of heredity upon mental traits were known to be
identical to its influence upon physical traits, and if in
addition it could be assumed that physical traits develop
in complete independence of environmental factors.

Willoughby (17), in his investigation of family resemblance cited in the preceding section, also obtained data
on sibling relationships in the eleven mental tests which
he administered. The subjects for this part of the study
were 280 siblings, ranging in age from seven up. The
average and range of the correlation coefficients for the
different tests were as follows:

	Average r (11 Tests)	Average r (Verbal Tests)	Average r (Non-Verbal Tests)	Range in r
Brother-brother	.44	.50	.37	.18 to .58
Sister-sister	.45	.40	.52	.26 to .63
Unlike-sex siblings	.36	.38	.35	.24 to .54

It is noteworthy that the like-sex siblings gave higher
correlations than the unlike-sex. This difference, although
small, suggests the greater community of environment
furnished within the family for like-sex siblings. As was
the case with parental correlations, the sibling correlations
exhibit a pronounced variation from test to test, and in
two of the three sibling groups, the average correlation is
higher for the verbal than for the non-verbal tests.

In their extensive investigations of honesty in school-children, May and Hartshorne (12) computed sibling correlations on four types of deception tests. A total of 734 pairs of siblings in seven groups were measured. The correlations,[1] differing somewhat with the group and the test, ranged from .208 to .445. May and Hartshorne minimize the part played by environment in these sibling resemblances, their main argument resting on the finding that socio-economic level of the home did not correlate very highly with honesty scores. Other less easily observable aspects of home environment may, however, be much more significant than socio-economic level in the development of such character traits.

It would seem that the correlations in test performance of siblings reared together, although uniformly positive and reliable, show a marked variation in amount. Among the major factors which determine this variation may be mentioned the nature of the test and in particular its relative dependence upon environment and training, the homogeneity of the sampling, and the age of the subjects. In regard to the factor of age, it is apparent that the older the subjects, the longer will environmental influences have been operative. Whether such influences will have a leveling or a differentiating effect, however, will depend upon the specific circumstances in each case.

REFERENCES

1. Danielson, F. H., and Davenport, C. B. *The Hill Folk.* Cold Spring Harbor: Eugenics Record Office Memoir No. 1, 1912. Pp. 56.
2. Dugdale, R. L. *The Jukes: a Study in Crime, Pauperism,*

[1] One type of deceptive behavior, *viz.*, securing help contrary to instructions on a test taken at home, gave much higher sibling correlations, but this was definitely affected by collusion, the siblings either helping one another or encouraging each other in the use of forbidden aids.

Disease, and Heredity. N. Y.: Putnam, 1910 (1st ed. 1877). Pp. 120.

3. Estabrook, A. H. *The Jukes in 1915.* Washington: Carnegie Institution, 1916. Pp. 85.

4. Estabrook, A. H., and Davenport, C. B. *The Nam Family.* Cold Spring Harbor: Eugenics Record Office Memoir No. 2, 1912. Pp. 85.

5. Galton, F. *Hereditary Genius: an Inquiry into Its Laws and Consequences.* London: Macmillan, 1914. Pp. 368.

6. ——. *Natural Inheritance.* London: Macmillan, 1889. Pp. 254.

7. Goddard, H. H. *The Kallikak Family: a Study in the Heredity of Feeblemindedness.* N. Y.: Macmillan, 1921 (1st ed. 1912). Pp. 121.

8. Gordon, K. "Psychological Tests of Orphan Children," *J. Del.,* 1919, 4, 46–55.

9. Hart, H. "Correlations between Intelligence Quotients of Siblings," *Sch. and Soc.,* 1924, 20, 382.

10. Hildreth, G. H. "The Resemblance of Siblings in Intelligence and Achievement," Teachers College, Columbia Univ., *Contrib. to Educ.,* 1925, No. 186. Pp. 65.

11. Jones, H. E. "A First Study of Parent-Child Resemblance in Intelligence," *27th Yearbook, Nat. Soc. Stud. Educ.,* 1928, Part I, 61–72.

12. May, M. A., and Hartshorne, H. "Sibling Resemblance in Deception," *27th Yearbook, Nat. Soc. Stud. Educ.,* 1928, Part II, 161–177.

13. Pearson, K. "On the Laws of Inheritance in Man: II. On the Inheritance of the Mental and Moral Characters in Man, and Its Comparison with the Inheritance of Physical Characters," *Biom.,* 1904, 3, 131–190.

14. Pearson, K., and Lee, A. "On the Laws of Inheritance in Man: I. Inheritance of Physical Characters," *Biom.,* 1903, 2, 357–462.

15. Pintner, R. "The Mental Indices of Siblings," *Psychol. Rev.,* 1918, 25, 252–255.

16. Thorndike, E. L., and staff. "The Resemblance of Siblings

in Intelligence," *27th Yearbook, Nat. Soc. Stud. Educ.*, 1928, Part I, 41–53.

17. Willoughby, R. R.   "Family Similarities in Mental Test Abilities," *27th Yearbook, Nat. Soc. Stud. Educ.*, 1928, Part I, 55–59.

18. Winship, A. E.   *Jukes-Edwards: a Study in Education and Heredity.* Harrisburg, Pa.: Myers, 1900. Pp. 88.

19. Woods, F. A.   *Mental and Moral Heredity in Royalty.* N. Y.: Holt, 1906. Pp. 312.

CHAPTER V

SPECIAL FAMILY RELATIONSHIPS

In the present chapter, a survey of psychological studies on twins and foster children will be presented. These two types of investigation of familial resemblance have been selected for a more detailed treatment because of the special facilities which they offer for the analysis of the relative contribution of hereditary and environmental factors. Twins and foster children may be said to represent the two extremes of hereditary similarity. In the case of *identical twins*, heredity is completely alike for the two individuals, so that any differences between them may be attributed directly to the operation of different stimulating conditions. *Foster children*, on the other hand, bear no hereditary resemblance to their adopted parents or to any other children with whom they are reared. These subjects therefore reveal the contribution of environmental influences in any similarity which they may exhibit to their foster parents or foster siblings.

The observation and measurement of *fraternal* or non-identical twins also offer a fruitful approach to this general problem. Such twins are no more alike than ordinary siblings in respect to heredity. They have, however, been exposed to the same prenatal environment. Since they are of the same age, they are also subjected to postnatal stimulation which is much more similar than in the case of ordinary siblings. They would thus seem to offer a sort of "environmental control" in the analysis of the sibling resemblances ordinarily observed. Similarly, the cases of identical twins who have lived apart from early infancy may be regarded as an "hereditary control" for identical twins reared together in the usual way. Both of these groups have the same degree of hereditary community; any differences in amount of resemblance are therefore attributable directly to environmental variations.

THE PSYCHOLOGICAL STUDY OF TWINS

Twins have long been acclaimed as particularly good material for the analysis of behavioral resemblance.[1] The arguments which have been put forth in the effort to prove the major potency of heredity on the basis of twin resemblance may be summarized under five headings. A brief critical evaluation of each will be given.

The first argument is based on the relative degree of resemblance of twins and of siblings. The closer resemblance of the former cannot, however, be attributed indiscriminately to their more similar heredity. It is true that, in respect to general home background and schooling, the environment of siblings is about as similar as that of twins. But the attitude of the parents towards an older and a younger sibling, the attitude of the children towards each other, and the specific events and vicissitudes occurring at any one life period for each child will differ far more for siblings than for twins. Conditions of this sort, operating differentially from a very early age, may be even more important than economic level or formal schooling in the development of the child's mentality and character.

A second type of comparison is that between older and younger twins. It is often argued that if environment were a significant factor in the resemblance of twins, then this resemblance should be closer in the older twins

[1] For a discussion of the biology and physiology of twins, cf. Newman (10, 11).

who have been exposed for a longer period to the equalizing environmental influences. As has been repeatedly pointed out above, however, it is impossible to generalize regarding the particular direction which environmental influences will take. Thus it seems very probable that in the case of twins, early environment may have a strongly equalizing effect, whereas later environment may produce differentiation. Prenatal environment, to be sure, is very similar in such cases. In infancy and early childhood, the twins are usually treated in much the same way. As the children grow older, however, any differences between them tend to be noted and emphasized for practical reasons, and the twin begins to learn that he must lead his own life and develop as an individual if he is to be well-adjusted. It would seem that a drop, rather than a rise, in correlation with age is to be expected on environmental grounds.

In some of the more recent studies the attempt has been made to classify twins into identical and non-identical, or fraternal. The comparison of these two types of twins in mental traits has furnished a third approach to the analysis of hereditary and environmental factors. It will be recalled that identical twins develop from a single fertilized ovum and therefore have identical heredity, whereas fraternal twins are no more similar than ordinary siblings in their hereditary constitution, although they develop simultaneously. It would seem that the difference in degree of resemblance of identical and non-identical twins could be attributed directly to heredity. The environment of fraternal twins is doubtlessly more uniform than that of siblings born at different times. But is it necessarily as homogeneous as that of identical twins? It must be remembered that fraternal twins are often of unlike sex, and the differential treatment of the two sexes may enter in to render their environment dissimilar. This may prove a very potent differentiating influence in the development of the two children. The physical differences themselves which characterize the fraternal as contrasted with the identical twins may further encourage differential reactions towards the former, especially during the important earlier ages when the identical twins are probably still being confused by their associates.

A fourth analysis is based upon the relative degree of twin resemblance in traits differing in their susceptibility to training. Such a comparison is very illuminating, provided the traits are not simply classified in respect to their dependence upon school training. Home environment is far more significant than formal schooling in determining twin or any other family resemblance. In those tests which depend primarily upon school training, we should expect unrelated children to resemble each other nearly as much as related children. This is especially true in studies in which all of the subjects are in the same community and hence exposed to fairly uniform schooling.

Lastly, twin resemblances in mental and in physical traits have been compared. A similarity in degree of correlation in the two cases is customarily regarded as evidence that the mental resemblances are independent of environment. This is based on the argument proposed by Pearson in his discussion of sibling correlations. The fallacy inherent in such a conclusion has already been discussed in the preceding chapter.

TWIN RESEMBLANCES IN MENTAL TRAITS

As early as 1875, Galton (3) compared the characteristics of about 80 pairs of twins, by means of questionnaires. The first quantitative investigation on the mental resemblance of twins was conducted by Thorndike (14). Six simple mental tests were administered to 50 pairs of twins between the ages of 9 and 15, and to a similar group of siblings.[1] On 39 of the twin pairs physical measurements were also obtained for comparative purposes. The correlations on the entire group of twins range from .69 (cancellation of A's) to .90 (naming opposites of words). The correlations are higher, in general, in those tests more susceptible to home surroundings and cultural level.

Sibling correlations were found on only three of the six tests and were all much lower than the corresponding twin correlations, their values being .32, .29, and .30. The twins were further classified into an older (age 12–14) and a younger group (age 9–11). The average correlation was .70 for the older and .83 for the younger. Finally, the average twin correlation on eight physical traits proved to be .76, as compared to an average of .78 for the mental traits. Thorndike gave a strongly hereditarian interpretation to all of these findings, relying upon the arguments outlined above.

Lauterbach (5), who tested 212 pairs of twins with eight mental tests and in addition obtained several physical measures on them, reports an average correlation of .67 between like-sex [2] twins and .41 between unlike-sex or fraternal twins in mental traits. The average correlation for older twins (157–328 months) was .55 and for younger (90–156 months) .54. The resemblances were higher, on the whole, in physical traits, the average correlation in four such traits being .77 and .55 for like-sex and unlike-sex groups, respectively.

Merriman (8) tested 200 pairs of twins with the Stanford-Binet, National Intelligence Test, and a modified

[1] Number and age not specified.   [2] Probably identical twins in most cases.

form of Army Beta.[1] Separate correlations were computed
for like-sex and unlike-sex twins, as well as for a younger
(5–9 years) and an older (10–16 years) group. The correlations of the entire group were very close to .80 on all three
tests. Like-sex twins gave consistently higher correlations
than unlike-sex, their correlations on the Stanford-Binet
being .867 and .504, respectively, on the National Intelligence Test .925 and .867, and on Army Beta .908 and .732.
In the majority of comparisons, the correlations were
higher in the younger than in the older group, although the
number of cases employed in these correlations was frequently small and inconsistencies were necessarily present.

In an investigation on identical and non-identical
twins, Tallman (13) administered the Stanford-Binet to
158 pairs of twins and 199 siblings between the ages of
3 and 20. The average difference in I.Q. between the
siblings was 13.14, and this dropped to 11.96 when only
siblings who were less than two years apart in chronological age were included. In computing the average difference between twins, Tallman combined her data with
those of Merriman [2] and obtained a final average of 7.07,
only about one-half as large as the sibling difference. In
this combined group, there were 84 pairs of unlike-sex
twins. The average I.Q. difference of these twins was 8.48.
The like-sex group contained 178 pairs and gave an average difference of 6.42. In the like-sex group, 63 pairs were
classified as identical twins, on the basis of general physical resemblance as well as coloring of hair, eyes, and skin.
The average difference of these identical twins was 5.08,
as contrasted to a difference of 7.37 for 39 non-identical
twins in the like-sex group.

[1] Not all of the children took all three tests.
[2] Cf. above; 105 pairs of twins in Merriman's group were given the Stanford-
Binet.

Hirsch (4) reports an average I.Q. difference of 13.8 points between 58 pairs of "dissimilar" or fraternal twins, and 2.3 points between 38 pairs of "similar"[1] twins. Correlations of I.Q.'s were .97 for similar and .53 for dissimilar twins. These findings, together with the fact that the average I.Q. difference of 4 pairs of similar twins living apart was only 3.5 points, led Hirsch to a rather strongly hereditarian interpretation. Only the results on the twins living apart could, however, be regarded as crucial, and these were unfortunately based on very inadequate data. Apart from the small number of cases, a serious objection to these data is that the period of separation was too short to allow much differentiation. The separation, furthermore, occurred so late in life as to have practically no significance in the development of the individual, the twins in each pair having been first separated at the ages of 12, 18, 29, and 33 years, respectively!

McNemar (7) administered five tests of motor skills to 98 pairs of male twins in junior high school. On the basis of physical criteria, 46 pairs were clearly classified as fraternal and 47 as identical. The twin correlations ranged from .39 to .56 for the fraternal group, and from .71 to .95 for the identical. Continued practice in three of the tests produced no significant change in correlation in the identical group and a rise on two tests in the fraternal group. McNemar concludes from these data that hereditary factors play the major part in twin resemblances in motor abilities. Insofar as sensory and muscular development is involved in such functions, this finding is not especially surprising. In no case, however, could such a conclusion be carried over to other kinds of activity.

[1] Probably identical.

Case Studies of Identical Twins Reared Apart

The study of twins reared apart *from an early age* furnishes an excellent opportunity for the analysis of hereditary and environmental factors. If the twins are identical, heredity can be regarded as constant. The operation of similar environmental influences is limited to prenatal life and to the brief postnatal period during which the twins may have lived together. Although not to be ignored, the community of environment in such cases is certainly much less than that commonly found among twins. Naturally, the number of twins available for observation under these conditions is very small. For this reason, the case history method has proved the most fruitful, since it is best suited to a thorough analysis of all the available information on relatively few subjects. The first report of a pair of identical twins reared apart was published in 1925 by Müller (9). The main facts of this report are reproduced below.

A pair of identical female twins were separated at the age of two weeks and brought up by different families. The twins did not see each other until they were 18 years old, and even after that age they only met for short visits. At the time of examination, they were 30 years of age. The environment of the two girls presented certain major differences as well as similarities. Twin J completed high school and had some summer university work; she has taught school, is married, and has a child. Twin B had only four years of formal education. At the age of 15, she took up clerical work and has been engaged in an active business career ever since. Her foster family moved about a good deal. Twin B did not have as many social contacts as her sister. Both read profusely as children, and both had been energetic, popular, and active in club work in their communities. On Army Alpha and Otis Advanced Test of Intelligence, the twins obtained very similar scores. Marked differences were found, however, on personality tests, speed of free association, and tests of motor speed and coördination. The differences were in general such as would be expected from the variations noted in their environments.

Following the report by Muller, there have appeared a series of very illuminating case studies by Newman.[1] Nine of these have been published to date and more are being collected. In all cases the twins have been separated from infancy or very early childhood. Psychological tests were administered in every instance, so that some quantitative data are available to supplement the general observations. The findings varied from one case to the other. Some twins were found who resembled each other in most traits; others showed close resemblance in certain characteristics and differences in others; and still others exhibited marked discrepancies in all traits, intellectual, emotional, and even in such physical conditions as general health and bodily vigor.

These variations are not surprising. The accidental separations of everyday life to which a pair of twins may be subjected are not to be viewed in the same light as an experimentally controlled separation. In the latter, *every effort would be made to render the environments of the pair as unlike as possible, in order to make the test more crucial and the findings more clear-cut.* In the cases reported by Newman, however, a certain element of chance entered into the selection of environments. Thus certain pairs of twins may have been accidentally adopted into homes which differed widely, others reared in surroundings which shared a few important features, and still

---

[1] For complete accounts, the reader is referred to Newman (12). Freeman and Holzinger coöperated with Newman in the psychological parts of these observations.

others exposed to environments which, although geographically separate, may have been fundamentally alike in their influence upon the growing child.

Unless the cultural milieu and educational facilities of the children are sufficiently different, one cannot be sure that any similarity between them is the result of heredity alone. This is particularly true of a degree of ability which is not far removed from the average. Thus, hundreds of children can be found with an I.Q. of 110, all of whom come from different families and live in different homes. Nor does equality of score on an intelligence test indicate mental identity, since the same total score may be obtained by subjects differing in specific abilities. The use of total scores on complex intelligence tests allows sufficient leeway to obscure a moderate amount of individual variation. The fact that twins reared apart from early infancy may obtain very similar I.Q.'s does not, therefore, constitute proof that intelligence is independent of environmental influence. On the other hand, it is obvious that even a single case of unmistakeable variation between twins known to be identical in hereditary constitution is conclusive evidence that psychological characteristics are susceptible to environmental factors. This is, in fact, equivalent to stating that if an event occurs once, the possibility of its occurrence has been demonstrated.

As an illustration of Newman's findings, a detailed account of two cases is given below. These cases were selected because the differences in environment were sufficiently large to give clear-cut results.

CASE IV (12, p. 200): Female twins, separated at the age of five months and reared by relatives; 29 years old when examined. Mabel had led the life of an active farm woman on a prosperous farm. Mary had lived largely a sedentary life in a small town, clerking in a store during the day and teaching music at night. Mabel had only an elementary school education, while Mary had had a complete high school course in an excellent city school. At the time of examination, a vast difference was noted between the twins in intellectual, emotional, and physical traits. Physically, Mabel is described as robust, muscular, and in perfect health, while Mary was underweight, soft-muscled, and in poor general condition; Mabel weighed 138½ lbs., Mary only 110¾ lbs. Intellectually, an equally striking difference was found, but in favor of Mary whose Stanford-Binet I.Q. was 106 as compared with 88 for her sister. Even larger differences were obtained in some of the other tests. Temperamentally, these twins are described as no more alike than two persons chosen at random.

CASE VIII (12, p. 202): Female twins separated at three months of age and reared in the home of a maternal uncle and the latter's brother-in-law, respectively; examined when about 15 years old. M lived in a small town where she knew nearly everybody and had many friends and playmates. Her foster father was well educated and had a cultured home, involving good books, good music, etc. R was brought up in a large city, but she was kept closely at home and had few friends. Her home environment is described as narrow and "unstimulating," neither of her foster parents having had much education. Formal schooling differed little in the two cases, M being in grade 10A and R in 10B at the time of examination. The physical environment is reported as being about the same for both. When examined, the two girls showed a remarkable similarity in physical characteristics. Mentally, there was a large difference, M doing consistently better on all tests. The Stanford-Binet I.Q.'s were 92 and 77 for M and R, respectively. Temperamentally, the differences were also large, as shown both by scores on personality tests and by general behavioral observations. R is described as timid and retiring, with a marked lisp in her speech, and apparently unhappy. M, on the other hand, seemed quite normal in emotional development.

FOSTER CHILDREN

Another approach to the analysis of heredity and environment has been made through the examination of large groups of foster children. Three such studies have been conducted to date, one by Burks at Stanford University, another by Freeman and his associates at the University of Chicago, and a third and most recent by Leahy at the University of Minnesota. Burks and Leahy offer rather strongly hereditarian interpretations of their findings, whereas Freeman lays much greater stress upon environmental factors. A brief analysis of each study will throw some light upon the reasons for such apparent discrepancies.

Burks (1) administered the Stanford-Binet to 214 foster children and 382 foster parents, one or both parents being tested in each family. A control group of 105 children and 205 natural parents were similarly examined. The study was carefully controlled from many angles. All of the foster children were placed in their adopted homes under the age of 12 months, and at the time of testing they were between 5 and 14 years of age. The control group was quite accurately matched with the foster group in respect to age of children and parents, educational, occupational, and social status of the parents, and cultural level of the home. In both groups, all subjects selected for investigation were White, non-Jewish, English-speaking Americans, British, or North Europeans, and all were residents of three districts in California. Each foster child lived in the home of a married couple both of whom were alive and living together at the time. The same specification was applied to the control group. In addition to the Stanford-Binet M.A.'s, information was obtained on cultural level of the home, educational, vocational, and other characteristics of the parents, home activities and care of the children, and parents' ratings on intellectual and personality traits of the children. Data on the natural parents of the adopted children were also examined whenever available.

The correlation between mental ages of parents and children in both foster and control groups is reproduced below; the correlation between child's mental age and cultural index of the home is also given.

r *between Child's M.A. and:*	*Foster*	*Control*
Father's M.A.	.07	.45
Mother's M.A.	.19	.46
Cultural index of home	.25	.44

From these and similar correlations between child's M.A. and various other conditions, Burks concludes that heredity is much more important than environment in determining individual differences on intelligence tests. On the basis of further statistical analyses of the data, she estimates that, "the total contribution of heredity . . . is probably not far from 75 or 80 per cent" (p. 308). She also suggests that, "The maximal contribution of the best home environment to intelligence is apparently about 20 I.Q. points, or less, and almost surely lies between 10 and 30 points. Conversely, the least cultured, least stimulating kind of American home environment may depress the I.Q. as much as 20 I.Q. points" (p. 309).

In the investigation by Leahy (6), the same general procedure was followed as in Burks' study, with a few improvements. Thus the Otis Self-Administering Test (Intermediate Form) was substituted for the Stanford-Binet in testing the parents, this test being better adapted to the adult level than the Stanford-Binet. The matching of the experimental or adopted group with the control group was done very meticulously, each adopted child being paired with a control child of the same sex, mental age (within 6 months), paternal occupation, and father's and mother's schooling. All subjects were White, non-Jewish, and of North European extraction. The children in both groups were reared in communities of 1000 or more inhabitants, 95% of the group living in communities of over 10,000. All of the foster children were legally adopted by a married couple. The age of adoption was placed even lower than in Burks' study, all of the children in the experimental group having been placed in the foster homes at the age of 6 months or younger. At the time of investigation, the children ranged in age from 5 to 14, the average ages being 9.3 years for the adopted and 9.4 for the control group. There was a total of 194 children in each group.

The general results of Leahy's study are in agreement with those of Burks. The correlations of child's I.Q. with father's and mother's Otis scores and with a cultural index of the home are reproduced below. Corresponding figures are shown for foster and control groups.

r between Child's I.Q. and:	Foster	Control
Father's Otis score	.19	.51
Mother's Otis score	.24	.51
Cultural index of home	.26	.51

Various other comparisons were made which lead the author to conclude, with Burks, that heredity is the major factor in the determination of intellectual level.[1]

[1] The Woodworth-Mathews Personal Data Sheet for measuring emotional instability was also administered to both the experimental and control groups. It is unfortunate, however, that no personality measures were obtained on the parents, with which the children's scores might have been correlated. Curiously

In spite of the care with which these investigations were conducted, there still remain too many disturbing factors for a conclusive analysis of hereditary and environmental influences. Thus the groups tested were admittedly very homogeneous in respect to economic, cultural, and educational status. Both Burks and Leahy point out that more marked environmental differences might produce larger intellectual deviations and that the results hold only for children brought up in the general run of American homes.

In the second place, the possibility still remains that a group of children living with their natural parents might not furnish a perfect control for foster children. The attitude of foster parents towards a child may differ in some essential ways from that of own parents. In some cases, the contact of foster parent and child may not be as close or intimate as that of a child and his natural parents. The fact that in both studies the foster child's mental level correlated higher with the cultural index of the home than with mother's intellectual level, and higher with the latter than with father's intellectual level, whereas all three correlations are very similar or identical in the control group seems to support such a suggestion. The child himself, if he knows of his adoption, may react differently towards his foster parents than he would towards his own parents.[1] Social expectancy may also enter into and com-

enough, Leahy concludes that environment plays a far greater part in the development of personality traits than in the case of intelligence. The basis for such a conclusion is the absence of significant correlations in both experimental and control groups between Woodworth-Mathews score of child and parent's intelligence or cultural index of home. It is difficult to follow the author's logic in such a conclusion. Surely we should not expect a very high correlation between intellectual and personality traits, regardless of the hereditary or environmental determination of such traits.

[1] In Burks' group, 35% of the children had been told of their adoption, in Leahy's group, 50%.

plicate the situation. Parents as a rule expect their own children to resemble them in intellectual and emotional development and this expectation may be manifested in their behavior towards the child, as well as in the attitude of other relatives and associates. As the child develops, his observers constantly call attention to points of family resemblance, real or imagined; he is frequently reminded of ancestral characteristics which are held up to him as his heritage. Such social influences are absent or greatly reduced in the case of foster children. Who knows what motivational differences might thereby arise, which would subsequently leave their mark upon the development of abilities?

In another extensive investigation on foster children, Freeman *et al.* (2) present data from a variety of comparisons. A total of 401 children was employed. All subjects were residents of Illinois. Both White and Negro children were included, but the number of the latter was small. The ages at adoption were much higher than in Burks' study, although over half of the entire group were under three years old when committed. The children were tested with the Stanford-Binet and the International Group Mental Test;[1] the foster parents were given the Otis Self-Administering Test[2] and a specially constructed vocabulary test covering many fields of knowledge. Field workers collected data on education, vocation, and cultural level of the foster parents, and conditions of the foster home. Information on the natural parents was obtained through visits, interviews with acquaintances, and examination of case records.

In order to facilitate various comparisons, the children

---

[1] Specially devised as a universal test of intelligence and relatively independent of specific cultural environment.

[2] A common verbal group test of intelligence.

were classified into four overlapping groups, and the major results on each reported separately. Group I, the *pre-test group*, consisted of 74 children who had been tested before adoption and who had lived in the same foster home until the time of the second examination. The average age of these children at adoption was eight years. The main data furnished by this group relate to gains in score from the first to the second testing. The average I.Q. showed a small but fairly reliable [1] rise from 91.2 to 93.7. When the group is subdivided into those adopted into the better and those adopted into the poorer foster homes, the former show a clear-cut improvement in I.Q., the latter no change. Similarly, the younger children proved more susceptible than the older to a change of surroundings. The relevant data are summarized below (2, p. 119).

Cultural Rating of Home	N	Average I.Q. First Test	Second Test
17 to 30 (Better homes)	33	95.2	100.5
7 to 16 (Poorer homes)	41	88.0	88.1
Age of Child on Second Test			
12–4 or older	37	89.7	89.3
Under 12–4	37	92.8	98.0

Although the average gains are small, the consistency of these results lends them significance.[2]

Group II, the *sibling group* was composed of 125 pairs of siblings, each adopted into a *different* foster home and separated for a period of 4 to 13 years. The average age at which the siblings became separated was 5 years-

---

[1] A gain of 2.5 ± .8, or over three times as large as its P.E.

[2] Freeman points out, furthermore, that the actual gains are somewhat larger than appears from these figures, since Stanford-Binet I.Q.'s show a slight drop with age owing to certain peculiarities of the test itself. He estimates that 5 points should be added to these gains in I.Q. in order to obtain a more correct picture.

4 months. The I.Q.'s of these siblings correlated only .25, in contrast to the correlation of about .50 ordinarily found between siblings reared in the same home (cf. Ch. IV). The scores of 63 siblings adopted into homes receiving significantly different cultural ratings correlated only .19; those of siblings adopted into similar homes correlated .30. These results are particularly striking when it is recalled that the siblings had lived together during the important years of early childhood.

The third group included all *foster siblings*, i.e., two unrelated children living in the same home. This, in turn, was subdivided into a group of 40 pairs consisting of a foster child and an own child of the foster parents, and a group of 72 pairs of unrelated foster children. In the former, a correlation of .34 was found between I.Q.'s of the two children in each pair; in the latter, the correlation was .37. These correlations are actually higher than those between true siblings adopted into different foster homes.

Finally, all of the children were included in one composite group of 401 cases. This composite, labeled the *home group* by Freeman, was employed chiefly in making general comparisons between foster child's intelligence and social adjustment, and such factors as foster parents' intelligence and cultural level of the foster home. In the entire group, a correlation of .48 was found between child's I.Q. and cultural rating of the foster home. The correlation of child's I.Q. with Otis score of the foster father was .37 (N = 180) and with that of the foster mother .28 (N = 255). These and other similar correlations again suggested the relatively large influence of environment upon intelligence test performance.[1]

---

[1] The specific results cited in the above discussion are all based on the Stanford-Binet and the Otis tests. The International and the vocabulary tests yielded very similar results in all cases in which they were employed.

The analyses carried out in the four groups yield results which corroborate each other closely. The data appear very conclusive. A difficulty in the way of a clear-cut interpretation is, however, the presence of a possible *selective factor* in adoption. Thus the more intelligent persons, with more cultured homes, may tend to adopt the more intelligent children. This would produce an entirely spurious correlation between intelligence of foster parents and children as well as between cultural level of the home and child's I.Q. Freeman recognizes this difficulty, but attempts to show that such selection is very insignificant. An examination of the application blanks submitted by the foster parents showed that factors other than intelligence were usually considered. Health, sex, race, and physical appearance were more often specified than intellectual level. When the latter was mentioned, it was only to require that the child be of "normal" intelligence, but no more specific account was taken of degree of intelligence. This request, furthermore, was made equally often by people who were themselves intellectually inferior as by those who were superior. Finally, in over 80% of the cases, very little information was available at the time of adoption about the intelligence of the child or of his natural parents. In the case of the 74 children for whom I.Q.'s were available before adoption (cf. above), there is evidence that such I.Q.'s were employed in placing the children, *but this group constituted only a small portion of the total group of 401 cases.*

If the studies of Burks, Leahy, and Freeman are evaluated together, it appears that the rôle of environment in the development of intelligence cannot be dismissed. Beyond this, however, it is impossible to generalize because of special difficulties inherent in each study. In Freeman's investigation, the factor of selection may have operated, although Freeman asserts that its effect was probably negligible. In Burks' and Leahy's studies, in which the age of adoption was much lower and selective factors were thus more completely eliminated, the only comparisons made were not very conclusive. As has already been pointed out, the evaluation of the foster data in terms of the control data was not perfectly justifiable, since the parent-child relationships were probably dissimilar in the two groups. It is unfortunate that Burks' and Leahy's groups of foster children, with their obvious advantage of lower adoption age, could not have been submitted to the same varied analyses employed by Freeman. A comparison of siblings adopted under the age of one year into different foster homes, for example, would have been very valuable. It would have been quite difficult, however, to find a sufficiently large number of such siblings meeting the required specification in respect to adoption age. If one requirement is met, another must be sacrificed. It would seem, then, that the study of foster children has not yet proved as fruitful an approach to the problem of heredity and environment as it had promised to be.

REFERENCES

1. Burks, B. S. "The Relative Influence of Nature and Nurture upon Mental Development; a Comparative Study of Foster Parent-Foster Child Resemblance and True Parent-True Child Resemblance," *27th Yearbook, Nat. Soc. Stud. Educ.*, 1928, Part I, 219–316.

2. Freeman, F. N., Holzinger, K. J., and Mitchell, B. C. "The Influence of Environment on the Intelligence, School Achievement, and Conduct of Foster Children," *27th Yearbook, Nat. Soc. Stud. Educ.*, 1928, Part I, 103–217.

3. Galton, F. *Inquiries into Human Faculty and Its Development.* London: Macmillan, 1883. Pp. 387.

4. Hirsch, N. D. M. *Twins: Heredity and Environment.* Cambridge: Harvard Univ. Press, 1930. Pp. 158.

5. Lauterbach, C. E. "Studies in Twin Resemblance," *Genetics,* 1925, 10, 525–568.

6. Leahy, A. M. "Nature-Nurture and Intelligence," *Genet. Psychol. Mon.,* 1935, 17, 236–308.

7. McNemar, Q. "Twin Resemblances in Motor Skills, and the Effect of Practice Thereon," *J. Genet. Psychol.,* 1933, 42, 70–99.

8. Merriman, C. "The Intellectual Resemblance of Twins," *Psychol. Mon.,* 1924, 33, No. 5. Pp. 58.

9. Muller, H. J. "Mental Traits and Heredity," *J. Hered.,* 1925, 16, 433–448.

10. Newman, H. H. *The Biology of Twins.* Chicago: Univ. Chicago Press, 1917. Pp. 185.

11. ——. *The Physiology of Twinning.* Chicago: Univ. Chicago Press, 1923. Pp. 230.

12. ——. "The Effects of Hereditary and Environmental Differences upon Human Personality as Revealed by Studies of Twins," *Amer. Naturalist,* 1933, 67, 193–205.

13. Tallman, G. G. "A Comparative Study of Identical and Non-Identical Twins with Respect to Intelligence Resemblances," *27th Yearbook, Nat. Soc. Stud. Educ.,* 1928, Part I, 83–86.

14. Thorndike, E. L. "Measurement of Twins," *Arch. Psychol.,* 1905, 1. Pp. 64.

CHAPTER VI

THE EFFECTS OF TRAINING

A distinction has frequently been made between development through specific practice or training in a given activity and development through maturation or growth. Such a distinction does not imply a dichotomy between inherited and acquired behavior. Thus maturation is not regarded as independent of environmental stimulation of a general sort, nor is learning necessarily considered to be exclusively determined by environmental factors. When we speak of growth, we usually think of a definite sequence of developmental stages in the structural characteristics of the individual. As the child grows older, for example, his height increases, his bodily proportions are altered, and many other well-known physical modifications occur. Such changes take place regardless of the specific training which the individual may have had.

As structures become altered with age, so we may expect their functions to undergo change. With stronger muscles, the older child can learn to walk, climb stairs, sit up, and perform various other tasks much more readily than his younger brother. It is logical to expect that certain types of activity will in general appear at fairly definite stages, since they require a specific degree of structural development for their execution. Very intensive training at an earlier age may produce almost negligible effects when compared to the achievements of an older child with only a minimum of training.

Since such a large share of infant behavior consists in the acquisition of motor skills and sensori-motor coördinations, activities which are closely linked to structural factors, growth rather than practice seems to play the major part in early behavioral development. It is quite a different matter, however, to use the concept of growth to describe the intellectual and emotional development of the older child. Such a concept has nevertheless been commonly employed in interpreting age changes in mental test performance, and the curves plotted to portray these changes graphically have been labeled "mental growth curves." Such growth curves are difficult to interpret for many reasons and their use has led to much technical controversy.

An equally confused issue centers about the question of the effect of growth or practice upon the extent of individual differences. Do people differ more among themselves when their general level of performance is high or when it is low? Will subjects become more alike or more unlike with training? Is variability greater among older or among younger individuals? In all of these phases of the problem of training and growth in relation to individual differences, there have appeared numerous investigations. But the results are very inconclusive and frequently misleading.

In the present chapter will be discussed those investigations which are primarily concerned with the effects of *specific training* upon performance. In such studies, some effort is made to bring about a change in behavior under experimentally controlled conditions. Those investigations which simply present observations or measurements made on different age groups without any attempt to alter the course of development will be given in the following chapter.

EXPERIMENTS ON INFANT DEVELOPMENT

In the course of extensive and carefully controlled observations and experiments conducted at the Yale Psycho-

Clinic, Gesell [1] has established developmental norms of infant behavior for different ages. Since the behavior repertory of the child during the first few years of life consists so largely in the exercise of simple sensory and motor functions, most of the data are drawn from this type of activity. Gesell concludes from various findings that such activities depend chiefly upon growth or maturational factors. Among his evidence he cites observations on pre-term and post-term babies. Infants born prematurely, before the normal nine-month gestation period, do not reach the developmental level of the normal newborn child until the age of one month. Similarly, a baby born after a ten-month gestation period will be as far advanced in its behavior at birth as a normal one-month old child. Yet the differences in opportunity for specific practice in prenatal and postnatal environment are obviously large.

Gesell likewise points to the consistency of developmental sequences as evidence for maturation. In the development of prehension behavior, for example, the successive stages come in the same order and at approximately the same ages in different children. Observation of the child's reactions towards a small sugar pellet showed that both in visual fixation and in hand and finger movements, characteristic behavior was displayed at successive ages.

Training experiments also tended to corroborate the same general view. A series of experiments were conducted by the "method of co-twin control" whereby one member of a pair of identical twins is subjected to intensive training in some activity while the other is used as a control subject and prevented from exercising the function under investigation. In one such experiment (7,

[1] Cf., e.g., 6 and 7.

p. 654), stair-climbing and "cube behavior" (including prehension, manipulation, and constructive play with cubes) were studied on a pair of identical female twins, 46 weeks old at the beginning of the experiment. The trained twin (T) was put through a daily 20-minute training period in both types of activity for six weeks. At the end of this period, the control twin (C) who had had no specific training in these functions proved equal to T in cube behavior. In stair-climbing, a difference was found. Whereas T was a relatively expert climber, her sister could not reach the top of a five-tread staircase even with assistance. Two weeks later, however, still without any previous training, the control twin was able to climb to the top unassisted. At this age (53 weeks), twin C was herself given a two-week training period, at the end of which she approximated T in her climbing skill. Thus, because of the higher level of maturational development, a two-week training period at 53 weeks of age proved to be nearly as effective as a six-week training period at 46 weeks.

Experiments on intensive training in infancy have also been conducted by McGraw (10). A pair of male twins [1] were observed from birth to the age of 22 months. Jimmy, the twin who appeared stronger and better developed at birth, served as the control, his activity being approximately that of a normal infant during the earlier period and possibly a little more restricted than normal later. The other twin, Johnny, was put through intensive daily training from the age of 20 days. Both twins lived at home but were in the laboratory between 9 and 5 o'clock for five days a week. The performance of the trained twin in each task was compared throughout the period

[1] Originally believed to be identical although subsequent physical characteristics threw doubt upon this designation.

of the experiment with that of the untrained control twin.

Specific exercise was found to have little or no effect upon a group of activities including simple reflexes, such as suspension-grasping, as well as crawling and creeping, erect walking, sitting, prehension, and others. Marked improvement resulted, however, from practice on a group of somewhat more complex functions such as skating, jumping, swimming, diving, ascending and descending inclines, getting off stools, and manipulating and climbing stools and boxes to reach an objective. Although a certain amount of sensory and muscular development obviously helps in the latter functions, their performance seems to depend largely on specific training. The independence of the former group of functions from practice confirms many of Gesell's findings. For the execution of these simpler functions, the presence of structures of a certain degree of development seems to be sufficient or nearly sufficient.

In an experiment by Dennis (4), the opposite procedure of restricting training was followed. Two female infants, who happened to be fraternal twins although this was not essential to the present experiment, were reared in the experimenter's home under controlled conditions from one to 14 months of age. During this period, all opportunity to stand or sit was eliminated and opportunities to grasp objects were reduced to a minimum. Comparing the behavior of these infants at successive periods of the experiment with norms established by Gesell and others, Dennis found marked retardation in these functions. The infants were unable to stand, sit unsupported, or grasp a dangling ring at the ages reported as "normal" for each activity.

These experiments indicate some of the major trends revealed by the study of infant behavior. There are some activities which depend so largely upon structural conditions, such as sensory, muscular, or neural development, that their performance is almost completely unaffected by specific exercise. When more complex and less structurally fixed activities are investigated, however, the effect of training is apparent. It should also be borne in mind in interpreting the above experiments that conditions were never perfectly controlled. For practical reasons, it is impossible either to determine or to observe all the stimulation to which the infant is exposed. In McGraw's study, for example, no control was exerted over the infants' activities during the time they spent at home. Finally, even if specific practice is rigidly prevented, the influence of the more or less random and general training which the infant obtains in the course of everyday activity cannot be ignored. Thus, for example, the greater effectiveness of training in stair-climbing when applied at a later age may result as much from the fact that the older child has used his muscles more in various general activities, as from his more advanced age.

Mention should also be made of experiments on infrahuman organisms, both by the method of special training and that of restricted practice. In their general implications, the findings are very similar to those on human infants. Certain functions, such as the flying of birds (13) or the swimming movements of tadpoles (2), for example, have been found to depend almost exclusively upon structural development. Other activities require a moderate amount of specific exercise together with a certain level of physical development for their normal execution; still others depend very largely upon the nature of the training and specific stimulation to which the organism is subjected, and are affected only in a very general way by maturational factors.

THE EFFECTS OF SPECIAL TRAINING AND COACHING UPON MENTAL TEST PERFORMANCE

Attempts have also been made to investigate the effect of specific training upon functions, such as memory or intelligence test performance, which are more complex and less directly related to sensori-motor development. Most of these experiments have been conducted on children of elementary school age. Gates (5) studied the effect of continued practice upon memory span for digits. Two groups of schoolchildren, selected so as to be equivalent in age, number of boys and girls, Stanford-Binet I.Q., school grade, teachers' estimates of scholastic maturity, and scores on several memory tests, were given an initial test in digit span. The children in the Practice group were then put through individual practice in recalling digits on each of 78 days extending over a period of five months. At the end of this period, both Practice and Control groups were given a final test. The average scores on initial and final tests are reproduced in Table IV.

TABLE IV

THE EFFECTS OF PRACTICE UPON MEMORY SPAN FOR DIGITS

(After Gates, 5, pp. 454–456)

Group	Initial Test	Final Test	After a Lapse of 4½ Months	After Common Practice for 22 Days
Practice	4.33	6.40	4.73	5.73
Control	4.33	5.06	4.83	5.92

Both groups show improvement, but the Practice group is clearly ahead, manifesting a gain which normally requires a six-year period, according to the Stanford-Binet norms for this function. Four and one-half months after the final test, both groups were again tested, by a different examiner. This time the Practice and Control groups were approximately equal. Finally, the two groups were subjected to 22 days of practice, at the end of which both showed improvement and in approximately equal degree. It was also found that the training in digit span had no effect on performance in other types of mental tests.

From these findings, Gates concludes that training is highly specific, consisting in the acquisition of special skills and techniques, and that it does not alter the growth of the underlying mental functions. It is unfortunate that in most studies on experimentally administered practice, all effects not directly resulting from such practice are attributed indiscriminately to growth or maturational phenomena, the influence of the vast amount of other training which the child is receiving in the course of everyday life being disregarded.

In Gates' experiment, the fact that the Control group also improved, although to a lesser extent than the Practice group, suggests the effect of other intervening experiences rather than growth. This explanation is further corroborated by the finding that both groups drop to an equal level when retested later by another examiner. The drop may have resulted from the time of year at which the tests were administered, or from other factors incidental to the school situation. The closeness with which the child attends to the material and the effort he puts forth to concentrate on the task of memorizing are very important factors in determining his span; and it seems entirely plausible that such factors should be affected both by the attitude of the particular examiners and by the sum total of school experiences which the child has had. It is noteworthy that the $4\frac{1}{2}$-month period preceding the drop in score included the summer vacation, which is definitely an environmental and not a maturational incident. The marked susceptibility of a function like memory span to training, which this experiment demonstrated, seems in itself to minimize maturational factors. To assume the existence of some underlying hypothetical capacity of memorizing which remains unaltered while performance on a memory span test rises and falls seems totally unwarranted by the facts and not a very clarifying procedure in any event.

Several investigations have been conducted to determine the effect of special training or coaching upon Stanford-Binet scores. In three studies (3) carried out under the direction of Terman at Stanford University, children were given instruction and practice for several weeks on material either identical or similar to some of the tests in the Stanford-Binet scale. The groups were small, varying from 10 to 26, but in each study the trained group was carefully matched with a control group by "pairing" the subjects. All experiments clearly demonstrated the possibility of teaching a child to perform tests which he was formerly incapable of doing because of age or mental level. The influence of this improvement upon the I.Q. obtained on the whole scale differed in the three studies, being most evident, as would be expected, in that study [1] in which the trained functions overlapped with the largest number of Stanford-Binet tests. In this study, furthermore, retests after a six-week period, during which neither group had received any training, showed the practice group to have retained its advantage over the control group.

A more direct investigation on the effects of coaching is reported by Greene (8). Three groups of children were given the Stanford-Binet. The subjects in one of these groups were then coached on the specific tests in which

[1] I.e., the study by Casey (3, pp. 431–433).

they had failed. A second group was coached on material similar but not identical to that in the Stanford-Binet. *No child in either group was coached for over two hours altogether.* The third group served as a control, receiving no special training in the test material. All groups were retested at intervals of three weeks, three months, one year, and three years after the initial tests. The average I.Q.'s of each group on the initial test and each of the four retests are given below (8, p. 425). The results obtained in two schools, A and Y, have been kept separate since a slightly different method of coaching was employed in each.

Test	School A			School Y		
	Control (N = 9)	Coached (N = 18)	Similar (N = 17)	Control (N = 17)	Coached (N = 11)	Similar (N = 16)
I. Initial	82.33	84.22	101.35	98.05	98.55	101.06
II. 3 weeks	88.22	107.94	109.47	100.18	133.09	107.81
III. 3 mos.	87.78	103.17	113.41	97.76	114.55	104.31
IV. 1 year	86.56	94.28	106.76	100.40	113.73	106.88
V. 3 years	85.44	88.67	106.71	96.18	102.82	98.75

It will be noted that whereas the control groups show only irregular fluctuations from time to time, the coached groups in both schools undergo a marked improvement on the second test which followed shortly after the coaching period. This improvement is retained on successive retests, although in ever decreasing amount. The gradual drop in I.Q. observed in the coached groups may be owing partly to forgetting of the coached material and partly to the fact that, as the children grew older, they were tested to an increasing extent at higher age levels *in which they had not been coached.* That the latter is probably the major factor is demonstrated by a comparison of the coached groups in the two schools. In school A, the children were coached more intensively on fewer tests; in school Y, they were coached on two additional higher levels. Thus the effects of coaching in school Y should not be "outgrown" as readily as in A. The average I.Q.'s do in fact show that the dropping off does not occur as rapidly in Y as in A. The groups trained on similar material also show an immediate improvement which gradually disappears on successive retests. As would be expected, the gains in these groups are much smaller throughout than in the groups which had been directly coached.

All of these studies indicate the very great extent to which mental test performance may be influenced by training. Such findings suggest vast possibilities regarding the part played by the incidental and often accidental training of everyday life. That the effects of a brief period of training are not permanent seems to be quite beside the point. *When training is discontinued*, we should naturally expect the improvement to fall off because of forgetting. If, furthermore, children are tested in different functions at successive ages, as they are to a large extent in the Stanford-Binet, the effects of training will not be manifested over a long period. It is futile to expect that a brief period of highly specific instruction or practice should raise the "general mental level" of the child, especially since such a mental level is itself a manifold of widely diverse and loosely interrelated functions. Training does have a very real effect, however, upon the individual's performance on specific mental tests. And this is of prime importance since all our observations regarding the subject's psychological make-up are ultimately derived from such concrete behavior.

THE PROBLEM OF PRACTICE AND INDIVIDUAL DIFFERENCES

Since it has been demonstrated that training can bring about a pronounced change in mental test performance, a further question may be raised regarding the differential effects of such training upon individual subjects. Will the initially better individuals benefit more than the initially poorer? Will subjects tend to maintain the same relative standing in the course of training? Do individual differences increase or decrease with practice? If these questions are still unanswered, it is not for dearth of data, for they have been repeatedly investigated with a wide variety of materials, methods, and subjects.[1] The entire problem is so beset with technical difficulties, however, as to have even been declared insoluble by some. The crux of the matter is that entirely opposite conclusions can be drawn if the results are expressed in different forms, a fact which has cast an aura of artificiality over all the data.

In the present section will be given a brief survey of the major issues involved in the problem of practice and variability. These must be considered before any attempts are made to examine the particular findings. The data are meaningless unless evaluated in terms of the specific questions which we wish to answer and the methodology necessitated by such questions. This section may seem somewhat of a technical digression, but it cannot be eliminated from any analysis of the effects of practice upon individual differences. Attempts to present only a simplified summary of results have proved exceedingly misleading, since the reviewer in such cases must either arbitrarily omit many of the data or offer conflicting conclusions with no possibility of reconciling them.

Many of the difficulties of this problem are inherent in any comparison of variability, either from trait to trait (cf. Ch. II) or from one condition to another. As is true

---

[1] For summaries of the relevant literature, the reader is referred to Kincaid (9), Peterson and Barlow (11), Reed (12), and Anastasi (1).

in all of these cases, if a solution is to be found it must be stated in terms of a specifically defined situation. Much of the controversy and confusion seems to have arisen from the attempt to go beyond the concretely established facts and discuss a sort of disembodied abstract "variability" which is expected to be independent of the particular situation in which it has been measured.

In any analysis of the effect of practice upon individual differences, it is necessary to ascertain at the outset what is meant by *equal practice*. If all individuals are permitted to practice for an equal period of time, the slower worker will be at a disadvantage since he will have received practice on less material than the faster individual. The use of an equal amount of material, on the other hand, places a handicap on the faster worker who will necessarily spend less time in training than the slower person. The *amount limit* method, giving the advantage to the initially poorer individual, favors a decrease in variability with practice, whereas the *time limit* method favors an increase.

Each method answers a somewhat different question. The best criterion for choosing between the two seems to be a practical one. Equal training, as the term is used in everyday life, usually refers to equal time spent in training. When a person takes a "course" in music, or golf, or Spanish conversation, he is given a specified *number* of lessons, each of the same duration. No adjustment is made for the fact that during that period the number of times a piano key is touched or a golf ball is hit, or the number of words spoken differs widely from one individual to another.

A second problem which confronts us is the form in which the scores are to be expressed. In Table V are illustrated three alternative ways of reporting the *same*

TABLE V

Various Ways of Expressing the Effects of Practice

1. *Amount Scores*	*Subject*	*Number of Items Completed during a 1-Minute Trial*		*Gain in Items per Trial*
		First trial	Last trial	
	A	20	30	10
	B	12	20	8
2. *Time Scores*	*Subject*	*Average Time in Seconds to Complete One Item*		*Gain in Time per Item*
		First trial	Last trial	
	A	3″	2″	1″
	B	5″	3″	2″
3. *Time Saved per Trial*	*Subject*	*Gain in Items per Trial*	*Time Initially Required for Each Item*	*Gain in Time per Trial*
	A	10	3″	30″
	B	8	5″	40″

scores obtained by two subjects, A and B, with the time limit method. In this table, A represents an initially faster worker and B an initially slower one. It will be noted that the relation between the gains of the initially better and poorer subjects differs in each method. When the scores are expressed as amount of work done per unit of time, the gain of the better subject appears larger than that of the poorer one. This will tend to make variability increase with practice. If, on the other hand, these same scores are expressed as time per unit of work, the slower individual will seem to gain more.

This apparent contradiction becomes intelligible if we realize just what time and amount scores are measuring. Since the slow worker requires more time on each item, *for every additional item which he completes within the given period after practice he will be saving much more time, than the faster worker.* Thus, if it took the slow worker B 5 seconds to complete one item at the beginning of practice and if he can complete 8 more items after practice than he could before, he has gained the equivalent of 8 × 5 or 40 seconds per trial. The faster worker A, on the other hand, added 10 items to his score, but he only required 3 seconds per item at the outset, so he has gained 10 × 3 or 30 seconds (cf. method 3, Table V). The gain in time *per item* (method 2, Table V) favors the slower worker even further, since it does not take into account the fact that during any one trial this unit gain in speed is manifested *more often* by the faster than by the slower worker, the former completing more items.

It is apparent, then, that the problem of practice and variability must be further defined in terms of the measure of progress employed. If a choice is to be made among the various measures, amount scores will prove more serviceable because of their wider applicability. In a "speed" test, amount scores can be employed interchangeably with time scores. In a "power" test, however, in which the items are arranged in an order of progressively increasing difficulty, a time score would be meaningless. If, for example, in a 30-minute test consisting of 10 problems, all the subjects attempt all the problems but the number of correct solutions ranges from 1 to 10, it would be absurd to report that the average time per problem ranged from 30 minutes to 3 minutes. The better subjects worked no faster than the poorer subjects since all members of the group tackled all the problems.

Finally, even after the scores have been found, there remains a difficulty in the treatment of the data. A lively controversy has been going on regarding the use of relative or absolute measures of variability in practice experiments. When absolute measures are used, such as the standard deviation, or gross gains made by initially high and low individuals or groups, variability tends to *increase* with practice. When, on the other hand, relative measures are employed, such as the coefficient of relative variability,[1] or some measure based upon relative or percentage gains, then variability *decreases* with practice in most cases. The fundamental objection against the use of relative measures has already been discussed in a previous chapter (cf. Ch. II). It was there demonstrated that, since scores on most current psychological tests are not measured from an absolute zero point of performance, any ratios or quotients computed with such scores may be entirely misleading; the addition of a few easy items at the lower end of the scale might completely reverse the relationship between the obtained values.

Thus it would seem that absolute measures of variability are preferable for a purely negative reason, if for no other. Since relative measures are ruled out by the use of arbitrary starting points in the tests, no alternative is left. We may, however, inquire more directly into the logic of using absolute or relative measures in practice experiments. The argument in support of relative measures is that, since the numerical size of scores changes in the course of practice, the scores are not expressed in the same units throughout and hence absolute measures will not be comparable from trial to trial. Through chance alone, the argument runs, absolute variability will *increase* when the size of scores increases and *decrease* when the scores decrease, such changes being therefore of the nature of a statistical artifact.

It is perfectly true that, other things being equal,

<hr>

[1] $\dfrac{100\ S.D.}{Average}$

numerically larger scores will exhibit greater variability. Obviously, if the standard deviation of a distribution of time scores is 10 minutes, the standard deviation of the same scores expressed in seconds will be 600. For the same reason, the standard deviation of the number of A's cancelled in one minute cannot be compared directly with that of the number of additions performed during an equal period, since the latter scores would be much smaller.[1]

This type of argument does not necessarily hold, however, when the same test is given to different groups or to the same group under different conditions, such as before and after practice. Let us suppose that the average score of a certain group I on an intelligence test is 25 points and that of group II 50 points. It does not necessarily follow from this difference in averages that group II will have a larger standard deviation than group I. In fact, the opposite might very likely be the case. If group I, for example, consisted of unselected third grade public school children and group II of superior sixth grade children in a private school, the latter would probably have a lower standard deviation. Similarly, one could assemble without too much difficulty two groups of men, whose average heights were 64 and 72 inches respectively, but whose standard deviation was 8 in both cases. It would be quite absurd to insist that the taller group is "actually" less variable in height than the shorter, or to suggest that the inches used in measuring height had in some mysterious fashion changed in value from group I to group II. It would seem that the comparison of variability before and after practice is more similar in principle to the above examples than to the measurement of variability in different tests. The use of absolute measures in this connection is therefore justifiable.

[1] Cf. Ch. II for a fuller discussion.

Typical Experimental Findings on Practice and Variability

If the problem be formulated in specific terms, we can legitimately inquire into the effects of practice upon individual differences. For reasons of convenience, as discussed above, we may arbitrarily define equal practice as equal time spent in practice and express scores in terms of amount done per unit time. Variability is to be measured in absolute terms, for the reasons stated in the preceding

TABLE VI

Averages and Standard Deviations of Scores on Successive Trials [1]

(After Anastasi, 1, pp. 40–42)

Trial	Cancellation		Symbol-Digit		Vocabulary		Hidden Words	
	Average	S.D.	Average	S.D.	Average	S.D.	Average	S.D.
1	40.63	6.78	41.15	7.58	39.06	6.84	43.58	6.94
2	44.99	6.42	47.63	7.38	46.30	6.03	44.63	6.90
3	47.00	6.60	52.69	7.30	45.22	6.95	49.00	7.52
4	48.00	6.52	54.57	8.04	47.74	5.88	51.25	7.74
5	50.75	6.60	57.90	7.94	49.19	6.86	54.49	7.86
6	50.30	6.68	58.63	8.34	48.80	6.78	55.12	8.24
7	51.68	6.62	61.02	8.66	52.06	7.22	58.18	9.28
8	52.74	7.04	62.25	8.44	48.97	7.89	60.40	8.90
9	53.06	7.28	63.79	8.08	51.59	7.16	61.30	9.10
10	55.83	7.24	64.52	8.36	52.50	8.34	64.40	10.22
11	54.70	7.24	65.22	7.94	53.08	8.90	62.19	10.46
12	55.08	7.22	65.70	9.40	55.35	8.10	63.26	10.96
13	56.09	7.70	67.04	8.06	54.54	7.98	67.02	11.36
14	55.50	7.12	67.51	8.40	54.74	7.26	68.47	12.96
15	57.88	7.54	67.78	8.72	56.02	8.49	69.28	11.44
16	56.67	7.70	69.13	9.78	56.48	8.46		
17	57.01	7.32	68.19	8.92	57.83	8.59		
18	57.62	7.58	68.81	8.80	56.63	9.13		
19	57.08	7.36	69.17	8.40	56.97	8.89		
20	59.60	7.88	70.07	9.98	59.28	8.87		

[1] The scores on all of these tests were transmuted into an equal unit scale and are thus directly comparable from one test to the other.

paragraph. Under these conditions, the findings of different experimenters agree very closely. An investigation by Anastasi (1) illustrates the general methods and findings of such studies.

Four groups, each comprising from 114 to 200 college students, were given continuous practice in one of four tests. The tests included A-Cancellation, Hidden Words,[1] Symbol-Digit Code Learning, and Vocabulary Learning.[2] The practice consisted of 15 4-minute trials in Hidden Words and 20 2-minute trials in each of the other tests, a different group of subjects being employed for each test. The average scores and standard deviations of the scores on each trial are reproduced in Table VI.

It will be readily seen that the standard deviations rise with practice in every test. It was also found that individuals tend to maintain the same relative standing in the group in the course of practice, the correlations between initial and final scores of the same subjects being consistently positive and usually high. For the four tests, these correlations were:

Cancellation	.6725
Symbol-Digit	.2981
Vocabulary	.5073
Hidden Words	.8239

Such correlations indicate a tendency for the individual who is best in the group at the outset to remain at the top after practice, for the one who is lowest to remain at the bottom, and so on. This is commonly found to be the case in all experiments on practice.

Both the tendency to maintain the same relative position during practice and the increase in absolute variabil-

[1] Subjects were to underline all four-letter English words which were "hidden" in a page of pied type.
[2] Subjects learned, by the method of paired associates, a "vocabulary" of nonsense syllables; the test is similar to code learning, but more difficult.

ity are illustrated graphically in Figure 25. This shows the *learning curves* of two subjects on the Hidden Words test. The subjects were selected near the extremes of the distribution, the differences between their initial scores

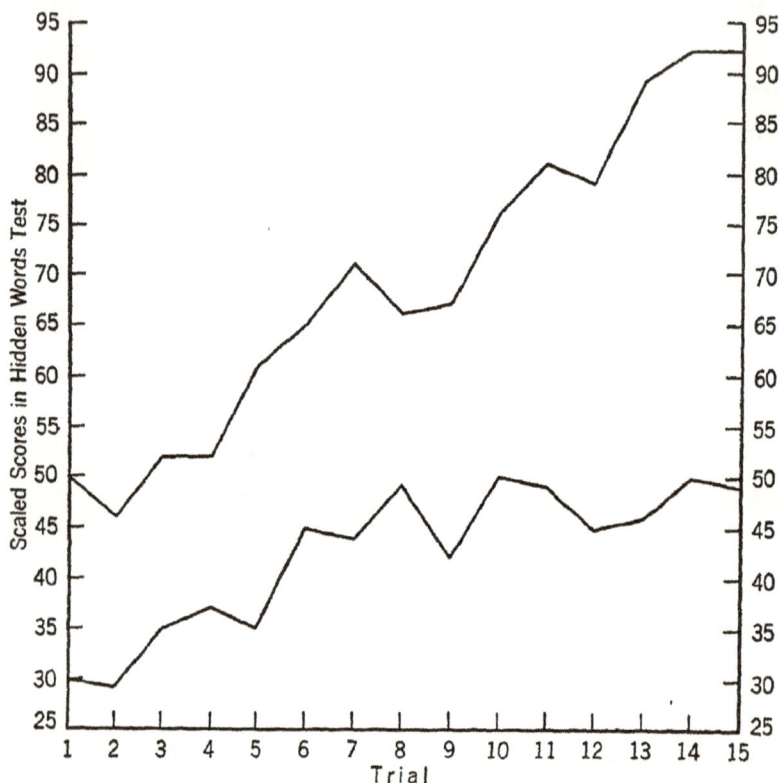

FIG. 25. LEARNING CURVES OF TWO SUBJECTS, ILLUSTRATING DIVERGENCE WITH PRACTICE. (Unpubl. data from investigation of Anastasi, 1.)

being very large. It will be noted that the curves do not at any time cross and that they diverge with practice, the differences between the two individuals being much larger on the fifteenth trial than they were on the first.

It has been frequently assumed that if individual differences in performance *increase* with practice, they can be attributed to hereditary differences; whereas if they *decrease*, they must have resulted, in large part at least, from inequalities of past training and environmental stimulation. It is argued that when subjects undergo a prolonged period of equal training, the differences in their past experience with the given task are thereby wiped out. This assertion is open to question. The influence of environmental factors upon the development of the individual is ordinarily cumulative. If one individual's past experience has made him more proficient than another in a certain task, we should expect him to be better fitted to profit from instruction for that very reason. Susceptibility to training can itself be environmentally determined, and if so determined there is no reason to assume that it will disappear with additional training. The individual who has been handicapped by a poor environment may lack the necessary intellectual tools to profit from instruction. Thus, had the Wild Boy of Aveyron (cf. Ch. III) and a boy of the same age from a middle class English home been put through an identical one-year course in the reading of French, the differences in their abilities to read that language would have been far greater at the end of the course than at the beginning. It is obviously unnecessary to assume an hereditary basis of individual differences in order to account for the increase in variability in such an example. The more the individual has learned in the past, the more he will be able to learn in the present. To use a rather crude analogy, we might say that practice does not add to the individual's ability, but multiplies it.

REFERENCES

1. Anastasi, A. "Practice and Variability: a Study in Psychological Method," *Psychol. Mon.*, 1934, 45. Pp. 55.
2. Carmichael, L. "A Further Experimental Study of the Development of Behavior," *Psychol. Rev.*, 1928, 35, 253–260.

3. Casey, M. L., Davidson, H. P., and Harter, D. I. "Three Studies on the Effect of Training in Similar and Identical Material upon Stanford-Binet Test Scores," *27th Yearbook, Nat. Soc. Stud. Educ.*, 1928, Part I, 431–439.

4. Dennis, W. "The Effect of Restricted Practice upon the Reaching, Sitting, and Standing of Two Infants," *J. Genet. Psychol.*, 1935, 47, 17–32.

5. Gates, A. I. "The Nature and Limit of Improvement Due to Training," *27th Yearbook, Nat. Soc. Stud. Educ.*, 1928, Part I, 441–460.

6. Gesell, A. *Infancy and Human Growth.* N. Y.: Macmillan, 1928. Pp. 418.

7. ———. "The Individual in Infancy." Ch. 16 in *The Foundations of Experimental Psychology*, C. Murchison, ed. Worcester: Clark Univ. Press, 1929. Pp. 907.

8. Greene, K. B. "The Influence of Specialized Training on Tests of General Intelligence," *27th Yearbook, Nat. Soc. Stud. Educ.*, 1928, Part I, 421–428.

9. Kincaid, M. "A Study of Individual Differences in Learning," *Psychol. Rev.*, 1925, 32, 34–53.

10. McGraw, M. B. *Growth: a Study of Johnny and Jimmy.* N. Y.: Appleton-Century, 1935. Pp. 319.

11. Peterson, J., and Barlow, M. C. "The Effects of Practice on Individual Differences," *27th Yearbook, Nat. Soc. Stud. Educ.*, 1928, Part II, 211–230.

12. Reed, H. B. "The Influence of Training on Changes in Variability in Achievement," *Psychol. Mon.*, 1931, 41. Pp. 59.

13. Spalding, D. A. "Instinct: with Original Observations on Young Animals," *Pop. Sci. Mo.*, 1902, 61, 126–142.

CHAPTER VII

MENTAL GROWTH

As will be subsequently shown, the distinction between investigations of training and those of mental growth is a superficial one. It is only for convenience, therefore, that the former were discussed in the preceding chapter, while the latter will be surveyed in the present one. The data of the two chapters should be considered as a whole. A few studies are difficult to classify into one or the other category; this is especially true of experiments on very young children, such as those reported in Chapter VI. For the purposes of the present discussion, however, we may regard studies of "growth" as those in which mental progress at successive ages is observed and charted, with no attempt to alter the normal course of development.

The Growth Curve

Growth curves were first plotted to show the development of physical traits, such as height, weight, bodily proportions as indicated by various indices, and the like. An example of such a curve, showing the changes in height in groups of tall, average, and short girls between the ages of 5 and 17, is given in Figure 26. As a descriptive technique for portraying more vividly the course of development of structural characteristics, the growth curve has proved serviceable and intelligible. The physical data are relatively easy to interpret and unambiguous. By analogy, however, attempts have been made to plot curves of "mental growth," a procedure which has brought additional confusion into an already difficult problem.

At best these curves are only a descriptive summary of changes produced by a multiplicity of factors; by lumping all such factors together and giving them a semblance of systematic growth, the main issues are only obscured.

Two general methods have been followed in the study of age changes in mental traits. The more direct ap-

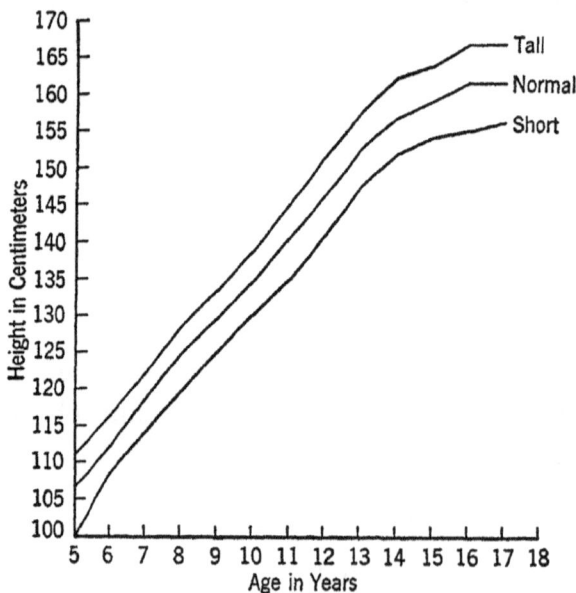

FIG. 26. GROWTH CURVES IN HEIGHT.
(After Baldwin and Stecher, 1, p. 13.)

proach is to retest a group of individuals at successive ages, a very laborious and time-consuming procedure. This method is also open to the objection that specific practice effects may operate in successive administrations of the same test or closely parallel forms. The more common method is to test different age groups at the same time. The average score of each age group is then regarded as indicative of the normal course of development at successive age levels. Such a procedure is subject to serious selective factors, since the different age groups may not be comparable. An illustrative study by each method will be described briefly.

In one of the most extensive investigations of "mental growth," Teagarden (13) tested 408 subjects between the ages of 12½ and 20. The standing of the group as a whole on intelligence tests showed them to be typical of American children and adolescents, their median Stanford-Binet I.Q. being 93.5, with a range from 61 to 136. All subjects were given the Stanford-Binet, Army Alpha, Pressey Senior Classification [1] and Stenquist Mechanical Aptitude Tests. Growth curves were plotted for each test. Apart from many irregularities resulting from selective factors, as well as certain differences from test to test, the curves in general exhibited the typical *negative acceleration* or slowing up at the upper age levels. A composite curve for the four tests is reproduced in Figure 27.

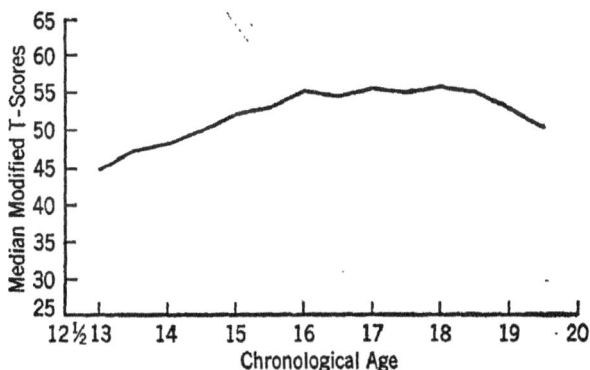

Fig. 27. COMPOSITE GROWTH CURVE ON FOUR MENTAL TESTS.
(After Teagarden, 13, p. 78.)

Development seemed to progress in a fairly regular course. Individual differences increased with age, variability being higher in the older age groups.

Baldwin and Stecher (1) administered the Stanford-Binet to a group of 143 normal and superior children

[1] A group test of "general intelligence."

between the ages of 5 and 14. The study differed from Teagarden's in many respects. The group was younger and included more children at the higher intellectual

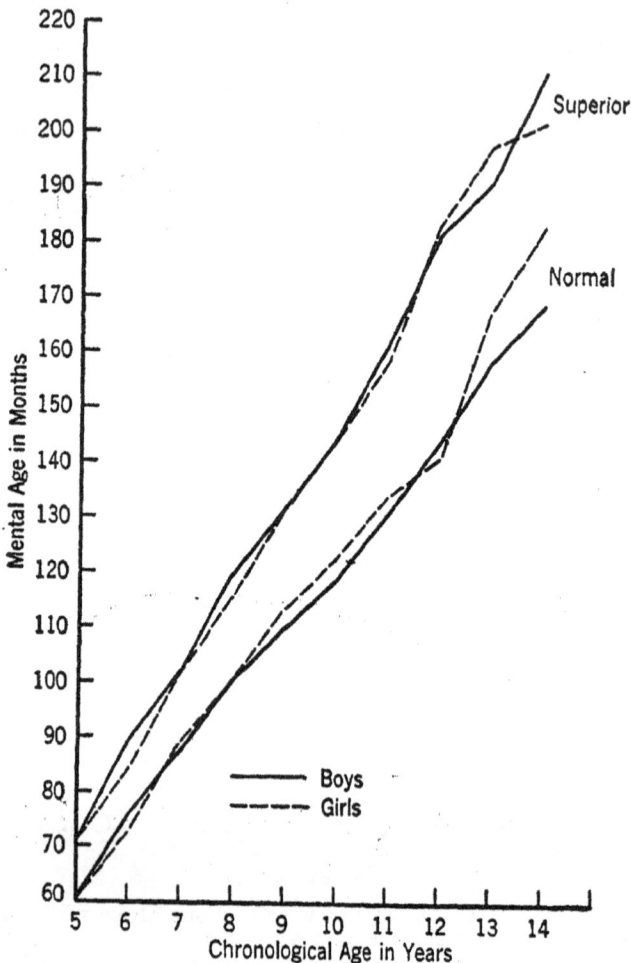

FIG. 28. GROWTH CURVES OF NORMAL AND SUPERIOR CHILDREN IN STANFORD-BINET MENTAL AGES. (After Baldwin and Stecher, 1, p. 11.)

levels, the I.Q.'s ranging from 90 to 167. The retest technique was employed, each child being tested from two to five times within a four-year period. Growth curves were plotted exclusively in terms of mental ages.

In constructing these curves, the retest data were combined with data on equivalent groups of children at different age levels, so that the curves are not based on the same subjects throughout the age range. In Figure 28 will be found the growth curves, plotted separately for normal and superior boys and girls. It will be seen that these curves resemble straight lines very closely and do not exhibit the usual negative acceleration. The curves of the normal and superior groups diverge with age, again indicating an increase in variability with age.

The problem of the effect of age upon the extent of individual differences is subject to the same difficulties as that of practice and variability. Since most studies have employed amount scores, absolute variability has usually been found to increase with age, as it does with training. In the interpretation of the growth curve itself as a picture of the course of mental development, additional and more serious difficulties are met. The weaknesses inherent in both the retest method and the equivalent group method have already been mentioned. It is the latter and cruder method which has more frequently been followed for reasons of convenience. The choice of subjects also affects the type of curve obtained. When only younger children are tested, for example, the curve may resemble a straight line because it represents only the first part of the growth curve and is cut off before the negative acceleration becomes sufficiently large to be conspicuous.

When a complex scale such as the Stanford-Binet is employed, the same abilities are not measured throughout the age range. At the upper age levels, for example, this scale is much more heavily loaded with verbal tests. It has also been pointed out that the form of the curve of mental growth may differ with the difficulty of the test.

In a relatively easy task, performance will improve rapidly during the first few years and more slowly later on as a perfect score is approached. In a relatively difficult task, on the other hand, or a task which requires a certain degree of general information or mastery of techniques before it can be properly executed, progress will be slow at first and much more rapid at the upper age levels. The latter task would thus give a positively rather than a negatively accelerated curve. This has been illustrated by Freeman (5) by means of performance curves of successive school grades on easy and difficult sentences in the Trabue Sentence Completion Scale. The curves for five representative sentences of different degrees of difficulty are shown in Figure 29.

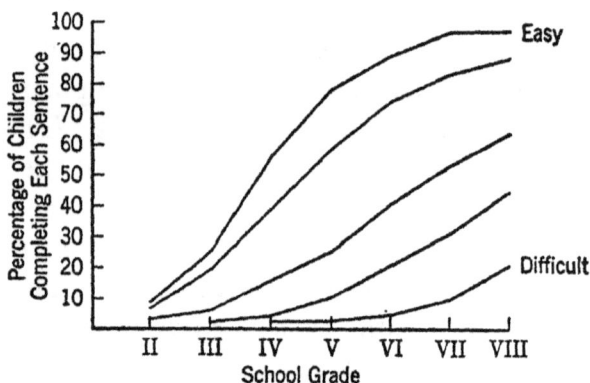

FIG. 29. GRADE PROGRESS CURVES FOR COMPLETION OF SENTENCES OF VARYING DIFFICULTY. (After Freeman, 5, p. 336.)

A further source of variation in the form of the growth curve is to be found in the units in terms of which the curve is plotted. The use of mental ages, as in the study by Baldwin and Stecher reported above, is particularly misleading. It can be readily demonstrated that if average mental age is plotted against chronological age, *the result must be a straight line*, unless the test is not sufficiently well standardized or is unsuited to the group upon which it was employed. To obtain a mental age growth curve which approximates a straight line simply serves to show that the test fulfills its purpose satisfactorily, since an age scale is constructed in such a way that the average child will progress one year in mental age during each year of life. Thus the successive mental age units are adjusted so as to rule out automatically any differences in the amount of improvement from year to year and are completely unsuited to an analysis of the course of mental development. The units in which a growth curve is plotted should be equal throughout the range; otherwise they will present a completely distorted picture. Various statistical devices have been suggested in order to arrive at a "true" picture of the course of mental development, but these techniques are still immersed in much technical controversy.[1]

It is apparent that for many reasons the available curves of mental growth are of doubtful significance. Apart from technical difficulties, however, we may question even the concept of a growth curve in the analysis of mental development. What such a curve actually shows is the *performance* of the individual at different ages in some

---

[1] Thorndike (15, pp. 463–466) presents a negatively accelerated curve to indicate the general trend of development in scores on the CAVD Intelligence Examination, which is scaled in equal units from approximately absolute zero. This curve, however, represents a very rough estimate based on data from many widely varying groups of subjects who had taken different levels of the test.

Thurstone (17) plotted the Stanford-Binet scores of 4208 children between the ages of 3 and 17, in terms of "absolute scale units," a scaling technique which he had devised particularly for the study of mental growth. The curve he obtained was *positively accelerated* at the lower age levels and *negatively accelerated* at the upper.

Courtis (3) has suggested a unit which he calls the *isochron* for the measurement of growth. He defines an isochron as one one-hundredth of the total time required for maturation. In plotting a growth curve, he takes the developments made in equal intervals of the total maturation period as equal. When isochrons are substituted for conventional units of achievement and plotted against age, a *straight line* is obtained as the growth curve.

standard test situation. Such a curve does not differ in any essential respect from a *learning curve*. In both cases, the subject is tested under similar conditions at successive intervals and his progress is charted on the curve. Learning curves, to be sure, usually cover a shorter period of time than growth curves, although a practice experiment could conceivably extend over several years. The major difference between learning curves and growth curves seems to be that in the former the subject is given special training under rigidly controlled experimental conditions, while in the latter he is left to his own resources. Thus it would seem that a mental growth curve is at best a practice curve obtained in the absence of controlled conditions.[1] It reflects the cumulative effects of the random training and experience of everyday life, without adding anything essentially new to the picture.

It follows from this discussion that growth curves are specific to the cultural milieu in which they are obtained. If the learning conditions differ from one group to another, the curves of mental growth should likewise be expected to differ. It might be suggested that the mental growth curve could still serve a useful purpose as a descriptive device. As such it would indicate the general course of development to be expected *under given cultural conditions*, and would characterize individuals of different age levels *within a specific group*. For this purpose, however, it seems that a more useful and intelligible picture could be obtained by observing cross-sections [2] of the

---

[1] This seems to be in general agreement with the view expressed by Courtis (3, 4), who regards growth as development under constant environmental conditions, and subsumes practice curves under the heading of growth curves. It seems to the writer, however, that the issues involved would be better clarified if growth curves were regarded as a type of practice curve, rather than *vice versa*.

[2] Cf., e.g., the interesting descriptions of the individual at various ages given by Hollingworth (7).

TABLE VII

FREQUENCY DISTRIBUTIONS OF ARMY ALPHA SCORES WITHIN SUCCESSIVE AGE GROUPS
(After Jones and Conrad, 8, pp. 240, 251)

Score	|| 10	11	12	13	14	15	16	17	18	19–21	22–24	25–29	30–34	35–39	40–44	45–49	50–54	55–59
200–										2								
190–																		
180–								I										I
170–									I	2	I	I	I	I			I	
160–							I		2	6		2		3	4	2	2	2
150–						I	5	4	2	2	I	2	3		3	I	2	I
140–			2			I	I	3	2	4	3	2	2	I	4	5	I	I
130–			I	I			5	I	I	5		4	2	4	6	3	2	
120–			2	2	2	2	4	6	3	I	3	4	5	7	7	I	7	
110–		2	8	4	I	4	6	5	I	6	4	I	9	8	5	5	3	I
100–			7	3	4	3	6	2	6	6	4	8	7	6	6	3	3	2
90–	3	2	5	7	4	2	8	4	I	3	3	6	7	5	5	4	3	2
80–		2	10	9	5	6	3	7	5	9	3	12	5	7	9	7	2	5
70–		II	9	6	13	9	5	3	3	5	2	10	2	II	10	5	4	2
60–		II	16	14	I	8	10	4	3	10	6	12	II	5	5	8	5	5
50–		3	4	9	9	8	5	4	8	7	3	6	12	5	7	II	6	2
40–		8	I	5	7	6	5	2	I	II	2	9	8	9	8	3	6	2
30–		II		6	4	3	5	4	5	I	4	3	8	6	5	4	7	6
20–		I		5	3	3	4		I	I	3	I	7	8	3	2	3	
10–		I			2	3	4		I	6	I	2	6	7	3	4	2	
0–9		4			I	2	3			I	I	I	5	3	6			I
Aver.	44.4	45.8	56.7	60.5	75.7	85.7	93.5	96.6	97.0	100.7	91.8	90.5	87.0	85.1	92.2	80.7	81.3	78.6
S.D.	23.5	23.4	23.4	27.0	28.3	32.3	39.0	38.0	41.6	45.5	41.6	38.6	44.0	42.5	44.7	39.3	43.1	40.1

Age

individual's behavior at various intervals, rather than tracing isolated traits through successive years.

Adult Intelligence

Lively discussion has been stimulated by the question of intellectual maturity and decline. Popular indignation or alarm was aroused when, on the basis of the army testing data, the report was voiced about that the average American male had the mentality of a 14-year-old child. This simply meant, of course, that the comparison of Stanford-Binet and Army Alpha scores of a representative group of soldiers in the United States army indicated that the average individual does not improve beyond the age of 14 in performance on common intelligence tests. These findings have subsequently been questioned, however, more recent investigations such as those of Teagarden (13) and Thorndike (14) having placed the "limit of intellectual growth" in the late teens or early twenties. In general, mental development seemed also to continue longer in subjects of higher educational level.

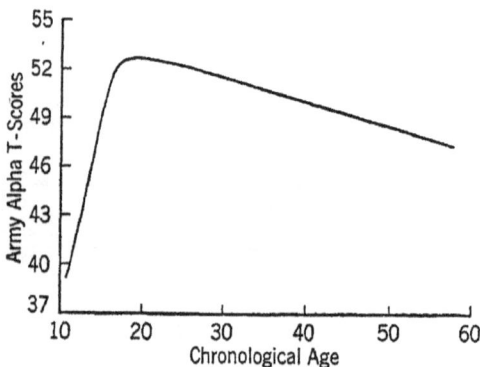

FIG. 30. Smoothed Curve of Rise and Decline of Army Alpha Scores in Rural New England Groups. (After Jones and Conrad, 8, p. 241.)

A closely related question concerns the decline of mental activity. Jones and Conrad (8) gave the Army Alpha to 1191 individuals between the ages of 10 and 60, living in 19 villages in rural sections of New England. In Table VII are shown frequency distributions as well as averages and standard deviations of successive age groups. The age changes in average score are shown graphically in Figure 30. It will be seen that the average score rises from 44.4 at age 10 to 100.7 at 19–21. Beyond this there appear irregular and small drops. Even for the oldest group tested, the drop is not very large. Selective factors may account in part for these findings. Among the older groups there were more individuals who pleaded exemption from the test because of failing eyesight, difficulty in reading, and similar reasons. The less intelligent and less energetic older subjects, furthermore, were less likely to come to the community centers where the tests were given, as was evidenced by the fact that subjects tested in their own homes showed a much sharper age decline than those tested in community centers. An analysis of age curves of the different tests in Army Alpha revealed fundamental differences from test to test, the curves for "naming opposites" and "general information," for example, showing *no decline with age.*

In regard to variability, it should be noted that individual differences were large at all ages, as shown both by the distributions and by the size of the standard deviations. Overlapping of different age groups is very marked, the range of scores within any one age group being much greater than the largest average difference between groups. Finally, the standard deviation shows a fairly clear-cut tendency to rise with age, even though selective factors would tend to make the older groups tested more homogeneous than the younger. It is interesting to find that the standard deviations of the older groups are larger than those of the younger in spite of the fact that the averages decrease with age. For example, the 50–54 year group has an average of 81.3, slightly lower than that of the 15 year group which is 85.7. The standard deviation of the former, however, is 43.1 as compared to 32.3 for the younger group. Thus the changes in standard deviation with age seem to be something more than a statistical artifact which might result from the changes in size of scores. As the individual has more experiences and is subjected to a wider variety of environmental stimulation with increasing age, more possible sources of variation are thereby introduced and individual differences will continue to increase indefinitely.

Willoughby (19), in his investigation of family resemblances in mental traits, also compared averages and standard deviations on each of 11 tests[1] for successive age groups from childhood to 60 years. The scores again rose until the late teens or early twenties. Beyond that age, however, the different tests presented somewhat varying pictures. A marked decline in score was found in tests of series completion, analogies, opposites, substitution learning, history-literature information, and making comparisons. In arithmetic reasoning, on the other hand, no decline was exhibited. The latter task is one which is more useful and more frequently met in everyday life. The decline of the older groups in most tests which do not enter into ordinary adult activities could be attributed to the fact that the *formal education of the older subjects is more remote and probably less in amount.* The general level of education has increased phenomenally during the past 50 years, a fact which cannot be ignored in comparing older and younger groups.

Miles and Miles (9) conducted a comprehensive survey of age changes in intelligence test scores. A total of 823 persons ranging in age from 7 to 94 were given a special adaptation[2] of the Otis Self-Administering Intelli-

---

[1] See Ch. IV for fuller description.

[2] Consisting of the first 60 items of the test, given with a 15-minute time limit. The scores so obtained, however, were found to correlate highly with scores on the 30-minute test, on various groups.

gence Test. The averages and standard deviations shown in Table VIII are based on 617 adults of both sexes tested in one city and are typical of the general findings. The averages show practically no change between 15 and 29; between 30 and 50 there are very small but consistent decreases; beyond 50 the decline is more rapid and continues up to the highest age group tested. Variability indicates no consistent change with age unless it be a slight increase during the middle period between 40 and 50, as compared to the youngest and oldest groups. This is in general agreement with the findings of other studies reported above. Wide individual differences were observed within all age groups, with marked overlapping.

TABLE VIII

AGE CHANGES IN OTIS SCORE: N = 617

(After Miles and Miles, 9, p. 53)

Age	Number of Cases	Average	S.D.	Age	Number of Cases	Average	S.D.
15–19	51	38.50	8.04	55–59	56	28.74	9.04
20–24	40	38.10	7.04	60–64	50	27.94	11.16
25–29	40	39.22	8.20	65–69	53	24.22	9.64
30–34	43	35.26	10.32	70–74	42	23.78	10.48
35–39	44	35.06	8.44	75–79	26	20.46	8.56
40–44	48	33.82	11.36	80–84	13	14.50	9.40
45–49	42	34.50	11.04	85–89	5	15.30	9.60
50–54	63	30.98	11.64	90–94	1	15.50	....

The correlations between each individual's score and his age brought out the same trends suggested by the comparison of averages. The correlation throughout the entire adult age range, from 20 to 95, was approximately —.50, showing a clear-cut tendency for the older persons to make lower scores.[1] When only individuals between

[1] Similar results have recently been obtained in a study on a small group of "mentally normal" hospital patients who were submitted to an intensive testing program (18).

15 and 55 are included, the correlation is −.283; when only the older subjects between 50 and 95 are employed, the correlation rises to −.372. This suggests a more rapid rate of decline during the upper ages, thus corroborating the findings on averages. The fact that all the correlations are far from a perfect −1.00 is attributable to the wide individual variation within age groups and the overlapping of different age levels.

As a further analysis of age changes, the subjects were classified into four groups in respect to the amount of formal education which they had received. In Figure 31 will be found the four curves, A to D, showing the average score of each educational group at successive decades between 20 and 80. The groups were constituted as follows:

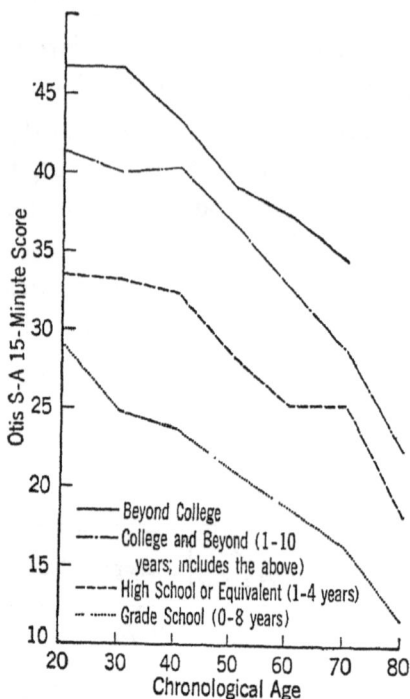

Fig. 31. Age Changes in Intelligence Test Score at Different Educational Levels. (After Miles and Miles, 9, p. 70.)

Group A—four years of college plus additional graduate or professional training

Group B—one year of college and higher (includes group A)

Group C—one to four years of high school or its equivalent

Group D—eight grades of elementary school or less.

Although all groups show a decline from the lower to the upper age levels, *this decline is smaller for the higher educational groups.* The curves do not cross, individuals in the higher educational groups obtaining higher average scores than those in the lower groups at all ages. It is also interesting to note that the lowest point on curve A, reached by the 70 year group is still higher than the highest points of curves C and D. Thus a 70-year-old person who had pursued at least one year of graduate work would be expected to score higher than a 20-year-old elementary or high school graduate. The significance of this finding will be elaborated below, in conjunction with other data.

ADULT LEARNING [1]

In a series of varied and extensive experiments on adult learning, Thorndike (16) found no appreciable decline in this ability between the ages of 20 and 45. Several groups of adults were put through a long period of training in different tasks and their progress was observed. The groups varied from an intellectually and educationally superior group of graduate students, through more nearly average subjects attending evening high schools and secretarial schools, to a somewhat inferior group of Sing Sing prisoners. The major findings have been summarized in Table IX. In each task, the gain through practice made by an older group (35 or over) has been expressed as a percent of the gain made by a younger group (20–24) under the same conditions. Thus, if the percentage is 100 it indicates that the two groups made equal gains; if it is less than 100, the younger group gained more; if over 100, the older gained more.

---

[1] For a comprehensive survey of studies on adult learning, the reader is referred to Ruch (11).

It is apparent from the data of Table IX that age differences in favor of the younger group are larger in the more meaningless rote learning tests and are absent or reversed in the more practically useful and meaningful functions. In most tasks, the older person could compensate for any deficiency in learning capacity by greater interest and effort and by a larger fund of relevant past

TABLE IX

AGE DIFFERENCES IN LEARNING ABILITY

(After Thorndike, 16, p. 103)

Group	Task	*Percentages:* Gain of older group / Gain of younger group × 100
Graduate Students	1. Drawing lines of given length, blindfolded	64
	2. Writing with wrong hand	72
	3. Transcribing words in code	81
	4. Memorizing code used in 3	61
	5. Learning Esperanto	79
	6. Memorizing paired numbers and syllables	64
	7. University studies	over 100 (estimated)
Prisoners of Inferior Educational Status	1. Number-letter substitution from key	104
	2. Elementary school studies	88
	3. Special addition practice	96
Evening High School Students	1. High school studies: English, algebra, civics, etc.	87 *
Secretarial School Students	1. Typewriting	Approximately 95 *
	2. Stenography	" 100 *

* Older group was 30 or over, rather than 35 or over.

experience. Thorndike gives many examples of this fact, in addition to his main findings. Thus the group of university students progressed over twice as fast in learning Esperanto [1] as 9- to 18-year-old pupils in a good private school, although the former had spent less than half as much time as the latter in studying the language. Similarly, the adult prisoners learned elementary school subjects faster than average schoolchildren.

In the attempt further to interpret his results, Thorndike suggested that two of the tasks employed with the university group, *viz.*, drawing lines blindfolded and incidental learning of a code, measured "sheer modifiability," or learning ability, more directly than the other tasks, since they were relatively independent of past experience. Drawing chiefly from the findings on these two tests, he ventured the estimate that there is a decline in "sheer modifiability" of approximately 15% between the ages of 22 and 42, a negligible loss of less than 1% a year. He also presents, on this basis, an estimated curve of age changes in "sheer modifiability" from childhood to middle maturity. This curve is reproduced in Figure 32.

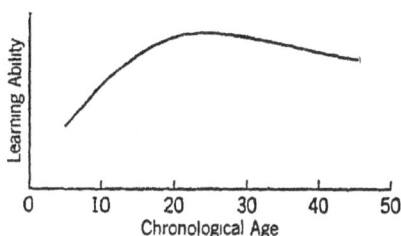

FIG. 32. ESTIMATED CURVE OF AGE CHANGES IN LEARNING ABILITY. (After Thorndike, 16, p. 127.)

The study of adult learning was extended into the higher age levels by Ruch (12). Three groups of subjects were employed, 40 in each of the age groups 12 to 17, 34 to 59, and 60 to 82. The tasks to be learned included two motor and three verbal. Of the motor tests, one involved a simple visuo-motor coördination in direct vi-

---

[1] One of the proposed "universal languages," characterized by a very systematic and logical structure in contrast to current languages.

sion; [1] the other consisted of the same task performed in mirror vision, thus involving the establishment of re-actions which were opposed to the subject's past experi-ence. All of the verbal tasks involved the learning of paired associates. The first consisted of word pairs having some meaningful connection, such as *nest-owl*, *soft-chair*. The second was made up of "nonsense" material, such as $A \times M = B$, $N \times M = C$, and was thus relatively neutral in regard to past association. The third necessi-tated the breaking down of old associations, the material consisting of false multiplications, such as $3 \times 4 = 2$, $3 \times 1 = 1$.

In Table X will be found the averages and standard deviations of the three groups on each test. Without a single exception, the averages show a progressive decline from the young to the middle and from the middle to the old group. The age differences are largest, however, in those tests which are hindered by ordinary past experi-ence and smallest in those which are aided by such experience.

TABLE X

AVERAGE SCORES OF THREE AGE GROUPS ON LEARNING TESTS
(After Ruch, 12, p. 277)

Tests	Averages			Standard Deviations		
	Young	Middle	Old	Young	Middle	Old
Motor learning:						
1. Direct	2857.0	2805.0	2392.0	244.3	287.2	415.9
2. Mirror	771.9	740.0	406.2	214.2	286.2	166.1
Paired associates:						
1. Meaningful	134.7	123.7	111.6	4.26	18.28	26.79
2. Nonsense	78.5	62.8	37.9	23.72	27.95	25.62
3. False multipli-cations	106.1	76.1	49.4	19.45	29.00	24.07

[1] A modified form of the Koerth pursuit rotor, in which the subject must follow a rapidly and irregularly moving object with a stylus.

Ruch demonstrates this by comparing the critical ratios[1] of the differences for each test. These are shown below for the differences between young and old groups, middle and old, and young and middle, respectively.

	Y–O	M–O	Y–M
Motor: Direct vision	6.1	5.4	0.9
Motor: Mirror vision	8.5	6.4	0.6
Meaningful associates	5.4	2.3	3.9
Nonsense associates	7.2	4.0	2.9
False multiplications	11.6	4.7	5.9

In both the Y–O and M–O comparisons, the results appear to be very consistent. Mirror vision learning shows greater age decline than direct vision learning; within the paired associates, there is a progressive rise in difference as we go from the meaningful associations, through the neutral nonsense material, to the interference material of the third test. The comparison of young and middle groups yields somewhat less consistent results, probably because these differences are all small and not very significant.

An examination of the standard deviations in Table X reveals a rather consistent *rise* in variability with age, in spite of the equally consistent drop in averages. The standard deviations of the oldest group are all larger than those of the youngest with only one exception, *viz.*, the mirror vision test. In the case of the middle group, all standard deviations are higher than those of the youngest, with no exceptions. These findings are in agreement with the analysis of age and variability given previously.

[1] Critical ratio = $\dfrac{\text{difference}}{\sigma_{\text{difference}}}$, a common statistical device for estimating the "reliability" of a difference. When the critical ratio is equal to 3 or more, it indicates that the obtained difference could not have resulted from chance errors of sampling, and such a difference is therefore regarded as reliable.

TRAINING AND GROWTH

We may now attempt to synthesize the findings of these various investigations and to evaluate them in the light of the studies on training discussed in the preceding chapter. If we think of all mental development in terms of learning, the diverse findings both on the upper limit of mental growth and on the decline of ability can be fitted into an intelligible pattern. It might be objected that the learning curve shows no decline, whereas age curves do. This apparent inconsistency results, however, from an incomplete statement of the situation. The problem will be considerably clarified if we speak of age changes in specific tasks, as we do in the case of learning, rather than discussing mental development in general. It is quite true that the cumulative effects of learning in everyday life will increase proficiency indefinitely in certain tasks, but such learning will just as surely interfere with the performance of other tasks. If the general effect of any specific act of learning upon all of the individual's behavior is considered, it becomes apparent that learning may cause a decline as well as a rise in achievement.

The decline in performance on most psychological tests with age is no longer surprising when we realize the resemblance of all such tests to school work. We should therefore expect that the longer the individual has been out of school, the more chance he has had to forget what he learned as a child, *through interference from other activities*.

Although in his everyday life the adult may be employing much that he learned in school, he is at the same time losing many school habits, such as working with a specific time limit, following directions literally although he may see little sense in them, and especially working with materials which may be meaningless and of no apparent use to him. When a schoolchild is confronted with a psychological test, the novelty, strangeness, and apparent purposelessness of many of the things he is asked to do will not disturb him unduly, since at that age he is still doing many things for which he can see no immediate value. Such tasks are accepted by the child as part of his everyday work. Not so with the adult. The older he grows, the more he concentrates only on those activities which are either of practical significance or directly pleasurable to him. The reaction of many adults to intelligence tests, as contrasted to that of schoolchildren, illustrates this difference. To most adults, such a test is either foolish or entertaining. The adult is far more sensitive to the apparent impracticality of the situation than the child who is used to taking tests which to him are almost equally meaningless.

That adult ability does not decline in all tasks is demonstrated by the obvious improvement in functions related to the individual's daily work. The achievements of many people progress along a continuously rising line throughout life.

Nor can a distinction be legitimately made between the *extent* of a person's abilities, which increases constantly with age, and the *level* or difficulty of task which he is capable of mastering.[1] The latter is definitely dependent upon the former. As was brought out in the discussion of practice and variability, the more an individual has learned, the better able he is to learn. A problem which is commonly regarded as difficult and which can be solved by only a few individuals is one which involves the synthesis of more numerous and varied types of learned behavior.

[1] Such a distinction has been suggested by Thorndike (15).

We should say, for example, that the derivation of a formula which requires a knowledge of arithmetic, algebra, trigonometry, and calculus is more difficult than one which can be derived simply by the application of principles of arithmetic and algebra. If we define the difficulty of a task objectively in terms of the number of people who can perform it correctly, it will unquestionably prove to be a function of the number of different specific abilities involved. Even if a more subjective, popular definition of difficulty were suggested, it would doubtlessly be found to hinge upon the same principle.

Many of the previously reported findings are clarified by such a view of mental development. Thus the slower decline in intelligence test performance of adults who have had a longer period of schooling is to be expected when we recall that such education is relevant to the tasks on the tests themselves. The formal education which is characteristic of our culture is of a verbal and abstract sort and it is from these fields that intelligence tests draw predominantly for their material. All groups have been constantly subjected to training, but of a different sort. In a test of manual operations, for example, we should expect a more rapid decline with age among the "better educated" professional classes than among certain groups of factory workers.

For the same reason, the limit of intellectual improvement, as measured by common intelligence tests, will be reached later by those groups which continue their formal schooling to a later age. This has been repeatedly demonstrated in studies on the "point of cessation" of mental growth. Corroboration of the proposed interpretation of age changes in mental traits can also be found in the experiments on adult learning. Thus it will be recalled that Thorndike found a difference in rate of decline between the more "meaningless" and the more "meaning-ful" and useful tasks; and Ruch found a similar difference between those tasks which were aided and those which were hindered by the common training furnished in our culture.

Finally, mention should be made of a possible physiologically determined decline in mental activity with age, apart from changes correlated with learning. The effect of the deterioration of necessary structures doubtlessly plays a part in the marked and sharp decline in all psychological functions which frequently characterizes very late old age or senescence.[1] Such obvious handicaps as failing vision and hearing, and muscular and neural deterioration can hardly fail to affect all the individual's activities. These changes, however, do not set in to an appreciable extent until very late in life and consequently cannot very plausibly be offered as an explanation of the decline in mental test performance during earlier maturity. There are cases, furthermore, in which serious structural handicaps during old age have been compensated to a remarkable degree by interest, effort, and the advantages of past experience. The wide individual differences found at different ages also bespeak the potency of specific environmental circumstances rather than physiological conditions characteristic of a given life period.

It would seem that the physical handicaps of senescence are of the same nature as the physical inadequacies of the immature child; they set the upper limits of behavioral development at a given chronological period, but they do not determine the degree to which such limits will be approximated. It seems, also, that these physically set

---

[1] For a discussion of the physiology of old age, and for descriptive accounts of behavior in senescence, the reader is referred to Child (2), Hall (6), and Hollingworth (7).

limits are always much higher than is commonly suspected, since training and stimulating conditions can at all ages accomplish surprising results.

REFERENCES

1. Baldwin, B. T., and Stecher, L. I. "Mental Growth Curves of Normal and Superior Children," *Iowa Univ. Stud. Child Welfare*, 1922, 2, No. 1. Pp. 61.

2. Child, C. M. *Senescence and Rejuvenescence*. Chicago: Univ. Chicago Press, 1915. Pp. 481.

3. Courtis, S. A. "Maturation Units for the Measurement of Growth," *Sch. and Soc.*, 1929, 30, 683–690.

4. ——. *Growth and Development in Children* (repr. from *Advances in Health Educ.*). N. Y.: Amer. Child Health Assoc., 1934. Pp. 180–204.

5. Freeman, F. N. *Mental Tests*. N. Y.: Houghton Mifflin, 1926. Pp. 503.

6. Hall, G. S. *Senescence*. N. Y.: Appleton, 1923. Pp. 517.

7. Hollingworth, H. L. *Mental Growth and Decline*. N. Y.: Appleton, 1927. Pp. 396.

8. Jones, H. E., and Conrad, H. S. "The Growth and Decline of Intelligence," *Genet. Psychol. Mon.*, 1933, 13, 223–298.

9. Miles, C. C., and Miles, W. R. "The Correlation of Intelligence Scores and Chronological Age from Early to Late Maturity," *Amer. J. Psychol.*, 1932, 44, 44–78.

10. Miles, W. R. "Age and Human Ability," *Psychol. Rev.*, 1933, 40, 99–123.

11. Ruch, F. M. "Adult Learning," *Psychol. Bull.*, 1933, 30, 387–414.

12. ——. "The Differentiative Effects of Age upon Human Learning," *J. Gen. Psychol.*, 1934, 11, 261–286.

13. Teagarden, F. M. *A Study of the Upper Limits of the Development of Intelligence*. N. Y.: Teachers College, Columbia Univ., Bur. Pub., 1924. Pp. 112.

14. Thorndike, E. L. "On the Improvement in Intelligence Scores from Thirteen to Nineteen," *J. Educ. Psychol.*, 1926, 17, 73–76.

15. Thorndike, E. L., and staff. *The Measurement of Intelligence.* N. Y.: Teachers College, Columbia Univ., Bur. Pub., 1926. Pp. 616.

16. Thorndike, E. L., *et al. Adult Learning.* N. Y.: Macmillan, 1928. Pp. 335.

17. Thurstone, L. L., and Ackerson, L. "The Mental Growth Curve for the Binet Tests," *J. Educ. Psychol.*, 1929, 20, 569–583.

18. Weisenberg, T., Roe, A., and McBride, K. E. *Adult Intelligence.* N. Y.: Commonwealth Fund, 1936. Pp. 155.

19. Willoughby, R. R. "Family Similarities in Mental Test Abilities," *Genet. Psychol. Mon.*, 1927, 2, 235–277.

CHAPTER VIII

THE RELATIONSHIP BETWEEN MENTAL AND PHYSICAL TRAITS

In the discussion of age changes in mental traits during childhood as well as senescence, mention has been made of certain upper limits of development set by physical condition. As was repeatedly pointed out, such structurally imposed limitations are less important than is commonly supposed, since the individual rarely attains the degree of development set by his physical capacity at any age. We may still inquire, however, whether physical differences *among individuals* exert an appreciable influence upon their mental differences. It is apparent that extreme sensory defects, for example, can so profoundly handicap the individual that even special training will not bring him up to a normal level of performance. Similarly, other parts of the reacting organism may, by their deficiency or superior condition, play a part in the development of mental traits. It should be kept clearly in mind, however, that structural characteristics, insofar as they are shown to influence mental development, can be regarded only as *necessary conditions;* the presence of a required physical factor does not in itself determine behavioral development, but simply makes the latter possible if the proper stimulation is available.

The question of the relationship between mental and physical characteristics has long proved a fascinating one to man. The field has abounded with fanciful speculations and vain hopes that a person's character or intelligence could be "read" from physical signs. Recently, the problem has been approached more empirically and objectively and a sizable body of data has been accumulated on the relationship between various structural, physiological, or sensory conditions and psychological traits. There are a number of well-known types of mental and emotional disorders which are directly traceable to the effects of drugs or infection on the nervous system, the deterioration of tissues, and the like. Thus general paresis results from syphilitic infection, delirium tremens from excessive habitual use of alcohol, cretinism from a deficiency of the thyroid gland, encephalitis lethargica [1] from a bacterium which is believed to enter through the nasal passages. Many other similar conditions could be enumerated.

In the present discussion, however, we shall deal only with the milder degrees of variation commonly found within the normal range of individuals. We are not concerned with more extreme and pathological conditions, since they are relatively rare and their effects upon behavior are more obvious. The major findings on the relationship of behavior traits to cranial and facial characteristics, body build, physiological conditions, and sensory defects will be surveyed briefly and illustrative investigations reported. Some further data on anatomical characteristics with special reference to theories of constitutional type will be presented in the following chapter.

CRANIAL MEASUREMENTS

Popular interest in the size and shape of the skull was considerably stimulated by the pseudo-science of phrenology,[2] initiated by Gall in the eighteenth century.

---

[1] Often popularly called "sleeping sickness," although not identical with African sleeping sickness.

[2] For a discussion from the viewpoint of a practicing phrenologist, see Fowler (4).

Phrenology was based on a false notion of the functions of the various parts of the cerebral cortex. Thus the phrenologists claimed that each part of the brain controlled a particular intellectual or moral function such as mechanical ingenuity, veneration, domestic impulses, and other equally complex and vaguely defined activities. They asserted further that the over- or underdevelopment of such characteristics could be detected by examining the protrusions on the skull. The location of a particular "bump" was taken to mean that the function whose cortical area was supposed to be beneath it was over-developed in the given individual.

It would seem unnecessary to refute such an obviously untenable doctrine were it not for its still widespread popularity among the general public and its lucrative current practice by quack "vocational counsellors" and similar soothsayers of modern times. In the first place, phrenology is founded on the erroneous assumption that there is a perfect correspondence between the shape of the skull and that of the brain; this is hardly to be expected in view of the several layers of membrane and the cerebro-spinal fluid which intervenes between the two. Size, furthermore, cannot be regarded as a sufficient index of degree of development in the nervous system; the latter seems to depend more closely upon the complexity of interrelation of the microscopical nerve cells. Experiments on cortical localization have demonstrated a connection between certain muscle groups or sense organs and certain brain areas; but this is quite unlike the phrenologist's attempt to map out complex personality traits.

Phrenologists have also tried to show that cranial capacity as a whole, or total brain size, is related to intelligence. As in all their data, however, they draw their evidence from selected examples. It is true that a certain type of idiot, the microcephalic, has a very small skull, but there are also idiots with normal or very large skulls. A few men of genius may be found with very large brains,[1] but some are likewise found with small brains. The question can only be settled by accurate measurement of large numbers of unselected cases.

Investigations on the relationship between cranial capacity and intellectual achievement have generally yielded negative results. In a number of studies in which average cranial dimensions of bright and dull groups were compared, the data are ambiguous and difficult to interpret.[2] The differences between the averages are always extremely small and occasionally inconsistent from one comparison to another. In many cases the measures taken on the living skull were not good indices of brain capacity. The groups employed varied widely in age and, especially when children are included, this may produce a spurious relationship between size of head and intelligence since the older subjects will have larger heads and at the same time will obtain higher scores on intelligence tests. Finally, the estimates of intelligence were frequently crude and unreliable.

The first well controlled study on cranial measurement in which adequate correlational analysis was employed is that of Pearson (17). Measures of head length, head breadth, and cephalic index [3] were obtained on three

---

[1] A frequently quoted example is Daniel Webster, whose head circumference measured 24½ inches.

[2] For a survey of these data, see Paterson (16).

[3] Cephalic Index $= \dfrac{100 \times \text{head width}}{\text{head length}}$. Length of head is measured from the space between the eyebrows to the farthest projection at the back of the head; head width, or breadth, is the distance from left to right sides, measured from the points of maximal protrusion above each ear. The following is a common classification of cephalic index:

Dolichocephalic, or long-headed	C.I. below 75
Mesocephalic, or medium-headed	C.I. between 75 and 80
Brachycephalic, or broad-headed	C.I. above 80

groups, including 1010 Cambridge University students, over 2200 12-year-old schoolboys, and over 2100 12-year-old schoolgirls.[1] It will be noted that age was held constant among the children by selecting only 12-year-olds. The subjects were classified into intellectual levels on the basis of teachers' ratings and scholastic records. The correlations between intellectual level and cephalic index were −.06, −.04, and .07 among the university students, schoolboys, and schoolgirls, respectively. For length of head, the correlations in these three groups were .11, .14, and .08, and for breadth of head .10, .11, and .11. These correlations speak for themselves, being too low in every case to indicate any appreciable trend. The very low and inconsistent correlations with cephalic index lend no support to a frequently proposed theory that the "long-headed" individuals, with a low cephalic index, are the more intelligent, nor to the opposite view, also occasionally voiced, that the "broad-headed," with high cephalic index, are the more intelligent.

More recent investigations by the correlation method have in general substantiated Pearson's findings. Murdock and Sullivan (14) report a correlation of .22 between head diameter, obtained by averaging maximum head width and maximum head length, and I.Q.[2] on about 596 elementary and high school pupils. By the use of I.Q.'s and by the conversion of physical measurements into deviations from the average of each age-sex group, the influence of age was held constant. Sommerville (27) found correlations of .10, .03, and .09 between head length, head width, and head height, respectively, of 100 male college students and their scores on the Thorndike Intelligence Examination for High School Gradu-

---

[1] The number of cases differed slightly for each measure.
[2] Found from a number of group intelligence tests.

ates. The correlations were no higher between intelligence test scores and cranial capacity as estimated from the three given head dimensions. Employing one standard formula for the computation of cranial capacity, Sommerville obtained a correlation of .11 with intelligence test score; with another formula, the correlation was .10. Reid and Mulligan (23) found a correlation of .08 between cranial capacity and scholastic achievement on 449 male medical students in Scotland. Cranial capacity was calculated by taking the product of head length, breadth, and height, with allowance for thickness of different parts of the cranium. Scholastic achievement was determined by performance on standardized examinations in three courses which were taken by all the students.

It seems quite definitely established, then, that no appreciable relationship exists between intellectual performance and either absolute head size or head shape, as determined by the cephalic index. Some dissenting voices are still heard, advocating the use of cranial measurement in the diagnosis of intellectual defect,[1] but their evidence is very ambiguous and their arguments are untenable and inconsistent. Further data on more detailed cranial conformation will be presented in the following section in conjunction with facial measurements.

FACIAL CHARACTERISTICS

There are at present many firmly entrenched beliefs regarding the "meaning" of various facial and other bodily characteristics. The high forehead as an index of intellectual talent, the shifty gaze to denote deceitfulness, the firm chin and square jaw of determination, the tapering fingers of the artist, and a host of other traditional

[1] Cf., e.g., Porteus (21).

associations which the reader can easily name have found their way not only into poetry and fiction but into the snap judgments and "hunches" of everyday life. We also frequently hear of alleged personality differences between blondes and brunettes, between blue-eyed and brown-eyed persons, or between those with a "convex" and those with a "concave" profile. Most of these beliefs are joined loosely under the general term "physiognomy." The latter is still being practiced as a financially profitable "system" of character analysis.

A series of very accurate investigations to check many of the assertions of physiognomy were conducted under the general direction of Hull (12). The relationship between convexity of profile and several personality traits, which is stressed by many commercial physiognomists,[1] was studied by Evans (3). The subjects were 25 college women, all of whom were members of the same sorority. Such a group was chosen because of their close acquaintance with each other and their resulting ability to rate each other with a fair degree of accuracy. For the same reason, all individuals who had not been members long enough to be well-known were excluded from the study. Each girl ranked the remaining 24 in six personality traits, including optimism, activity, ambition, will power, domination, and popularity. The average or consensus rank of all 24 judges on each girl was computed as a final estimate for each trait. The subjects were also rated in a similar way for degree of blondness. A specially devised mechanical instrument was employed to read off directly the "angle of convexity" of the profile. In order not to omit any possibilities, convexity was measured in five different ways, such as whole face, upper face only, con-

[1] Cf., e.g., Blackford, K., and Newcombe, A. *The Job, the Man, the Boss.* N. Y.: Doubleday, Page, 1919 (p. 154).

vexity without including the nose, and so on; height of forehead was also measured.

The correlations between each of the measures of convexity or height of forehead and each of the six personality traits were low and often inconsistent with expectation; that is, a correlation which would have been expected to be negative on the basis of the physiognomists' claims was positive, and vice versa. The highest correlations were a +.39 between convexity of whole face with nose omitted and "activity" rank, and a −.39 between height of forehead and "will power" rank. Even these correlations, however, are not significant in view of the small number of subjects, and they could have resulted from chance errors of sampling. The correlations for blondness range from +.28 with will power to −.26 with optimism. These are also too low to be significant.

A further point to bear in mind in evaluating these correlations is that the existence of a widespread bias among the judges regarding the association of facial and personality characteristics might in itself produce a correlation. Since tests were not available for the traits under consideration, it was necessary to resort to associates' judgments; but this procedure is inconclusive when prevalent popular beliefs are present.

Facial and cranial measurements were combined in a study by Sherman (25). A group of 78 freshmen in an engineering college were measured by means of a specially designed "radiometer." A total of 15 distances and 4 angles were obtained on each subject, and each of these measures was then correlated with academic grades as an index of scholastic achievement. The correlations with the combined grades on all courses ranged from −.26 to +.34. It is interesting to note that height of forehead correlated −.15 with academic grades. This corroborates the low negative correlations found by Evans between height of forehead and several personality traits which might be expected to manifest themselves in school work. If such a tendency were established, it would indicate a reversal of the popular notion of a "high-brow"!

Various similar studies have been conducted by many investigators. In Hull's laboratory, an investigation was carried out to determine whether there is any relationship between the shape of the hand and a number of traits suggested by "chirognomists." The results were definitely negative. Numerous experiments have been conducted to discover whether it is possible to judge intellectual or emotional traits from photographs, as we should expect if these traits were manifested in facial characteristics. All of these investigations, although revealing many interesting cases of agreement among judges which suggest widespread popular beliefs or a conventionalized facial symbolism, showed no agreement with independent criteria of the traits, such as intelligence test scores or observations of behavior.

It should be pointed out in conclusion that even when significant correlations are found between certain facial or cranial characteristics and psychological traits, as in the case of a few of Sherman's measures, the correlations are still too low to give any information about *individuals*. They simply indicate a general trend in the group which may result from a few extreme cases. Insofar as the correlation is far below 1.00, it shows that there are many individual exceptions to the general trend. The presence of such exceptions or reversals of relationship proves that whatever influence any physical factor may exert upon behavioral development is very minor and can easily be obscured by other more potent factors.

A further fact to note is that as long as a certain notion

is widely prevalent regarding the association of a given physical characteristic with a mental or emotional trait, this may in itself influence the individual's development. If a person is commonly mistrusted by his associates and is not given any responsibility, it is difficult for him to be open and sincere; if a child is regarded as dull and stupid, he may easily come to believe it himself and act accordingly. The social and motivational influence of a widespread prejudice cannot be ignored. A vicious circle is initiated by such a situation; the more widespread the prejudice, the more effective it will be and the more evidence can therefore be found which seems to support it.

From these considerations it is apparent that any relationship which may exist between facial characteristics and psychological traits cannot be large. Even the very low degree of correlation occasionally found is far from being conclusively established because of many uncontrolled factors. Should a slight correspondence be proved between certain facial or cranial conformations and behavior, it has been suggested that such association may result from a common dependence of both types of characteristics upon some underlying condition. The activity of the endocrine glands offers possibilities for such a connection. In certain extreme pathological cases as, for example, thyroid deficiency, the resulting condition includes characteristic physical as well as mental symptoms. It is barely possible that certain facial characteristics, as well as emotional or intellectual traits, are influenced within their normal range of variation by over- or underactivity of some endocrine gland. This, of course, is only speculation. The field of endocrinology is far too complex and too young to offer any clear-cut answers to such a query.

Body Build

Gross bodily dimensions, proportion of trunk and limbs, height in relation to weight, and similar structural characteristics have also been suggested as possible indices of intellectual or emotional status. Since much of the material in this field has been collected to test out the various "type theories" proposed from time to time, the discussion in this section will be supplemented in the following chapter. Only the data on gross size and absolute measures will be treated here, the material on relative proportions and body type being reserved for Chapter IX.

Similarly, we are not concerned with gross malformations and pathological conditions. Many of these conditions, with which anyone who has seen circus "freaks" is familiar, have been definitely attributed to glandular disorders. Thus gigantism, a condition in which the individual may attain a height of seven or eight feet,[1] results from oversecretion of a pituitary hormone; dwarfism, or stunted growth in which the bodily proportions are normal, is produced by insufficient pituitary secretion. No definite intellectual defect has been demonstrated in these cases. Cretinism, associated with an underactive thyroid, is characterized by abnormal bodily development and proportions as well as by intellectual defect, sluggishness, and other behavioral disturbances. If we exclude cases which manifest obvious glandular dysfunctions or other pathological conditions, we still find a wide range in height and weight within the general population. It is into the relationships of these variations with behavioral characteristics that we now wish to inquire.

As in the case of cranial measurements, interest in body build has long been manifested. The search for a possible

[1] The "giant" with the Ringling Bros.-Barnum & Bailey circus is reported to be 8 feet, 6½ inches tall.

relation between body dimensions and intellect probably received a strong impetus from the popular view that the intellectually gifted were deficient in other respects, and in particular that such individuals were weak, puny, and physically inferior. This notion of compensation was cherished widely because of its consoling character—it was no doubt accepted as the device of a benevolent nature to "even things up." In the effort to overthrow these unfounded beliefs, early research workers swung to the opposite extreme and asserted that the intellectually ablest were also the physically ablest, and that a close correspondence exists between physique and mental ability.

Galton (5), for example, suggested that the number of physically superior individuals among his groups of eminent men (cf. Ch. IV) was greater than in the general population. Many studies on large groups of children have subsequently appeared which relied upon the comparison of averages for their conclusions.[1] Such investigations agree in finding a slightly higher average height and weight among the intellectually superior groups than among the normal, and slightly higher for the normal than for the dull. Intelligence was usually estimated quite crudely from school status or teachers' ratings. The differences in averages were invariably so slight and the overlapping of groups so large that the degree of correlation between height or weight and intelligence would necessarily be negligible.

Investigations on the physical status of the feebleminded or the intellectually gifted child have yielded results which are equally difficult to interpret. When averages are compared, the feebleminded appear to be definitely below the norms in height and weight, and the bright children above the norms. In Terman's extensive investigation (29)

[1] For a summary of this literature, see Paterson (16).

on gifted children,[1] a slight tendency was noted for the subjects to be above the age norms for American-born children in height and weight. L. S. Hollingworth (11) compared the heights of three groups, each composed of 45 children between the ages of 9 and 11. In the "superior" group were only children whose I.Q.'s were above 135 (median I.Q. = 151), in the "normal," those with I.Q.'s between 90 and 110 (median I.Q. = 100), and in the "inferior," those with I.Q.'s below 65 (median I.Q. = 43). The subjects in the three groups were carefully equated, each child in the one group being "matched" with a child in the other two groups in respect to age, sex, and racial background,. so that the influence of these factors was ruled out. In Table XI will be found a frequency distribution showing the number of children in each group who fell within successive class-intervals in height, as well as the average height of each group.

TABLE XI

DISTRIBUTIONS AND AVERAGES OF HEIGHT IN INTELLECTUALLY
SUPERIOR, NORMAL, AND INFERIOR GROUPS
(After L. S. Hollingworth, 11, p. 80)

Height in Inches	Frequencies		
	Group A (Median I.Q. = 151)	Group B (Median I.Q. = 100)	Group C (Median I.Q. = 43)
55–59	12	2	1
50–54	30	30	18
45–49	3	13	23
40–44	0	0	3
Average height	52.9	51.2	49.6

Norsworthy (15), in her comprehensive survey of the characteristics of the feebleminded, obtained measures of

[1] Cf. Ch. XIII for fuller report.

height and weight on 157 mental defectives in special classes and in various institutions. She found the same slight differences in averages, with marked *overlapping*, 44% of the mentally defective children exceeding the median of normal children in weight and 45% in height.[1] Goddard (7) collected extensive data on the height and weight of about 11,000 mentally defective individuals, ranging in age from early infancy to 60 years, in 19 American institutions for the feebleminded. In Figures 33 and 34 are reproduced curves showing the average height and weight of successive age groups within four intellectual levels; the data on boys are given in Figure 33, those on girls in Figure 34. It will be noted that the curves of the four intellectual groups are practically identical at the lower age levels; the lower average height and weight of the mentally deficient groups becomes apparent only as adolescence and maturity are approached.

Several factors may enter in to complicate the analysis of institutional data on the feebleminded. In the first place, those individuals with physical as well as intellectual defects are more likely to be committed to an institution. The feebleminded person who is physically fit or superior is less likely to be sent to an institution at all and more likely to leave the institution after he has received several years of training. Such individuals will have a greater chance to succeed in a routine occupation requiring strength and a good physique, with a minimum of thought and planning. The operation of such a selective factor might explain the divergence of Goddard's height and weight curves with age. Since only institutional cases were tested, the inferiority at the upper ages could have resulted from the fact that the physically strongest and ablest had

---

[1] Complete overlapping would have been indicated if 50% of the feeble-minded group had exceeded the normal median.

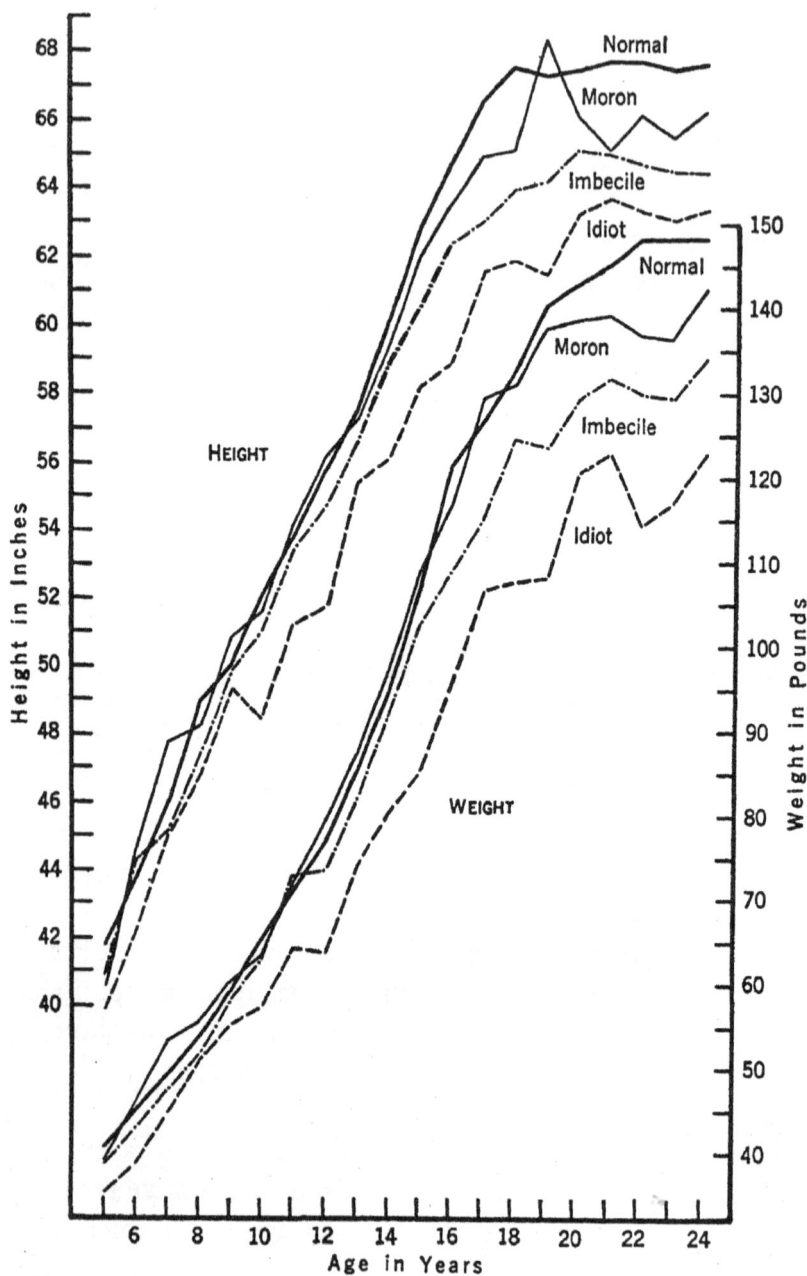

FIG. 33. AVERAGE HEIGHT AND WEIGHT OF FEEBLEMINDED AND NORMAL
BOYS AT SUCCESSIVE AGES. (After Goddard, 7, p. 228.)

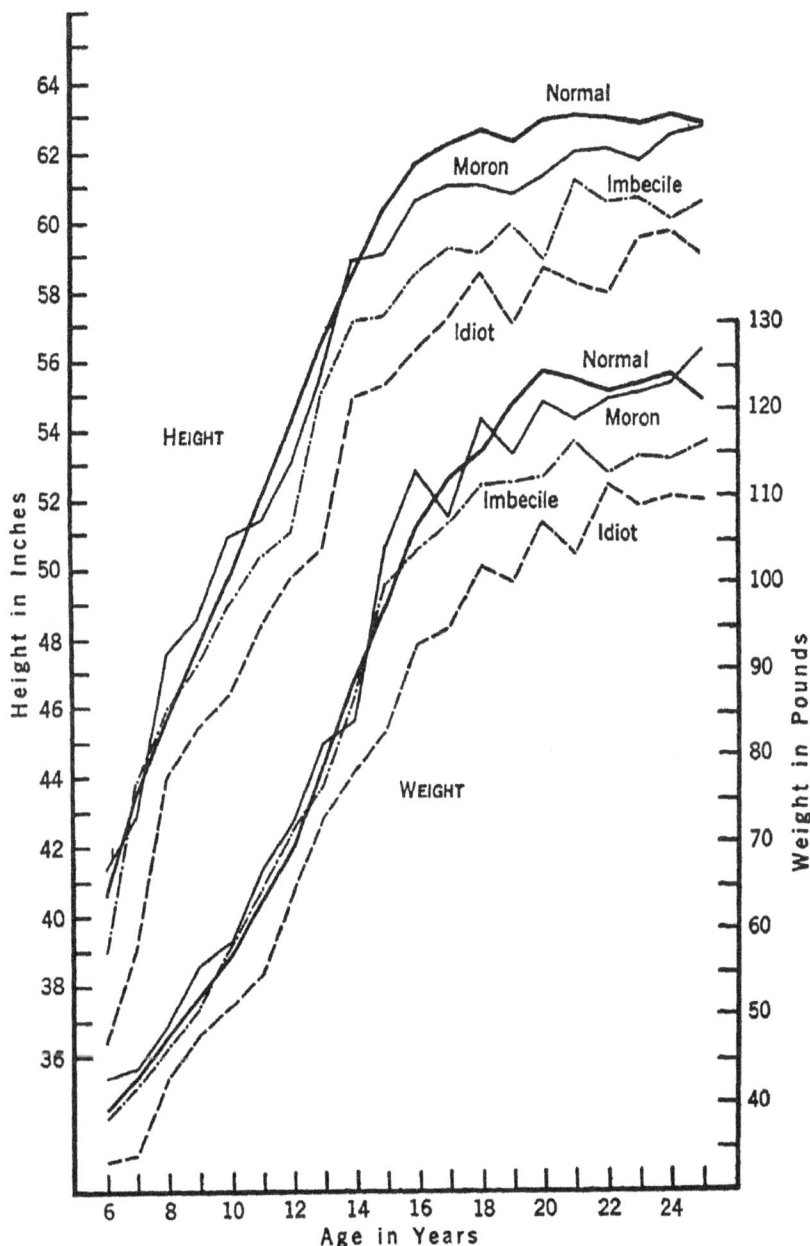

FIG. 34. AVERAGE HEIGHT AND WEIGHT OF FEEBLEMINDED AND NORMAL GIRLS AT SUCCESSIVE AGES. (After Goddard, 7, p. 229.)

left the institution. In addition, the norms in terms of which these groups are evaluated may not be comparable at successive ages. As such norms are usually established on schoolchildren because of their greater accessibility for measurement, the norms at higher ages are frequently derived from high school students, a distinctly select group in respect to the general population. Finally, when fairly low grade feebleminded subjects are employed, it is very likely that several cases presenting special conditions such as cretinism are included and this would serve further to complicate the issue.

A few representative results obtained more recently by the use of the correlation technique within "normal" groups will be reported as more conclusive. Murdock and Sullivan (14), in the investigation cited above [1] found a correlation of .16 between I.Q. and weight (N = 595) and one of .14 between I.Q. and height (N = 597). In an investigation on 58 children in the kindergarten and 57 in the fourth grade, Gates (6) reports a correlation of .06 between Stanford-Binet mental age and height, and .10 between Stanford-Binet mental age and weight.[2] Pearson and Moull (18) correlated height and weight with estimates of intelligence in groups of 616 Jewish boys and 580 Jewish girls living in London; the correlations between intelligence and height were .12 for boys and .11 for girls, and between intelligence and weight, .15 for boys and .07 for girls. None of these values indicates a significant degree of relationship.

Data on older subjects have yielded the same general results, the correlations often being even lower since the groups were more select and covered a narrower range.

---

[1] In the section on cranial measurements.
[2] These correlations are the averages of four separate correlations for kindergarten boys and girls, and fourth grade boys and girls.

Brooks (2), employing 1118 subjects between the ages of 13 and 20, in the third year of junior high school, the normal school, or the freshman year of college, correlated measures of height and weight with performance on several standardized group intelligence tests. Since correlations were computed separately for the two sexes and for several age groups, the subjects were classified into 17 groups ranging in number of cases from 16 to 139. The height correlations ranged from −.09 to +.26; those of weight ranged from −.31 to +.26. Finally, in the study by Sommerville (27) on college freshmen described above,[1] a correlation of .16 was found between intelligence and standing height, .13 between intelligence and sitting height, and .10 between intelligence and weight. The majority of these correlations are positive but so low as to indicate little or no appreciable relationship between general bodily size and intellectual level when selective factors and other irrelevant conditions are ruled out.

PHYSIOLOGICAL CONDITIONS

Attempts have also been made to investigate the effects upon mental efficiency of various physiological conditions, such as general health, malnutrition, defective breathing, and focal infection from diseased tonsils, dental caries, and other sources. One of the first comprehensive surveys of the relative frequency of physical defects among children of differing intellectual level was made by Ayres (1). A total of 3304 schoolchildren between the ages of 10 and 14 were classified into dull, normal, and bright groups on the basis of school progress. The percentage of children in each category having various common defects is shown below (1, p. 74). The percentage having any defect at all, as well as the average number of defects per child, are also given.

---

[1] Section on cranial measurements.

Nature of Defect	Dull	Percentages Normal	Bright
Enlarged glands	20	13	6
Defective vision	24	25	29
Defective breathing	15	11	9
Defective teeth	42	40	34
Hypertrophied tonsils	26	19	12
Adenoids	15	10	6
Other defects	21	11	11
Defective	75	73	68
Average number of defects per child	1.65	1.30	1.07

With only one exception every comparison reveals a consistent decrease in frequency of defects from the dull to the normal and from the normal to the bright group. The one exception is defective vision which shows the opposite relationship from all the other defects, being most frequent among the bright and least frequent among the dull subjects. The greater studiousness of the academically superior child may be more conducive to eye-strain and thus account for this inconsistency. Perhaps the most noteworthy finding of this investigation is the extremely low degree of relationship indicated between physical defect and scholastic achievement.

Little or no relationship has been found between mental traits and such conditions as general health and malnutrition. This problem has been very extensively investigated in England by Pearson and his students, with consistently negative results. Correlations between these general physical conditions and ratings of intelligence on schoolchildren in various social and economic levels invariably proved to be very close to zero.[1] In this country, Hoefer and Hardy (10) conducted an intensive investigation on 343 third and fourth grade schoolchildren between the ages of 8 and 11. All the children were American-born

[1] Cf., e.g., Pearson and Moull (18).

Whites; none was feebleminded and none physically deformed. Thus the influence of extraneous factors was
considerably reduced. Yearly measurements were made
on the subjects over a period of three years. At these
times, each child was examined by a physician, anthropometric measurements were taken, and finally the Stanford-
Binet and the Stanford Achievement Test in school subjects were administered. Below will be found the major
data relevant to the problem under consideration.

General Physical Condition:	Number of Cases	Initial I.Q.	Average Monthly Gain in M.A.
1. Good	145	104	1.30
2. Improved	131	105	1.25
3. Poorer	27	99	1.12
4. Poor or fair	40	101	1.11
Condition of Tonsils:			
1. Tonsillectomy *before* initial test	78	107	1.28
2. Tonsillectomy *after* initial test	64	104	1.33
3. Normal tonsils	53	103	1.20
4. Improved tonsils	30	102	1.20
5. Diseased tonsils	118	102	1.19

The children were classified into four groups on the basis
of general health as determined by the physician. This
classification was made in terms of the relative condition
at the beginning and end of the experiment. Thus "good"
physical condition means "good" both at initial and final
examination; "improved" and "poorer" indicate the direction of change; and "poor or fair" refers again to an
unchanged condition on both occasions. The subjects
were also divided into five groups on the basis of the condition of their tonsils, as indicated. In each case, the
average initial I.Q. of the group is given, as well as the
average monthly gain in mental age months during the
experimental period. The intellectual differences among

the groups are in all cases too small to be of much significance, and the relative status of the physically better and poorer groups is often inconsistent with expectation.

In view of the frequent exaggerated claims made for the effect of diseased tonsils upon intellectual status, a direct and well controlled investigation of this specific problem was conducted by Rogers (24). The subjects included 530 public school boys between the ages of 6 and 14. All had been given the Stanford-Binet as a part of the regular school routine. On the basis of an examination by the school nurse or physician, the children were classified into two groups, the one composed of 236 boys whose tonsils were sufficiently diseased to require treatment, and the other of 294 boys whose tonsils were either not defective or so slightly defective as not to deserve treatment. The average I.Q.'s of the normal and defective groups proved to be 95.4 and 94.9, respectively. The percentage distribution of the two groups is given in Figure 35. The practically complete overlapping of these groups is apparent from an examination of the distribution curves.

In order further to check upon any possible influence of tonsillar condition upon mental development, 28 boys whose tonsils were subsequently removed were retested with the Stanford-Binet after a six months' interval. The gain in I.Q. made by this group was compared with that of a control group of 28 boys who suffered from diseased tonsils but who had not been operated upon. The operated group made an average gain of 2.25 I.Q. points as compared to an average gain of 3.28 in the control group. Finally, it was possible to test 21 subjects after an interval of from 10 to 17 months following the operation. The average gain in I.Q. made by this group was 3.0 points, while a control group of 21 cases gained 6.2 points. It is

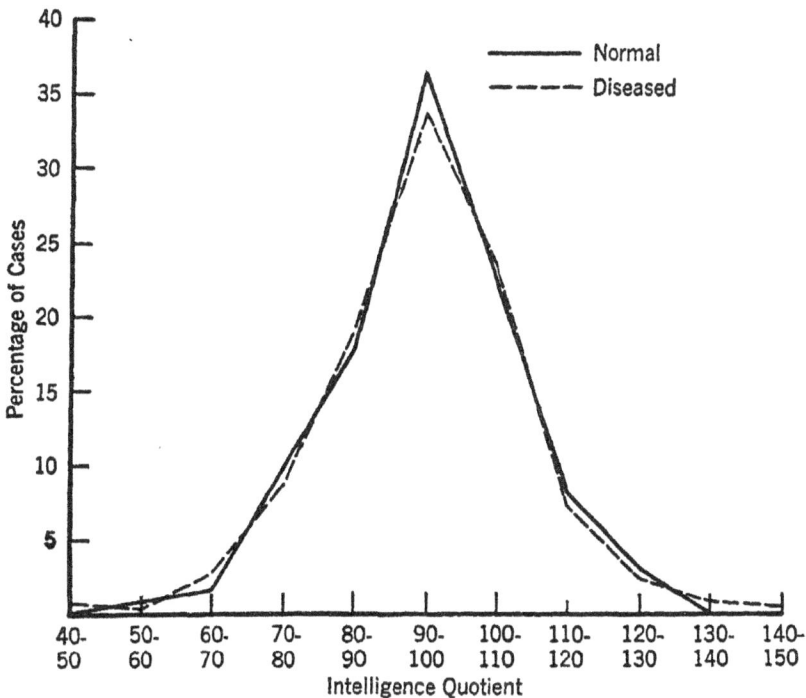

FIG. 35. PERCENTAGE DISTRIBUTION OF I.Q.'S OF BOYS WITH NORMAL
AND DISEASED TONSILS. (Data from Rogers, 24, p. 29.)

very doubtful whether further retests after a longer delay
would reveal any effect of the tonsillectomy on intellectual
development. The lack of significant intellectual inferiority of the defective group as compared to the normal
group at the outset and the absence of any improvement
in I.Q. which could be directly attributed to the removal
of diseased tonsils are mutually corroborative in demon-
strating a lack of relationship between mental level and
this particular physical condition.

Extravagant statements have appeared from time to
time in the popular press and elsewhere regarding the
effects of dental caries (decayed teeth) upon mental functions. Although there is relatively little information on
this question, what there is seems to point to a complete

lack of relationship. Pearson and Moull (18), for example, report a correlation [1] of .15 between number of carious teeth and estimates of intelligence on a group of 617 Jewish boys and a similar correlation of .10 on 581 Jewish girls living in London.

A rather suggestive study on this problem was conducted by Kohnky (13). Two fifth grade classes in the same school, closely similar in all respects, were selected for the experiment. One class, consisting of 38 children, served as the control group. The other, comprising 40 children, received all possible dental attention during the school year. This included dental treatment whenever needed, toothbrush drills, dinners to afford opportunity to teach proper mastication, inspection by the school nurse, home visits by a social worker, etc. A series of sensori-motor and simple mental tests were administered to both groups in October and in May. The differences in gain made by the control and experimental groups were very slight and inconsistent, in a few cases the control group making the larger gain.

It is commonly believed that hookworm (*Necator americanus*) infection produces mental defect, sluggishness, and apathy. Because of the very common occurrence of this infection among schoolchildren in certain parts of the country, it has attracted the attention of educators. Several studies have indicated a tendency for children with hookworm infection to be duller than those not so afflicted. An investigation by Smillie and Spencer (26) gives typical results. A group of 118 children in grades 3 to 7 of three rural schools in a hookworm "area" were given the Otis Intelligence Test. Their scores were trans-

---

[1] The two variables correlated in this study were so arranged that a positive correlation would indicate more carious teeth among the less intelligent individuals.

muted into I.Q.'s in order to eliminate the disturbing factor of age. On the basis of medical tests, it was possible also to determine the degree of hookworm infestation for each child. Below are given the average I.Q.'s of children in five categories, ranging from a normal group who showed no trace of hookworm infection to the most heavily infected group (from 26, p. 319).

Intensity of Infection	Number of Cases	Average I.Q.
Normal	17	90.2
Very light (1–25) [1]	40	88.3
Light (26–100)	27	86.4
Moderate (101–500)	23	84.1
Heavy (501–2000)	10	76.3

Although the differences in averages are appreciable if extreme groups are compared, the overlapping of all groups is large. When individual scores rather than group averages are considered, a correlation of .30 [2] is obtained between I.Q. and degree of hookworm infestation.

This correlation, although not high, indicates a somewhat closer degree of relationship than has been found between mental level and any of the other physiological conditions so far discussed. The analysis of results obtained in investigations on hookworm suggests the operation of a factor which is probably present, although to a lesser extent, in all studies on the relationship between mental and physical characteristics. The individuals of inferior physical condition in general tend to come from a poorer social level; their environment is deficient in opportunity for mental development as well as in sanitary conditions, facilities for medical attention, proper food and home care, and so forth. This is particularly well illustrated by hookworm, a condition which is prevalent

[1] Estimated number of hookworms.
[2] Computed by Paterson (16, p. 196), from the data of Smillie and Spencer.

among individuals of low social status and flourishes in very poor and backward rural districts. The environmental background may be the common underlying factor which leads both to the physical and to the mental conditions. This could in itself account for what little relationship is found between physical condition and mental level.

Sensory Defects

Finally, we may inquire into the effects of sensory deficiencies upon behavioral development. Visual and auditory defects are the most serious sensory handicaps for man. Since our culture is built to such an enormous extent upon a foundation of language, and the latter is acquired chiefly through the eye and the ear, the significance of deficiencies in these particular sensory fields is apparent. Sensory limitations have a much more direct bearing upon behavior than the other kinds of physical deficiency discussed above. Environmental stimulation is cut off by blindness or deafness; the individual so afflicted is psychologically "isolated" from cultural contacts in the same sense as the wolf children of India or Kaspar Hauser, described in Chapter III. We should therefore expect a fairly pronounced behavioral deficiency to be associated with such sensory defects.

Relatively little progress has been made in the psychological testing of the *blind*.[1] Hayes (9) has adapted the Stanford-Binet for testing the blind and has also administered several group intelligence and educational achievement tests to blind subjects. In general, blind children test below the norms for children of normal vision; their average I.Q. has been estimated at about 90, as compared to 100 for children in general. A much

---

[1] Cf. Pintner, (20, Ch. XIX) and Haines (8).

greater percentage of children classified as distinctly feebleminded are also found among the blind. There seems to be no evidence for the popular belief that the blind have a finer discrimination than the normal in other senses, such as hearing or touch. The remarkable feats often accomplished by blind persons through the use of other senses result from a more efficient use of sensory cues rather than in a superiority of the senses themselves. Through prolonged training, an individual may acquire the ability to respond to very slight cues which are ordinarily ignored. Such seems to be the case among the blind.

Minor visual defects seem to have little or no effect upon intellectual development. It will be recalled that in Ayres' survey, for example, the percentage of visual defects was slightly larger among the accelerated and slightly smaller among the retarded children than among children of normal age-grade location. It should be noted, however, that unlike deficiencies in other sensory fields, visual defects are frequently corrected by the use of lenses. If the child wears glasses from a very early age, the stimulational handicap resulting from his sensory deficiency will be eliminated. If the relation between sensory defect and intellectual development is attributable entirely to the psychological "isolation" produced by sensory limitations, we should not expect to find any mental inferiority when the sensory deficiency has been compensated by artificial means.

The *deaf* have proved to be even more backward than the blind in the abilities measured by intelligence tests. This is very likely owing to their greater difficulty in the acquisition of language. The language ability of the deaf in general has been found to be very deficient, and as a result their whole educational progress is much slower. Even when oral instructions are eliminated, the deaf cannot be tested by means of the ordinary intelligence tests because of their serious language handicap.

Reamer (22), for example, reports an average retardation of five years in standardized educational tests among deaf children. Pintner (19), in a nation-wide survey of the deaf, found an equally wide discrepancy between the educational achievement of deaf and hearing children. Comparing the performance of deaf children at different ages with norms on hearing children, he obtained the following:

Age	Average Score Expressed as an "Educational Age"	Educational Quotient
12	7 years–9 months	65
13	8 years–1 month	62
14	8 years–9 months	63
15	9 years	60

Thus, the average 15-year-old deaf subject made a score equivalent to that of the average 9-year-old hearing child, and so on for the other ages. The educational quotient given in the third column is to be interpreted analogously to the I.Q.

In the same investigation it was found that the congenitally deaf or those who became deaf during the first few years of life manifested greater educational retardation than those who acquired deafness later in life, the most marked differences being observed between the three-year and the five-year groups. Those subjects in whom the onset of deafness was postponed until the fifth year had had an opportunity to attain a certain level of linguistic development before the necessary stimulation was cut off.

In the effort to rule out language handicap, specially devised performance and non-language tests have been employed with deaf children. In one very comprehensive investigation by Pintner (19), a total of 4432 children, 12

years of age or older, were tested in 41 schools for the deaf
by means of the Pintner Non-Language Test. This test
involves no language in any part, the directions being
given by demonstration and pantomime. The average
score made by children in each age group was transmuted
into a mental age and from these, I.Q.'s were computed.
The results are summarized below:

Age	Average M.A.	Average I.Q.
12	10 years	83
13	10 years–6 months	81
14	11 years	79
15	12 years	80

If these averages be compared to those obtained with
educational tests (cf. above), the greater inferiority on the
latter will be apparent. The elimination of even written
language from the test situation has reduced the handicap
of the deaf child, but it has not eliminated it. By cutting
off an important source of environmental stimulation,
deafness has produced a more widespread effect than just
a linguistic deficiency. The subject is backward in all
intellectual tasks, whatever their nature.

Mention should also be made of the deaf-mute. These
individuals present a very striking illustration of the influence of environmental stimulation in the development
of a function. Never having heard the human voice, the
deaf-mute is unable to speak *although his vocal organs may
be perfectly normal.* The presence of human vocal organs
does not in itself lead to the development of human speech,
any more than any other structure insures the presence of
the function ordinarily associated with it. Vocal organs
of a certain type are a necessary but not a sufficient condition for the acquisition of speech. That the deficiency of
the deaf-mute is a stimulational one is demonstrated by
the cases in which such persons have been taught to speak

through the use of other cues. The remarkable results obtained in a few such cases, of which the blind deaf-mute Helen Keller is probably the most famous example, again testify to the importance of training in behavioral development. When even such intense structural handicaps as complete blindness and deafness have been overcome by intensive training to such an extent that the individual is capable of normal or even superior intellectual achievement, the factor of structural limitation seems to lose much of its potency.

In regard to milder hearing deficiencies, there is some evidence to suggest a possible effect upon intellectual status. Sterling and Bell (28) tested 1860 schoolchildren between the ages of 8 and 17 with an audiometer.[1] Having arbitrarily defined a "significant loss of hearing" as a loss of nine or more units from the average reading on the audiometer scale, these investigators found such a hearing deficiency among 2.9% of the retarded children and only 1.2% of those in the normal age-grade location. Similarly, when the children were divided into those doing excellent school work, those whose work was satisfactory, and those whose work was unsatisfactory, the percentage of children with hearing deficiency in each group was 1.6, 1.7, and 2.2, respectively. I.Q.'s were available on 585 of the total group of children. When these subjects were classified on the basis of intelligence test performance, the following results were obtained:

I.Q.	Percentage of Children Showing a Significant Loss of Hearing
Above average	0.6
Normal	1.6
Below average	3.7

[1] A very accurate standardized instrument for determining the weakest, or least intense, audible sound for each ear.

Although very small, these differences are interesting in view of the fact that the hearing deficiencies under consideration were not so serious as to produce a marked stimulational handicap.

GENERAL EVALUATION

In the light of the various findings on the relationship between mental and physical traits which have been surveyed in the preceding sections, we may inquire into the possible nature of such a relationship. We are confronted in the first place with certain abnormal conditions of the organism which have characteristic physical as well as behavioral symptoms. It is unwarranted, however, to generalize from the association found in such pathological cases to a possible connection among individuals in general. To take an obvious and extreme illustration, an individual whose legs have been amputated to the knee is unable to dance; we cannot conclude from this, however, that length of leg is correlated with dancing ability and that those persons with longer legs will be the better dancers within a group.

Aside from the relationships which have been demonstrated in pathological conditions, surprisingly little is known directly, although much has been inferred, regarding the operation of physiological factors in behavioral development. In the field of endocrinology, for example, much remains to be learned. Too often what has been offered as a stimulating hypothesis for further research has been interpreted by the layman as an established fact. The same may be said in regard to nerve physiology. The field abounds in speculation and the experts still disagree. At such a stage, it is definitely premature to venture a systematic analysis of behavior in terms of the nervous system.

If we turn from the observation of pathological cases and speculations on the physiological mechanisms underlying behavior to data collected on normal groups, we still meet difficulties. Many of the investigations on this problem have been inadequately controlled. Through the misinterpretation of statistical techniques, slight general trends in groups have been erroneously attributed to individual cases. It will be recalled, for example, that the small differences in group averages, which were regarded as significant by many early workers, actually showed only a negligible relationship when the individual scores were correlated. The pronounced overlapping of groups was often ignored. Age differences were occasionally present within the groups, thus producing a spurious connection between certain physical characteristics and mental level.

Finally, the factor of social status is probably of the utmost importance in any investigation on the relationship of physical and mental condition. The individual of superior social level, coming from a better home, will have richer opportunities for intellectual development and at the same time receive better physical care. He will be brought up under more sanitary conditions and will have less chance of contracting disease than the less fortunate child reared in a city slum or a poor rural district. This factor is probably responsible to a large extent for what little positive correlation has been found between mental and physical traits.

Bearing in mind the fact that direct investigation on normal groups has generally yielded very low positive correlations between mental and physical characteristics and that this correlation would be still further reduced if social status were held constant, we shall examine two possible interpretations of such a relationship. On the one hand we have the theory voiced by Galton and others in the attempt to refute the popular notion of "compensation." This theory interprets the positive correlation between mental and physical traits in terms of some general quality of the organism which underlies all forms of development. It assumes that "good things go together" just on general principles, that the person who is superior along one line tends to be superior in others because of the quality of some common developmental factor.

An alternative explanation is based on the *direct behavioral handicap* introduced by physical deficiencies. This handicap can take many forms. In the case of sensory deficiencies, there is a partial stimulational isolation of the individual. Malnutrition, poor health, and other general physiological conditions reduce endurance, increase fatiguability, affect muscular development, and generally lower the efficiency of work. These conditions, if sufficiently prolonged, would be expected to retard intellectual development to a certain extent. Physical defects or discomforts also prove a powerful distraction and would thus make it more difficult for the child to concentrate on his school work or other tasks. Finally, certain striking facial, cranial, or bodily characteristics which have acquired a specific significance through some traditional belief or superstition may affect the individual's subsequent intellectual and emotional development, because of the social attitudes which they engender.

In conclusion, it would seem that there are adequate reasons to account for the very slight positive correlations found between mental and physical traits, simply on the basis of direct behavioral handicap. There is no need to invoke a mysterious underlying quality which produces the all-around "good" person or the all-around deficient individual.

REFERENCES

1. Ayres, L. P. "The Effect of Physical Defects on School Progress," *Psychol. Clinic*, 1909–10, 3, 71–77.

2. Brooks, F. D. "The Organization of Mental and Physical Traits during Adolescence," *J. Appl. Psychol.*, 1928, 12, 228–242.

3. Evans, A. L. *The Alleged Relations between the Face and the Character.* Unpub. A.B. Thesis, Univ. Wisconsin, 1921 (also reported in Hull, 12).

4. Fowler, O. S. *Human Science or Phrenology.* Phila.: Nat. Pub. Co., 1873. Pp. 1211.

5. Galton, F. *Hereditary Genius.* London: Macmillan, 1914. Pp. 379.

6. Gates, A. I. "The Nature and Educational Significance of Physical Status and of Mental, Physiological, Social, and Emotional Maturity," *J. Educ. Psychol.*, 1924, 15, 329–358.

7. Goddard, H. H. "The Height and Weight of Feebleminded Children in American Institutions," *J. Nerv. and Mental Diseases*, 1912, 39, 217–235.

8. Haines, T. H. "Mental Measurements of the Blind," *Psychol. Mon.*, 1916, No. 1. Pp. 86.

9. Hayes, S. P. *Terman's Condensed Guide for the Stanford Revision Adapted for the Blind.* Watertown, Mass.: Perkins Inst. for the Blind, 1930.

10. Hoefer, C., and Hardy, M. C. "The Influence of Improvement in Physical Condition on Intelligence and Educational Achievement," *27th Yearbook, Nat. Soc. Stud. Educ.*, 1928, Part I, 371–387.

11. Hollingworth, L. S. *Gifted Children, Their Nature and Nurture.* N. Y.: Macmillan, 1926. Pp. 374.

12. Hull, C. L. *Aptitude Testing.* Yonkers-on-Hudson: World Book Co., 1928. Pp. 535.

13. Kohnky, E. "Preliminary Study of the Effect of Dental Treatment upon the Physical and Mental Efficiency of Schoolchildren," *J. Educ. Psychol.*, 1913, 4, 571–578.

14. Murdock, K., and Sullivan, L. R. "A Contribution to the

Study of Mental and Physical Measurements in Normal Children," *Amer. Phys. Educ. Rev.*, 1923, 28, 209–215; 276–280; 328–330.

15. Norsworthy, N. "The Psychology of Mentally Deficient Children," *Arch. Psychol.*, 1906, No. 1. Pp. 111.

16. Paterson, D. G. *Physique and Intellect.* N. Y.: Century, 1930. Pp. 304.

17. Pearson, K. "Relationship of Intelligence to Size and Shape of the Head and Other Mental and Physical Characters," *Biom.*, 1906, 5, 105–146.

18. Pearson, K., and Moull, M. "The Problem of Alien Immigration into Great Britain, Illustrated by an Examination of Russian and Polish Jewish Children," Part II, *Ann. Eugenics*, 1925–26, 1, 56–127.

19. Pintner, R. "A Mental Survey of the Deaf," *J. Educ. Psychol.*, 1928, 19, 145–151.

20. ——. *Intelligence Testing: Methods and Results.* N. Y.: Holt, 1931. Pp. 555.

21. Porteus, S. D., and Berry, R. J. A. "Intelligence and Social Valuation, a Practical Method for the Diagnosis of Mental Deficiency and Other Forms of Social Inefficiency," *Vineland Training Sch. Res. Pub.*, No. 20, 1920. Pp. 100.

22. Reamer, J. C. "Mental and Educational Measurements of the Deaf," *Psychol. Mon.*, 1921, 29, No. 3. Pp. 130.

23. Reid, R. W., and Mulligan, J. H. "Relation of Cranial Capacity to Intelligence," *J. Roy. Anthr. Inst.*, 1923, 53, 322–331.

24. Rogers, M. C. "Adenoids and Diseased Tonsils, Their Effect on General Intelligence," *Arch. Psychol.*, 1922, No. 50. Pp. 70.

25. Sherman, E. B. *An Experimental Investigation concerning Possible Correlation between Certain Head Measurements and University Grades.* Unpub. A.B. Thesis, Univ. Wisconsin, 1923 (also reported in Hull, 12).

26. Smillie, W. G., and Spencer, C. R. "Mental Retardation in School Children Infested with Hookworms," *J. Educ. Psychol.*, 1926, 17, 314–321.

27. Sommerville, R. C. "Physical, Motor, and Sensory Traits," *Arch. Psychol.*, 1924, No. 75. Pp. 108.

28. Sterling, E. B., and Bell, E. "Hearing of School Children as Measured by the Audiometer and as Related to School Work," *U. S. Public Health Reports*, U. S. Health Service, 1930, 45, 1117–1130.

29. Terman, L. M. *Genetic Studies of Genius.* Stanford Univ., Calif.: Stanford Univ. Press, 1925. Vol. I. Pp. 648.

CHAPTER IX

THE QUESTION OF CONSTITUTIONAL TYPES

The relationship between mental and physical traits has also been considered from the point of view of *constitutional types*. In the effort to simplify the almost infinite observable variations among individuals, certain basic human types have been proposed. A specific individual can then be described as a more or less close approximation to one of a small number of types. Such constitutional types are offered as a characterization of the individual as a whole, in all his physical, intellectual, and emotional traits, and are not to be envisaged in terms of any isolated qualities of the organism. There is also a strong presumption of an innate or hereditary basis to the development of types. Thus a theory of constitutional types implies a certain degree of conformity among the various characteristics of the individual, these characteristics being ultimately attributed to an underlying innate tendency.[1]

Type theories have been eagerly seized upon by the general public as a short-cut to the understanding of human nature. The layman is impatient with the slow, meticulous methods of science. This is particularly true in psychology, because of the more intimate and immediate bearing which this science has upon man's everyday life. The terminology of type theories has become such

---

[1] The concept of types has also been employed in the description of specific functions, as in Galton's classification of individuals in regard to their predominant field of imagery, i.e., visual, auditory, olfactory, etc. (3). Such types, however, do not characterize the personality as a whole, and are not to be confused with the constitutional biotypes under consideration.

an integral part of our language that it is almost impossible for us to speak about people without reference to some hypothetical categories. Sooner or later we inadvertently lapse into this practice. The popular tendency to make sharp distinctions, together with the previously discussed efforts to "read" character and mentality from physical signs, has done much to keep "types" alive.

In view of their wide and persistent practical influence, type theories should be closely examined and submitted to experimental analysis. Recently there has been a revival of interest in the problem of constitutional types among psychologists. In the present chapter, we shall survey briefly some of the best-known type theories, inquire into their psychological implications, and examine some representative data collected to support or test their claims.

Type Theories

The first clearly formulated attempt to classify individuals into basic types was probably that of the Greek physician, Hippocrates, in the fifth century B.c. Hippocrates proposed a two-fold division into *habitus apoplecticus* and *habitus phthisicus*. The former corresponds to a thick-set, heavy body build, susceptible to apoplexy and similar physical disorders; the latter is characterized by a long, slender body and susceptibility to respiratory diseases such as tuberculosis. Because of the predominantly medical interest of its exponent, this classification was based primarily upon relative susceptibility to different kinds of physical ailments. Such an approach has, however, persisted to the present, many current type theories taking susceptibility to various physical or mental disorders as their starting point.

The second century Greek physician Galen, frequently

called the father of modern medicine, is responsible for the well-known classification of "temperaments" into the sanguine, the choleric, the phlegmatic, and the melancholic. These terms have achieved great popularity as descriptive figures of speech, although one wonders how often they are still being taken literally. The theories of both Hippocrates and Galen were founded upon a biochemical approach to personality. Thus Hippocrates attributed the development of his two types to the relative proportion of "fire" and "water" elements in the individual's make-up. Galen ascribed his four temperaments to the excess of one or another of four "humors" or body fluids.

Passing to more modern times, we find a wide variety of type concepts in literature, art, philosophy, medicine, anthropology, or any other field in which man is the central figure. The English anthropologist Walker,[1] in 1852, wrote of "nutritive beauty," "locomotive beauty," and "mental beauty." In the following year, Carus,[1] a German zoölogist, described three bodily types. These were the phlegmatic, in whom the region of the digestive organs is prominent, the athletic, with strongly developed bones and muscles, and the asthenic, with narrow chest, a long body, and poorly developed skeleton and musculature. In France, several type theories have been proposed, chief among which is that of Sigaud [1] and his students. Sigaud recognized four types, which he designated the digestive, the muscular, the respiratory, and the cerebral. Manouvrier [1] suggested a division into makroskele and brachyskele, or narrow skeleton and broad skeleton. MacAuliffe [1] offered the *type plat* (flat) and the *type rond* (round).

In Italy, Viola (cf. 19) formulated a theory which has

[1] Cf. Wertheimer and Hesketh (28).

become familiar to psychologists through the researches of Naccarati (19, 20, 21) and others in America. Viola's types include the macrosplanchnic, the normosplanchnic, and the microsplanchnic. The macrosplanchnic individual possesses a large trunk which is excessively developed in comparison with the length of the limbs; in such a body type, the horizontal dimensions are relatively large, the vertical relatively small. The microsplanchnic, on the other hand, has a small trunk and long limbs, the vertical dimensions being relatively in excess of the horizontal. Between these two extremes is the normosplanchnic, who exhibits a proportionate and harmonious development of trunk and limbs. Viola suggested a series of body measurements to be employed in classifying individuals into these types. Naccarati (19) subsequently devised a *morphologic index* as a single numerical expression of body build. This index is computed as follows:

$$\text{M.I.} = \frac{\text{length of one arm} + \text{length of one leg}}{\text{volume of trunk}}.$$

The trunk volume is determined by a series of rather elaborate measurements.

According to Viola's theory, the macrosplanchnic represents an overdevelopment of the nutritional or "vegetative system" contained within the trunk. The microsplanchnic, on the other hand, is characterized by an overdevelopment of the "animal system," consisting of the musculature, nervous system, and skeleton. Intellectual and emotional differences are attributed to the two types, because of the relative activity of the vegetative and animal systems which are regarded as independent and even antagonistic in their action. The macrosplanchnic is regarded as representing a lower evolutionary level than the microsplanchnic because of the greater morphologic resemblance of the former to the newborn and of the latter to the adult. Naccarati (19), in his elaboration of Viola's theory, also suggests that the microsplanchnic corresponds to a hyperthyroid condition and should therefore be expected to manifest the various characteristics associated with overactivity of this gland.

Pende (cf. 28) has more recently proposed a classification into hypervegetative and hypovegetative biotypes, which, as the terms imply, has much in common with Viola's theory. A definite endocrine basis is offered for this theory.

In America, Davenport (2) has classified individuals into the fleshy, the medium, and the slender biotype. Stockard (26) distinguishes between the linear and the lateral types, which he ties up with the activity of the thyroid. The linear type is described as active, energetic, and nervous, but emotionally controlled; such individuals grow rapidly and reach puberty at a relatively early age. The lateral type is less active and grows at a slower rate. The former type of individual is also characterized by a dolichocephalic skull, the latter by a brachycephalic one. Mention should also be made, from the psychological side, of the famous distinction proposed by William James (8) between the "tender-minded" and the "tough-minded" individuals, a distinction which bears a certain resemblance to the introvert-extrovert classification to be discussed shortly.

Pavlov (22), the Russian physiologist, has suggested a type classification in terms of the nervous system. On the basis of observations made in the course of his conditioning experiments on dogs, he proposes two predominant, opposed types, corresponding to extreme tendencies toward excitation or inhibition, respectively. Intermediate, less pronounced types are also described. Pavlov points to a resemblance between the classification so obtained and the classical division into sanguine, melancholic, phlegmatic, and choleric temperaments. He suggests that, "Until a rigid scientific classification is fully established for all the various types of central nervous system . . . we may be permitted to make use of the ancient classification of the so-called temperaments" (22, p. 286).

Type psychology has flourished most vigorously in Germany. Numerous variations and ramifications of type theory have been formulated by contemporary German psychologists. Weidenreich (27), after a survey of the current type psychologies, has attempted to reduce all types to two, namely, the leptosome, with long, narrow body, and the eurysome, with short, thick-set body. Jaensch (cf. 12, 14) has proposed a classification of constitutional types on the basis of eidetic imagery. The eidetic image is a peculiarly vivid and detailed memory image [1] which is experienced by some individuals. Eidetic imagery has been found to be most common in late childhood and to disappear gradually during adolescence, although it has also been discovered among some adults. The eidetic image may be a photographic replica of the original object, or it may differ from the latter in certain characteristic ways. Jaensch and his co-workers maintain that eidetic images are not a pathological phenomenon, but represent a normal stage in the development of many individuals.

Jaensch recognizes two types of eidetic individuals. In the first type, the image can be called up, banished, and altered voluntarily. The eidetic image in such cases may be nothing more than a visualized idea and it is

---

[1] Eidetic images have usually been investigated in the visual field, although it has been claimed that they are equally common in other senses.

accepted as natural and normal by the individual. In the second type, the image usually arises spontaneously and may persevere in spite of efforts to banish it; voluntary alterations in the qualities of the image are often impossible. Such images do not come up very frequently and are often regarded as unpleasant and even uncanny by the subject. Jaensch considers these two eidetic types to be distinct constitutional types, manifested in many bodily and mental traits and characterized by basically different "psychophysical reaction systems." The eidetic characteristics are simply taken as convenient starting points in the classification. The first of the two types described above has been designated the B-type, because of its alleged resemblance to the Basedow syndrome,[1] and the second the T-type, owing to the similarity of some of its manifestations to the condition of tetany.[2]

Jung's introvert and extrovert types are well-known (9). In the extrovert, the "psychic energy" is turned outward to the objective environment. In the introvert, it is turned inward to a subjective world. The extrovert is predominantly oriented in all his actions, thoughts, interests, and feelings, by the objects and people about him. His beliefs and opinions are guided by the mores of his group. The introvert, on the other hand, is governed by subjective factors; all his behavior has a subjective, inner reference. Jung regards these two types as fundamental biological contrasts. They denote for him basic attitudes which characterize all aspects of the individual's psychological make-up.

---

[1] A condition characterized by prominence of the eyeballs, enlargement of the thyroid gland, muscular tremors, rapid heart action, and more or less profound mental disturbance; believed to be caused by overactivity of the thyroid gland.

[2] A motor disorder, including muscular tremor, muscular spasms, and sometimes uncoördinated muscular contractions following upon an effort to make a voluntary movement; attributed to insufficient secretion of the parathyroid gland.

Jung's types have become more widely known, however, in terms of their emotional and social manifestations. Thus the introvert is usually thought of as an emotionally shut-in individual who shuns social contacts, prefers to work alone, and finds more pleasure in imaginative work than in a life of action. The extrovert suggests the "salesman" type, who meets people easily, is happiest in a social situation, friendly, and interested in his fellow-beings. Jung regards introversion and extroversion as characterizations of *normal people*. In extreme forms, to be sure, they would predispose the individual to mental disorders which are opposite in their symptoms.[1] The fundamental distinction, however, is not made on the basis of these mental disorders. The susceptibility to one or another form of insanity is considered simply one more manifestation of the basic type.

Kretschmer's type theory (15) has probably been the most influential in stimulating research. Physically, Kretschmer classifies individuals into four groups, the pyknic, athletic, leptosome, and dysplastic. The *pyknic* type of body build is short and thick-set, with relatively large trunk and short legs, round chest, rounded shoulders, and short hands and feet. The *athletic* has a more proportionate development of trunk and limbs, well-developed bones and muscles, wide shoulders, and large hands and feet. The *leptosome* is generally characterized by small body volume in relation to height. He is tall and slender, with relatively narrow chest, long legs, elongated face, and long, narrow hands and feet. In the *dysplastic* category are placed all individuals who present some marked abnormality of physical development, disproportion, glan-

---

[1] This distinction has been stressed by McDougall, who states for example: " . . . persons of the extrovert temperament seem more liable, under strain, to disorder of the hysteric or dissociative type; those of introvert, or shut-in, temperament to disorder of the neurasthenic type" (17, p. 28).

dular imbalance, or other defect. Kretschmer suggests a wide variety of physical measures to be used, in conjunction with the clinical diagnosis of the experimenter, in differentiating between these bodily types.

The basic contention of Kretschmer's theory is that there exists a relationship between the body types which he describes and two essentially opposed "temperaments," the cycloid and the schizoid. The cycloid individual manifests personality traits which in extreme cases would be classified under the circular, or manic-depressive, form of insanity; the schizoid tends toward schizophrenia, or dementia præcox. Kretschmer claims that the cycloid is usually pyknic, whereas the schizoid is leptosome or, less frequently, athletic. Although originally applied to different forms of mental disorders, this theory has subsequently been extended to normal individuals who manifest no personality disturbance. The terms cyclothyme and schizothyme have been employed to denote these two normal biotypes. The former is described as social, friendly, lively, practical, and realistic; the latter as quiet and reserved, more solitary, timid, and shut-in. It will be noted that these descriptions correspond closely to Jung's extrovert and introvert types.

Throughout these various type systems we can detect a general dichotomy between two opposed constitutional types. From the standpoint of physique, the distinction is one between the long narrow body, with relatively long limbs, and the short stocky build, with relatively large trunk and short limbs. In respect to personality, we are offered at the one extreme the expansive, sociable, easy-going, and practical man, and at the other the more taciturn, unsociable, intellectually independent, or idealistic type. Occasionally, more than two categories are given, but the additional types are usually found to be either intermediate degrees or modifications of the major ones.

In some theories, the structural classification is emphasized; in others the behavioral one is foremost. Many of the theories draw upon pathological conditions either for striking examples or for their starting points, so that we frequently find susceptibility to a given class of physical or mental disorders as an outstanding characteristic of each type. In many cases, too, the various physical and personality types have been linked to the problem of race and attempts have been made to attribute racial differences to the predominance of one or another constitutional type within each group. Discussion of this phase of the problem will be postponed to Chapter XV.

The concept of types is a broad one. We have been here concerned only with theories of constitutional biotypes as described in the opening paragraph. For this reason, no mention has been made of such theories as that of Spranger (25),[1] who describes six fundamental types of individuality, namely the theoretical man, the economic man, the æsthetic man, the social man, the man of power, and the religious man. These "types" are regarded as meaning-tendencies or values in terms of which an individual's responses to his environment are to be understood. They are ideal types or schemata of understanding, rather than empirically observable biotypes.

IMPLICATIONS OF TYPE PSYCHOLOGY

Type theories have been most commonly criticized because of their attempt to classify individuals into sharply divided categories. As was pointed out in Chapter II, such a procedure implies a *multi-modal* distribution

[1] Cf. also the discussion by Klüver (13).

of traits. The introverts, for example, would be expected to cluster at one end of the scale, the extroverts at the other end, and the point of demarcation between them should be clearly apparent. Actual measurement, however, reveals a uni-modal distribution of all traits, which closely resembles the bell-shaped normal curve.

Similarly, it is often difficult to classify a given individual definitely into one type or the other. The typologists, when confronted with this difficulty, have frequently proposed intermediate or "mixed" types to bridge the gap between the extremes. Thus Jung suggested an ambivert type which manifests neither introvert nor extrovert tendencies to a predominant degree. Observation seems to show, however, that the ambivert category is the largest, and the decided introverts and extroverts are relatively rare. The reader is referred, for example, to the distribution curve obtained by Heidbreder with an introversion questionnaire administered to 200 college students (Ch. II). It will be recalled that the majority of scores were intermediate and that as the extremes of either introversion or extroversion were approached, the number of cases became progressively smaller. The curve, too, showed no sharp breaks, but only a continuous gradation from the mean to the two extremes. As was indicated in Chapter II, the same may be said of all other measurable traits of the individual, whether social, emotional, intellectual, or physical.

It is apparent, then, that insofar as type theories imply the classification of individuals into clear-cut classes, they are untenable in the face of a mass of indisputable data. Such an assumption, however, is not necessarily inherent in all systems of human typology. It is more characteristic of the popular versions and adaptations of type theories than of the original concepts. To be sure, type psychologists have often attempted to categorize individuals, but this was not an indispensable part of their theories; their concepts have occasionally been sufficiently modified to admit of a normal distribution of traits.

The suggestion has been offered that type theories may refer simply to varieties or breeds of man, which were originally pure "biotypes." Through successive generations of interbreeding, mixed types have been produced which now outnumber the remaining specimens of pure types. It is well known that through the mechanism of heredity, interbreeding will in the long run produce a larger number of mixed than pure individuals. The same applies to interbreeding among the proposed human biotypes. This situation would then present a normal distribution of traits, with the largest number of individuals in the center of the distribution, corresponding to the numerically largest "mixed" group.[1] Thus the form of the distribution curve cannot in itself indicate the composition of the group. The normal curve might be obtained with a single intermediate type and minor deviations from it, or it might result from the mixture of several pure biotypes.

The only essential implication in this concept of biotypes seems to be a certain organization among the various characteristics of the individual. Thus a relationship would be expected between body build, emotional reactions, and intellectual traits. If there exist diverse biological types of man, each manifesting its own peculiarities in physique, personality, and intellect, we should find a certain degree of conformity among these characteristics of the individual. When so conceived, the problem of types is ultimately reducible to a considera-

---

[1] A particularly lucid statement of this point of view can be found in Klineberg et al. (10).

tion of the relationship between structural and behavioral qualities. It is not, however, concerned with isolated traits, but with the composite picture of the individual as a whole.

Insofar as the existence of human biotypes cannot be determined from the form of the distribution curve, the question may be raised regarding available techniques of typological investigation. One method involves the classification of individuals into distinct groups on the basis of personality tendencies, and the subsequent comparison of these groups in regard to physique. This technique has been employed largely with abnormal cases in the effort to check the assertions that a given physique predisposes the individual to a certain kind of mental disorder. Thus, for example, the relative number of pyknics and leptosomes among individuals manifesting different forms of insanity has been compared and evaluated in terms of the expected association.

A second method is based on the correlational analysis of measurements collected on large normal groups. Various physical indices of body build have been worked out for this purpose. Such indices are then correlated with test scores or ratings on crucial personality traits. A high correlation would be evidence for the conformity implied by type theories.

Finally, efforts have been made in a few studies to identify and select "pure types" and then investigate thoroughly the characteristics of these individuals. The types are chosen on the basis of physical characteristics, so as to represent "good specimens" in this one respect. The physically contrasting groups are then compared in emotional and intellectual reactions. This method rests upon two questions. First, can individuals be found who correspond to the alleged biotypes in all their physical, intellectual, and emotional characteristics? Secondly, when persons are put into classes on the basis of clear-cut and extreme physical diversities, will they also exhibit corresponding differences in other traits? It will be noted that the second question is similar to that which underlies the study of types among the psychotic and neurotic. In the present method, however, the classification is employed on normal rather than on pathological cases, and physical rather than emotional traits are taken as the starting point. Some of the major investigations by each method will be surveyed in the following sections.

EVIDENCE FROM ABNORMAL CASES

Kretschmer originally formulated his theory of constitutional types from observations on psychotic patients. In comparing the body build of schizophrenics and manic-depressives, he has consistently found a greater proportion of leptosomes among the former and pyknics among the latter. Recently Kretschmer (16) has compiled data from several investigators on over 4000 abnormal cases, with the following results:

Body Type	Schizophrenic	Manic-Depressive
Pyknic and mixed pyknic	12.8%	66.7%
Leptosome and athletic	66.0	23.6
Dysplastic	11.3	0.4
Unclassifiable	9.9	9.3

It is apparent that by far the largest percentage of schizophrenics fall into the leptosome and athletic categories, and an equally large percentage of manic-depressives fall into the pyknic and mixed pyknic class.

Wertheimer and Hesketh (28) measured 65 male patients chosen at random from two American institutions for the insane. Of these, 11 had been clearly diagnosed as manic-depressive and 23 as schizophrenics. The major part of the investigation was therefore confined to these cases. The subjects were first classified into Kretschmer's body types on the basis of general observation. A series of 53 anthropometric measurements were then taken and various bodily indices computed. One of these indices was ultimately selected as the most satisfactory [1] and adopted as the chief basis of classification. A close correspondence was found between the two procedures. Those individuals classified as pyknic by the experimenter's diagnosis invariably had indices under 255; those classified as leptosomes had indices over 270. There was no overlapping in the indices of these two groups. By either method of classification, however, the number of decided pyknics or leptosomes was small, most individuals falling into the intermediate athletic or mixed groups, as would be expected.

The percentages of persons of each body type found in the schizophrenic and manic-depressive groups are given below:

Body Type	Schizophrenic (N = 23)	Manic-Depressive (N = 11)
Pyknic	4.3%	45.5%
Pyknoid	13.0	36.4
Athletic	26.1	9.0
Leptosome-athletic-mixed	34.8	0.
Leptosome	17.4	0.
Unclear	4.3	9.0

These data again show a marked predominance of pyknic types among the manic-depressives. The schizophrenics scatter over a wider variety of body type, but the greatest number fall in the leptosome and athletic groups.

[1] $\text{Index} = \dfrac{100 \times \text{leg length} \times 10^3}{\text{transverse chest diameter} \times \text{sagittal chest diameter} \times \text{trunk height}}$
(cf. 28, p. 415).

The chief difficulty in interpreting the results of these and similar investigations on psychotic cases is inadequate control of the age factor. Schizophrenia is more common among younger subjects, whereas older people are more susceptible to manic-depressive psychoses. It is also a well-established fact, which Kretschmer himself recognizes, that older subjects tend more toward the pyknic body build, younger subjects toward the leptosome. To be sure, pyknics may be found among young people, and leptosomes among older groups; and many individuals retain the same type of body build throughout life. But the general trend is sufficiently marked to produce an entirely spurious relationship between body build and psychotic tendencies. For this reason, it is essential that age differences be ruled out in any comparison of the body type of different psychotic groups.

In a recent investigation by Garvey (5), 130 manic-depressives and 130 dementia praecox, or schizophrenic, patients were selected so that the two groups would be closely matched in age. Only clear cases, classified with complete agreement by the hospital staff (not including the experimenter), were employed. When the patients were divided into heavy and slender types on the basis of general observation, some evidence was found for Kretschmer's claims. The association, however, is reported as too slight to permit body type to be regarded as diagnostic of psychosis. Extensive physical measurements were taken and several ratios between horizontal and vertical bodily dimensions were computed. All showed an *almost complete overlapping* of the two psychotic groups. Not only were the averages closely similar, but the range and the general form of the distribution were practically identical in the two groups.

Naccarati (20), in the effort to check upon Viola's

hypothesis, measured 100 male Italian psychoneurotics between the ages of 25 and 40. The number of normo-splanchnics is reported as being smaller in this group than in normal groups. The neurasthenics had a larger proportion of microsplanchnics (long, slender type), while macro-splanchnics predominated among the "emotional psycho-neurotics." Under the latter category Naccarati includes cases of hysteria, anxiety neuroses, and traumatic neuroses. Averages of some of the most significant physical measurements as well as the average age of the two groups are given below.

Group	Morphologic Index	Total Volume of Trunk	Length of Extremities	Age
50 Neurasthenics	456.64	30.43	133.35	32.16
50 Emotional psycho-neurotics	362.06	37.36	128.80	33.94

It will be noted that the neurasthenic group has a lower average age than the emotional psychoneurotics. This might account in part for the greater tendency to micro-splanchny among the former. No account is given of the method of obtaining or diagnosing the subjects, a fact which makes interpretation of the findings difficult.

Although not dealing with abnormal patients, a subsequent investigation by Naccarati and Garrett (21) may be mentioned in this connection. The subjects were 54 male college students between the ages of 18 and 25. The general approach was similar to that of the other investigations reported in this section. The subjects were classified into three groups on the basis of number of neurotic symptoms indicated on the Woodworth Personal Data Sheet.[1] The investigators also obtained ratings

---

[1] The students were also given the Pressy X–O and the Downey Will-Temperament tests, but the results were difficult to interpret, probably because of the inadequacy of these tests when applied to college groups.

by the class instructor and self-ratings of each student
on physique (including bearing, apparent health, vigor,
strength, and endurance), intelligence, emotional stability, and aggressiveness. Morphologic indices were computed for each subject. The average Woodworth P.D.
score for each group is shown below, together with the
averages and S.D.'s of the morphologic indices. It will
be recalled that a high morphologic index indicates micro-
splanchny, a low morphologic index macrosplanchny.

	Group I (N = 18)	Group II (N = 16)	Group III (N = 20)
Woodworth P.D. Score: Average	6.9	14.2	24.8
Morphologic Index: Average	498.5	495.0	460.8
Morphologic Index: S.D.	61.3	57.5	56.0

It will be noted that group III, composed of the most
neurotic individuals, has a much lower average morphologic index than the other two groups. The self-ratings
and instructors' ratings agreed closely with each other
and with the test results. The average differences among
the three groups were slight but in the expected direction.
Thus, in emotional stability, group I was rated as the most
stable and group III as the least stable. Similarly, group I
was rated as most intelligent, group III least intelligent.
These data seem to support Viola's contentions in a
general way. The macrosplanchnics appear less intelligent
and have a more pronounced tendency to neuroticism
than the microsplanchnics. Several reservations should,
however, be borne in mind. The groups are small; age
may have differed appreciably among the three categories;
and finally, much overlapping in morphologic index is
indicated by the large S.D.'s. Variations in body build
within each group were larger than the differences between
the averages.

A very comprehensive investigation on the relationship between body type and psychotic disposition was recently conducted by Burchard (1). A total of 407 male White patients from several institutions for the insane were selected for the survey. Of these, 125 were clearly diagnosed as schizophrenes by the hospital staff, and 125 as manic-depressives. The remaining 157 patients manifested a variety of psychotic and neurotic conditions and were employed as a control group. The subjects in all three groups were classified into pyknics, athletics, and leptosomes by "general impression." Comparisons were also subsequently made in respect to several anthropometric measures and indices. Only seven dysplastics were found in the entire sampling, and these were eliminated from further consideration. All other subjects were retained, any intermediate or mixed types being assigned to the morphological type which they resembled most closely. Below are given the percentages of pyknics, athletics, and leptosomes found in the manic-depressive, schizophrenic, and control groups, respectively, when the "impressionistic" method of classification was employed.

Morphological Type	Percentages		
	Manic-Depressives	Schizophrenes	Control
Pyknic	63.2	36.3	55.6
Athletic	8.8	17.7	11.3
Leptosome	28.0	46.0	33.1

The general trend of these figures seems to be in agreement with Kretschmer's theory. Not only are the greatest percentage of manic-depressives pyknics, and the greatest percentage of schizophrenes leptosomes, but the control group occupies a position intermediate between these two groups in all percentages. When the schizophrenes and

manic-depressives are compared in terms of anthropometric measures, a certain amount of differentiation is
also revealed. Perfectly reliable differences between the
averages of the two groups were found in three out of
nine physical measures and in two out of three bodily
indices. The overlapping of the groups in all of these
measures was nevertheless very large. This is illustrated
in Figure 36, which shows the frequency distributions on

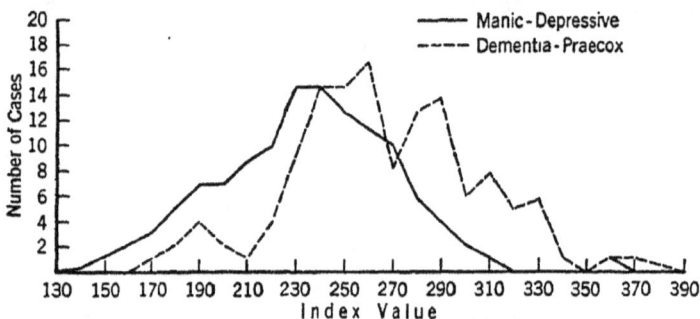

Fig. 36. Frequency Distribution of 125 Manic-Depressives and 125
Schizophrenes on the Wertheimer-Hesketh Index of Body Build.
(After Burchard, 1, p. 47.)

Wertheimer-Hesketh index of body build (cf. above).
This index yielded the largest differences between the
two groups. It is apparent that, in spite of the statistically significant differences in averages, schizophrenes can
be found who are much more pyknic than certain manic-
depressives, and *vice versa.*

Even the differences in averages between the two groups
may be owing to other factors which have not been controlled. Burchard recognized this difficulty and undertook a detailed analysis of his manic-depressive and
schizophrene groups. In regard to racial and national
background, occupation, and educational status, no appreciable or consistent differences could be discovered.
In age, however, the differences were very large, the average ages of schizophrenic, control, and manic-depressive

groups being 30.97, 42.90, and 49.65 years, respectively. Further analysis revealed a definite relationship between age and body build. This factor seems to have accounted largely, although not entirely, for the group differences found.

Since the age factor plays such an important part in all studies on constitutional type, we may examine more closely Burchard's data on this problem. Below will be found the average Wertheimer-Hesketh indices of subjects falling in successive decades within the entire sampling as well as within each psychotic group.

Average Wertheimer-Hesketh Indices

Age	Entire Group	Schizophrenes	Manic-Depressives	Control
15–19	306.11	297.25	262.66	321.00
20–29	275.10	279.77	252.00	273.48
30–39	260.82	272.00	256.33	253.86
40–49	249.34	252.50	246.52	249.41
50–59	253.68	277.50	247.29	257.16
60–69	236.50	243.33	241.67	228.75

These averages indicate a definite tendency towards a more pyknic body build with advancing age. This is manifested *within each disease group,* as well as in the entire group. Further corroboration of this finding is furnished by the correlation of −.256 obtained between age and index value in the entire sampling. Much of the difference observed between the two psychotic groups can therefore be attributed to age. It should be noted, however, that within each decade the schizophrenes have a higher average index than the manic-depressives. To be sure, the differences are considerably reduced by ruling out age, and the control group no longer retains its intermediate position, but a certain difference in the expected direction remains. Burchard himself is very cautious in interpreting these findings, concluding ". . . that age is a very important conditioning factor upon the morphological habitus and that—although the type of psychosis apparently play(s) an important rôle—the relative weights of the two factors remain in considerable doubt" (1, p. 65).

CORRELATIONAL STUDIES ON NORMAL GROUPS

It has frequently been objected that one cannot generalize from a slight correspondence between body build and certain forms of insanity to a relationship between personality traits and bodily characteristics of normal individuals. The comparison of average values, furthermore, or of the percentage frequency of bodily types among different groups may exaggerate a very slight degree of association. Such comparisons tell us little about individual cases. For these reasons, a number of investigators have resorted to the correlation coefficient to obtain an exact quantitative measure of the amount of relationship within a group.

The correlation coefficient is affected not only by the *presence or absence* of clear-cut types within a group, but also by the *degree* to which a given typal characteristic is exhibited. This method seems to rest upon a slightly different principle than that underlying group comparisons. Thus if morphological index were found to correlate highly with intelligence, it would mean not only that the clearly microsplanchnic are more intelligent than the clearly macrosplanchnic, but also that within the intervening range, the more microsplanchnic the individual, the more intelligent he will be. A lack of relationship between intelligence and body build within the intermediate mixed groups will considerably lower the correlation which would be obtained if only "pure types" were included.

Naccarati (19) found a correlation of .356 between morphologic index and Thorndike Intelligence Examination for High School Graduates within a group of 75 college men. In the same study, height-weight ratios [1] were computed for 221 college men ranging in age from 17 to 22, all of whom had taken the Thorndike test. The correlation between this ratio and intelligence proved to be .230.

The slight positive correlation between height-weight ratio and intelligence would seem to support the claim that the microsplanchnic, or tall, slender individual, tends to be more intelligent. The age factor, however, must again be considered. Upon further statistical analysis of the data, it was discovered that the correlation of .230 resulted largely from a negative correlation between *weight* and *intelligence test score* within this group.[2] The more heavily built, stocky individuals at the age levels under consideration tend to be the *older* members of the group. Similarly, the older individuals *within any one academic level* are usually the duller ones. It therefore seems very likely that even the low degree of correspondence found between height-weight ratio and intelligence is attributable to an uncontrolled age factor and cannot be accepted as proof of a relationship between body type and mentality.

Subsequent investigations by a similar method have likewise cast doubt upon Naccarati's conclusions. Heidbreder (6) checked Naccarati's hypothesis on a group of 1000 White, native-born college freshmen, consisting of 500 men and 500 women. Scores on the Minnesota

---

[1] The height-weight ratio has frequently been substituted for the more elaborate morphologic index, for the sake of expediency, since the two indices are closely related. Naccarati (19), for example, found a correlation of .70 between the two in a group of 75 students, and a correlation of .75 in another group of 50.

[2] Subsequently computed by Hull (7, pp. 142–143), from Naccarati's published data.

College Ability Tests were correlated with the height-weight ratios obtained by careful measurements on each subject. This correlation proved to be only .03 in the group of men and .04 in the women's group. Similarly, the correlation between height-weight ratio and scores on each of the five subtests of the intelligence examination closely approximated zero, ranging from −.07 to +.10.

In the effort to discover whether the use of the more elaborate morphologic index in place of the height-weight ratio might yield more positive evidence for Naccarati's view, Sheldon (23) conducted an elaborate investigation on 434 freshman men. All subjects were White; age varied between 17 and 22. Twelve measurements were carefully made on each individual and from them were computed the morphologic indices, in the manner described by Naccarati. The correlation between these indices and scores on a common group intelligence test for college freshmen was .14. Correlations of the morphologic index with each of the nine subtests in the examination ranged from −.02 to +.12. These findings corroborate closely those obtained by Heidbreder with the height-weight ratio.

In a further investigation of morphologic types, Sheldon (24) correlated morphologic index and ratings on five personality traits within a group of 155 freshman men. Each student was rated by five upperclassmen who belonged to the same fraternity as the subject. The judges had thus had considerable opportunity to observe the student's everyday behavior in many situations and were fairly well qualified to rate him. The consensus of all five judges was taken as the final rating for each individual. Below will be found the correlations between morphologic index and ratings on each trait.

Trait Rated	Correlation with Morphologic Index
Emotional excitability	.00
Aggressiveness	—.08
Leadership	—.14
Sociability	—.22
Perseverance	.01

On the whole, these correlations are too low to indicate an appreciable degree of relationship between bodily type and personality traits. The correlations of morphologic index with leadership and sociability are, however, suggestive. These two correlations indicate a tendency for the more heavily built individual to be more sociable and more of a leader. This may again be owing to a disturbing age factor, inasmuch as the older individuals within such a group might well be expected to manifest these characteristics.

A comprehensive investigation including both intellectual and personality traits was conducted by Garrett and Kellogg (4). The subjects were again male college freshmen. Morphologic indices were computed with measurements taken from three standard photographs of each subject. These photographs, taken in connection with gymnasium routine, showed three different views of the individual in the nude. The morphologic indices computed from the photographs correlated .81 with height-weight ratios obtained from direct measurements on 219 students. On this basis, the authors felt justified in their use of the photographs for the sake of expediency. The "photographic" morphologic indices, as well as the height-weight ratios from direct measurements, were correlated with scores on the Thorndike Intelligence Examination for High School Graduates, the Woodworth Personal Data Sheet, and the George Washington Social Intelligence Test, with the following results:

Test	Morphologic Index (from photographs)		Height-Weight Ratio (from direct measurements)	
	Number of Cases	Correlation	Number of Cases	Correlation
Thorndike Intelligence Test	219	.07	219	.10
Woodworth P.D. Sheet	151	.05	150	.09
Social Intelligence Test	123	−.06	122	.05

None of these correlations is sufficiently large to indicate a significant degree of relationship.

INVESTIGATIONS ON "PURE TYPES"

The study of constitutional types through the correlation technique has yielded consistently negative results. As has already been pointed out, however, this may be owing to the presence of a predominantly large group of mixed types in whom no consistent relationship between physique and mental or emotional traits is to be found. For this reason, advocates of type psychology have deplored the use of correlation. It has also been argued that even when indices are employed in lieu of isolated dimensions, the investigator is not getting a picture of the individual's physique in its totality. And the latter is essential in any concept of constitutional types.

Most of the numerous German investigations on types have proceeded by *selecting* good specimens of each type on the basis of physical measurements or observations and then administering a variety of psychological tests to the groups so obtained. By this method, for example, the conclusions have been reached that pyknics are more distractable than leptosomes, that they have a greater perception span, a better incidental memory, respond "synthetically" rather than "analytically" to a difficult perception, are more sensitive to colors than to forms, are superior in motor tasks except when these require delicacy of movement, and give more extroverted responses. These are among the major differences reported by German investigators.[1] Relatively little stress is placed by the latter upon differences in general intelligence between the types.

Many of these studies are open to serious criticism and it is therefore difficult to evaluate their findings. The groups employed are frequently small. Averages are reported with no indication of variability within each group or of amount of overlapping between groups. Quantitative data are frequently lacking and only descriptive observations reported. The tests are often inadequate or poorly standardized. The groups themselves, selected chiefly on the basis of physical type, frequently differ in other essential respects. Thus the relative proportion of men and women may not have been constant in all the groups. The pyknics, furthermore, may have been older than the leptosomes, and this age difference could account for the observed psychological differences. Little or no attempt has been made to control this factor, in some studies the subjects ranging from adolescents to sexagenarians. Social and cultural background may have also affected the results. There is some evidence, for example, that leptosomes are found more commonly among the higher social and educational levels. Since there are also intellectual and possibly emotional differences among these classes, the factor of social level should be ruled out.

Mohr and Gundlach (18) conducted an intensive quantitative investigation on a group of male convicts in the Illinois State Prison. A total of 600 men was measured, out of which 89 were selected as good representatives of leptosome, athletic, and pyknic types. In arriving at this

[1] For a survey of many of these investigations, see Klineberg et al. (10).

classification, the investigators employed all the anthropometric measures suggested by Kretschmer, as well as a general observational diagnosis of body type. Each subject was given the Army Alpha as well as about a dozen simple psychological tests suggested by the German workers as diagnostic of constitutional type. Such tests were included as speed of tapping and of writing, visual reaction time, cancellation, substitution, color fusion, Rorscharch ink blots, etc.

A striking difference in average Army Alpha score was found among the three groups. This is shown below, together with the number of cases in each group and the average ages.

Body Type	Number of Cases	Average Age	Average Army Alpha Score
Leptosome	19	28.55	96.5
Athletic	26	28.65	79.2
Pyknic	44	34.75	57.9

The correlation between Army Alpha score and an index of body build was found to be −.34, which further corroborates the above results. Although not very high, this correlation indicates a significant tendency for the tall, slender individuals to obtain higher scores. Similarly, in many of the other tests the differences among the groups were large enough to be statistically significant. It will be noted, however, that there is a marked difference in age among the three groups, the pyknics being on the average a little over *six years* older than the leptosomes or athletics. In view of the tendency for Army Alpha scores to decrease with age (cf. Ch. VII), therefore, the pyknic group would be expected to obtain lower scores. The cultural and racial composition of the three groups is not stated, and these factors may also account for some of the observed differences in test performance.

More recently, Klineberg, Asch, and Block (10) have

attempted to compare Kretschmer's body types under more rigidly controlled conditions. The study was limited exclusively to college students, so that variations in age and in social and educational level were largely reduced. The first group was composed of 153 male college students, with an average age of 19 years-9 months. All were attending the same institution and were very homogeneous in respect to racial and cultural background. The subjects were classified into leptosome and pyknic categories on the basis of experimenter's diagnosis as well as five indices computed from anthropometric measurements. Each subject was given the Otis Self-Administering test of intelligence, an emotional adjustment test, and a series of six tests designed to measure alleged characteristics of the two opposed constitutional types.

It was possible to obtain two groups which were clearly differentiated in respect to physique. This is illustrated by the frequency distribution curves of the leptosome and pyknic groups in Pignet Index,[1] reproduced in Figure 37.

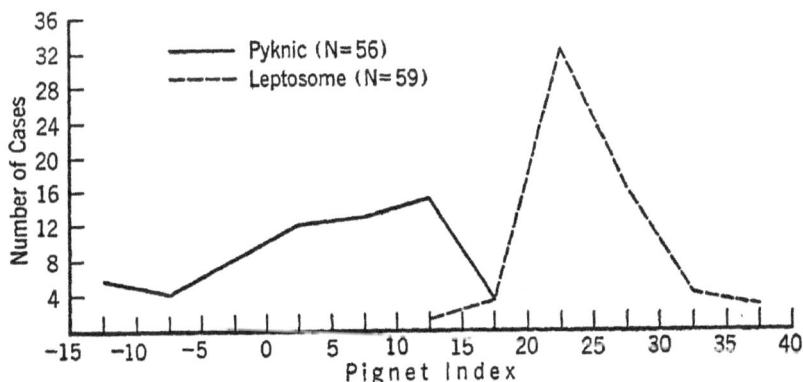

Fig. 37. Distribution of Scores of Leptosomes and Pyknics on the Pignet Index. (After Klineberg, Asch, and Block, 10, p. 180.)

[1] Pignet Index = Height — (weight + chest circumference).
Note: This formula is printed incorrectly in the study under consideration (11, p. 164). We assume this was a misprint, and that the correct formula was employed in the computations.

This index was found to differentiate more clearly between the groups than any of the other physical measures employed. It will be noted that overlapping is virtually absent. In sharp contrast to this distribution is that given in Figure 38, which shows the scores of leptosomes

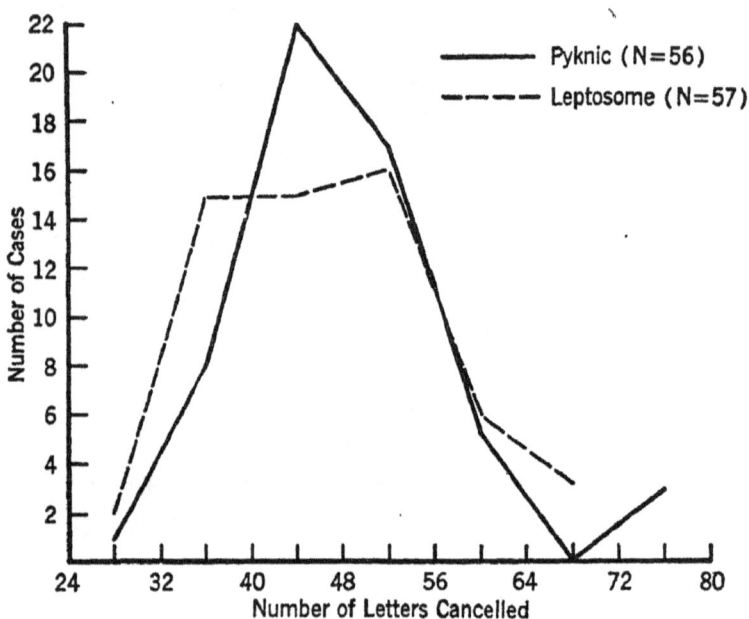

Fig. 38. Distribution of Scores of Leptosomes and Pyknics in Letter Cancellation. (After Klineberg, Asch, and Block, 10, p. 180.)

and pyknics in one of the psychological tests, *viz.*, cancellation of letters. In this case, the two groups overlap almost completely. Similar results were obtained with all of the other tests. In no case were the differences between the two groups statistically significant. Correlation of measures on 110 cases confirmed these findings. The correlations between physical indices and test scores were all close to zero. Intercorrelations of the various psychological tests were also negligible. If the underlying conformity implied by type theories were present, a fairly close correspondence should have been found among the various diagnostic tests. Viewed from any angle, the results are completely negative.

A parallel study was conducted on 79 women students in one college, all of whom were between the ages of 16 and 20. Various physical measures, as well as scores on the Scholastic Aptitude Test were already available on these subjects. They were given, in addition, an emotional adjustment test and three simple tests suggested by the German type studies. It proved impossible to classify the subjects into bodily types, since all fell within the leptosome range. As a result, only the correlation technique could be employed.[1] As in the study on men, the correlations between test scores and physical indices were too low to be of any significance.

A very thorough investigation of personality traits in relation to physical type has recently been conducted by Klineberg, Fjeld, and Foley (11).[2] The subjects were again students, selected from several colleges in New York City and its environs. A total of 200 men and 229 women were examined. Within each of these groups, the subjects who fell in the upper and those who fell in the lower 25% of the distribution of Pignet Index were selected as leptosomes and pyknics, respectively. This gave 50 leptosomes and 50 pyknics among the men, and 57 leptosomes and 57 pyknics among the women.

That the groups so obtained were clearly differentiated in physique is shown by an examination of other physical measures and indices found for all the subjects. In both male and female groups, the differences between leptosomes and pyknics were statistically reliable in all physical

---

[1] As a subsidiary analysis, the subjects were classified into "leptoid" and "less leptoid," and average scores on these two groups were computed. This procedure could not, however, be expected to yield very significant results.

[2] The writer is indebted to Drs. Klineberg, Fjeld, and Foley for making available to her the unpublished data of this study.

measures except standing and sitting height and the ratio between these two. Not only were the differences between averages very large and reliable in all other physical measures or indices, but the ranges showed little or no overlapping. In regard to age, the male pyknics proved to be slightly older on the average than the leptosomes, the average age of the male leptosomes being 20.17 years and that of the male pyknics 21.08 years. In addition to being very slight, this age difference is such as to *exaggerate* any of the alleged psychological differences between leptosomes and pyknics. Hence such an age discrepancy loads the dice slightly in favor of Kretschmer's hypothesis and would make *negative* findings all the more conclusive. Among the females, the age difference was negligible, the leptosomes averaging 19.73 and the pyknics 19.23 years.

All subjects were given the *Bernreuter Personality Inventory*. This test was scored with six keys, yielding measures of as many different though more or less interrelated aspects of personality, *viz.*, neuroticism, self-sufficiency, introversion, dominance, self-confidence, and sociability.[1] The *Allport-Vernon Study of Values* was also administered. This test is designed to measure the relative prominence of six basic interests or motives in personality, the theoretical, economic, æsthetic, social, political, and religious. As will be noted, this classification is based on Spranger's proposed list of evaluative attitudes (cf. above). All subjects were further given a specially devised test of *suggestibility*. In addition, it was

[1] Statistical analysis has recently shown that the Bernreuter test can be regarded as measuring two fundamental, independent traits which have been labeled self-confidence and sociability (cf. Flanagan, J. C. *Factor Analysis in the Study of Personality*. Stanford Univ., Calif.: Stanford Univ. Press, 1935. Pp. 103). The other four scores, although not mutually independent, were included in this study since they correlate highly with scores on other current personality tests and correspond to more familiar psychological terminology.

possible to administer two other tests to many, but not all, individuals. One of these was an *honesty* test, showing the number of times the subject cheated on what seemed to be an information test (Maller Test of Sports and Hobbies). The other was a specially constructed *persistence* test which measured the length of time the individual worked on an insoluble finger maze before giving up.

In Table XII will be found the average scores of both male and female leptosomes and pyknics on each test. Critical ratios are also given to show the reliability of the differences between the averages. It will be recalled that if the critical ratio has a value of 3 or more, the difference is regarded as statistically significant. In interpreting the data of Table XII, it should be borne in mind that on the Bernreuter test, the positive scores indicate a greater degree of the trait named, the negative scores a lesser degree. Thus in neuroticism, for example, a *higher positive* score indicates a *more neurotic* individual, a *higher negative* score a *less neurotic* individual. In introversion, the positive scores indicate a tendency toward introversion and the negative scores a tendency toward extroversion. The same is true of the other traits; the end of the scale corresponding to the positive scores is the one from which each test was named. In the Allport-Vernon test, the higher scores indicate greater prominence of the particular "value" in question. In suggestibility, the higher scores show a greater susceptibility to suggestion. In the persistence test, likewise, the higher scores show greater persistence. On the honesty test, the scores were expressed in such a form that the higher values corresponded to the more "honest" individual who cheats less often.

The data of Table XII are clearly negative as regards type theories. None of the leptosome-pyknic differences, in either male or female groups, is reliable. In the male groups, the critical ratios range from 0.005 to 2.22; in the female groups, the range is from 0.09 to 2.22. None of the differences is three or more times as large as its standard error. All the obtained differences could therefore have resulted from chance errors of sampling. In each sex group, there is only one critical ratio which reaches or exceeds a value of 2, and this occurs *on a different test* in the two cases. In the male group, the largest critical ratio was obtained on the honesty test, which gave a critical ratio of only 0.25 in the female group. Similarly, the largest critical ratio in the female group is found with the "social values" score on the Allport-Vernon scale and this gives a critical ratio of only 0.39 in the male group.

It might also be pointed out that in several comparisons the differences between leptosomes and pyknics are contrary to expectation. For example, the male leptosome group appears more "sociable" on the Bernreuter and seems to have a higher sense of "social value" according to the Allport-Vernon scale, than does the male pyknic group. The average scores of all the groups, furthermore, fall very close to the norms for college men and women in general. Finally, the ranges of the leptosome and pyknic groups were nearly identical, showing an almost complete overlapping of distributions on all personality tests.

To be perfectly cautious, one might conclude that the problem of constitutional types remains an open question. All the better controlled studies by any of the three methods described above have, however, yielded overwhelmingly negative evidence. In those studies which have reported positive results, it is a relatively easy matter to find uncontrolled factors which *could*, in themselves, have produced the observed differences in alleged typal characteristics. Since the concept of types seems to

TABLE XII

AVERAGE SCORES OF LEPTOSOME AND PYKNIC GROUPS ON
PERSONALITY TESTS

(After Klineberg, Fjeld, and Foley, 11)

Test	Male			Female		
	Lepto-some (N = 50)	Pyknic (N = 50)	Critical Ratio of Difference	Lepto-some (N = 57)	Pyknic (N = 57)	Critical Ratio of Difference
Bernreuter						
1. B_1N: Neuroticism	−37.50	−39.76	0.14	−40.51	−45.60	0.34
2. B_2S: Self-sufficiency	+34.30	+29.22	0.49	− 0.26	+18.02	1.88
3. B_3I: Introversion	−14.98	−17.88	0.30	−18.47	−27.00	0.95
4. B_4D: Dominance	+39.20	+42.18	0.26	+30.32	+38.54	0.72
5. F_1C: Self-confidence	− 8.54	− 8.46	0.005	+ 4.67	−13.67	1.19
6. F_2S: Sociability	+ 1.22	− 6.66	0.62	−29.79	−18.39	0.97
Allport-Vernon Study of Values						
1. Theoretical	31.82	31.46	0.23	28.57	29.32	0.54
2. Economic	28.67	29.98	0.96	27.42	26.71	0.61
3. Æsthetic	27.27	28.40	0.61	34.77	32.91	1.15
4. Social	32.29	31.82	0.39	30.25	32.63	2.22
5. Political	30.30	31.72	1.08	29.65	29.54	0.09
6. Religious	29.65	26.62	1.47	29.34	28.89	0.28
Suggestibility	11.02	10.82	0.23	11.89	11.43	0.56
Persistence *	6.00	10.94	2.22	6.94	8.71	1.32
Honesty *	97.58	94.77	1.61	99.00	99.14	0.25

* Not all subjects were given these tests.

have proved unsuccessful in explaining the organization of traits within the individual, we may now inquire into the latter question from a more empirical viewpoint. An analysis of *variations within the individual*, to be discussed in the following chapter, will serve as a background for this problem.

REFERENCES

1. Burchard, E. M. L. "Physique and Psychosis: an Analysis of the Postulated Relationship between Bodily Constitution and Mental Disease Syndrome," *Comp. Psychol. Mon.*, 1936, 13, No. 1. Pp. 73.

2. Davenport, C. B. "Body-Build and Its Inheritance," *Carnegie Inst. Wash. Publ.*, No. 329, 1923. Pp. 176.

3. Galton, F. *Inquiries into Human Faculty and Its Development.* London: Macmillan, 1883. Pp. 387.

4. Garrett, H. E., and Kellogg, W. N. "The Relation of Physical Constitution to General Intelligence, Social Intelligence, and Emotional Stability," *J. Exper. Psychol.*, 1928, 11, 113-129.

5. Garvey, C. R. "Comparative Body Build of Manic-Depressive and Schizophrenic Patients," *Psychol. Bull.*, 1933, 30, 567-568 (see also p. 739).

6. Heidbreder, E. "Intelligence and the Height-Weight Ratio," *J. Appl. Psychol.*, 1926, 10, 52-62.

7. Hull, C. L. *Aptitude Testing.* N. Y.: World Book Co., 1928. Pp. 535.

8. James, W. *Pragmatism, a New Name for Some Old Ways of Thinking.* N. Y.: Longmans, 1907. Pp. 309.

9. Jung, C. G. *Psychological Types* (transl. by H. G. Baynes). N. Y.: Harcourt, Brace, 1924. Pp. 654.

10. Klineberg, O., Asch, S. E., and Block, H. "An Experimental Study of Constitutional Types," *Genet. Psychol. Mon.*, 1934, 16, 140-221.

11. Klineberg, O., Fjeld, H., and Foley, J. P., Jr. "An Experimental Study of Personality Differences among Constitutional, 'Racial,' and Cultural Groups." (To appear.)

12. Klüver, H. "An Analysis of Recent Work on the Problem of Psychological Types," *J. Nerv. and Mental Diseases*, 1925, 62, 561-596.

13. ——. "The Problem of Type in 'Cultural Science Psychology,'" *J. Philos.*, 1925, 22, 225-234.

14. ——. "Studies on the Eidetic Type and on Eidetic Imagery," *Psychol. Bull.*, 1928, 25, 69-104.

15. Kretschmer, E. *Physique and Character* (transl. from 2nd ed. by W. J. H. Sprott). N. Y.: Harcourt, Brace, 1925. Pp. 266.

16. ——. *Körperbau und Charakter* (Tenth edition). Berlin: Springer, 1931. Pp. 240.

17. McDougall, W. *Outline of Abnormal Psychology.* N. Y.: Scribner's, 1926. Pp. 572.

18. Mohr, G. H., and Gundlach, R. H. "The Relation between Physique and Performance," *J. Exper. Psychol.*, 1927, 10, 117–157.

19. Naccarati, S. "The Morphologic Aspect of Intelligence," *Arch. Psychol.*, No. 45, 1921. Pp. 44.

20. ——. "The Morphologic Basis of the Psychoneuroses," *Amer. J. Psychiat.*, 1924, 3, 527–545.

21. Naccarati, S., and Garrett, H. E. "The Relation of Morphology to Temperament," *J. Abn. and Soc. Psychol.*, 1924–25, 19, 254–263.

22. Pavlov, I. P. *Conditioned Reflexes: an Investigation of the Physiological Activity of the Cerebral Cortex* (transl. and ed. by G. V. Anrep). Oxford Univ. Press: Humphrey Milford, 1927. Pp. 430.

23. Sheldon, W. H. "Morphologic Types and Mental Ability," *J. Pers. Res.*, 1927, 5, 447–451.

24. ——. "Social Traits and Morphologic Types," *J. Pers. Res.*, 1927, 6, 47–55.

25. Spranger, E. *Types of Men* (transl. by P. J. W. Pigors). Halle: Niemeyer, 1928. Pp. 402.

26. Stockard, C. R. "Human Types and Growth Reactions," *Amer. J. Anat.*, 1923, 31, 261–288.

27. Weidenreich, F. *Rasse und Körperbau.* Berlin: Springer, 1927. Pp. 187.

28. Wertheimer, F. I., and Hesketh, F. E. "The Significance of the Physical Constitution in Mental Disease," *Medicine*, 1926, 5, 375–463.

CHAPTER X

VARIATION WITHIN THE INDIVIDUAL

The study of variations from trait to trait within the individual is of both practical importance and theoretical significance. When a child is classified as intellectually inferior on the basis of, let us say, Stanford-Binet I.Q., there is still much that remains to be known about his mentality. Is he equally inferior in all respects or does he exhibit significant discrepancies in his mental development? Is he normal or even superior along some specific lines? Similarly, in the case of a child of very high I.Q., we may inquire in what ways he is superior. How uniformly does he excel the average child in intellectual performance? The intelligence test, furnishing a single summary figure to characterize the child's general mental level, often obscures important facts. Two individuals obtaining the same total score may present very different "mental pictures" when their performance along specific lines is analyzed.

The skilled clinician or mental tester has always taken this into consideration in interpreting test scores. The child's performance on the different parts of an intelligence scale and even, when feasible, on several different kinds of tests, is carefully analyzed before a final judgment is offered. In this way, the practical common sense of the examiner is brought in to remedy a deficiency in the test itself. There is a rapidly growing realization, however, that the question of variation among the individual's abilities deserves serious and systematic consideration and should be investigated in its own right. This problem is gradually coming to be regarded as even more important than the establishment of the individual's general level of performance.

In planning an educational program for a given individual, or in helping him to choose a vocation, it is of the greatest importance to know his strong and his weak points. Total scores on intelligence tests can be used only in a very crude and general sort of educational and vocational guidance. In the comparative study of groups, such as the sexes or different racial or cultural groups, a consideration of the general level of ability may also prove misleading. Let us suppose, for example, that one such group excels markedly in ability A and the other in ability B. If both are examined with an intelligence test which samples abilities A and B to an equal extent, no difference in total score will appear between the two groups. Essential and large differences might thus be concealed by the practice of lumping a number of tasks indiscriminately in the effort to arrive at the general mental average called "intelligence."

Much confusion has likewise been introduced into the interpretation of test results by the common tendency to take labels too seriously. Thus, if two tests are labeled measures of "intelligence," it is assumed that they are measuring the same characteristic of the individual. It is therefore most disconcerting to discover that the same child may appear dull in one intelligence test and above average in another. Such cases are, however, found. Since intelligence scales consist of a more or less random sampling of different tasks, the specific abilities covered by the various tests may differ. Some tests, for example, may be more heavily "loaded" with verbal items, others with mechanical items. Even successive levels of the same test occasionally involve different abilities. Thus the

Stanford-Binet draws more heavily from the verbal field at the higher year levels than it does at the lower. The same child tested with the Stanford-Binet at different ages might be favored at one time and handicapped at another because of the particular abilities called into play.

If the individual's abilities were all more or less on a dead level, a single summary score would be quite informative. But if appreciable variation in the individual's standing in different traits is the rule, then such a score is crude at best and may upon occasion be definitely misleading. It is essential, therefore, to inquire into the extent of variation within the individual. The data on this question have been gathered from a variety of sources. Case studies are available of individuals who exhibit marked asymmetry of development along different lines. Such individuals can be found among the feebleminded and the intellectually superior, as well as among the normal. Quantitative measurements have also been made on the extent of variability from trait to trait in large random samplings. Finally, correlational analysis throws some light upon this problem. Typical data obtained by these various approaches will be examined.

THE "IDIOT SAVANT"

Among the feebleminded, persons are occasionally met who display an exceptional talent along some specific line. Such individuals have been designated "*idiots savants*" (wise idiots). This term has been criticized for being somewhat misleading. The usual *idiot savant* is neither particularly wise nor an idiot. He is not sufficiently deficient to be classified as an idiot, but is frequently found at the moron or borderline level. And he is "wise" only in a very limited field. In the practical management of his own life he is ordinarily a complete failure. Many of the *idiots savants* in institutions for the feebleminded were physically awkward or uncouth, had a serious sensory deficiency, or were reputed to be emotionally unstable or irresponsible. Otherwise they might have been able to shift for themselves with a little assistance, by capitalizing their special talent. As is true of all extreme deviations in the distribution of any trait, *idiots savants* are relatively rare. Because of their striking quality, however, such cases attract a good deal of attention, so that a number of fairly complete descriptive accounts are now available.

The special talent of the *idiot savant* may be observed in practically every type of mental activity. Mechanical aptitude, ability in drawing and painting, a phenomenal memory, arithmetic proficiency, a special gift in music, all are represented. The one field from which *idiots savants* seem to be conspicuously absent is that of linguistic or verbal aptitude.[1] This fact throws some light upon our concept of general intelligence. As will be more fully demonstrated in the following chapter, the latter is very largely *identified* with verbal ability. Most intelligence tests are composed, to a very great extent, of verbal tasks. Success in the practical business of everyday life is also more closely linked to linguistic facility than to other traits. A serious deficiency in the power of verbal expression will thus brand an individual as incompetent from many points of view. Conversely, a person who is especially proficient in verbal traits may thereby compensate for deficiencies along other lines and will rarely, if ever, find his way into an institution for the feebleminded. No

---

[1] Feebleminded individuals have been described who could repeat long quotations in several foreign languages, without error and with perfect accent. But these cases probably represent a more specific abnormal phenomenon and cannot be regarded as having superior linguistic endowment in the usual sense. Such individuals, for example, are frequently unable to read or write. (Cf. Barr, 4, for a report of such a case.)

other single talent seems to be such a saving grace in our civilization.

Several cases of special talent in pictorial art have been found among the feebleminded. Such individuals are able to execute excellent reproductions of well known paintings. Occasionally this talent passes beyond mere copying and suggests real creative genius. Such a case is that of Gottfried Mind (35, p. 336), diagnosed as a cretin imbecile. His mental deficiency was manifested from an early age. He was unable to learn to read and write. His movements were awkward, his hands large and rough, and his general appearance that of the traditional mental defective. Since he showed considerable talent for drawing, he was given some instruction in this field. His subsequent success in pictorial art was phenomenal. Because of his excellent drawings of cats, he came to be known as "The Cats' Raphael." In addition, he produced drawings and watercolor sketches of deer, rabbits, bears, and groups of children, which were remarkable for their life-like quality and masterly execution. His fame spread throughout Europe and one of his pictures of a cat and kittens was purchased by King George IV of England.

An equally remarkable case is that of J. H. Pullen, who has been called "The Genius of Earlswood Asylum" (35, pp. 340–345). This individual had extraordinary mechanical ingenuity coupled with talent in drawing and carving. In other respects he was very deficient. He did not talk until the age of seven, and for a long time only uttered the word "muvver." His speech was always imperfect, and he is reported as being very deaf. He was taught by his family to write and to spell the names of simple objects, and this constituted the extent of his schooling. From an early age, he spent much of his time in drawing or in carving ships out of pieces of firewood, occupations in which he showed considerable proficiency. At the age of 15, he was admitted to Earlswood Asylum, where he was put to work in the carpenter's shop and soon became an expert craftsman. During his sixty-six years at the asylum, he produced an impressive array of beautiful and highly ingenious objects, including crayon drawings, carvings in ivory and wood, excellent models of ships, and various mechanical devices. Occasionally he even designed his own instruments to help him in his work.

One of Pullen's constructions was a representation of a gigantic human form, thirteen feet high. This full-fashioned "robot" could be made to execute a variety of movements such as raising the arms, rotating the head, protruding the tongue, opening and shutting mouth or eyes, etc. Another remarkable construction was a model of a ship, beautifully executed in the minutest detail. This model required over three years for its completion and attracted universal admiration when exhibited. Pullen's work revealed artistic imagination as well as mechanical ingenuity, skill in planning, and painstaking execution. Being cut off from many ordinary sources of stimulation by deafness, it is probable that he concentrated all his efforts from childhood upon the development of this one remarkable talent. In regard to general personality development, he is described as childish and immature, emotionally unstable, and lacking in common sense.

Special talent in music has also been repeatedly observed among the feebleminded. A very striking case (35, p. 339) of exceptional musical ability combined with serious defect in other respects is that of a woman in the Saltpetrière, a famous French institution for the feebleminded and the insane. This patient was an imbecile, blind from birth, a cripple, and affected with rickets. She was, however, able to sing without error any selection which she had heard. It became customary for her fellow-inmates to come to her so that she might correct their mistakes in singing. She attracted wide attention, and one day the composers Liszt and Meyerbeer visited her "singing class" to bring their encouragement and consolation.

Recently, a similar example of musical talent has been investigated by the use of standardized intelligence tests (cf. 26). This was the case of a boy admitted to a feebleminded institution at the age of 14. He came from an intellectually superior family which included many musically gifted individuals among its members. As a child, the subject was intellectually normal and manifested his musical talent from an early age. When three years old, he had pneumonia and meningitis, and since then he underwent steady mental deterioration. Upon admission, his I.Q. was 62; at the last testing, it had dropped to 46. He was then over 20 years of age and had a mental age of 7 years-5 months. His memory was unimpaired, however, and he retained his excellent musical ability. Although never known to compose a piece, he could play difficult music by ear and was also able to read difficult musical compositions at sight.

The feats of memory performed by some feebleminded individuals have often attracted notice. Tredgold (35, p. 337), for example, describes a 65-year-old mental defective in Earlswood Asylum with a remarkable memory for historical facts. He could repeat the dates of birth and death and the essential facts of the life of any prominent character in history. This knowledge was acquired largely by rote, through poring over all available books on biography and history. It was not, however, a matter of sheer meaningless repetition, as was shown by the subject's responses when questioned on the material. Another patient at the same institution showed an excellent memory for dates and occurrences which had come within his own experience. He proved a useful source of reference on local happenings in the institution.

Arithmetical prodigies have also been found among the ranks of the feebleminded. Usually, the skill manifested is confined to the mechanics of computation. Thus the subject may perform long and complicated calculations within a very short time and without the aid of paper and pencil. A favorite feat is to determine the number of minutes a person has lived, from a knowledge of his age or date of birth. Multiplication of three-place numbers, naming square roots and cube roots of four-place numbers, and similar difficult operations have also been executed within a few seconds. In some cases, this numerical aptitude goes beyond routine computation, as is indicated by the individual's ability to solve mathematical problems expressed in fairly elaborate and confusing terms.

Asymmetry of Development in "Normal" Individuals

Asymmetry of mental development is not to be regarded as characteristic of the feebleminded. It is equally common outside of institutions and among those classified as normal or superior on the basis of intelligence test performance. As was found in the case of the feebleminded, verbal traits are closely linked with what is termed "general intelligence" and therefore offer no examples of special talent. Children who are deficient in reading or spelling are usually inferior on intelligence tests.[1] Occasionally, a young, bright child is a poor speller because of his distaste for the routine drill necessary to master this school subject, but the inferiority is usually overcome. Juvenile authors, furthermore, have invariably been children of very high I.Q.[2] In many other traits, however, marked

[1] Cf. L. S. Hollingworth (16, Ch. IV and V).   [2] Cf. 17, Ch. IX, for examples.

discrepancies have been found between the child's alleged "general mental level" and his ability along specific lines.

Musical aptitude seems to have little or no relationship to superior intelligence. This was clearly shown in a study by L. S. Hollingworth (18) on 49 intellectually gifted children. All of the subjects were enrolled in special classes conducted for children with I.Q.'s of 135 or higher. The median Stanford-Binet I.Q. of this group was 153 and the range extended from 135 to 190. In chronological age, the children corresponded closely to the group of fifth grade schoolchildren upon whom the Seashore tests of musical sensitivity [1] had been standardized. Accordingly, the scores of the intellectually superior children on these tests were expressed as percentiles of Seashore's fifth grade group. The average percentile scores thus obtained on each test are given below.

Test	Average Percentile Score
Pitch	47
Intensity	50
Time	58
Consonance	48
Tonal memory	52

A percentile score of 50, it will be recalled, corresponds to the middlemost score of the standardization group and thus represents a "normal," or average, performance. The closeness to 50 of all the average percentile scores of the superior group indicates that musical aptitude is distributed among these children in very much the same fashion as in any group of the same age, chosen at random. Although in intelligence test performance these subjects were all within the upper 1% of the general population,

[1] For a description of these tests, cf. Seashore, C. E. *The Psychology of Musical Talent.* N. Y.: Silver, Burdett, 1919. Pp. 288.

their individual percentile scores on the music tests ranged from zero to 98.

Case studies of arithmetical prodigies and "lightning calculators" suggest that numerical aptitude is likewise distributed independently of general intelligence. Many such cases, from the early Greeks to the end of the last century, have been brought together by Scripture (31) and later by Mitchell (27). In regard to their achievements along other lines, or their practical ability to succeed in everyday life, mathematical prodigies run the gamut from genius and eminence of the highest order to mental dullness. A few would no doubt be classified as "borderline" or lower on current intelligence tests. At the other extreme are such men as Gauss and Ampère, whose exceptional talents covered a wide range, and who have made distinguished contributions in mathematics and allied fields. These men were "lightning calculators," but also possessed very superior ability along many other lines. For the present purpose, however, we are concerned with cases of asymmetrical development in which prodigious arithmetic powers are coupled with mediocrity or deficiency in other respects.

Henri Mondeaux (cf. 31), the untutored son of a poor woodcutter, is a famous example of remarkable arithmetic ability in an otherwise dull person. In his childhood he received no instruction, but was sent to tend sheep at the age of 12. While engaged in this occupation, he amused himself by counting and arranging pebbles; by this means he learned to carry out arithmetic operations. He worked out for his own use many special devices and aids to computation. After long exercises at these calculations, he offered to tell people he met the number of seconds in their ages. At this time, a schoolmaster became interested in him and offered to instruct him. Unfortunately the boy had a very poor memory for names and addresses and he spent nearly a month searching the city before he was able to locate his benefactor. Mondeaux was subsequently exhibited by his teacher at several colleges and universities and in 1840 he was presented before the Academy of Sciences at Paris. His was not merely a talent for routine calculation. He demonstrated his ability to solve, by ingenious devices of his own making, complex problems such as the following:

> There is a fountain containing an unknown quantity of water; around it stand people with vessels capable of containing a certain unknown quantity. They draw at the following rate: the first takes 100 quarts and $\frac{1}{13}$ of the remainder; the second takes 200 quarts and $\frac{1}{13}$ of the remainder; the third 300 quarts and $\frac{1}{13}$ of the remainder, and so on until the fountain is emptied.

Mondeaux gave the correct answer to this problem in a few seconds and then explained the method whereby he had arrived at the solution.

A similar case is that of Tom Fuller, a Negro slave brought from Africa at the age of 14. He could neither read nor write and received no formal instruction. As in the case of Mondeaux, his arithmetic was entirely self-taught. It is reported of him that when asked how many seconds a man had lived who is 70 years-17 days-12 hours old, he gave the answer, after $1\frac{1}{2}$ minutes, as 2,210,500,800 seconds. One of his questioners had meantime been computing with paper and pencil and informed Fuller that he had arrived at a different number, which he read off. At this, the Negro immediately pointed out that his questioner had forgotten to allow for leap years!

A few cases of "lightning calculators" have been directly observed and investigated by psychologists.[1] The informa-

[1] Cf. Binet (6) and Lindley and Bryan (23).

tion thus obtained, as well as the careful analysis of available reports on arithmetic prodigies, has brought to light certain characteristics of these individuals which may account for their talent. In most cases, the individual has worked out a number of short-cuts and special devices which enable him to compute far more efficiently than is ordinarily possible. Secondly, such individuals have usually memorized many more number combinations, such as squares, cubes, roots, products, etc., than are at the disposal of the average man. Arithmetical prodigies invariably manifest a very keen interest and fascination for numbers; as a result, they devote much time to analysis of computation methods and drill which would otherwise prove very monotonous. Many also seem to have a large perception span which enables them to grasp a long series of numbers simultaneously, as well as vivid imagery, making possible "mental computation" without the aid of paper and pencil.

The examples which have been reported suffice to illustrate the existence of extreme asymmetries of mental development. It is apparent that talent along certain lines is not incompatible with mediocre or inferior status in others. The cases so far described represent extreme deviations which for that reason are easily recognizable. Other instances of special talents or deficiencies, not so striking as to attract widespread attention, but revealed by the application of quantitative techniques of measurement, will be found in the following section.

THE INDIVIDUAL PSYCHOGRAPH

In the effort to obtain a more objective and concrete picture of variations within the individual than is furnished by the general impression of the examiner, a *psychograph*, or *profile chart*, of the individual may be drawn up. The psychograph shows at a glance the relative standing of the subject on any number of tests or other measures. The individual's scores on all tests must first be transmuted into *comparable units*. This is the fundamental step in any attempt to study variations within the individual. The psychograph itself, in the sense of a pictorial representation, could easily be dispensed with. The same information, although in a less vivid form, could be got from an examination of a set of scores obtained by the individual, *provided that all scores are expressed in the same terms*. It is in this latter respect that the judgment of the examiner needs to be supplemented by quantitative techniques. Confronted with a set of scores, some of which are expressed in seconds, others as number of words recalled, and still others as number of problems correctly solved, the clinician would be at a complete loss.

Comparable measures can be obtained in several ways. If all the tests have been standardized in terms of age, each score can be expressed as a *mental age*.[1] In many situations, however, this is not feasible. Some tests, especially in the field of personality, do not exhibit large or systematic age changes. The range of variation within one age group might thus be greater than the largest difference between the average performance of age groups. The application of the mental age concept to adult subjects, furthermore, is a rather questionable practice.

A commonly employed and generally applicable measure is the *percentile score* (cf. Ch. II). A percentile, it will be recalled, gives the percentage of individuals whose scores fall at or below that obtained by the given subject. Percentiles are determined once and for all in the process

---

[1] A mental age psychograph is employed at the N. Y. C. Children's Hospital, an institution for the feebleminded. (Cf. Poull, L. E. "The Psychographic Method in Clinical Practice." *J. Appl. Psychol.*, 1936, 20, 161–164.)

of standardization. The test is administered to a large group, representative of the population upon which it will ultimately be employed, and the percentage of individuals who score at or below each point is determined. Thus, if on an arithmetic reasoning test, 10% of the subjects correctly solve *three problems or less*, then any child who completes three problems correctly receives a percentile score of 10. A percentile scale divides the group into 100 classes, each composed of *the same number of persons*. Any subject subsequently taking the test is then placed into one of these classes, the poorest corresponding to the first percentile and the best to the 100th percentile. A subject who receives a percentile rating of 100 has obtained the highest score reached in the standardization group, but not necessarily the maximum score possible on the test. Similarly, a zero percentile rating does not mean a zero score; it signifies only that the subject's score is lower than that obtained by any member of the standardization group.

Scores from different tests can also be made comparable by the use of *standard measures*.[1] In this case, the subject's score is expressed as a deviation above or below the average of a given group. Thus if his original score falls exactly at the average, he receives a standard score of zero. If he is better than average, he receives a *plus* score, if poorer than average, a *minus* score. The unit in terms of which the scores are reported is the standard deviation (S.D.) of the distribution. Thus, if the average of the distribution is 35 and the S.D. 10, and if a given subject obtains a score of 45 points, his standard score would be +1, or one standard deviation above the group average $\left(\frac{45 - 35}{10} = 1 \right)$. Similarly, if another subject receives a score of 30 on the same

[1] Cf. Kelley (21), pp. 114–117.

test, his standard score would be $-.5\left(\dfrac{30-35}{10}=-.5\right)$.
If the distribution of scores on the different tests can be assumed to be of the same general shape, approximating the normal bell-shaped curve, the standard scores computed from them will be directly comparable.[1]

It should be borne in mind that none of these techniques for converting scores into comparable measures yields a scale of equal units. They simply express, in terms which are more or less intelligible, the *relative position* of the individual in different tests, but they do not furnish a precise statement of the actual *amount* of trait difference represented by the various scores. Thus, it will be recalled that the mental age unit corresponds to the average change in score occurring during a one-year period. Successive mental ages will not, therefore, represent equal increments of ability. We know that an M.A. of 6 indicates a higher standing than an M.A. of 5, and that an M.A. of 10 indicates a higher standing than one of 9, but we cannot conclude that the amount of difference is the same in both cases.

Nor can percentile scores be interpreted as equal ability units. As was shown in Chapter II, such an interpretation would imply that the distribution of the trait measured is rectangular. Since, however, traits are distributed according to the normal bell-shaped curve, individuals will cluster more closely at the center of the distribution and scatter as the extremes are approached. As a result, a difference of one percentile point at the extremes corre-

[1] Hull (19) has described a technique for obtaining comparable measures by transmuting the original scores into a distribution with any desired average and S.D. This procedure is based upon the same principle as standard measures. Its chief advantages lie in the fact that the scores can be expressed in more familiar terms than by the use of standard measures, and that negative values, decimals, etc., can be eliminated.

sponds to a much greater difference in amount of the trait than does a difference of one percentile point nearer the center. The difference between an individual who receives a percentile rating of 90 in height and one who receives a percentile rating of 91 is much greater, *in actual inches*, than the difference between two individuals receiving percentile ratings of 50 and 51.

Similarly, standard scores do not represent equal units. By subtracting a constant (the average) and dividing by a constant (the S.D.), we do not alter the scores in any essential way. The set of measures is simply transmuted into a different system of expression, as when pounds are changed to kilograms. But the standard scores so obtained retain any inaccuracies or inequalities which were present in the original measures.[1]

In addition to the different ways of expressing comparable scores, there are a variety of ways in which the psychograph itself can be plotted. Illustrations of different kinds of psychographs will be found in Figures 39–45. Figure 39 shows a *horizontal bar diagram*. It will be noted that no scores are available for the subject on a number of tests listed in the psychograph. The use of horizontal bars which are not joined is necessary in such a case, since a continuous line would be inapplicable. The boy whose abilities are pictured in this psychograph exhibits a fairly clear-cut tendency to excel in motor performance. His score becomes progressively poorer as we pass from the strictly motor, through sensori-motor and perceptual, to more highly "intellectual" or verbal functions. His "men-

---

[1] Equal units can, of course, be obtained by the use of *scaling techniques*. This, however, is a laborious procedure, requiring the testing of a large, representative, and normally distributed sampling of individuals. The question of equal units is no more essential, furthermore, for the measurement of trait variability than for any other problem involving mental tests. It has been brought up in this connection solely because of a rather common tendency erroneously to treat transmuted measures as equal unit scales.

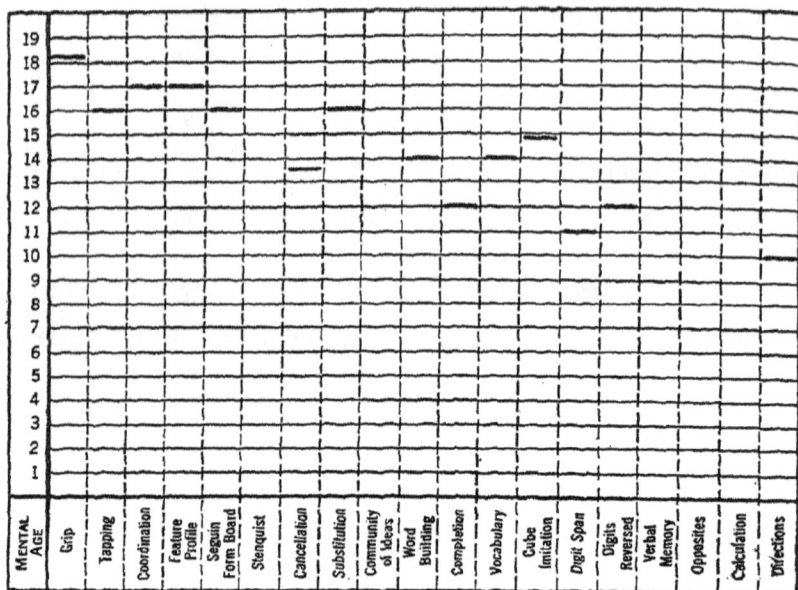

FIG. 39. HORIZONTAL BAR PSYCHOGRAPH. SCORES ARE IN TERMS OF MENTAL AGES. (After H. L. Hollingworth, 15, p. 208.)

tal age" on the different tests ranges from 11 years in a test of following written directions to slightly over 18 in hand grip.

Figure 40 illustrates the use of a *circular psychograph,* plotted in terms of percentile scores. The center of the circle corresponds to a zero percentile, the outermost circumference to 100 percentile, and the middlemost corresponds to an average performance. The radii indicate the individual's relative standing in different functions. This psychograph shows a boy, slightly above average in intelligence, who is fairly uniform in most of the traits measured. With one exception, his percentile ratings vary between 45 and 70. In mechanical aptitude, this boy seems to have a special talent, obtaining a percentile score of 95 on the Stenquist Mechanical Aptitude Test.

Figures 41–45, inclusive, illustrate the *continuous line psychograph.* In Figure 41 will be found the psychograph

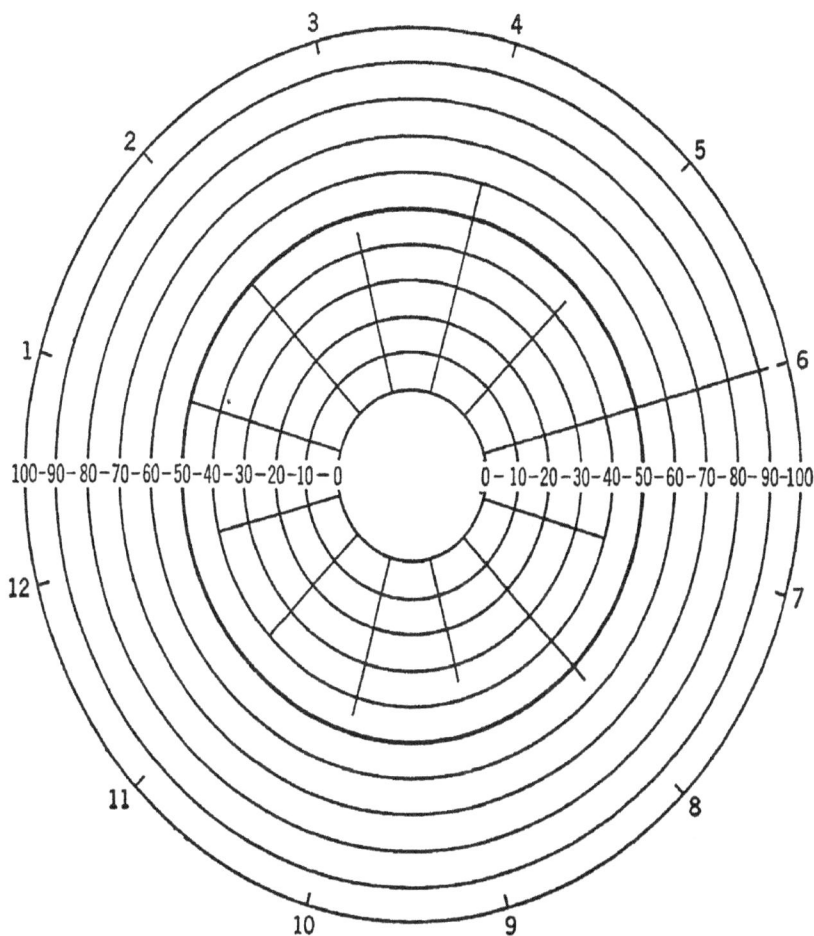

1. Stanford-Binet
2. Trabue Completion Test
3. Cancellation
4. Digit-Symbol
5. Opposites
6. Stenquist Mechanical Ability Test
7. Tonal Memory
8. Pitch
9. Time
10. Intensity
11. Healy Pictorial Completion
12. Grip in Hand

FIG. 40. CIRCULAR PSYCHOGRAPH, IN WHICH THE MEDIAN CIRCUMFERENCE DENOTES THE AVERAGE PERFORMANCE AT THE GIVEN AGE. SCORES ARE IN TERMS OF PERCENTILES. (After L. S. Hollingworth, 16, p. 41.)

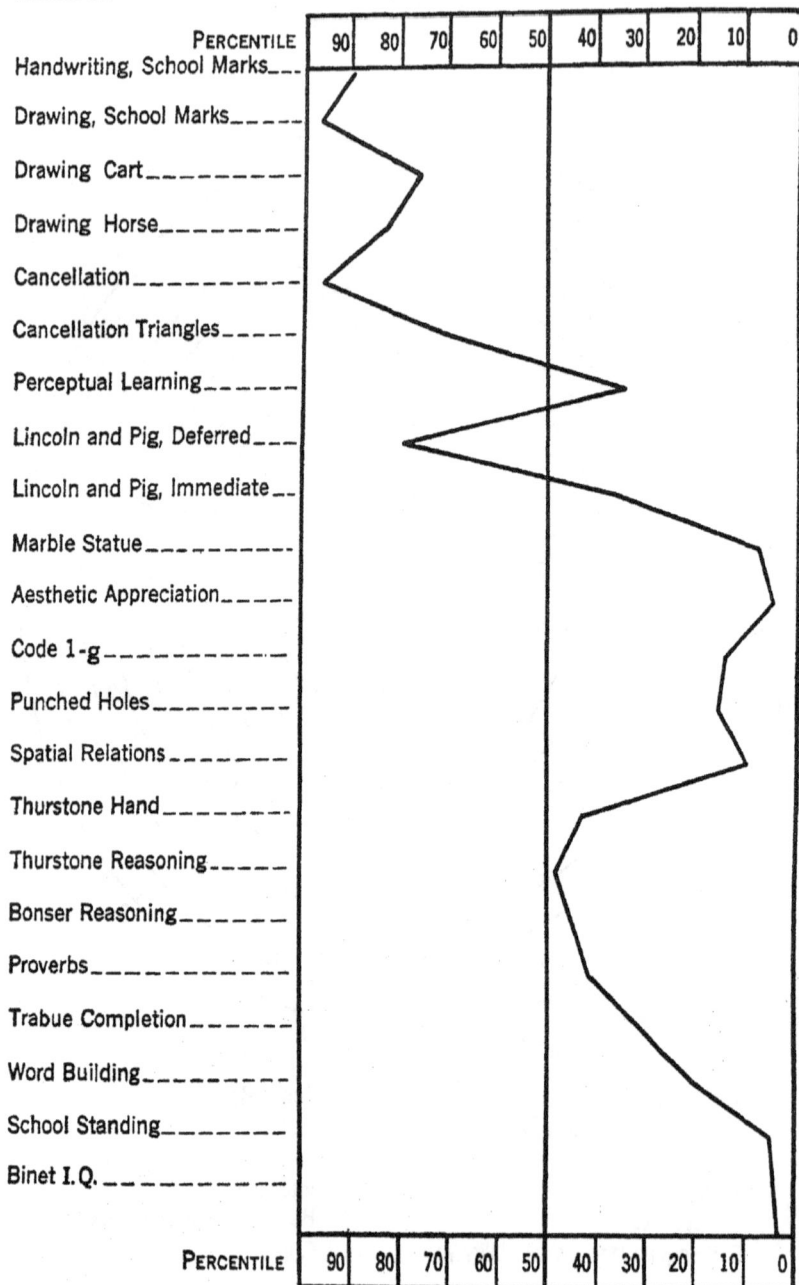

FIG. 41. PSYCHOGRAPH OF AN INTELLECTUALLY BACKWARD CHILD WITH A SPECIAL TALENT IN REPRESENTATIVE DRAWING. (After Manuel, 24, p. 100.)

of a girl who falls within the lowest 10% in I.Q. and in school standing, and is below average in most verbal tests of intellectual functions. But she exhibits exceptional talent in representative drawing. When tested, this girl was in the sixth grade at the age of 14. Many members of her family were reported as interested and talented in drawing or painting. Figure 42 shows the psychograph of

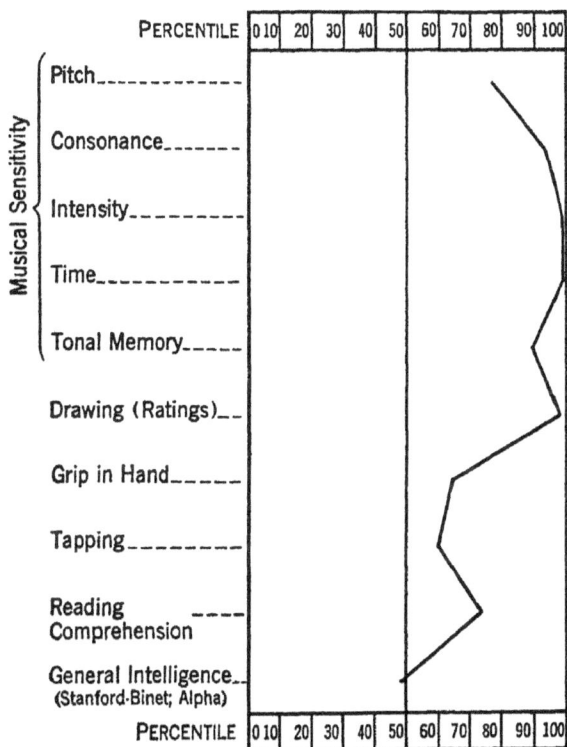

FIG. 42. PSYCHOGRAPH OF A CHILD OF MEDIOCRE INTELLIGENCE WITH SPE-CIAL ABILITY IN REPRESENTATIVE DRAWING. (After L. S. Hollingworth, 16, p. 175.)

a 14-year-old girl of average general intelligence, with exceptionally high ratings in music and drawing. This subject was referred for psychological examination because she was doing poorly in school. She had been attending a superior private school in which the average I.Q. was 120, a fact which accounts for her apparent backwardness. In this school, she had been receiving good grades only in music and drawing. In Figure 43 is given the psychograph

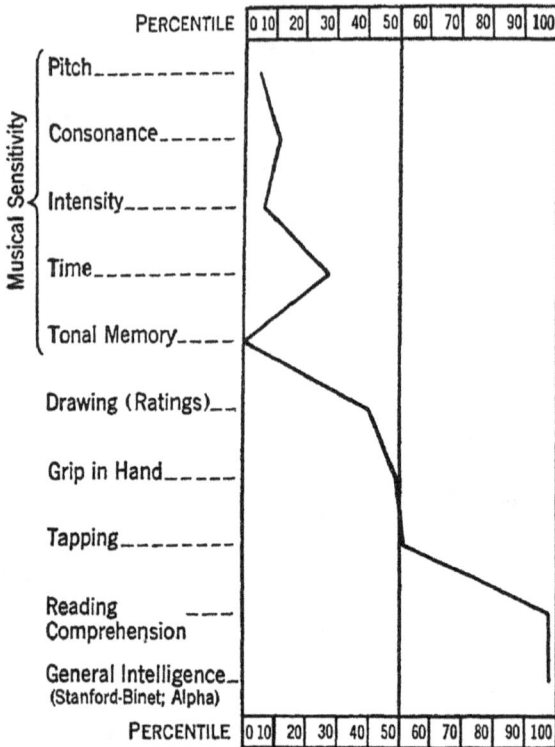

FIG. 43. PSYCHOGRAPH OF A CHILD WITH SPECIAL DEFECT IN MUSIC, COMBINED WITH VERY SUPERIOR GENERAL INTELLIGENCE. (After L. S. Hollingworth, 16, p. 179.)

of a 10-year-old schoolboy. On intelligence tests this boy ranked close to the 100th percentile, having an I.Q. of 151. In reading, arithmetic, and elementary science, his school work was excellent. In music tests, on the other hand, he ranked consistently low; his music teacher regarded him as a complete failure and advocated that he repeat the grade.

Figures 44 and 45 have been plotted in terms of standard scores. Both are taken from a series of psychographs con-

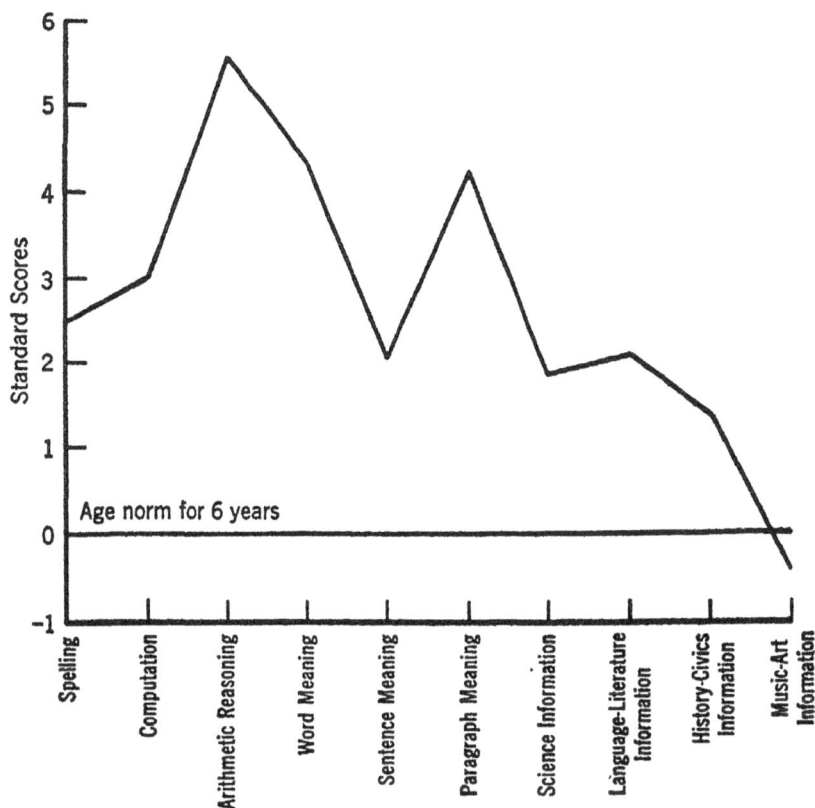

FIG. 44. PSYCHOGRAPH OF AN INTELLECTUALLY SUPERIOR SIX-YEAR-OLD SCHOOLGIRL. (After DeVoss, 8, p. 350.)

structed by DeVoss (8) on children who had been selected for their high intellectual level.[1] The psychograph in Figure 44 is that of a girl with a Stanford-Binet I.Q. of 192. This child, although above her age norm in all of the tests but one, exhibits marked discrepancies among her scores. She is highest in arithmetic reasoning and also shows unusual ability in tests involving reading comprehension. In four information tests dealing with science, language and literature, history and civics, and music and art, she obtained much lower scores. In the last named test, her

[1] Part of the group employed by Terman in his extensive investigation or gifted children (cf. Ch. XIII).

score was even slightly *below* her age norm. In Figure 45 is the psychograph of a schoolboy with an I.Q. of 155, who presents a very different mental picture. He is best in

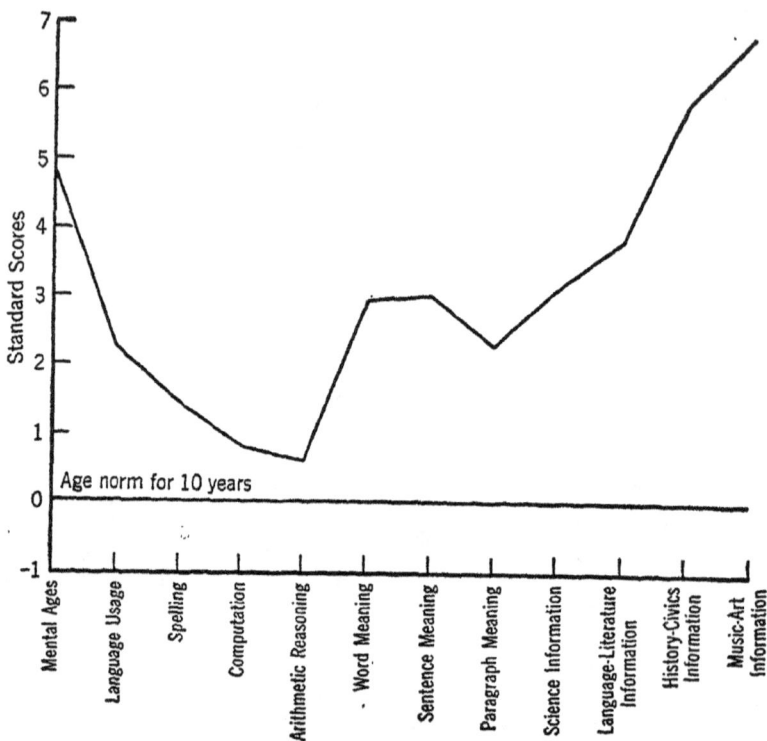

FIG. 45. PSYCHOGRAPH OF AN INTELLECTUALLY SUPERIOR TEN-YEAR-OLD SCHOOLBOY. (After DeVoss, 8, p. 360.)

music-art information, second best in history-civics information, and poorest in arithmetic reasoning and computation. These examples illustrate the fact that intellectually superior children, although above their age norms in most mental tests, *may be much farther above average in some traits than in others.*

THE MEASUREMENT OF TRAIT VARIABILITY

The term *trait variability* has been suggested by Hull (20) to designate variability from trait to trait within the individual. This is to be distinguished from *individual variability* which refers to the differences among individuals in a single trait. All of the statistical techniques commonly employed to measure the amount of individual variability can be applied to the measurement of trait variability, provided that the scores on different tests are expressed in the same units.

In a study by Hull (20), an attempt was made to measure the amount of variability in different traits and compare it with the amount of individual variability on single tests. The scores of 107 high school freshmen on 35 tests were obtained.[1] The tests included several subtests from intelligence scales, as well as tests of motor characteristics, perception, attention, and personality traits. Each of the 35 sets of scores was transmuted into a distribution with an average of 81 and an S.D. of 7 by a method similar in principle to that employed in obtaining standard scores (cf. Hull, 19). The particular values chosen for average and S.D. are arbitrary and were selected chiefly because of their similarity to school grades.

With these converted scores, the S.D. of each individual's scores in the 35 tests was computed as a measure of the amount of trait variability. There were thus obtained as many S.D's as there were subjects, *viz.*, 107. The average of these 107 S.D.'s proved to be 6.33. Hull compared this figure with the S.D. of 7 which, in the scale of units employed, represents the *individual variability* in any one of the tests. After allowing for possible chance errors of sampling and measurement, Hull estimated that trait variability is about 80% as great as individual variability. The exact relationship obtained between these two forms of variability is, however, affected by the homogeneity of

---

[1] The original data were collected by C. E. Limp in connection with an investigation of shorthand and typewriting aptitudes.

the group employed. The more homogeneous the group, the smaller will be the original S.D.'s representing individual variability in raw scores. Because of the transmutation technique employed, this will automatically make the deviations within the individual appear larger. The group of high school freshmen upon whom Hull's data were obtained was a fairly representative sampling, covering a wide range. His results are therefore typical of what would be found on many groups. A universal estimate of the amount of trait variability can never be arrived at, however, because such a measure depends in a peculiarly intimate fashion upon the nature of the group within which it is obtained.

It is nevertheless apparent from this study that a large amount of trait variability may be found within a group of normal individuals *who were not selected on the basis of asymmetrical development*. The amount of trait variability also differed with the individual. Some subjects displayed much more uniformity than others in their performance on different tests. The individual S.D.'s of trait variability ranged from 4.3 to 9.09. The distribution of scores of each individual on the 35 tests seemed to follow the general form of the normal curve. Most of the individual's scores clustered about his own average, only a few scores deviating markedly from it in either direction. Finally, no relationship was found between the individual's general level of ability and the extent of his trait variability. There was no tendency for either the brighter or the duller individual within this group to exhibit more marked asymmetry of abilities. The correlation between each individual's average score on all the tests and his trait variability was only .03.

DeVoss (8) conducted an investigation to determine whether gifted children are any more specialized in their intellectual abilities than normal children. A group of 100 subjects were selected on the basis of mental age from a larger group of "gifted children" employed by Terman (cf. Ch. XIII). The mental ages of DeVoss' group ranged between 14 and 15-5, with an average of 14-8; the chronological ages ranged from 8-6 to 11-1. The average I.Q. was 149.4, and the range from 136 to 180. In school grade, the children were scattered from the third to the eighth grade, inclusive. These subjects were compared with a control group of 96 unselected eighth grade schoolchildren of approximately the same *mental ages* as the superior group. Both groups were given the Stanford Achievement Test, consisting of seven subtests on different school subjects, as well as information tests in special fields. All scores were reduced to standard measures.

Examination of the inter-test variations within each subject's scores revealed many differences large enough to be significant. By means of a specially devised statistical formula,[1] it was possible to estimate how large a trait difference might be obtained simply through the operation of chance factors, such as inadequacies in the tests employed. Upon the application of this formula, it was discovered that a large percentage of the trait differences fell beyond the chance limits and must therefore represent a true discrepancy in the individual's standing in the traits compared. In Table XIII are given the percentage of trait differences, in both the gifted and control groups, which fell outside of the distribution of differences expected by chance. The percentages in the gifted group are given above the diagonal, those in the control group below the diagonal. The tests which are being compared are indicated in the top row and first column to the left. Thus,

---

[1] A formula for the computation of the P.E. of the difference between an individual's standard scores on any two tests.

in the gifted group, 24% of the differences between scores on arithmetic reasoning and computation fell beyond the chance limits; the corresponding percentage for the control group is 34%, and so on.

TABLE XIII

PERCENTAGE OF TRAIT DIFFERENCES AMONG 100 GIFTED AND 96 CONTROL CHILDREN WHICH FALL OUTSIDE OF THE CHANCE DISTRIBUTION *

(After DeVoss, 8, p. 325)

Tests to Be Compared	Arithmetic Computation	Arithmetic Reasoning	Word Meaning	Sentence Meaning	Paragraph Meaning	Language Usage	Spelling	Science Information
Arithmetic computation		24	32	31	34	37	26	33
Arithmetic reasoning	34		30	31	31	38	29	29
Word meaning	39	30		13	24	25	26	23
Sentence meaning	40	26	13		26	24	28	29
Paragraph meaning	35	26	14	17		33	27	34
Language usage	39	33	24	23	17		30	32
Spelling	31	36	28	33	25	30		30
Science information	35	20	24	25	21	30	31	

* Gifted group above the diagonal: upper right-hand block. Control group below the diagonal: lower left-hand block.

It will be noted that in every test pair compared there are found differences over and above those expected by chance. This is true of both gifted and control groups. The percentages of such differences are also closely similar in the two groups, test by test. In the gifted group, the percentages vary from 13 to 37, in the control group from 13 to 40. The average percentages are 28.89 and 27.82 for gifted and control groups, respectively. Out of the 28 inter-test comparisons given in Table XIII, the gifted group has the larger percentage of excess differences 13 times, the control group has the larger percentage 12 times, and the two have identical percentages in 3 cases. Thus there seems to be no appreciable or consistent difference in trait variability between intellectually normal and superior children.

Evidence from Correlation

The examination of extreme examples of asymmetrical development, as well as the measurement of trait variability within individuals in general, suggests that superior talents in one line may be associated with inferior abilities in other respects. It is not to be concluded from this, however, that compensation is the rule. Superior standing in one trait does not *imply* inferiority in another. We have cited only examples in which individuals with a high standing in a certain trait *A* make a poor showing in a second trait *B*. We could with equal facility find cases in which the individual is superior in *A* as well as *B*, or superior in *A* and average in *B*. This, in fact, is what we mean by a *zero correlation*. If various abilities are specific and mutually independent, so that an individual's standing in one tells us nothing about his relative standing in another, we should expect the correlation between such abilities to be zero or very low. Correlation thus offers another approach to the analysis of trait variability. We may now turn to a consideration of some typical correlational results on the various traits suggested by case studies and psychographic analysis.

In regard to the specificity of musical aptitude, certain

findings with the Hevner tests of music appreciation are illuminating. In a group of 74 college students, Hevner (13) obtained a correlation of −.17 between one form of her music appreciation test and the Minnesota College Ability Test. The latter is very similar in its content to current intelligence examinations adapted to the college level. In the music appreciation test, four versions of parts of 24 musical compositions are rendered on the piano. These versions include the original and four distortions. One is a simplification of the music in which many of the tones are omitted, so that the music sounds bare, hollow, and uninteresting. In a second version, the music is elaborated by introducing additional tones into the chords and by ornamentation, so that the piece is overdone, confusing, and "frilly." In a third version, the melodic progression or phrasing is altered, the music being thereby rendered formless and unbalanced. The subject is required to state, in each case, which of the four versions he prefers. This test has been found to be quite diagnostic of musical aptitude, correlating highly with other music tests and independent criteria.

The same subjects were given another form of the music appreciation test which included 48 items presented in only two versions, the original and one distortion. The correlation between intelligence test performance and scores on this test proved to be −.15. The low negative correlations of these tests with intelligence would suggest a slight tendency for the more "intelligent" subjects to be inferior in music appreciation. The correlations are too low, however, to indicate a significant trend and the two traits can be regarded as practically unrelated.

Intelligence has also been found to have little or no relationship with performance on the Seashore tests of musical sensitivity. In an investigation (9) on 230 college

students, I.Q.'s were estimated from scores on the Otis
Self-Administering and Army Alpha. These I.Q.'s were
correlated with scores on each of the Seashore tests, with
the following results:

Musical Test	Correlation with I.Q.
Pitch	.32
Intensity	.01
Time	.13
Consonance	.09
Tonal memory	.10
Rhythm	.12

Aptitude in pictorial art shows a similar independence
of general intelligence. Meier (25) obtained a correlation
of −.146 between the Terman Group Test of Intelligence
and an art judgment test, within a group of 55 high school
students. The same test correlated −.018 with Thorndike
Intelligence Test among 53 college students. Both correlations are sufficiently low to indicate an absence of relationship between the two traits. The art judgment test consisted of a series of pairs (or larger groups) of pictures
reproduced in black and white. Within each pair (or
group), one picture was the original, the other (or others)
a variation which disrupted the organization of the picture
by altering its symmetry, balance, harmony and unity,
rhythm, or similar features. The subject was to indicate
which picture he preferred in each case.

In the effort to discover the relationship between drawing ability and other traits, Ayer (3) conducted an investigation on 51 high school students. The subjects were
shown a turkey feather and were asked to: (1) make a
representative drawing of it, (2) diagram it, and (3) describe it verbally. Twenty-four hours later, they were
again required to draw a diagram of the feather from
memory and also to answer certain questions about it

(retention test). Each subject's performance on all five tests was scored independently by 10 judges in order to arrive at a final estimate of his score. The various correlations computed among these scores are reported below.

Representative drawing and verbal description	—.271
Representative drawing and diagramming	—.052
Diagramming and verbal description	.231
Representative drawing and retention	—.022
Verbal description and retention	.234
Diagramming from memory and retention	.433

As would be expected, the only positive correlations are those between diagramming (immediate or delayed), verbal description, and retention. These tasks have a good deal in common, since they all involve careful analytic observation of the object. Little or no artistic talent is required in diagramming. The only task which implies drawing ability to any appreciable extent is representative drawing. This, it will be noted, shows very little correlation with the other tasks. All the correlations computed by Ayer with representative drawing are negative. Two are too low to indicate the presence of any relationship; the third, although also low, suggests the possibility that those subjects who rendered a good representative drawing may have overlooked certain details and concentrated chiefly on a general impressionistic observation.

Mechanical aptitude seems also to be a special ability. Stenquist reports a correlation of .230 between the Stenquist Assembling Test and a composite score from six verbal intelligence tests in a group of 267 seventh and eighth grade boys. Although reliably higher than zero, this correlation indicates only a very slight degree of relationship. The Stenquist Assembling Tests involve the construction of common mechanical objects such as a lock, bicycle bell, chain, and mouse trap, from given parts.

In a very extensive and thorough investigation on mechanical aptitude conducted at the University of Minnesota (cf. 29), various correlations were computed between mechanical tests and intelligence. I.Q.'s were estimated from scores on the Otis Intelligence Test. The correlation between these I.Q.'s and a mechanical aptitude battery,[1] composed exclusively of apparatus or manipulation tests, proved to be only .13 within a group of 100 Junior High School boys. Anastasi (1) obtained a correlation of .07 between a vocabulary test and the Minnesota Paper Form Board Test among 225 male college students. The latter is a paper-and-pencil test of the ability to handle spatial relations. Vocabulary tests, which measure the subject's understanding of word meanings, have been found to correlate so highly with the majority of common intelligence tests as to be practically interchangeable with them. From these examples, it is apparent that in large groups of subjects of different age and academic level, only a very low positive correlation exists between spatial or mechanical ability and the verbal type of intelligence test. When the mechanical problems are presented verbally, the correlations with intelligence tests are usually higher because of the common influence of the comprehension of verbal directions, knowledge of words, and general facility with verbal material.

Of the special aptitudes suggested by case studies, only numerical ability remains to be examined. In spite of the indisputable presence of "mathematical prodigies" who are deficient in other respects, numerical ability has not usually been classed with special aptitudes. Arithmetic tests are also frequently included in intelligence scales. Recent correlational analysis has demonstrated,

---

[1] A series of tests each of which is given an optimum weight and combined so as to give the best possible estimate of the trait measured.

however, that the relationships between verbal and numerical tests are much lower than those within either group of abilities. In many investigations, the correlations between verbal and numerical tests were no higher than those between verbal tests and the various special aptitudes discussed above.

Kelley (22) obtained a correlation of .09 between a reading comprehension test and a test of arithmetic reasoning in a group of 140 seventh grade children. Schneck (30) tested 210 college men with 5 verbal and 4 numerical tests. The average of the correlations between all possible pairs of verbal tests was .4920; the corresponding average correlation for the numerical tests was .3383. When verbal and numerical tests were paired off, the average of the correlations so obtained was only .1441. Even this rather low positive correlation probably resulted from the fact that in at least one of the numerical tests, the problems were expressed in verbal terms, and in all of the tests the directions were given verbally. Anastasi (1) found a correlation of −.01 between arithmetic reasoning and vocabulary among 225 male college students. In a subsequent investigation by the same author (2) on 140 college women, all possible correlations were computed among two verbal and two numerical tests. The correlation between the two verbal tests (vocabulary and analogies) was .65, and that between the two numerical tests (arithmetic reasoning and number series completion) .58. The average of four correlations obtained by pairing each of the verbal tests with each of the numerical was only .16. These various findings suggest that verbal and numerical tests seem to be measuring two "special aptitudes" in the same sense as the other tests discussed above.

No mention of personality traits has been made in this

chapter. This is because the independence of personality and intellectual traits is now quite generally recognized. Emotional instability, for example, may be found over a wide range of intellectual levels. Insanity among highly gifted persons is not unknown. Extreme emotional disorders are perhaps not as common among the intellectually ablest as among more mediocre individuals because the former can exert somewhat more control over social, economic, and other aspects of their environment and are therefore less frequently subjected to conflicts or frustrations. At the same time, certain forms of insanity are rare among low grade mental defectives because these individuals have too restricted a mental life to experience much stress or strain.

Moral or character development seems also to be very largely independent of ability. Criminals are not significantly differentiated from non-criminals in intellectual status. This was demonstrated in an extensive investigation by Murchison (28) in which the Army Alpha was administered to 3954 native-born White men [1] in the penitentiaries of five states. The distribution of the scores of this group coincided very closely with that of the army draft from the same five states. Among juvenile delinquents, many investigations have revealed no intellectual deviation when the subjects are compared with a non-delinquent group of the same cultural and economic level (cf., e.g., Slawson, 32). In the course of extensive experimentation with large groups of schoolchildren, Hartshorne and May (10, 11) found very low correlations between intellectual level and tests of several character traits. The children were tested in practical everyday situations and without their knowledge. Among the

---

[1] Separate investigations were also conducted on smaller groups of foreign-born, Negro, and women prisoners.

character traits investigated were lying, cheating, stealing, charity, coöperativeness, persistence, and inhibition. When the questionnaire type of test was employed (cf. 12), the correlations with intelligence were much higher, owing to the common dependence of such tests upon verbal comprehension.

The administration of tests of social traits or emotional instability to large groups also reveals little or no relationship with intelligence. Thus, for example, no appreciable correlation has been found between intelligence test score and performance on the Colgate Tests of Emotional Outlets for measuring introversion and emotional instability. Within a group of 218 college students, a correlation of .02 was obtained between introversion scores and performance on the Thorndike Intelligence Test. The correlation between scores on the same intelligence test and number of neurotic symptoms proved to be .008 among 203 male subjects and −.12 among women (number not stated). Thurstone (34) reports a correlation of .037 between scores on his Neurotic Inventory and the American Council of Education intelligence test among 694 college freshmen. Bender (5) found a correlation of .0008 between scores on the same intelligence test and performance on the Allport Ascendance-Submission test in a group of 192 college sophomores. It is almost superfluous to discuss correlations between intelligence and personality tests, since in the construction of the latter a definite attempt is made *to avoid an appreciable correlation with intelligence*. The assumption is implicit in techniques of personality test construction that the traits to be measured are independent of intellectual status. That these efforts have usually succeeded testifies to the soundness of the assumption.

REFERENCES

1. Anastasi, A. "A Group Factor in Immediate Memory," *Arch. Psychol.*, No. 120, 1930. Pp. 61.
2. ——. "Further Studies on the Memory Factor," *Arch. Psychol.*, No. 142, 1932. Pp. 60.
3. Ayer, F. C. *The Psychology of Drawing.* Baltimore: Warwick and York, 1916. Pp. 186.
4. Barr, M. W. "Some Notes on Echolalia," *J. Nerv. Mental Diseases*, 1898, 25, 20–30.
5. Bender, I. E. "Ascendance-Submission in Relation to Certain Other Factors in Personality," *J. Abn. Psychol.*, 1928–29, 23, 137–143.
6. Binet, A. *Psychologie des grands calculateurs et joueurs d'échecs.* Paris: Hachette, 1894. Pp. 364.
7. Bronner, A. F. *The Psychology of Special Abilities and Disabilities.* Boston: Little, Brown, 1919. Pp. 269.
8. DeVoss, J. C. "Specialization of the Abilities of Gifted Children," in *Genetic Studies of Genius*, Terman, L. M., ed. (Vol. I, Ch. XII). Stanford Univ., Calif.: Stanford Univ. Press, 1925. Pp. 648.
9. Fracker, C. C., and Howard, V. M. "Correlation between Intelligence and Musical Talent among University Students," *Psychol. Mon.*, 1928, 39, 157–161.
10. Hartshorne, H., and May, M. A. *Studies in Deceit.* N. Y.: Macmillan, 1928. Book I, pp. 414; Book II, pp. 306.
11. Hartshorne, H., May, M. A., and Maller, J. B. *Studies in Service and Self-Control.* N. Y.: Macmillan, 1929. Pp. 559.
12. Hartshorne, H., May, M. A, and Shuttleworth, F. K. *Studies in the Organization of Character.* N. Y.: Macmillan, 1930. Pp. 503.
13. Hevner, K. "A Study of Tests for the Appreciation of Music," *J. Appl. Psychol.*, 1931, 15, 575–583.
14. Hoitsma, R. K., "Reliability and Relationships of the Colgate Mental Hygiene Tests," *J. Appl. Psychol.*, 1925, 9, 293–303.
15. Hollingworth, H. L. *Judging Human Character.* N. Y.: Appleton, 1922. Pp. 268.

16. Hollingworth, L. S. *Special Talents and Defects*. N. Y.: Macmillan, 1925. Pp. 216.

17. ——. *Gifted Children: Their Nature and Nurture*. N. Y.: Macmillan, 1926. Pp. 374.

18. ——. "The Musical Sensitivity of Children Who Test above 135 I.Q.," *J. Educ. Psychol.*, 1926, 17, 95–109.

19. Hull, C. L. "The Conversion of Test Scores into Series Which Shall Have Assigned Mean and Degree of Dispersion," *J. Appl. Psychol.*, 1922, 6, 298–300.

20. ——. "Variability in Amount of Different Traits Possessed by the Individual," *J. Educ. Psychol.*, 1927, 18, 97–104.

21. Kelley, T. L. *Statistical Method*. N. Y.: Macmillan, 1924. Pp. 390.

22. ——. *Crossroads in the Mind of Man*. Stanford Univ., Calif.: Stanford Univ. Press, 1928. Pp. 238.

23. Lindley, E. H., and Bryan, A. L. "An Arithmetical Prodigy," *Psychol. Rev.*, 1900, 7, 135.

24. Manuel, H. T. *A Study of Talent in Drawing*. Bloomington, Ill.: Public School Pub. Co., 1919. Pp. 152.

25. Meier N. C. "Æsthetic Judgment as a Measure of Art Talent," *Univ. Iowa Stud.: Series on Aims and Progress of Research*, 1926, 1, No. 19. Pp. 30.

26. Minogue, B. M. "A Case of Secondary Mental Deficiency with Musical Talent," *J. Appl. Psychol.*, 1923, 7, 349–352.

27. Mitchell, F. D. "Mathematical Prodigies," *Amer. J. Psychol.*, 1907, 18, 61–143.

28. Murchison, C. *Criminal Intelligence*. Worcester, Mass.: Clark Univ. Press, 1926. Pp. 291.

29. Paterson, D. G., *et al*. *Minnesota Mechanical Ability Tests*. Minneapolis: Univ. Minn. Press, 1930. Pp. 586.

30. Schneck, M. M. R. "The Measurement of Verbal and Numerical Abilities," *Arch. Psychol.*, No. 107, 1929. Pp. 49.

31. Scripture, E. W. "Arithmetic Prodigies," *Amer. J. Psychol.*, 1891, 4, 1–59.

32. Slawson, J. *The Delinquent Boy*. Boston: Badger, 1926. Pp. 477.

33. Stenquist, J. L. *Measurements of Mechanical Ability.* N..Y.: Teachers College, Columbia Univ., 1923. Pp. 101.

34. Thurstone, L. L., and T. G. "A Neurotic Inventory," *J. Soc. Psychol.*, 1930, 1, 3–30.

35. Tredgold, A. F. *Mental Deficiency.* N. Y.: Wood, 1922. Pp. 569.

CHAPTER XI

MENTAL ORGANIZATION

The lack of relationship between intelligence test performance and several mental functions (cf. Ch. X) raises a question as to what constitutes "intelligence." It will be recalled that the original purpose of intelligence tests was to sample a large number of different abilities in order to arrive at an estimate of the subject's general level of performance. Insofar as the individual's standing in specific functions differs, such a general estimate is unsatisfactory. It is apparent, however, that current intelligence tests do not even furnish an adequate estimate of the average ability of the individual, since they are overweighted with certain functions and omit others. Thus in the non-language and performance tests of intelligence, spatial aptitude plays the dominant rôle. Most paper-and-pencil tests, on the other hand, measure chiefly verbal ability and, to a slighter extent, numerical ability.

Since the latter type of test is by far the most frequently employed, the term "intelligence" has come to be used almost synonymously with verbal ability. Mental age on the Stanford-Binet, for example, has been found to correlate as highly as .91 with performance on the vocabulary test of the scale (cf. 28). This finding led Terman to suggest that "a mental age based on the vocabulary score alone would not be far wrong in a large per cent of the cases" (30, p. 454).

From another angle, most intelligence tests may be regarded as measures of scholastic aptitude, or *ability to succeed in our schools.* This is illustrated particularly well by the procedure commonly followed in validating intelligence tests. The term validity is used to denote the degree to which a test actually measures what it purports to measure. In the case of intelligence tests, validity is usually checked against school success as a criterion. Scores on the test are correlated with school grades or teachers' estimates of ability, and the higher these correlations the more valid the test is said to be.

Some rather illuminating data on the relationship between intelligence test performance and scholastic ability were brought together by Kelley (17, Ch. VIII). Availing himself of material gathered by several investigators, Kelley presents correlations between scores on several intelligence tests and performance on the Stanford Achievement Test. The latter is a carefully constructed and standardized test covering several school subjects and was designed for use in place of ordinary school examinations. The correlation of this examination with the National Intelligence Test proved to be .66; with Otis Intermediate Test of Intelligence, the correlation was .79; and with Illinois General Intelligence Test, it was .71. These correlations are practically as high as those obtained when different intelligence tests are correlated with each other. Thus Stanford-Binet and National Intelligence Test correlated .84, National Intelligence Test and Terman Group Test .79, and Stanford-Binet and Terman Group Test .75.

From these considerations, it would seem that "intelligence" is a very ambiguous, if not misleading, term to employ. Recently, there has been a tendency either to discard or to qualify the blanket term "intelligence" and to give more specific and more informative names to mental tests. Thus we find the Intelligence Scale CAVD, named after its four component parts, *C*ompletion, *A*rithmetic, *V*ocabulary, and *D*irections; this test claims to measure no more than the "CAVD segment" of intellect (cf. 41). The Minnesota College Ability Test and the Scholastic Aptitude Test constructed by the College Entrance Examination Board are also examples of the explicit recognition of the specific nature of the measuring instrument. In the latter test, the subject is now given a separate score in the verbal and numerical parts (cf. 21), a procedure which testifies further to the influence of studies of trait relationship upon test construction and interpretation. Thus emphasis is shifting from indices of so-called general intelligence to concrete behavior traits and their interrelations.

Such interrelationships among an individual's abilities are included under the rubric of *mental organization*. In investigating this problem, we are not only concerned with the establishment of the presence or absence of trait variations, but we are also interested in an exact formulation of the principles underlying the amount and direction of such variations. Through such an analysis, we shall be able to identify the basic components or unitary traits into which the individual's behavior may be resolved.

Theories of mental organization are very old. As long as philosophers have discussed the nature of mind, they have proposed theories to explain how the "parts" of the mind were related or organized. With these speculations, however, we are not concerned. It is only since the application of mental tests and quantitative methods that the relationships among the varied responses of the individual could be measured. The more recent theories have been offered as interpretations of specific evidence and hence have a more objective foundation.

Major Contemporary Theories of Mental Organization

The problem of mental organization was first placed upon an empirical basis with the publication of Spearman's 1904 article (26) in which were presented a theory and a new method of investigation.[1] According to Spearman's *Two-Factor Theory*,[2] all intellectual activities have in common one fundamental function which is called the *General* factor, or *g*. In addition, each activity has *Specific*, or *s* factors. The *s* factors are exceedingly numerous and strictly specific to each activity of the individual. No two activities can share specific factors, by definition. Spearman argued that such a theory is consistent with correlation results. Thus the presence of different specifics in every activity would explain the absence of perfect + 1.00 correlations; no two activities, however much they may depend upon the *g* factor, are entirely free from specifics. The fact that most abilities are positively correlated, on the other hand, is attributed to the ubiquitous *g*. Different proportions of *g* and *s* in each activity would produce a wide range of positive correlations, all higher than zero and lower than 1.00.

It follows from the Two-Factor theory that the aim of mental testing should be to measure the amount of each individual's *g*. If this factor runs through all abilities, it furnishes the only basis of prediction of the subject's performance from one situation to another. It would be futile to measure specific factors, since each operates in only one activity. Accordingly, Spearman proposed that a single test, highly "saturated"[3] with *g*, be substituted

---

[1] Discussed below.

[2] For a discussion of the main points of this theory and its modifications, see 27 and 28.

[3] Spearman employs the term "saturation" to denote the degree to which an activity depends upon the *g* factor.

for the heterogeneous collection of items in intelligence scales. He suggested that tests dealing with abstract relations, such as the analogies test, are the best single measures of *g* and could therefore be employed for this purpose.

In regard to the nature of *g*, Spearman offers only tentative suggestions. He proposes that *g* may be regarded as the general mental energy of the individual and the *s* factors as the "engines" through which it operates, or the specific neurone patterns involved in each activity. This interpretation of *g* and *s* is not, however, an integral nor a basic part of the Two-Factor theory. It might be noted that Spearman's *g* would also furnish a basis for the popular notion of general intelligence.

Even from the outset, Spearman realized that the Two-Factor theory must be qualified. When the activities compared are very similar, a certain degree of correlation may result over and above that attributable to the *g* factor. Thus in addition to the general and specific factors, there might be another intermediate class of factors, not so universal as *g* nor so strictly specific as the *s* factors. Such a factor, which is common to a group of activities but not to all, has been designated a *group factor*. In the early formulation of his theory, Spearman admitted the possibility of very narrow and negligibly small group factors. Following subsequent investigations by several of his students, he included much broader group factors of verbal ability and spatial or "practical" ability.

Finally, on the basis of a series of studies, additional *general* factors were suggested. These include *p* (perseveration), *o* (oscillation), and *w* (will), the last extending the theory to the field of personality traits. It has also been proposed by Spearman (cf. 28) that whereas *g* represents the total amount of mental energy at the subject's disposal, p may denote the inertia of such mental energy, and o the unsteadiness of its supply. Thus all three general factors may be but different manifestations or aspects of the same fundamental factor.

Spearman at present recognizes the presence of all three possible classes of factors, *viz.*, general, group, and specific. The chief differentiating characteristic of his theory seems to be its emphasis upon the g factor as the predominant influence in correlation and its relegation of group factors to a position of minor importance.

Thomson (31-34 and 7) has proposed a *Sampling Theory* of mental organization, which has undergone little or no change since its original formulation. Behavior, according to Thomson, depends upon a very large number of independent elements which he has occasionally identified with neurones or bonds between neurones. Any one activity of the individual depends upon or involves a particular *sample* or pattern of these elements. Correlation results from the *overlapping* of different samples of elements. There may thus be found any number of different types of factors, varying from the specific, through group factors of differing extent, to the general. Thomson has repeatedly illustrated, with data from dice throws,[1] how various factor patterns could result from overlapping samples of independent elements.

Improvement in an activity with practice, according to the Sampling Theory, is not due to improvement in the elementary abilities involved but in a more economical and efficient selection of these abilities. As a practical illustration of this, Thomson cites the well-known dropping out of unnecessary movements in the learning of a motor skill.

[1] Frequently employed in statistics as a means of obtaining purely random or "chance" data.

Thorndike's views on the relationships of mental traits seem to have run the gamut from extreme specificity to the opposite extreme of a single general factor. Thorndike's belief in strict specificity is ordinarily traced to his 1909 article with Lay and Dean (40) in which, after reporting very low correlations between tests of sensory discrimination and estimates of intelligence, Thorndike concluded: "In general there is evidence of a complex set of bonds between the psychological equivalents of both what we call the formal side of thought and what we call its content, so that one is almost tempted to replace Spearman's statement by the equally extravagant one that there is *nothing whatever* common to all mental functions, or to any part of them" (40, p. 368).

Similarly, in the 1914 edition of Thorndike's *Educational Psychology* (35) appeared the following statements: ". . . the mind must be regarded not as a functional unit, nor even as a collection of a few general faculties which work irrespective of particular material, but rather as a multitude of functions, each of which involves content as well as form, and so is related closely to only a few of its fellows, and to others with greater and greater degree of remoteness . . . we need to bear in mind the singularity and relative independence of every mental process, the thoroughgoing specialization of the mind" (35, pp. 366–367). Thorndike also pointed out that "the circumstances of training would seem to sometimes intensify and sometimes weaken original relations" (p. 371). It will be noted that the possibility of narrow group factors is admitted even in these early statements, and the influence of environment in altering the organization of abilities is suggested.

In 1921, following the analysis of intercorrelations among the subtests of Army Alpha and Army Beta,

Thorndike (37) suggested the possibility of fairly broad group factors, including numerical and spatial aptitudes among others. In a symposium on intelligence and its measurement (38) appearing in the same year, he stated: "We know that, taking people as we find them, the ability measured by verbal tests is not the same as the ability measured by non-verbal tests; and there is reason to expect other similar specializations" (38, p. 126). But in this case specialization means group factors of fairly broad extent. At the same time, more emphasis is shifted to the environment as an influence which might produce specialization. This is illustrated by the following statement: "All of the above,[1] of course, concerns individuals as we find them, products of nature and nurture. Spearman's doctrine might fit the *original* nature of intellect better. Certain factors, like ability to understand oral language, ability to read, ability to perceive objects in three dimensions, which occur to everybody as neither entering into all cognitive performances of a person nor entering into only a few very closely similar performances, might in original nature be absorbed into one unitary ability to learn" (38, p. 151).

Thorndike's frequently quoted analysis of intelligence into abstract, mechanical, and social "intelligences," within each of which is found "relatively great consistency" whereas "between one and another of these three there is relatively great disparity," also appeared at this time (36). It is doubtful, however, whether this analysis should be incorporated into a survey of Thorndike's basic theory since it was offered only as a practical suggestion to expedite testing. In any event, it falls in line with the above suggestions of broader group factors.

In *The Measurement of Intelligence* (41), Thorndike

---

[1] Referring to specialization.

swings all the way to a general factor theory with his
Quantity Hypothesis. This hypothesis "asserts that in
their deeper nature the higher forms of intellectual operation are identical with mere association or connection
forming, depending upon the same sort of physiological
connection but requiring *many more of them*. By the same
argument the person whose intellect is greater or higher
or better than that of another person differs from him in
having . . . simply a larger number of connections of
the same sort" (41, p. 415). Thorndike also proposes
that "we may be able for many purposes *to replace our
measurement via a sample inventory of tasks, by a more or
less direct measurement of C*" (41, p. 422). By "*C*" he
refers to the total number of connections which the individual can possibly have by original capacity. Attention
is called to the fact that this hypothesis limits itself to the
organization of original capacity, and that various other
relationships may be environmentally produced. The chief
difference between the Quantity Hypothesis and Spearman's theory seems to be that in the former the number
of possible connections is substituted for mental energy
as the interpretation of the general factor.[1]

Lastly, we may consider what can conveniently be
classified as *Group Factor*, or *Multiple Factor Theories*.
A group factor, it will be recalled, is one which is common
to only a group of activities; it is narrower in extent than
the general factor and broader than specifics. The publication in 1928 of Kelley's *Crossroads in the Mind of Man*
(18) paved the way for a large number of studies in quest
of particular group factors. Kelley contended, after a
critical analysis of the methodology and data of Spear-

[1] Recently, Thorndike has again emphasized specialization, on the basis of the
current findings on trait relationships. He points out, for instance, that many of
the recently proposed group factors "correspond interestingly" to "conceivable
biological realities" (cf. 39).

man, that the general factor is of relatively minor importance and can usually be attributed to the heterogeneity [1] of the subjects and to the common verbal nature of the tests employed. If a residual general factor be found when these influences are ruled out, Kelley claimed that it would probably be very small and insignificant. The major relationships among tests he attributed to a relatively small number of broad group factors. Chief among these were manipulation of spatial relationships, facility with numbers, facility with verbal material, memory, and mental speed.[2]

Methodological Problems

It is not within the scope of this book to discuss the mathematical techniques which have been developed and refined for the analysis of trait relationships. This material is of too technical a nature to be of interest to the general reader. It is, however, necessary to learn something of the general approach to the problem and of its limitations. The present section is intended to serve chiefly as an orientation for the proper understanding of the results to be subsequently reported.

Fundamentally, all techniques for the study of mental organization are based upon the correlation coefficient. This measure indicates the degree of relationship between two sets of scores, or the extent to which each individual's performance in one test corresponds to his performance in another test. Correlation, however, cannot analyze the

---

[1] The influence of heterogeneity upon correlation coefficients will be discussed in the following section.

[2] Various modifications of group factor theories have appeared. Thurstone (42) identifies himself with some form of group factor theory, although he has been more concerned with the development of methods than with the formulation of a definite interpretation. Variations of group factor theory have also been proposed by Garrett (14), Hull (16), Meili (20), and Tryon (43). For a fuller description of each, see Anastasi (5), Ch. I.

mutual interrelationships of a large number of variables. A correlation coefficient may indicate whether there is some factor common to a pair of tests, but it cannot show the presence of a single common factor through three, or four, or any larger number of tests. Let us suppose that all intercorrelations among three tests have been computed, with the following results: [1]

$$r_{12} = .60$$
$$r_{13} = .49$$
$$r_{23} = .70$$

Although all three correlations are positive and high, we cannot determine whether these three tests have one common factor or several common factors among them. Test 1 might share one factor A with test 2, and a different factor B with test 3; a still different factor C might constitute the common element between tests 2 and 3.

It was Spearman (26) who first demonstrated that from the *relationships among correlation coefficients* it is possible to discover the organization of any number of traits. The first method proposed by Spearman was the *hierarchal arrangement* of correlation coefficients. According to this criterion, if it was possible to arrange all the intercorrelations among a set of tests in such a way that they decreased consistently in size both along the rows and along the columns of the table, then the relationships among these tests could be explained entirely in terms of g and *s*. This was a relatively crude "inspectional" method of determining hierarchy. Subsequently, the computation of *intercolumnar correlation* was suggested as a convenient numerical index of hierarchy. The intercolumnar correlation is simply the correlation between columns of correlation coefficients. A + 1.00 intercolum-

---

[1] It is customary to denote the particular variables correlated by subscripts. Thus, r_{12} is the correlation between test No. 1 and test No. 2.

nar correlation would indicate a perfect hierarchal arrangement of the coefficients.

Finally, the intercolumnar correlation was replaced by the *tetrad criterion*. The latter gets its name from the fact that the tests are considered in sets of *four*. For every four tests, or variables, we can compute three tetrad equations as follows:

$$t_{1234} = r_{12} \times r_{34} - r_{13} \times r_{24}$$
$$t_{1243} = r_{12} \times r_{34} - r_{14} \times r_{23}$$
$$t_{1342} = r_{13} \times r_{24} - r_{14} \times r_{23}$$

Spearman and others have been able to prove mathematically that if all three tetrad equations are equal to zero,[1] then a single common factor is sufficient to account for the relationships among the four variables.

This was a decided step forward from the simple correlation coefficient. It was now possible to analyze the interrelationships of any number of variables by computing different sets of tetrads. The extension of the tetrad criterion beyond four variables can be easily demonstrated. Let us suppose that we have administered six tests to the same subjects. First, we compute the three tetrad equations with tests 1, 2, 3, and 4. If all three tetrads are equal to zero, we may conclude that the same factor which underlies tests 1 and 2 is also common to tests 3 and 4. Then if the tetrad criterion is likewise satisfied (i.e., all tetrads equal to zero) with tests 1, 2, 5, and 6, we know that the factor common to 1 and 2 is identical with that common to 5 and 6. Hence the same factor must be common to all six variables.

The introduction of this ingenious technique stimulated much research on mental organization, a problem which might otherwise have remained on the plane of unchecked

[1] Within their probable errors.

speculation. In its specific application and interpretation, however, the tetrad criterion has been the target of much criticism. Its chief critic has probably been Thomson. The latter has repeatedly pointed out and demonstrated that *the tetrad criterion can be satisfied without a g factor* (cf. 31, 32, 33). The satisfaction of the tetrad criterion merely indicates that the observed relationships among the given variables *could be explained* in terms of g and s. But they could also be accounted for by other factor patterns. In other words, tetrad equations can never disprove the possibility of alternative factor analyses of the variables.

The tetrad criterion is also inadequate in that it does not in itself indicate the magnitude or relative importance of the common factor in each variable. Similarly, when the presence of group factors is demonstrated,[1] the weights of these factors in the various tests cannot be determined. Recently, more elaborate and exact procedures have been evolved for the direct analysis of any factor pattern. These methods have become known under the name of *factor pattern analysis*.[2] Like tetrads, they are ultimately based upon certain relationships among correlation coefficients. It is possible by these methods to arrive at the "weight" or "loading" of each factor in each of the variables. A sample of such a factor pattern analysis is shown below.

In this factor pattern, the numbers below each factor show the weight of that factor in each test, or the degree to which performance in the test is attributable to that particular factor. Thus factor I has a large and positive weight in all four tests and is therefore a general factor

---

[1] I.e., when the tetrad equations are not equal to zero.
[2] Several different methods of factor analysis have been worked out; cf., e.g., Hotelling (15), Kelley (19), Thurstone (42).

TABLE XIV

A SAMPLE FACTOR PATTERN ANALYSIS
(After Hotelling, 15, p. 434)

Test	Factor I	Factor II	Factor III	Factor IV
Reading speed	.818	−.438	−.292	.240
Reading power	.695	−.620	.288	−.229
Arithmetic speed	.608	.674	−.376	−.193
Arithmetic power	.578	.660	.459	.143
Percentage of total variance attributable to each factor	46½%	36½%	13%	4%

common to all of these tests. Factor II reveals a differentiation between verbal and arithmetic ability, since it has positive weights in the two arithmetic tests and negative weights in the verbal ones. Factor III has positive weights in the two power tests and negative weights in the two speed tests, thus suggesting a possible distinction between speed and deliberation, or carefulness. The fourth factor is too small to be of any significance. The percentages given in the last row of the table indicate the relative importance of the four factors in all of the tests. Thus the first factor alone is sufficient to account for nearly one-half (46½%) of the relationships found among these four tests, the second factor for 36½%, the third for 13%, and the fourth for a negligible 4%.

It should be kept in mind that the same sort of qualifications made in the interpretation of tetrads applies to factor pattern analyses. In no case is the possibility of alternative explanations precluded. As Thomson has pointed out, with any given body of data, "innumerable factorial analyses are possible, and ... any choice between them must be made on psychological grounds" (34, p. 185). Any set of intercorrelations can be analyzed into factors in an infinite number of ways. In order to arrive at a determinate solution, certain "limiting conditions" must be imposed. The various current methods of factor analysis differ in their choice of limiting conditions, or postulates. It might be noted, however, that in actual practice the general results obtained by these different methods do not differ very significantly.

In concluding this very brief survey of methodological problems, mention should be made of the widely discussed question of heterogeneity. It has been repeatedly demonstrated, both empirically (cf. 10) and theoretically (cf. 13), that the size of a correlation coefficient is affected by the heterogeneity of the group of subjects upon whom the data were collected. The most obvious example is that of age heterogeneity. If the subjects range in age from 3 to 15 years, a high positive correlation will be found between even such diverse characteristics as size of the great toe and Stanford-Binet mental age. The same two measures would yield a zero correlation within a homogeneous age group such as, for example, 10-year-old children. Nor does heterogeneity necessarily raise the correlation coefficient. If a heterogeneous group composed of Chinese and Scandinavians were rated for height and for proficiency in the use of chopsticks, a fairly high *negative* correlation would be obtained between these two measures. The Chinese subjects would, in general, be shorter than the Scandinavians and definitely more adroit with chopsticks. Within either group, however, we should scarcely expect any correlation between these two characteristics.

Correlations which result from a marked degree of heterogeneity in the group are usually regarded as *spurious correlations*. It is difficult to decide, however, just what constitutes a permissible degree of heterogeneity. Obviously, all heterogeneity should not be eliminated, even if this were possible, since individual differences would thereby disappear and correlation would be meaningless. The desired degree of heterogeneity must be determined arbitrarily and on the basis of the particular problem under investigation. It should always be remembered, however, that a correlation coefficient, or any statistical measure derived therefrom, must be interpreted in the light of the particular group upon which it was obtained.

GROUP FACTORS

Perhaps the most general finding of the numerous and varied investigations on mental organization is the presence of group factors of varying extent. It will be recalled that all theories now admit the presence of such factors, although differing in the relative emphasis which they place upon them. There is scarcely a single well controlled study which has not revealed group factors of some sort. The individual's mental activities seem thus to be organized into a relatively small number of independent aptitudes which may combine in various ways in any one task.

Of the group factors proposed by Kelley (18), definite evidence has been found for the *verbal* and *numerical* factors (cf., e.g., 21, 24, 29). *Spatial aptitude* seems to be a composite of more than one independent factor. The administration of the extensive series of Minnesota Mechanical Aptitude Tests to groups of high school boys revealed a number of narrow group factors rather than one unitary factor in the ability to deal with spatial relations (22). Other investigations have indicated the presence of " *practical intelligence* " (1) which is predominant in the performance type of intelligence test. In addition, independent factors of " *mechanical aptitude* " (8) and of " *routine manual aptitude* " (9) have been tentatively established.

The latter is found among motor skills and manipulatory activities.

In regard to a possible common factor of *speed*, the data are very conflicting. In general, there seems little basis for expecting an individual who is fast in one sort of mental activity to be proportionately fast in others. Speed of performance seems to be quite highly specific and to depend upon the nature of each particular task. When evidence is presented for the existence of an independent group factor (cf., e.g., 11), such a factor is very small and is cut across by numerous other group factors.

The same is true of *memory*. Individuals cannot be characterized as possessing a good memory or a poor memory, since they do not manifest uniform powers of retention for different materials. A common factor through memory tests is found only when the tests are also similar in other respects. For example, if all are rote memory tests for relatively meaningless material and all the items are presented visually, then performance on such tests will show a common factor (cf. 2). In such cases, however, the same special devices or aids to memorization can be applied to all the tests. Thus if a subject evolves the device of forcing a meaningful association into the material, this will help him on all the tests and thereby produce a certain uniformity of performance. But such is not the case when memory is tested in a variety of situations, including recall and recognition of logical material, rote memory for numbers and for letter combinations, memory for tones, etc. (cf. 3).

In the measurement of personality, the same techniques of factor pattern analysis are being gradually introduced. Thus, for example, among the various items included in the Bernreuter Personality Inventory, two independent group factors, or "traits" have been identified (12). These have been tentatively described as *sociability* and *self-confidence*. Various investigators have undertaken factor pattern analyses of emotional stability, interests, and other phenomena of personality. Conclusions in regard to the organization of personality traits are still highly tentative, however, owing to the complex nature of the phenomena under investigation and to the relatively recent application of testing techniques to this field.

FORM VERSUS CONTENT

The reader may have noticed that those aptitudes which have been shown to be independent or differentiable traits are characterized by community of material or *content*. When the similarity among the tests was one of process, structure, or *form*, no clear-cut group factor could be discovered within them. Such was the case with speed and memory. Both may be tested with any kind of material. On the other hand, the clearly established verbal and numerical factors are definitely linked up with materials. A common factor will be found through verbal tests, regardless of what the subject is required to do with the words. The individual who ranks relatively high in verbal aptitude will excel in verbal memory, will be faster on a verbal test, more adept at perceiving relations which are expressed linguistically, and so on. Thus content factors cut across the boundaries of form and seem to be the most potent determiners of uniformity of response.[1]

Direct evidence for this conclusion can be found in

---

[1] No fundamental differentiation between form and content is implied by this. The distinction is simply a convenient practical one. To be sure, a group factor is simply an index of relationship among the individual's responses to concrete stimuli. Similarity in that aspect of the situation which is commonly designated as "material" or "content" seems to exert more influence upon such relationships, however, than similarity in any other aspect.

several studies which have employed tests differing both in form and in content. In an investigation with a wide variety of memory tests (3), for example, the specific materials of the tests were found to be much more effective in determining correlation than the methods of testing memory. Thus a logical recall and a logical recognition test, *both involving prose passages*, correlated .74 with each other; it should be noted that these two methods of testing memory are generally considered the most unlike. Similarly, the logical recall and recognition tests correlated .42 and .56, respectively, with a verbal analogies test. The correlations of these two memory tests with other memory tests, on the other hand, were much lower. Logical recognition correlated only .23 with nonsense syllable recognition, for example, although both tests employed the same method of testing memory.

In an investigation designed specifically to test the relative influence of "material" and "structure" in mental organization (25), more conclusive evidence for the same point was obtained. A series of 14 tests was administered to 186 male college students. In respect to material, four of the tests were numerical, four spatial, and five verbal. At least three "structural patterns" were represented, *viz.*, analogies, generalizations, and construction;[1] each of these occurred in all three types of material. A factor pattern analysis of the intercorrelations among these tests indicated that similarity of material was more influential than similarity of structure in producing group factors.

It is interesting to compare the empirically discovered group factors with the proposed mental "faculties" of the medieval Scholastic philosophers, which have found their

---

[1] Including such tests as sentence completion and number series completion, as well as spatial construction tests.

way into popular speech. Whereas the "faculty psychologists" spoke of attention, memory, judgment, reasoning, and similar mental processes, we now find group factors of verbal, numerical, and spatial aptitudes. The latter classification is one of content; the Scholastic was one of function.

SHIFTING COMPONENTS OF MENTAL LIFE

With the rapid accumulation of data on mental organization, certain definite discrepancies have been brought to light. Rather than being stable and universal, trait relationships have been found to vary from one type of subject to another. Spearman called attention to these differences in 1927, stating that, "Another important influence upon the saturation of an ability with g appears to be the class of person at issue" (27, p. 217). At this time, he also reported some data which suggested that among *older* as well as among *brighter* individuals, abilities were more specialized and the general factor played a relatively less dominant part.

Although the data of earlier studies are somewhat conflicting,[1] recent and more adequately controlled investigations have demonstrated a tendency for abilities to be more specialized among *older* subjects and among those in *higher educational levels*. Thus investigations on schoolchildren have usually shown the presence of an appreciable general factor (cf., e.g., 23). It is interesting to note that a large number of the studies by Spearman and his students were conducted on schoolchildren, a fact which might account in part for the insistence of these investigators upon the importance of the g factor. Studies on college groups (cf., e.g., 2, 3, 24), on the other hand, have indicated a much more pronounced specificity,

[1] Cf. Anastasi (5) for a discussion of these data.

with relatively narrow group factors. Recently, some suggestive data have also been presented to show diverse factor patterns among various *occupational groups* (cf. 20). Certain interesting correspondences were noted between the nature of the occupational activities and the organization of the individual's abilities.

Although these discrepancies originally led to controversy or confusion, they are now coming to be recognized as an important means of studying the nature of trait relationships. Thus two recent studies have been conducted with the explicit purpose of discovering age changes in mental organization. In one of these (14), three groups of schoolchildren, aged 9, 12, and 15 years, respectively, were given six memory tests as well as tests of motor speed and verbal, numerical, and spatial aptitudes. The intercorrelations among these tests tended to *decrease with age*, as is indicated by the average intercorrelations of .29, .26, and .14 obtained in the 9, 12, and 15 year groups, respectively. Factor pattern analyses revealed a large general factor whose weight decreased consistently from ages 9 to 15.

In the second study (6), a single group of children were retested after a lapse of three years.[1] Eight tests, including verbal, numerical, and spatial materials, were administered. Intercorrelations dropped from the first to the second testing, this decrease being greater in the correlations *between* verbal and numerical tests than in those *within* either group. Factor pattern analyses corroborated these findings. At both age levels, a large general factor was found, but its magnitude decreased consistently from 9 to 12.

---

[1] The initial data were collected in an earlier investigation (23) on mental organization with a group of 395 children. Of the latter, it was possible to obtain 161 for retesting three years later.

In both of these studies, the changes in mental organization may have resulted from a variety of conditions. The subjects differed in age, in general experience and training, and in academic level. It is therefore impossible to determine what brought about the change in mental organization. It might be argued that mental organization undergoes a progressive and regular alteration with age. On the other hand, the variations observed may have resulted from environmental stimulation and in particular from school instruction. The question can only be answered by an *experimental approach*. If the pattern of trait relationships can be experimentally altered, the influence of environmental stimulation upon mental organization will have been demonstrated.

This was undertaken in a recent experiment by the writer (5). The essential aim of the study was the alteration of a factor pattern by a brief, relevant, interpolated experience. Five tests, including vocabulary, memory span for digits, verbal reasoning of the syllogistic type, code multiplication, and pattern analysis,[1] were administered to 200 sixth grade schoolchildren. All subjects were then given *instruction* in the use of special techniques or devices which would facilitate performance on the last three tests only. This instruction was similar in its general nature to that received in the course of school work, as, for example, in the teaching of arithmetic operations, short-cuts of computation, etc. After a lapse of 13 days, parallel forms of all five tests were administered under exactly the same conditions as in the initial testing. Since the entire experiment covered such a short period, age changes were reduced to a minimum and other outside influences were more uniform than in any previous investigation on this problem.

---

[1] Predominantly a spatial ability test.

For convenience in discussing the data, we shall refer to vocabulary and memory span, the two tests in which no instruction was received, as "non-instruction" tests; the remaining three tests will be referred to as "instruction" tests. A comparison of the intercorrelations among the five variables in the initial and final testing showed practically no change in the correlation between the two "non-instruction" tests, a slight change in the correlations between "instruction" and "non-instruction" tests, and a marked change in the correlations among the three "instruction" tests. Factor pattern analyses [1] revealed a wide variation from the initial to the final testing. An examination of the weights of each factor in the five tests before and after instruction suggested that the changes were such as would have been expected from the nature of the interpolated experience.

All of the above investigations indicate that "factors" cannot be regarded as fixed and immutable. Nor can they be interpreted in terms of underlying psychological entities. A "factor" is simply a mathematical statement of observed relationships among a group of concrete behavior manifestations (cf. 4). And by relationship is meant nothing more than a tendency to concomitant variation. When we say that performance on two tasks is related, we mean simply that those individuals who excel in one tend also to excel in the other. To conclude any more than this from a factor pattern analysis is mere speculation.

THE RÔLE OF ENVIRONMENT

The possibility of artificial alteration of a factor pattern demonstrates the susceptibility of mental organization to experiential conditions. The experiment described in

[1] Computed by Hotelling's (15) method of principal components.

the preceding section reproduced, in a highly condensed form, the type of experience to which the child is exposed in the course of school work and other everyday activities. It is therefore entirely possible that factor patterns are determined in the first place by the nature of such experiences. The diverse factor patterns which have been found in different populations may thus have been environmentally produced. Insofar as the experiences of all of the groups employed in such studies have common features, certain fundamental similarities in their mental organization have been discovered. Insofar, however, as these experiences have varied from group to group, different patterns of mental organization were found. Thus a very widespread "verbal factor" could easily develop in our culture in which language plays so important a part in a wide variety of fields. If there were an educational system in which only woodcraft and poetry were taught, we might indeed find a "group factor" common to these two abilities and to no other. Those subjects who had spent more time and effort on their academic work would excel in both tasks, but not necessarily in other fields of activity. The experimental findings which have been reported furnish an illustration of how "group factors" might be produced or obliterated by the subject's experience.

It also follows that trait relationships may vary with age within the same individuals. As the subject's experiences accumulate throughout his life, certain alterations in the pattern of mental organization will take place. The relationships of performance in the same or similar situations will not remain constant over a long period of time. If the lapse of time is short, the influence of the intervening experience may be too slight to produce an appreciable difference in factor pattern. Over a long period, however, the cumulative effect will become apparent, as in the comparison of children with adults.

In summary, it would seem that the relationships among the individual's performance on a number of tests *at any one time* may be explained in terms of a small number of independent unitary factors. Under existing cultural conditions, a certain degree of uniformity of factor patterns is found because of a general environmental uniformity. Traditional educational curricula and vocational classifications have probably contributed much towards this uniformity. Thus in the young schoolchild, we find a large general factor through all types of activities which are taught in our schools, the so-called "higher mental processes." As the child grows older and specialization of function is encouraged, certain culturally determined differentiations appear. "Group factors" are produced in linguistic, mathematical, mechanical, and possibly other functions. These factors, however, are only a mathematical statement or conceptual simplification of the observed relations among concrete responses. And as such they may be expected to shift from time to time in the same subjects or from one population to another because of varying experiences.

Thus the rôle of environment is again forcefully demonstrated. In view of the dependence of the individual's behavioral development upon environmental stimulation, it is not surprising to find that the *relationships* among various classes of behavior are also environmentally determined. The existence of innate or fixed patterns of trait relationship could scarcely be expected when the traits themselves have been found to be so profoundly influenced by experiential conditions.

REFERENCES

1. Alexander, W. P. "Intelligence, Concrete and Abstract: a Study in Differential Traits," *Brit. J. Psychol., Mon. Suppl.*, No. 19, 1935. Pp. 177.

2. Anastasi, A. "A Group Factor in Immediate Memory," *Arch. Psychol.*, No. 120, 1930. Pp. 61.

3. ——. "Further Studies on the Memory Factor," *Arch. Psychol.*, No. 142, 1932. Pp. 60.

4. ——. "Some Ambiguous Concepts in the Field of Mental Organization," *Amer. J. Psychol.*, 1935, 47, 508–511.

5. ——. "The Influence of Specific Experience upon Mental Organization," *Genet. Psychol. Mon.*, 1936, 18, No. 4, 245–355.

6. Asch, S. E. "A Study of Change in Mental Organization," *Arch. Psychol.*, No. 195, 1936. Pp. 30.

7. Brown, W., and Thomson, G. H. *The Essentials of Mental Measurement.* London: Cambridge Univ. Press, 1925. Pp. 224.

8. Cox, J. W. *Mechanical Aptitude—Its Existence, Nature, and Measurement.* London: Methuen, 1928. Pp. 209.

9. ——. *Manual Skill—Its Organization and Development.* London: Cambridge Univ. Press, 1934. Pp. 247.

10. Cureton, E. E., and Dunlap, J. W. "Some Effects of Heterogeneity on the Theory of Factors," *Amer. J. Psychol.*, 1930, 42, 608–620.

11. DuBois, P. H. "A Speed Factor in Mental Tests," *Arch. Psychol.*, No. 141, 1932. Pp. 38.

12. Flanagan, J. C. *Factor Analysis in the Study of Personality.* Stanford Univ., Calif.: Stanford Univ. Press, 1935. Pp. 103.

13. Garrett, H. E., and Anastasi, A. "The Tetrad-Difference Criterion and the Measurement of Mental Traits," *Ann. N. Y. Acad. Sci.*, 1932, 33, 234–281.

14. Garrett, H. E., Bryan, A. I., and Perl, R. E. "The Age Factor in Mental Organization," *Arch. Psychol.*, No. 176, 1935. Pp. 31.

15. Hotelling, H. "Analysis of a Complex of Statistical Variables into Principal Components," *J. Educ. Psychol.*, 1933, 24, 417–441; 498–520.

16. Hull, C. L. *Aptitude Testing.* Yonkers-on-Hudson: World Book Co., 1928. Pp. 535.

17. Kelley, T. L. *Interpretation of Educational Measurements.* Yonkers-on-Hudson: World Book Co., 1927. Pp. 363.

18. ——. *Crossroads in the Mind of Man: a Study of Differentiable Mental Abilities.* Stanford Univ., Calif.: Stanford Univ. Press, 1928. Pp. 238.

19. ——. *Essential Traits of Mental Life.* Cambridge: Harvard Univ. Press, 1935. Pp. 145.

20. Meili, R. "Recherches sur les formes d'intelligence," *Arch. de psychol.*, 1930, 22, 201–284.

21. *N. Y. College Entrance Examination Board: Reports of the Commission on Scholastic Aptitude Tests,* 1926–1936.

22. Paterson, D. G., *et al. Minnesota Mechanical Ability Tests.* Minneapolis: Univ. Minn. Press, 1930. Pp. 586.

23. Schiller, B. "Verbal, Numerical, and Spatial Abilities of Young Children," *Arch. Psychol.*, No. 161, 1934. Pp. 69.

24. Schneck, M. M. R. "The Measurement of Verbal and Numerical Abilities," *Arch. Psychol.*, No. 107, 1929. Pp. 49.

25. Smith, G. M. "Group Factors in Mental Tests Similar in Material or in Structure," *Arch. Psychol.*, No. 156, 1933. Pp. 56.

26. Spearman, C. "'General Intelligence' Objectively Determined and Measured," *Amer. J. Psychol.*, 1904, 15, 201–293.

27. ——. *The Abilities of Man.* N. Y.: Macmillan, 1927. Pp. 415.

28. ——. "'G' and After—a School to End Schools." In *Psychologies of 1930,* C. Murchison, ed. Worcester: Clark Univ. Press, 1930. Pp. 339–366.

29. Stephenson, W. "Tetrad-Differences for Verbal Subtests Relative to Non-Verbal Subtests," *J. Educ. Psychol.*, 1931, 22, 334–350.

30. Terman, L. M. "The Vocabulary Test as a Measure of Intelligence," *J. Educ. Psychol.*, 1918, 9, 452–456.

31. Thomson, G. H. "A Hierarchy without a General Factor," *Brit. J. Psychol.*, 1916, 8, 271–281.

32. ——. "A Worked Out Example of the Possible Linkages of

Four Correlated Variables on the Sampling Theory," *Brit. J. Psychol.*, 1927, 18, 68–76.

33. ——. "On Complete Families of Correlation Coefficients and Their Tendency to Zero Tetrad-Differences: Including a Statement of the Sampling Theory of Abilities," *Brit. J. Psychol.*, 1935, 26, 63–92.

34. ——. "The Factorial Analysis of Human Abilities," *Human Factor*, 1935, 9, 180–185.

35. Thorndike, E. L., *Educational Psychology*. N. Y.: Teachers College, Columbia Univ., 1914. Vol. III.

36. ——. "Intelligence and Its Uses," *Harper's Magazine*, 1920, 140, 227–235.

37. ——. "On the Organization of Intellect," *Psychol. Rev.*, 1921, 28, 141–151.

38. ——. "Intelligence and Its Measurement: a Symposium," *J. Educ. Psychol.*, 1921, 12, 124–127.

39. ——. "The Organization of Mind," *Proceed., Forty-third Annual Meeting, Amer. Psychol. Assoc.*, 1935, 61–62.

40. Thorndike, E. L., Lay, W., and Dean, P. R. "The Relation of Accuracy in Sensory Discrimination to General Intelligence," *Amer. J. Psychol.*, 1909, 20, 364–369.

41. Thorndike, E. L., *et al. The Measurement of Intelligence*. N. Y.: Teachers College, Columbia Univ., 1926. Pp. 616.

42. Thurstone, L. L. *Vectors of Mind: Multiple-Factor Analysis for the Isolation of Primary Traits*. Chicago: Univ. Chicago Press, 1935. Pp. 266.

43. Tryon, R. C. "A Theory of *Psychological* Components—an Alternative to 'Mathematical Factors,'" *Psychol. Rev.*, 1935, 42, 425–454.

PART II

ANALYSIS OF MAJOR GROUP DIFFERENCES

CHAPTER XII

THE SUBNORMAL

In Part I we surveyed some of the major problems and findings on *individual differences* and attempted to unravel the factors and conditions which produce variation from one person to another. With this background, we may now turn to an examination of certain *groups* into which individuals are commonly classified. Such groupings have been built up through social and cultural traditions and illustrate the general tendency to employ rigid categories and sharp divisions. Thus individuals are popularly classed into the normal and the abnormal, the genius, the feebleminded, the insane, the neurotic. Psychological differences are expected, or at least sought, between the sexes or among nations or "races." Many other groupings can likewise be construed. A person can be classified, for example, in regard to religion, political affiliation, or even place of residence. Psychological differences might be expected between urban and rural populations, or between groups inhabiting regions of different geographical character, such as mountainous or flat, inland or coastal, cold or warm.

These various groupings, like all rigid classifications of individuals, are arbitrary and artificial. In all behavioral traits, people are distributed according to the normal bell-shaped curve and cannot be assigned to distinct categories. When the distributions of any two biologically or culturally differentiated groups, such as the sexes, or "racial" and national groups, are compared, the overlapping is so large as to render any difference between averages of doubtful practical significance. In such comparisons, the difference between the averages is far smaller than the range of difference within either group. *In the study of individuals, the only proper unit is the individual.* There is no short-cut to the understanding of people, no possibility of learning the behavioral peculiarities of a few broad groups into which any individual could then be conveniently pigeon-holed.

The multiple and complex determination of the individual's behavioral development should in itself make us skeptical regarding any simple systems of characterizing people. Yet it is an all too common practice to expect an individual to be dependable, or shiftless, or dull, or excitable, or poor in mechanics, or to ascribe to him dozens of similar characteristics, simply from the knowledge that such a person is a man or a woman, or that he belongs to a particular "race" or nation.

It is partly to clarify these very muddled popular notions that the empirical study of group differences ought to be undertaken. To be sure, a careful examination of the principles underlying individual variation in general should suffice to show the fallacies inherent in many popular claims regarding group differences. But when beliefs are as deep-rooted and emotionally tinged as those governing many group relations, they are not easily dislodged. Direct evidence on the nature of group differences is more convincing than deductions from generally established principles.

From a more theoretical point of view, the analysis of group differences is a valuable adjunct to the investigation of individual differences in general. The existence of culturally diverse groups may be regarded as furnishing a natural experiment in the production of human variability. If psychological differences among groups are investigated with reference to the factors which brought them about, the understanding of individual differences will have been considerably furthered.

In the present analysis of group differences, we shall be more concerned with fundamental concepts and methodological issues than with a cataloguing of results. The latter have little meaning unless critically evaluated. The data on group differences are difficult to interpret and have frequently led to opposite conclusions in the hands of different writers. It is of fundamental importance, therefore, that the special difficulties inherent in group comparisons be clearly realized and that the necessary cautions and controls be applied before making any generalizations. With a clear understanding of the problem, the reader will be in a position to make his own interpretation of any data which he may come across. And he will also be able to guard against the pernicious habit of overhasty generalization and to detect the fallacies in erroneous statements with which he may be confronted. Objective and critical habits of thinking are more urgently needed in the field of group differences than are randomly gathered data. Of the latter there is a sizable accumulation, while the former are all too frequently lacking even in supposedly scientific discussions.

Historical Views of Mental Disorder

The first traditional grouping with which we shall deal is that of *normal* and *abnormal*. From the earliest periods of human history, we find instances of conspicuous deviates whom we should now regard as feebleminded or insane.[1] Such individuals were generally considered to be distinct beings, either representing a lower order of humanity or

[1] For a historical survey of conceptions and treatment of insanity and feeblemindedness, see Farrar (9) and Hollingworth (14), Chs. 2 and 3.

"possessed" by spirits. These spirits were usually considered to be evil, although in certain cases they were looked upon as gods. This *demonological view* was particularly prevalent during the Dark Ages and reflects the influence of Christianity upon the thought of the period. At this time, it was Satan who was thought to "possess" the demented person. Such a condition was supposed to be visited upon the individual either as a punishment for his sins or as an ordeal to test his moral fortitude and religious faith. Thus many persons who were subsequently sanctified by the church experienced epileptic seizures, hysterical paralyses or anæsthesias, hallucinations, paranoid delusions, and similar well known symptoms of insanity. The treatment of mental disorders consisted of exorcism, physical abuse, or veneration, depending upon the particular theological doctrine which happened to be current or upon the specific circumstances of the subject's life.

The *medical view* of mental disorders, on the other hand, was put forth as early as the fifth century B.C. by the Greek physician, Hippocrates. The latter proposed that mental disorders result from disease or injury to the brain. He also wrote extensively on various classes of mental disorders and their probable physical bases. For many centuries, the doctrines of Hippocrates were accepted unquestionably. They were suppressed during the Dark Ages, together with most of the scientific knowledge of the Greeks, but were again resumed with the revival of scientific interest and the development of anatomy and physiology during the Renaissance. The medical conception of mental abnormalities is still prevalent at present, especially among psychiatrists.[1]

The *psychological study* of the abnormal is of relatively

[1] A psychiatrist is a physician who specializes in mental disorders.

recent date. Its approach to the problem is through a direct study of *behavior*. Behavioral disorders are explained in terms of behavioral principles, rather than by reference to some other realm or class of phenomena. *Abnormal psychology* is an empirical and direct study of extreme deviations in behavioral traits. As such it has been regarded as a branch of differential psychology.

THE CONCEPT OF ABNORMALITY

The term abnormal, which means literally "away from the norm," has been used to cover at least three distinct concepts.[1] First, we may consider the *anti-normative* view which regards as abnormal any deviation from the ideal or perfect condition. The norm in such a case is a goal or *desideratum* to be approximated by the existing conditions. To be "normal," according to this view, would be the exception rather than the rule. Such a use of the terms normal and abnormal is illustrated by a number of common expressions. To say that a person is one of the "lucky few" who have a normal skin or normal teeth, for example, implies an identification of normality with freedom from defects or other imperfections. Or to assert that few can remain normal under the stress and strain of modern life suggests that normality is an ideal state of perfect composure and stability.

A second view identifies abnormality with *pathological* or dangerous conditions. This usage is particularly common in medicine. To be classed as abnormal in this sense would have distinctly undesirable connotations. Such a view may be regarded as an adaptation of the anti-normative concept to meet practical and social requirements. The abnormal still represents a deviation from a perfect condition, but the deviation is now so great as to

[1] Cf. Hollingworth (14) and Foley (11).

present practical difficulties. The condition requires action of some sort for the protection either of the individual or of society. Thus a person who exhibits a few mild neurotic symptoms, such as a compulsion to avoid stepping on the cracks in the sidewalk or a slight twitching of the forehead, may elicit the remark: "a bit queer, yes—but not serious— nothing *really abnormal* about him." But let such an individual become so depressed over an imagined or exaggerated wrong that his work must be discontinued, or let him threaten a suspected enemy with physical violence, and he will immediately earn the appellation "abnormal." According to this view, only a very small number of individuals are abnormal, the large majority being indiscriminately classified as normal.

Both of the above views necessitate an arbitrary norm or standard. In the first, the norm is a theoretical ideal, in the latter a practical criterion of individual and social survival. A more objective and empirical approach to the problem is furnished by a purely *statistical* concept of abnormality. The norm in this case is the average. It is the usual and most common condition. The abnormal is the unusual, the relatively infrequent. The more infrequent a condition, furthermore, the more abnormal it is considered. Many conditions classed as abnormal in the pathological sense would also be regarded as statistically abnormal because of their relative rarity. On the other hand, the majority of those individuals classed as abnormal according to the anti-normative view would be considered *normal*, since they constitute the large, intermediate, and most representative segment of the population. Similarly, those who approximate the ideal or perfect state too closely would now be regarded as abnormal, since they deviate significantly from the ordinary, average individual.

It follows from the statistical view that the abnormal may be *either inferior or superior* to the normal. The abnormal corresponds simply to the two ends of the normal distribution curve. Since the curve is symmetrical, the superior deviate is just as abnormal as the inferior, in the sense that he is equally far from the norm. It is apparent that this is the only sense in which abnormality can be objectively determined and measured. To speak of inferiority and superiority implies evaluation in terms of specific biological and cultural requirements. Such evaluation is characterized by a certain degree of impermanence and subjectivity which often confuse the problem. A purely statistical concept of abnormality, on the other hand, limits itself to an incontrovertible and empirical criterion.

It is in the statistical sense that the term abnormal will be employed in the present discussion. In respect to any specific situation, the abnormal will be further subdivided into the subnormal and the super-normal. The present chapter will be concerned with the subnormal deviates. The super-normal will be considered in the following chapter on "genius." These two groups of extreme deviates should be constantly viewed in their proper perspective, as opposite ends of a continuous distribution curve.

It is noteworthy that the terms abnormal and subnormal are frequently employed interchangeably. In everyday speech, it has become almost impossible to use the word abnormal in its innocuous etymological sense. To congratulate a great scientist upon a recent discovery by informing him that we consider him extremely abnormal would probably be a breach of etiquette. Nor is this confusion restricted to popular usage. Most textbooks on abnormal psychology, for example, deal exclusively with the subnormal. A few make brief mention of the logical need for including "genius" in this category. Having acknowledged this fact, however, they then devote all subsequent chapters to the subnormal.

The identification of abnormality with subnormality may result in part from the influence of the anti-normative and pathological views. Such a confusion of terms also offers an interesting commentary upon human thought. It is an all too common practice to regard as inferior whatever differs from oneself. Mutual racial prejudices are a good example of this tendency. The strange paradox that several distinct groups may each regard themselves as superior to all the others is attributable to this human characteristic. To be too different from oneself must surely imply some sort of defect, otherwise one's self-respect would be too seriously impaired!

THE FEEBLEMINDED

Feeblemindedness represents the lower end of the distribution of intelligence. It is characterized by intellectual rather than emotional defect. The term feeblemindedness is not used, however, to cover deficiency in *any* ability. Thus an individual may be far below average in music, drawing, or even mechanical aptitude, and still be regarded as intellectually normal. *Feeblemindedness designates a deficiency only in those abilities which have proved essential for survival in our cultural milieu.*

As was indicated in the preceding chapter, *verbal ability* probably plays the dominant rôle in our conception of feeblemindedness. Linguistic aptitude has often been explicitly accepted as a criterion of mental deficiency. Thus Binet and Simon (4) wrote: "An idiot is a person who is not able to communicate with his fellows by means of language. He does not talk at all and does not understand." Similarly, Esquirol (cf. 14, p. 165) distinguished between three levels of feeblemindedness: (a) those making cries only; (b) those using monosyllables; (c) those using short phrases but not elaborate speech. Another classification which is still widely quoted (cf. 14, pp. 165–166) is that between: (a) Idiots, who are incapable of spoken language, and are limited to gestures; (b) Imbeciles, who are able to understand and employ spoken language; and (c) Morons, who are capable of acquiring also written language, but have difficulty with the more complex verbal and abstract concepts.

Feeblemindedness has been described from many points of view. Probably the most common definitions are the *sociological*, or economic, and the *psychometric*. A widely quoted schema of classification adopted in 1908 by the Royal Commission on the Feebleminded, of Great Britain (5), illustrates the *sociological* conception. This classification recognizes three grades of feeblemindedness, characterized as follows:

1. Idiot (low grade amentia)—"A person so deeply defective from birth or from an early age that he is unable to guard himself against common physical dangers."

2. Imbecile (middle grade amentia)—"One who, by reason of mental defect existing from birth or from an early age, is incapable of earning his own living, but is capable of guarding himself against common physical dangers."

3. Moron [1] (high grade amentia)—"One who is capable of earning a living under favorable circumstances, but who is incapable, from mental defect existing from birth or from an early age, (a) of competing on equal terms with his normal fellows, (b) of managing his affairs and himself with ordinary prudence."

[1] In England, the term "feebleminded" refers to the high grade aments, and "amentia" is used as a general term to cover all degrees of mental deficiency. The term "moron" has been substituted for "feebleminded" in the above definition, in accordance with the more familiar American usage.

The *psychometric* classification is more common among mental testers and admits of more quantitative definition. When applied only to adults, the differentiation is often made on the basis of *mental age*. Thus an adult whose mental age is three years or less is usually regarded as an idiot; between three and seven is the imbecile level; morons fall above a mental age of seven but fail to reach the average adult level. To make the classification applicable to children as well as adults, the limits have been expressed in terms of I.Q. Terman's classification (23, p. 79) is probably the most widely employed and has been reproduced below.

Designation	*I.Q.*
Dullness, rarely classifiable as feeblemindedness	80–90
Borderline deficiency, sometimes classifiable as dullness, often as feeblemindedness	70–80
Moron	50–70
Imbecile	20–50
Idiot	below 20

It should be borne in mind that these distinctions are purely arbitrary and are made only for practical convenience. There is no sharp dividing line either between the normal and the feebleminded, or between the various "levels" of feeblemindedness. The intellectual differences are of degree only and form a continuous gradation, although the social effects may differ qualitatively.

The feebleminded have also been classified in respect to physical characteristics. According to the early medical conceptions, feeblemindedness was a disease which was expected to show physical as well as mental symptoms. The percentage of feebleminded persons who present a distinct morphological picture proved, however, to be very small.[1] The large remaining majority had to be given

[1] Hollingworth, for example, estimates the number as only 10% (14, p. 159).

the unrevealing appellation of "simple amentia." The major clinical varieties of feeblemindedness which have been differentiated include microcephaly, hydrocephaly, cretinism, and Mongolism.

The *microcephalic* has an abnormally small, pointed skull, producing a characteristic "sugar-loaf" appearance. The *hydrocephalic* has a very large skull and an excessive amount of cerebro-spinal fluid intervening between the skull and the brain. The *cretin* has already been described in a different connection (cf. Ch. VIII). He is easily identified by his stunted physique, coarse thick skin, loss of hair, and other physical characteristics. This condition has been definitely linked with a thyroid deficiency and has been frequently relieved by repeated administration of thyroid extract in early childhood. *Mongolism* acquired its name from a certain facial resemblance to the Mongolian race. This similarity, it should be mentioned, is quite superficial and slight. The peculiar, narrow, slanting eyes characteristic of this type of ament were chiefly responsible for the alleged resemblance to the Mongolian face. This condition can also be distinguished by the shape of the skull and certain peculiarities of the tongue.[1]

Apart from the relatively small number of cases classifiable into these special clinical varieties, the feebleminded are not clearly differentiated from the normal in physical traits. Data relevant to this question have already been presented in Chapter VIII. It will be recalled that in such physical measures as height and weight, the differences between the averages of normal and feebleminded subjects were small and the overlapping large. It is true that in practically every comparison the feebleminded are con-

---

[1] For a comprehensive survey of these clinical varieties as well as the characteristics of the feebleminded in general, the reader is referred to Tredgold (25); see also 22, for a discussion of feeblemindedness in children.

sistently below normal in physical as well as mental traits (cf., e.g., 8, 20). But in evaluating these findings, we must bear in mind the influence of social and economic level upon both physical and mental development. In dealing with institutional cases, furthermore, the operation of selective factors must be taken into account.[1]

It has been repeatedly demonstrated that the feebleminded are not equally deficient in all functions and that the degree of their inferiority increases as we go from simple sensory and motor traits to complex intellectual processes, and especially "symbolic" activities (cf. 6, 14, 20). Norsworthy, for example, found that the percentage of feebleminded subjects out of a group of 157 who reached or exceeded the median score of normal groups was much greater in the simple sensory and perceptual functions than in abstract verbal tests. The same was true when the percentages who reached or exceeded the −1 P.E. point rather than the median were compared.[2] The data for both types of comparison are presented below (cf. 20, p. 68).

Function Tested	Percentage of Feebleminded Subjects Who Reached or Exceeded:	
	Median of Normal Group	−1 P.E. of Normal Group
Comparison of weights	18	28
Cancelling A's	9	18
Cancelling words containing *a* and *t*	1	14
Memory for unrelated words	6	18
Memory for related words	5	19
Association: part-whole	9	17
Association: genus-species	9	16
Association: opposites, form 1	0	0.9
Association: opposites, form 2	0	1

Similarly, Burt (6) collected data on the relative achievements of 143 mental defectives in different school

---

[1] Cf. Ch. VIII for a discussion of both points.

[2] In a normal group, 75% of the cases would reach or exceed −1 P.E.

subjects. Performance in each subject was expressed as
a ratio of the average achievement expected from normal
children of the same age. These ratios are reproduced
below.

School Subject	Educational Ratio
Spelling	.460
Reading comprehension	.489
Composition	.514
Reading: accuracy and speed	.534
Subtraction	.534
Division	.553
Addition	.565
Multiplication	.589
Writing: speed and quality	.609
Drawing	.649
Handwork	.697

It is apparent from this analysis of abilities along various lines that the feebleminded *as a group* are most deficient in verbal tasks. In arithmetic, their performance is
intermediate, and in activities involving mechanical aptitude or motor skill, they are closest to the norm. This
does not mean, however, that such a hierarchy of deficiency exists within the individual feebleminded person.
The same result might follow if there were *more* feebleminded persons deficient in verbal ability, fewer deficient
in arithmetic ability, and fewest in mechanical or motor
aptitudes. The relationship between such group averages
depends not only upon the relative amount of inferiority
displayed by each individual, but also upon the *number*
of persons who are inferior. Since verbal aptitude plays
such a large part in the criterion of feeblemindedness,
almost all persons in a feebleminded group will be definitely below normal in this trait. This consistent inferiority will of course produce a very low group average in
verbal traits.

In arithmetic aptitude, many will be below average, some may be normal, and a few even superior. The slight positive correlation between performance on arithmetic and verbal tests, as well as the fact that arithmetic tests are frequently included in scales of "general intelligence," would lead us to expect the *majority*, but not all, feebleminded subjects to be below the norms in arithmetic aptitude. This would result in a group average higher than that in verbal traits, but still considerably below normal.

In tasks involving motor skills or aptitude in mechanics, music, or pictorial art, we should expect the feebleminded to be distributed very similarly to a normal group, since these traits show little or no correlation with verbal ability or intelligence test performance. The majority would in this case be normal, only a small number inferior, and a few superior. As a result, the status of the group as a whole would be only slightly below normal. Thus it is apparent that the hierarchy of deficiency usually found in feebleminded groups is a result of the culturally imposed criterion of feeblemindedness as well as the organization of abilities.

The Insane

Insanity consists of a marked deviation in emotional or other personality traits. The individual, although intellectually normal or even superior, is unable to make a satisfactory adjustment because of serious personality disorders. Thus he may have delusions of persecution, which make him suspect all with whom he comes into contact of plotting against him, or delusions of grandeur, in which he believes himself to be Napoleon or some other favorite character. Such symptoms are classified under *paranoia*. Or he may develop such extreme introverted tendencies as to lose all contact with his fellow-beings and with occurrences about him, as in *dementia præcox*. His symptoms may consist of recurrent periods of extreme depression and excitement, as in *manic-depressive* insanity. These examples will suffice to show the varied forms which insanity may take. We are not here concerned with a classification of insanities, or *psychoses*, into the common clinical varieties, nor with an enumeration of symptoms. This material can be found in any standard textbook of psychiatry and in many books on abnormal psychology (cf., e.g., 17, 18, 19). We are concerned only with the general psychological nature of such psychoses.

In the first place, insanity is not to be confused with feeblemindedness. The insane are recruited from all intellectual levels. Many psychotics fall within the normal range of intelligence. Instances are not unknown among the highly gifted. And likewise, insanity may occur in feebleminded individuals, although for some psychoses, such as paranoia, a certain degree of complexity of mental life seems to be required. A number of psychotic conditions, such as dementia præcox, lead to intellectual deterioration, but there are others, such as paranoia, in which the subject may suffer no impairment of abilities.

As in the case of feeblemindedness, there is no sharp dividing line between insanity and normality. Sharp distinctions are made for practical purposes of confinement, treatment, and similar reasons, but close examination reveals a continuous, unbroken gradation from the thoroughly well-adjusted person to the conspicuously insane. Psychotic symptoms differ only in degree from the behavioral peculiarities of the normal individual. From the blissful optimist who trusts implicitly whomever he meets to the paranoiac who believes that the stranger who accidentally brushes against him is plotting his demise, there are all degrees of "suspiciousness." The same may be said of all other characteristics of the insane. A good example of this is the familiar case of the student who, upon reading a manual of psychiatry or attending a course in abnormal psychology, believes himself to be afflicted with each form of psychosis in turn. Most of us can discover in ourselves at least one characteristic of many types of insanity, in mild form. It is not normal, in the statistical sense, to be entirely free from all such slight peculiarities.

A fundamental distinction from the viewpoint of the psychologist is that between *organic* and *functional* disorders. Briefly, organic disturbances are those which can be definitely attributed to a structural deficiency. In functional disorders, on the other hand, there seems to be only a faulty operation or deficient action of apparently normal structures.[1] Thus general paresis has been definitely traced to the influence of syphilitic infection upon the nervous system; a group of psychoses have been shown to develop from excessive use of alcohol or drugs; injuries, or lesions, to certain parts of the brain or lower nerve centers lead to characteristic behavioral deficiencies. There remain, however, a large number of psychotic conditions for which no physical basis has been discovered. Some claim that the physical concomitants of such behavioral disorders are only undiscovered and that ultimately all will be adequately explained in structural terms.[2]

There is a growing conviction, however, especially

---

[1] This distinction, although generally employed only with reference to personality disorders, could be applied equally well to feeblemindedness. Cretinism, for example, represents an organic mental deficiency resulting from physical disorders. In nearly 90% of feebleminded cases, however, no structural deficiency can be discovered and the disturbance might be regarded as functional. In a few instances, as in isolation amentia, the functional nature of the disorder is clearly demonstrated.

[2] For a discussion of various forms of insanity from this point of view, see Moss and Hunt (19).

among psychologists, that these disorders may be purely functional in their origin and involve no structural impairment. If this be the case, we should seek the causes of psychotic conditions in the mechanism of learning and in the environmental conditions which have surrounded the individual.[1] This question is still a highly controversial one to which no final answer can be given as yet.

That many behavioral disorders are functional can, however, be clearly demonstrated. A number of tests have been suggested for diagnosing the functional nature of several types of symptoms (cf. 14, Ch. 10). Thus functional disorders are more often *intermittent* and *occasional* than organic disorders and may depend upon the presence of a specific situation or stimulus. The symptom may only be manifested, for example, in the presence of certain individuals or in a particular locality. Functional disorders are also more *variable*, exhibiting more individual idiosyncracy from one case to another. Functional symptoms of a motor or sensory nature can usually be detected because of their *anatomical impossibility*. The so-called "stocking and glove" anæsthesia, for example, is a loss of sensitivity in regions which are unitary only in popular thought, but do not correspond to any neurologically possible division. In certain types of symptoms, special methods of examination, employing unusual situations unknown to the subject, will also reveal the functional nature of the disorder.

Finally, a very striking characteristic of functional disorders is their susceptibility to various fantastic *methods of treatment*. In general, nearly any conceivable procedure or technique may cure such symptoms, *provided the patient is convinced of its efficacy*. The success of many systems of

---

[1] For a vivid analysis of the method whereby such disorders might be built up through learning, cf. Watson (26).

mental therapy which have achieved widespread publicity can be attributed to this peculiar characteristic of functional symptoms. Similarly, the sudden, startling, and miraculous "cures" effected at various shrines, one of the best known of which is that of Sainte Anne de Beaupré in Canada, testify to the functional nature of the disorders. Dramatic incidents are recounted of the blind who suddenly regained their vision, or of the crippled who abandoned their crutches and walked forth erect. The same results have occasionally been observed in a severe emergency, as when a supposedly hopeless cripple arises from his chair to save a loved one from drowning or fire.

The history of such cases usually reveals a certain obscurity of diagnosis. Physicians were baffled, the case was declared hopeless or a mystery, thus adding to the glamor of the "cure." What this suggests, however, is the functional nature of the disorder which naturally defied organic diagnosis and treatment.

In closing this brief survey, mention should be made of the fact that these disorders are no less "real" because they are functional. The subject may suffer just as acutely and be as seriously handicapped as if he had a definite structural deficiency. Similarly, such disturbances cannot be overcome merely by voluntary effort. Nor should they be confused with malingering. The subject himself is undergoing as vivid an experience as if he had an organic disorder and he may be completely unaware of the fact that his symptoms have no structural basis.

The Neurotic

Neuroses may be regarded as milder forms of personality disorder than the psychoses. They are also more generally regarded as functional in their nature than the latter. In their specific manifestations, they bridge the gap between the slightly maladjusted and emotionally unstable individual on the one hand and the distinctly insane on the other. On the basis of the normal distribution of behavioral traits, we should expect neurotics to be more numerous than psychotics, since they are nearer the center of the curve. This seems to be borne out by observation, although it is difficult to obtain accurate data on the relative incidence of such disorders because of loose methods of diagnosis.

A common classification of neuroses recognizes three major types differentiated on the basis of symptomatology, *viz.*, psychasthenia, neurasthenia, and hysteria. Typical *psychasthenic* symptoms are phobias, or abnormal fears, compulsions, obsessions, worries, restlessness, and irritability. *Neurasthenia* is characterized by such symptoms as dizzy spells, headaches, excessive feelings of fatigue, digestive disturbances, and the like. *Hysteria* covers motor and sensory disturbances, such as tremors, contractions, paralyses, loss of sensation, and heightened sensitivity, as as well as fits of unconsciousness, loss of memory, and similar somnambulistic disorders. It has been suggested (cf. 14, pp. 403–404) that psychasthenia represents a disorder on the intellectual, or symbolic, level, neurasthenia on the autonomic, or visceral, and hysteria on the postural.

Neuroses, like psychoses, bear little relation to intellectual level. Neurotic symptoms occur over a wide range of mentality. In Table XV will be found the mental ages of 1172 soldiers in the United States army during the World War who manifested various neurotic disorders. These mental ages were determined by a variety of ways, including Stanford-Binet, performance scales, Army Alpha, a series of five specially selected tests,[1] or a combination of more than one of these methods.

[1] Completion, opposites, substitution, word-building, and digit span.

TABLE XV

FREQUENCY DISTRIBUTION OF MENTAL AGES IN NEUROTIC GROUPS
(After Hollingworth, 13, p. 87)

M.A.	Hysteria	Constitutional Psychopathy	Neurasthenia	Concussion	Psychasthenia	Psychoneurosis *	Undiagnosed †
Failed	15	2	5	1	0	9	18
5–6	2	0	0	0	0	0	2
6–7	5	0	0	0	0	1	3
7–8	10	2	1	2	0	8	9
8–9	15	5	6	1	0	7	17
9–10	19	5	7	3	0	9	24
10–11	14	7	8	7	1	7	25
11–12	16	6	11	6	1	16	31
12–13	16	5	6	3	1	9	19
13–14	15	2	11	4	2	10	18
14–15	11	3	8	3	1	10	21
15–16	13	1	3	3	1	6	13
16–17	16	5	10	6	2	11	20
17–18	7	5	1	2	0	6	5
Over 18	3	0	6	0	1	5	7
Total	177	48	83	41	10	114	232

* Not classifiable into a specific sub-form.
† Undiagnosed at the time of testing, but believed to be chiefly neurotic.

It will be noted that all of the disorders occur over the
entire range of intelligence test scores, except psychasthenia, which seems to be absent below a mental age of
ten years. The various neurotic groups tend, however, to
cluster at different points on the scale. It has been suggested on this basis that intellectual level determines to a
certain extent the type of neurotic symptom which an
individual will develop. Thus duller subjects are expected
to be more susceptible to disorders of the hysteric type
and brighter subjects to psychasthenia; neurasthenia
occupies an intermediate position. The army data given

in Table XV yield the following median mental ages for these three groups.

Diagnosis	Numbes of Cases	Median M.A.
Hysteria	177	11.5
Neurasthenia	83	13.0
Psychasthenia [1]	10	14.0

In evaluating these group tendencies, one must not lose sight of the fact that there is much overlapping between the groups and wide variation of intellectual level within each type of neurosis. The group differences themselves may be variously interpreted. Environmental factors, for example, might prove adequate to account for the slight relationship found between intelligence and nature of neurotic symptom. Individuals of lower intellectual status usually come from inferior social, economic, and educational levels. The problems and difficulties which they encounter are thus of a different nature from those which confront individuals in a superior environment. The emotional disorders developed by such groups can reasonably be expected to differ accordingly.

One further point deserves mention in connection with the neuroses. One often hears the statement that neuroses are a product of the strain and stress of civilized life. The evidence cited is the appalling number of persons, now classed as neurotics, who visit psychiatrists or spend brief periods "recuperating" in sanatoriums. History, it is pointed out, bears little testimony to the presence of this class of individuals in former eras. The fallacy inherent in this argument is a common one. With the rapid development of psychology and psychiatry, there has come a more general *recognition* of neurotic conditions.

---

[1] It is of course difficult to generalize from only 10 cases, but data of other investigators agree in showing psychasthenics to have higher intelligence test scores than other neurotics.

These mild abnormalities may have always existed, but they passed undiagnosed until the present. The neurotic is not sufficiently maladjusted in most cases to attract much attention or demand urgent treatment. In the past, such individuals may have gone their unhappy way, probably unpopular or disliked among their fellow-beings, but bearing their difficulties unlabeled and unrecorded. Similarly, the more highly developed the methods of diagnosis, the milder will be the disorders which are detected and the more numerous the individuals classified as neurotic.

ABNORMALITY IN DIFFERENT CULTURES

Recent interest in the study of abnormal conditions in widely varying cultural milieux has revealed the fact that abnormality is *culturally defined*.[1] There are two distinct ways in which specific cultural standards determine what shall be considered abnormal. First, the *norm* will differ from one group to another, so that any one specific behavioral manifestation may occupy entirely different positions in different distribution curves. An example from physical traits will make this clear. If we ask whether a given individual is "tall" or "short," we may obtain very different answers when different groups are employed as a standard. The same individual might be abnormally tall when evaluated in reference to the distribution of Japanese subjects, and abnormally short in terms of the distribution of Scandinavians. Similarly, in certain groups violent displays of emotions are the rule and stolidity would be abnormal. In others, the reverse is true.

Secondly, culturally established standards determine which end of the distribution curve shall be termed super-

[1] For a comprehensive and systematic analysis of this problem, cf. Foley (11).

normal and which end subnormal. As has already been
pointed out, such a criterion is intrinsically cultural in
its nature. Comparative anthropology furnishes many
instances of behavioral deviations which are regarded as
unadaptive, pathological, insane, or mentally deficient
in one culture and are admired or revered in another.
Such behavior may be abnormal in both cases, in the
statistical sense, but its social evaluation and practical
value in the different cultures place it at opposite ends
of the scale. This point has been clearly expressed by
Benedict (1) who states:

> . . . it is probable that about the same range of individual
> temperaments are found in any group, but the group has
> already made its cultural choice of those human endowments
> and peculiarities it will put to use . . . the misfit is the
> person whose disposition is not capitalized by his culture. . . .
> It is clear that there is not possible any generalized descrip-
> tion of "the" deviant—he is the representative of that arc of
> human capacities that is not capitalized in his culture (p. 24).

The same point of view is further elaborated in a later
article (2) by Benedict, in which appear the following
statements:

> One of these problems relates to the customary normal-
> abnormal categories and our conclusions regarding them. In
> how far are such categories culturally determined, or in how
> far can we with assurance regard them as absolute? In how
> far can we regard inability to function socially as diagnostic
> of abnormality, or in how far is it necessary to regard this
> as a function of the culture?
> As a matter of fact, one of the most striking facts that
> emerge from a study of widely varying cultures is the ease
> with which our abnormals function in other cultures. It
> does not matter what kind of "abnormality" we choose for
> illustration, those which indicate extreme instability, or those

which are more in the nature of character traits like sadism or delusions of grandeur or of persecution, there are well described cultures in which these abnormals function at ease and with honor, and apparently without danger or difficulty to the society (p. 60).

As an example of behavior regarded as subnormal in our society, but valued and respected in other cultures, may be mentioned the conventional behavior of the Siberian shaman, or priest (cf. 7). Such phenomena as cataleptic seizures often constitute an essential component of the behavior of the shaman. Similarly, trances, extreme introversion bordering on dementia præcox, manic-depressive behavior, and homosexuality are fostered and considered the ideal norm of behavior in various cultures. Paranoia, with its delusions of grandeur and its extreme suspiciousness, may be identified in the behavior and traditional chants of many medicine men or tribal priests. Illustrations could easily be multiplied from a survey of the behavior of different peoples.[1] .

Abnormality in Infrahuman Organisms

It should also be noted that behavioral deviations sufficiently pronounced to be classified as abnormal in the statistical sense are not an exclusively human phenomenon. Marked deviates can be found in all species. Mental deficiency, as well as "unadaptive" behavior which may be characterized as psychotic or neurotic, has been observed in many animal forms. Abnormal reactions ranging from drowsiness and sleep to overexcitability and violent emotional displays have been observed in chimpanzees when the latter were confronted with an "overexacting" situation (cf. 3, Ch. VIII). Similarly, Pavlov (21) observed distinctly neurotic behavior in dogs in the

[1] Cf. Benedict (1, 2) and Foley (11).

course of conditioning experiments. Symptoms not unlike those of the human "nervous breakdown" appeared
when the animal was required to make too fine a sensory
discrimination, or to set up too many conditioned reactions within a short time, or to establish a conditioned
reaction when the two stimuli were separated by too long
an interval.

Homosexuality has been observed or experimentally
induced among doves, pigeons, guinea pigs, white rats,
and monkeys (cf. 12, 15). Several investigators (cf.,
e.g., 10, 12, 24) have reported instances of other types of
abnormal behavior among monkeys, such as habit residu-
als, temper tantrums, infantile reversions, and various
forms of sexual perversions. These constitute abnormalities in the sense that they differ conspicuously from the
usual behavior of the given species. Whenever the etiology
of such abnormal behavior could be definitely traced,
experiential or environmental factors were again found
to play a predominant part (cf. 10, 12, 15, 24).

The Nature of Abnormality

We may now collate the diverse facts of abnormal behavior reported in the preceding sections and attempt to
characterize the nature of abnormality. *First*, there is
nothing absolute about abnormality. The deviations
termed abnormal are *relative* and *continuous*. There is
no sharp or clear dividing line between the normal and
the abnormal, nor do abnormal symptoms differ qualitatively from normal behavior. Such symptoms are only
exaggerations of normal behavior.

Secondly, abnormality is *specific* (cf. 11). The individual may be quite abnormal in one trait and yet remain
very close to the group norm in others. This is true of
both intellectual and emotional traits and follows from

the organization of behavior traits within the individual (cf. Chs. X and XI).

Thirdly, psychological abnormality is to be defined in terms of behavior. In some cases, behavioral disorders may have structural concomitants, such as physical diseases, lesions, and malformations. But in the majority of cases no such physical basis can be discovered and it would only obscure the issue to attribute such behavioral manifestations to unknown organic causes. Analysis of the behavioral history and environmental stimulation of the individual, on the other hand, often reveals an adequate background for the development of the particular symptoms. Functional abnormalities are the special domain of the psychologist and should be studied directly, without vague, hypothetical reference to physical concomitants.

Fourthly, abnormal behavior involves the same psychological principles as normal behavior. *Abnormality is the normal result of certain stimulating conditions.* Such behavior is termed abnormal only because it conflicts with the needs or standards imposed by a given culture. This is illustrated by two facts of cultural anthropology, *viz.*, the *shifting norm* and the cultural evaluation of the *direction* of deviation.

REFERENCES

1. Benedict, R. "Configurations of Culture in North America," *Amer. Anthr.*, 1932, N.S. 34, 1–27.
2. ———. "Anthropology and the Abnormal," *J. Gen. Psychol.*, 1934, 10, 59–82.
3. Bentley, I. M. *The Problem of Mental Disorder.* N. Y.: McGraw-Hill, 1934. Pp. 388.
4. Binet, A., and Simon, Th. *The Intelligence of the Feeble-minded* (transl. by Kite, E. S.). Vineland, N. J.: Training School Publ. No. 11, 1916. Pp. 336.

5. "British Royal Commission on the Care and Control of the Feebleminded," *Report of the Commission.* London: Wyman, 1908.

6. Burt, C. *Mental and Scholastic Tests.* London: King, 1921. Pp. 432.

7. Czaplicka, M. A. *Aboriginal Siberia: a Study in Social Anthropology.* Oxford: Clarendon Press, 1914. Pp. 334.

8. Doll, E. A. *Anthropometry as an Aid to Mental Diagnosis.* Vineland, N. J.: Training School Publ. No. 8, 1916. Pp. 91.

9. Farrar, C. B. "Some Origins in Psychiatry," *Amer. J. Insanity,* 1907–08, 64, 523–552; 1908–09, 65, 83–101; 1909–10, 66, 277–294.

10. Foley, J. P., Jr. "Second Year Development of a Rhesus Monkey (*Macaca mulatta*) Reared in Isolation during the First Eighteen Months," *J. Genet. Psychol.,* 1935, 47, 73–97.

11. ———. "The Criterion of Abnormality," *J. Abn. and Soc. Psychol.,* 1935, 30, 279–291.

12. Hamilton, G. V. *An Introduction to Objective Psychopathology.* St. Louis: Mosby, 1925. Pp. 354.

13. Hollingworth, H. L. *The Psychology of Functional Neuroses.* N. Y.: Appleton, 1920. Pp. 259.

14. ———. *Abnormal Psychology: Its Concepts and Theories.* N. Y.: Ronald Press, 1930. Pp. 590.

15. Jenkins, M. "The Effect of Segregation on the Sex Behavior of the White Rat as Measured by the Obstruction Method," *Genet. Psychol. Mon.,* 1928, 3, 457–571.

16. Klineberg, O. *Race Differences.* N. Y.: Harper, 1935. Pp. 367.

17. Kraepelin, E. *Clinical Psychiatry: a Textbook for Students and Physicians* (abstr. and adapt. from Ger. ed. by A. R. Diefendorf). N. Y.: Macmillan, 1918. Pp. 562.

18. Morgan, J. J. B. *The Psychology of Abnormal People.* N. Y.: Longmans, Green, 1932. Pp. 627.

19. Moss, F. A., and Hunt, T. *Foundations of Abnormal Psychology.* N. Y.: Prentice-Hall, 1932. Pp. 548.

20. Norsworthy, N. "The Psychology of Mentally Deficient Children," *Arch. Psychol.,* No. 1, 1906. Pp. 111.

21. Pavlov, I. *Conditioned Reflexes: an Investigation of the Physiological Activity of the Cerebral Cortex* (transl. and ed. by G. V. Anrep). Oxford Univ. Press: Humphrey Milford, 1927. Pp. 430.

22. Pintner, R. "The Feebleminded Child." Ch. 20 in *Handbook of Child Psychology*. C. Murchison, ed. Worcester, Mass.: Clark Univ. Press, 1933. Pp. 956.

23. Terman, L. M. *The Measurement of Intelligence*. N. Y.: Houghton Mifflin, 1916. Pp. 362.

24. Tinklepaugh, O. L. "The Self-Mutilation of a Male *Macacus rhesus* Monkey," *J. Mammal.*, 1928, 9, 293–300.

25. Tredgold, A. F. *Mental Deficiency*. N. Y.: Wood, 1922. Pp. 569.

26. Watson, J. B. "Behavior and the Concept of Mental Dissease," *J. Phil., Psychol., and Sci. Method*, 1916, 13, 589–597.

CHAPTER XIII

GENIUS

The existence of genius has probably been recognized by man from earliest times. In order to be popularly acclaimed as a genius, however, an individual must possess very exceptional talents of the kind demanded by his culture. Since only the extreme deviates attract notice, they seem by the very rare quality of their attainments to stand off from the rest of mankind and constitute a distinct group. With the advent of more objective methods of observation and the development of testing techniques, the presence of lesser deviates who bridge the gap between the average man and the person of rare gifts has been demonstrated. Thus the popular belief in genius as a separate species arose in the same fashion as the similar belief regarding the feebleminded and it is being dispelled by the same methods.

The relationship between genius and eminence is a curious one. Many writers identify the two by the simple expedient of defining genius as the possession of "what it takes" to become eminent in our society. The eminent man is then considered a genius *ipso facto*. There would thus be as many kinds of genius as there are ways of succeeding in the particular society. The successful financier, for example, may be awarded an honorary university degree for his "financial genius," the victorious general for his "military genius." Society often creates a new form of "genius" in order to rationalize its allotment of eminence.

Almost any theory regarding the nature of genius could,

of course, be defended by restricting the term genius in some arbitrary way. The broadest and most objective definition of genius is that of *an individual who excels markedly the average performance in any field.* Social evaluation, however, invariably enters into the concept. Genius is defined in terms of specific social criteria and a cultural sense of values. In our society the more abstract and linguistic abilities are considered the "higher" mental processes. Similarly, certain lines of achievement enable the individual to earn the appellation of genius much more readily than others. Thus academic and scientific work, literature, music, and the plastic arts are rated higher than, let us say, roller skating or cooking.

To be sure, very exceptional accomplishments in the latter fields might be recognized as genius, after a fashion. An internationally famed roller skate acrobat or a renowned *chef-de-cuisine* might be called a genius and ranked higher than a mediocre scientist or painter. But in the former instances, *the attainments must be proportionately far greater* than in the latter in order that the individual may be designated a genius. And even when the term genius is applied to such cases, one feels that it is done only by courtesy and that the word is implicitly enclosed in quotation marks. It is apparent, therefore, that in order to have practical meaning, any definition of genius must recognize the selection of significant talents which has been made within a given cultural group.

A further question which has been vigorously debated is that of *general versus specific genius.* Is the man of genius one who manifests a well-rounded intellectual superiority or one who possesses a highly specialized gift? It follows from the organization of mental traits that this distinction is not a valid one. Since the intercorrelations of diverse abilities are neither highly positive nor highly negative, we should expect all degrees of generality of genius. A few individuals may excel highly in a large number of traits and thus appear to be all-around geniuses. Some will excel in only a few traits, and still others may have a single talent which is sufficiently pronounced to put them in the category of genius. There is no necessary relationship, either positive or negative, between excellence in one trait and in any other.

THEORIES ON THE NATURE OF GENIUS

Theories on the nature and causes of genius are legion. The genius has been credited with a wide variety of attributes, ranging from divine inspiration and a superhuman "spark" to imbecility and insanity. Among these diverse theories it is possible to discern four underlying viewpoints. These will be designated the *pathological, psychoanalytic, typological,* and *deviational.*[1]

Pathological theories link genius with insanity, racial degeneracy, and even feeblemindedness. This view was put forth by many of the ancient writers, among whom may be mentioned Democritus and Seneca. More recently, it received clear expression in the writings of Moreau (23), who claimed that all genius is a neurosis, and often a psychosis. Originality of thought, Moreau pointed out, is equally characteristic of all of these conditions. Essentially the same theory was later expanded by Nisbet (24) in England, who held genius to be a mere sport of nature or spontaneous variation which betrays a lack of adaptation to its environment.

The greatest impetus to the development of the pathological view of genius was probably furnished by the

---

[1] These terms are only employed as convenient designations and are not to be regarded as a sufficient characterization of any of the views. The terms "typological" and "deviational," for example, should be accompanied by qualifying adjectives, but the latter are omitted for the sake of conciseness.

Italian anthropologist, Lombroso (22). His book entitled *The Man of Genius* was translated into several languages and read widely at the turn of the present century. In it he attributed to the genius a wide variety of qualities which he regarded as indicative of species degeneration. Among them are included short stature, rickets, excessive pallor, emaciation, stammering, left-handedness, delayed development, and originality! He also claimed to have observed a certain similarity between the creative act of genius and the typical epileptic seizure.

Havelock Ellis (12) proposed a two-fold theory which recognizes the exceptional talents of genius but at the same time includes a certain essential deficiency in the complete picture. This deficiency he regards as some innate organic inaptitude which prevents complete adjustment to the activities of everyday life. He cites as examples motor incoördination, narrow specialization with attendant inferiority in other fields, impracticality, and similar deficiencies occasionally found in men of genius.[1]

The evidence presented in support of these views consists of illustrative examples of geniuses who manifested the alleged traits. Such evidence is open to all the criticisms of *selected cases*. A few individuals can be found to illustrate almost any theory. Only the objective observation of large numbers of unselected cases can furnish an adequate test of these assumptions. This type of evidence will be presented in a subsequent section.

Several factors can be cited which might erroneously suggest a linkage between insanity and genius. Thus many geniuses of high degree may become maladjusted in a society built up around the average man and his

---

[1] This theory might also be classified under the psychoanalytic viewpoints, owing to a certain resemblance to the Adlerian concept of organic inferiority in genius (cf. below).

needs. This is particularly noticeable in the case of a very superior child placed in a class of mediocre school-children. It is equally true of superior adults. Geniuses, furthermore, are often regarded as pathological by their fellow-men until the practical benefits of their work become tangible. Their achievements are ridiculed until they succeed. The familiar example of Fulton and his steamboat is a case in point. Occasionally, the genius has met with systematic and even violent opposition from the church or other organized bodies. Life under such conditions was not very conducive to the development of a stable and well-adjusted personality. Finally, it may be added that even when the genius is recognized and acclaimed as such, he is likely to be surrounded by such a blare of publicity that all his actions and idiosyncracies become common knowledge. As a result, any behavioral deviation too slight to attract attention in a less outstanding individual is pounced upon, discussed, and elaborated until it may assume the proportions of a neurotic or psychotic symptom.

Psychoanalytic explanations of genius emphasize motivational rather than intellectual characteristics. The psychoanalytic concepts of sublimation and compensation are brought in to account for the remarkable achievements of genius. Freud (cf. 10) regards the manifestations of genius as a sublimation or substitute outlet for a thwarted sex drive. He does, however, recognize the need for a certain degree of talent together with strong motivational factors. Adler (1) regards the exceptional accomplishments of genius as compensations for other inferiorities, usually of an organic nature. A favorite example is that of great orators, such as Demosthenes, who developed their talent by overcompensating for an initial habit of stammering or some similar speech defect.

The rôle of motivational factors in the development of genius cannot be ignored. Under certain conditions, a slight physical handicap may spur the individual on to greater efforts and thereby contribute indirectly to his success. Similarly, thwarted desires or emotional disappointments may cause some individuals to turn to intellectual pursuits as a consolation. Restriction of one's range of activities by physical defects, unpopularity, or other conditions may also lead to more intensive work and subsequent success along a particular line. These various motivational influences are very simple and clearly observable facts. The psychoanalytic theories, on the other hand, are burdened with vague concepts, fantastical allusions to Unconscious forces, and mystifying statements. The simple issues involved are greatly confused by such interpretations. These theories, furthermore, could only account for a relatively small number of geniuses. Nor do they offer a satisfactory interpretation of the *essential nature* of genius.

Those views which we have classified under the heading of *typological* regard genius as a distinct type differing qualitatively from the rest of the species. Such views are to be distinguished from the pathological and the psychoanalytic in that they regard the man of genius as essentially *superior* to the norm. No inferiorities of any sort are implicit in this concept. The achievements of genius, according to these theories, result from some process or condition which is entirely absent in the ordinary man. Such current expressions as "the spark of genius" reflect the popular influence of this point of view.

The typological approach, like the pathological, has a long history.[1] In the ancient world, genius was frequently attributed to divine inspiration. The Greeks spoke of a

[1] Cf. 17 and 29 for references.

man's "dæmon" which was supposed to possess divine powers and to furnish the inspiration for his creative work. Among those who discussed genius in these terms may be mentioned Plato and Socrates. Christianity advanced the view that genius was the inspiration of a selected mortal by God. Or, in some cases, it was Satan who provided the creative talents, especially when the inspiration was of a kind contrary to the dogmas of the church.

Qualitative distinctions are also common in literary and philosophical writings on the subject of genius. Mystic insights and unconscious intuitions have been attributed to the man of genius. In this connection may be mentioned the views of Schopenhauer, Carlisle, and Emerson.

In psychological discussions of genius, this point of view is much less common. G. Stanley Hall's proposal (16, p. 320) that the characteristics of genius are similar to those of the adolescent may be regarded as a qualitative distinction. Recently Hirsch (17) has put forth a distinctly qualitative view. He attempts to differentiate three "dimensions" of intelligence. The first dimension is perceptual and cognitive and is shared by man and the lower animals; the second is conceptual and is common to all of mankind; the third he designates "creative intelligence" and attributes only to genius.

Qualitative distinctions appeal to the imagination of the public. The genius whom the layman acclaims differs so greatly from the rest of mankind in his achievements that he seems to belong to another species. A careful analysis of the individual's abilities, however, will reveal no essentially new process. And only a brief unbiased search discloses the presence of intermediate degrees of capacity in all lines.

The *deviational* view regards genius only as the upper extreme of the normal distribution curve. The special "gifts" and "creative powers" of genius are possessed, to a much lesser degree, by all individuals. Distinctions are quantitative and not qualitative. Genius is defined in terms of concrete, measurable behavior rather than in terms of mystical entities. To be sure, the accomplishments of genius are not attributed to any single talent, but to a favorable combination of several intellectual, motivational, and emotional factors.

It follows from the deviational view that the origin of genius is to be understood in the same terms as that of all individual differences. Many writers on the subject of genius, such as Galton (13, 14), Terman (31, 32), Cox (8), L. S. Hollingworth (18), and Pintner (26, Ch. 15), lay the major emphasis upon hereditary factors. The observation that genius runs in families has probably given the greatest impetus to this view. In such cases the potent environmental influence exercised by family traditions and family contacts is overlooked. For an analysis of the operation of hereditary and environmental factors in the development of individual variations in general, the reader is referred to Chapters III, IV, and V.

METHODS EMPLOYED IN THE STUDY OF GENIUS

Psychological investigations on the nature and development of genius have followed a variety of procedures. These may be classified into: (1) biographical analysis, (2) case study, (3) statistical survey, (4) historiometry, and (5) mental measurement. In *biographical* studies, all available printed material on a given individual is examined in the effort to arrive at an understanding of the nature and origin of his genius. The investigation is limited to a single individual, who is usually chosen from the great men of the past. This method has been employed chiefly by psychoanalysts, but it is also occasionally used by psychologists.

The *case study* method consists of direct and controlled observations of a single living individual. Because of the difficulty of subjecting adult geniuses to such an investigation, this method has been applied almost exclusively to gifted children. Several such studies on contemporary child prodigies, and especially juvenile authors, have been initiated by psychologists.

The *statistical survey* method, like the biographical, is based upon an analysis of printed records. It differs from the latter method, however, in several essential respects. The purpose of statistical surveys of genius is to discover general trends in a large group, rather than to make an exhaustive analysis of a single case. All available information on a large number of men is obtained from biographical directories, encyclopedias, *Who's Who*, and similar sources. This material is occasionally supplemented from biographies. But the former sources are employed predominantly because of the more objective, reliable, and standardized nature of their data. It will be noted that in this method the criterion of genius is chiefly eminence.

The *historiometry* method makes use of all historical material on an individual or a group of individuals. The data are culled from a variety of sources, including biographies, directories, and original documents such as letters and diaries. The attempt is made to obtain as complete information as possible, especially on the childhood accomplishments of the great man. This material is then evaluated in terms of a more or less constant standard in order to arrive at an estimate of the individual's traits. This method was employed by Woods (34) in his study of mental and moral heredity in royalty. Terman (28) subsequently suggested an adaptation of historiometry whereby the recorded achievements are evaluated in terms of mental test standards and norms of performance for each age. From this, an estimate is obtained of the individual's I.Q. in childhood. Terman estimated by this method, for example, that the I.Q. of Francis Galton was approximately 200.

The *mental measurement* method consists of the direct study of large groups of intellectually superior children by means of mental tests. Extensive use is now being made of this method. The subjects are originally selected on the basis of intelligence test performance, and subsequent analyses are made with the aid of standardized intellectual, scholastic, and personality tests.

Each of these procedures contributes something which is lacking in the others. Similarly, each by itself suffers from special weaknesses. The statistical survey, historiometry, and mental measurement methods can be applied to large groups, and hence disclose general trends. They are also relatively free from selectional bias. The biographical and case study methods, on the other hand, give a more complete picture of the individual and enable one to note the specific action of various conditions upon the subject's development. The study of contemporary living geniuses makes direct observation possible and avoids the judgment errors and other inaccuracies which are inevitably present in historical material. On the other hand, carefully controlled observation on living geniuses offers many practical difficulties. A further disadvantage in the study of contemporaries is the possibility that the eminence of some may be short-lived and spurious and that others who are laboring in obscurity may be recognized as geniuses by posterity.

Finally, the relative advantages of studying adult geniuses and gifted children may be considered. To investigate intellectually superior children in the effort to discover the characteristics of adult geniuses seems somewhat indirect. Only a small number of such children, furthermore, will develop into adults who can be classified as geniuses. Children, however, are available for prolonged and controlled observation and testing which would be practically impossible with adults. A further advantage of the study of gifted children is that it offers a *genetic approach* to the problem. Such an analysis may go far towards clarifying the origin and nature of genius.

Surveys of Adult Genius

Investigations on genius through statistical surveys of printed records have been conducted in England by Galton [1] (13, 14) and Ellis (12), in France by de Candolle (9), Jacoby (21), and Odin (25), and in America by Cattell (4, 5, 6), Brimhall (2), and Clarke (7). Castle (3) conducted a similar survey on eminent women of all countries, but the data of this study are extremely tentative and quite difficult to interpret. The major findings of these studies will be summarized briefly.

The *social and occupational level* of eminent men has been generally found to be superior to the average of the entire population. Thus in Cattell's analysis of the occupations of the fathers of American men of science (5), the percentage engaged in the professions was far in excess of that in the general population. The relevant data are reproduced in the following table. Cattell himself gave a strongly environmental interpretation to these data, stating: "We may conclude that more than one-half of our men of science come from the one per cent of the

[1] Cf. Ch. IV for a discussion of specific procedure and results.

Occupational Group	Percentage in Each Occupational Group	
	Fathers of American Men of Science	General Population in 1850 [1]
Professions	43.0	3.1
Manufacture and trade	35.7	34.1
Agriculture	21.2	44.1

population most favorably situated to produce them. The son of a successful professional man is fifty times as likely to become a leading scientific man as a boy taken at random from the community" (5, p. 511).

A similar distribution of occupational level is to be found among the eminent men and women surveyed by Ellis (12). In Castle's study (3) of eminent women of all times and nationalities, it was reported that 33.1% had fathers in the "learned professions." Cox (8, p. 37) obtained the following distribution of paternal occupation in a group of 282 eminent men and women of all countries.

Occupational Level	Percentage
1. Professional and nobility	52.5
2. Semi-professional, higher business, and gentry	28.7
3. Skilled workmen and lower business	13.1
4. Semi-skilled	3.9
5. Unskilled	1.1
No record	0.7

The number of *eminent relatives* is also of interest in this connection. It will be recalled that in Galton's study (13), the 977 eminent men investigated had a total of 739 known relatives who had also achieved eminence. It will also be recalled that, in general, the closer the degree of relationship, the more numerous were the eminent relatives. Similar results were obtained in Brimhall's investigation (2) of family resemblance among American men of science.

[1] Corresponding roughly to the time when the fathers of the scientific men had pursued their vocations.

Rather suggestive evidence for an environmental interpretation of the development of genius is furnished by Cattell's analysis of the *place of birth* of American men of science (cf. 4, 6). In his 1906 report, Cattell pointed out that cities contributed a much greater proportion of men of science than did rural sections. Although at that time the urban population was about one-sixth of the rural population, it produced a quarter of the scientific men. Even more striking is the comparison of different states which varied widely in their educational facilities. Below are shown the relative number of scientists born in each of nine states. The latter have been chosen as the clearest examples of a definite trend which has been operative during the last three decades. Corresponding figures are shown for the original group of 1000 scientists selected in the year 1903 and for the group of 250 elected in 1932. All figures have been expressed in terms of 1000 entries to permit direct comparison (cf. 6, p. 1265).

Place of Birth	*Number of Cases* (*in terms of 1000 entries*)	
	1903	1932
Massachusetts	134	72
Connecticut	40	16
New York	183	128
Pennsylvania	66	48
Illinois	42	88
Minnesota	4	32
Missouri	14	40
Nebraska	2	20
Kansas	7	32

These data suggest several conclusions which are borne out by the complete results for all parts of the country (cf. 6). In the first place, there are marked discrepancies in the relative number of eminent scientists born in different parts of the country. Secondly, these differences in birthplace correspond very closely to differences in educational opportunities in various sections of the country. Thirdly, as educational facilities change, the frequency of scientists shows a corresponding change. In recent years, for example, there has been a phenomenal development of education in the mid-western states. The relative quality of education in such states has improved, new universities have been established, the number of students in institutions of higher learning has increased rapidly,[1] and a powerful tradition has been built up which fosters intellectual activity. These factors probably account for the definite rise in the number of scientists from mid-western states, as compared to the New England states which were formerly the undisputed center of the intellectual life of the country.

Of interest in connection with the pathological theories of genius is the relative frequency of *insanity* among the relatives of eminent men, as well as among the subjects themselves. In all well controlled studies in which the cases were not selected to prove a point, the incidence of intellectual and emotional disorders has been found to be consistently smaller among eminent men and their families than in the general population. In the group investigated by Ellis (12, p. 192), less than 2% were reported to have had either insane parents or insane offspring. Among the eminent individuals themselves, Ellis mentions 44 cases of emotional disorder out of a total group of 1030. Of these, only 13 could be definitely classed as insane during the active period of their lives; 19 were either insane for a short period or manifested very mild disorders; and 12 developed senile dementia in old age (cf. 12, pp. 189–190).

---

[1] Cf., e.g., Eells' analysis of the "center of population" of higher education from 1790 to 1920, which showed a westward movement at the rate of 60 miles per decade (11).

Other facts which have been brought to light by these surveys relate to *age of parents at the time of birth of the child, order of birth*, and similar "vital statistics." It has been proposed, for example, that older parents have intellectually superior children (cf. 27). From a somewhat different angle, Lombroso (22) claimed that geniuses are the offspring of aged parents and offered this as further evidence of the pathological nature of genius. The data on this question are difficult to interpret because of the complicating factor of social level. People in the higher social classes, from which geniuses are most frequently recruited, tend to marry later and therefore have children at a later age. For this reason average ages are in themselves inconclusive. Among American men of science, Cattell (5, III) found 35 years to be the average age of the father at the time of the subject's birth. For English men of science, Galton (14) found the corresponding figure to be 36 years. Ellis (12) gives 37.1 years for his group of British men and women of eminence. In all of these groups, however, the range of parental ages at birth is extremely wide. In the majority of cases the parents were in the prime of life at the time of the subject's birth, contrary to Lombroso's contention.

Somewhat more conclusive is the analysis of order of birth within the family. In general the eminent individual is most often the oldest or first-born child in the family. Next in order of frequency comes the youngest child, intermediate children having the least chance of becoming eminent (cf. 12, 35). These findings are in direct contradiction to the proposed theory that older parents have intellectually more gifted offspring. It would seem that, within the same family, the superior child is most likely to be born when the parents are younger. This finding may be interpreted in cultural terms. The first born has traditionally enjoyed privileges in our society that his younger siblings may not have had. More is usually expected of the oldest son. If a choice must be made for economic reasons, the oldest child is usually allowed to complete his education, in preference to the younger children. These conditions might be sufficient to produce a slight degree of relationship between birth order and achievement.

The Early Mental Traits of Genius

The childhood of great men, viewed retrospectively, has been the source of much controversial discussion. There is a popular belief [1] that many geniuses were dull in childhood. Several examples are cited in support of this contention. Darwin was considered by his teachers to be below average in intellect. Newton was at the bottom of his class. Heine was an academic failure, revolting against the traditional formalism of the schools of his time. Pasteur, Hume, von Humboldt, and other equally famous men were unsuccessful in their school work.

An examination of the available biographical material in such cases shows that the intellectual defect was inferred from scholastic achievements of a rather narrow scope. The intellectually superior child may be just as maladjusted in school as the dull or borderline case. Schools adapted to the average child may be unsuited to the highly gifted pupil in many ways. The monotonous drill and rote memorization which constituted such a large part of school work in the days when men like Darwin or Hume attended school would prove particularly irksome to a bright child. Darwin, for instance, seems to have been more interested in his collections of insects than in memorizing Latin declensions, much to the annoyance of

[1] Also proposed by Lombroso (22).

his teachers. Thus it is often impossible to accept the recorded opinions of parents or teachers regarding the intellectual status of great men in childhood.

More accurate information can be obtained from factual records of the *specific behavior* of the individual at various ages. An early attempt to conduct such an analysis of the boyhood of great men was made by Yoder (35). Fifty cases, representing a wide variety of occupations or fields of eminence, were selected from the great men of six countries. All of the subjects were born in the eighteenth or nineteenth centuries, except Newton, Swift, and Voltaire, who were born in the seventeenth. In general Yoder found that ill health in childhood was often exaggerated by the earlier biographers and that this condition was not so prevalent as is supposed. Feeble or delicate health may, however, offer advantages in some cases by stimulating reading and intellectual pursuits. Dickens was a good example of this. In regard to intellectual status, Yoder reports that excellent memory and vivid imagination were often exhibited by great men from early childhood.

A very painstaking and comprehensive study of the childhood of great men was conducted by Cox (8). Terman's adaptation of the historiometry method was employed. Through the examination of several thousand biographical references, information was gathered on the traits of 301 eminent men and women born between 1450 and 1850. Particular attention was given to childhood behavior, such as age of learning to read, letters and original compositions which may have been preserved, early interests, etc. Any special circumstances which might have influenced the subject's development were also noted. The material so collected was analyzed and evaluated independently by three trained psychologists.

Each investigator estimated the lowest I.Q. compatible with the given facts for every subject, and the average of these three independent judgments was taken as the final minimum I.Q. estimate for the given individual.

After allowing for certain inaccuracies in the data, Cox concludes that the average I.Q. for the group "is not below 155 and probably at least as high as 165" (8, p. 217). The estimated minimum I.Q.'s ranged approximately from 100 to 200. The same geniuses cited by Lombroso and others as instances of early mental inferiority were invariably found to give evidence of high I.Q.'s during childhood. Among these may be mentioned Lord Byron, Sir Walter Scott, and Charles Darwin, whose estimated I.Q.'s proved to be 150, 150, and 135, respectively. Among those receiving I.Q.'s above 180 were Goethe, John Stuart Mill, Macaulay, Pascal, Leibnitz, and Grotius.

In addition to intellectual superiority, Cox emphasizes the importance of favorable personality traits in the development of genius. Among such traits she mentions "persistence of motive and effort, confidence in their abilities, and great strength or force of character" (8, p. 218). Eminent relatives, superior home background, and opportunities for education and intellectual contacts are also stressed.

Thus it seems that genius is usually foreshadowed by the intellectual and temperamental traits of childhood. The geniuses of tomorrow are probably to be found among the gifted children of today. This consistency of superior accomplishment has been interpreted as an indication of the hereditary determination of genius. It might, on the other hand, be regarded simply as illustrative of the major importance of *early environment*. The nature and direction of the individual's subsequent abilities are largely determined by the circumstances of his early life.

It may be for this reason that the achievements of the adult are reflected in the interests and proclivities of his childhood.

The Child Prodigy [1]

Since geniuses have generally displayed superior talents in childhood, a direct study of gifted children should prove relevant. The traditional or popular concept of the "child prodigy" is that of a weak, sickly, unsocial, and narrowly specialized individual. His achievements are expected to be of the nature of intellectual "stunts" and to have little or no practical value.

One of the earliest recorded cases of such a child prodigy is that of Christian Heinrich Heineken, whose achievements are described by his teacher in an old German book published in 1779 (cf. 26, pp. 352–353). At the age of 10 months this child was able to name objects in pictures. Before the age of 12 months he had memorized many stories in the book of Moses. At 14 months he knew the stories of the Old and New Testaments. At 4 years of age he could read in his native language, had memorized 1500 sayings in Latin, and also knew French. At this time he was able to perform the four fundamental arithmetic operations, and he knew the most important facts of geography. His fame spread throughout Europe and he was summoned to appear before the King of Denmark. True to the traditional picture, however, Christian Heinrich was a sickly child, and at the age of 4 years-4 months he died.

Contrary to popular belief, the case of Christian Heinrich is not typical. As an example of a highly gifted child

---

[1] A discussion of *teaching methods* suitable for gifted children is beyond the scope of this volume. For a number of studies on this problem the reader is referred to the *Twenty-third Yearbook of the National Society for the Study of Education* (36).

who developed into a healthy and successful adult may be mentioned Karl Witte (cf. 33). Born in Lochau, Prussia, in 1800, this "child prodigy" lived until he was 83, having retained his excellent intellectual powers to the end. Karl was literally educated from the cradle. His father was convinced of the efficacy of early training and undertook to prove this with his son. The child was never taught "baby talk." All the games he played were games of knowledge. When only 8 years old, he read with apparent pleasure the original texts of Homer, Plutarch, Virgil, Cicero, Fénelon, Florian, Metastasio, and Schiller. He matriculated as a regular student at Leipzig at the age of 9. Before his fourteenth birthday he was granted a Ph.D. Two years later he was made a Doctor of Laws, being at the same time appointed to the teaching staff of the University of Berlin.

Karl Witte's father, in discussing the boy's education, wrote:

> . . . he was first of all to be a strong, active, and happy young man, and in this, as everybody knows, I have succeeded. . . . It would have been in the highest degree unpleasant for me to have made of him preëminently a Latin or a Greek scholar or a mathematician. For this reason, I immediately interfered whenever I thought that this or that language or science attracted his attention at too early a time (33, pp. 63–64).

Karl seems not to have been in the least vain or spoiled. He never paraded his knowledge, was modest and unpretentious, and not infrequently tried to learn from his companions what they knew better than he. He had many playmates of his own age and we are told that: "He got along so well with them that they invariably became very fond of him and nearly always parted from him with tears in their eyes" (33, p. 187).

Recent case studies of gifted children by psychologists likewise lend no support to the view that such children are inferior in other respects. The gifted "juvenile author," Betty Ford, obtained a Stanford-Binet I.Q. of 188 when tested at the age of 7 years-10 months (cf. 30). She ranked high in all other intellectual and educational tests, but showed a special interest and talent for the composition of prose and poetry. This child was reported to be in excellent health and free from physical defects. She was found to be a year or so accelerated in physical development.

Betty Ford's superior linguistic abilities were apparent from an early age. At 19 months she could express herself clearly and also knew the alphabet. By her eighth birthday she had read approximately 700 books, including such authors as Burns, Shakespeare, Longfellow, Wordsworth, Scott, and Poe. By this age she had also written over 100 poems and 75 stories. The following is a specimen of her literary products, written at the age of 7 years-11 months and entitled "Fairy Definition":

> Fairies are the fancies of an imaginative brain
> Which wearying of earthly realities aspires to
> Create beings living only in thought
> Endowing the spirits thus created
> With all genius for giving Happiness.

A case which attracted wide attention a few years ago is that of a boy known in the psychological literature as E——. When first tested at the age of 8 years-11 months, E—— obtained a mental age of 15-7, which gave him an I.Q. of 187. He also did well on all other tests except those involving manual dexterity. He is reported as being strong and healthy, but not much inclined to indulge in games and sports. At the age of 12 he was admitted to Columbia College. On the Thorndike Intelligence Examination for High School Graduates, he ranked second among 483 competitors. During his freshman year at college all his academic grades were B or better, with the exception of physical education, in which his grade was C. He is described as being a "good sport" and getting along well with the other students. He received his A.B. degree at 15, being also admitted to Phi Beta Kappa. At 16 he obtained his M.A. degree, and at 18, when the final report appeared, he was well advanced towards the Ph.D. degree. On the CAVD Intelligence Examination, his score was 441, which falls approximately in the upper $\frac{1}{4}$ of 1% of college graduates. Thus during the ten-year period over which he was investigated, E—— showed no tendency to drop below the high intellectual level indicated by his initial I.Q.

These cases are typical examples of intellectually superior children. Exceptional talents in childhood are not incompatible with good health, physical vigor, longevity, or a well-rounded personality. To be sure, puny, timid, and sickly children can be found among the gifted, as among the intellectually normal or dull. But such cases are very few and cannot be regarded as representative of the group as a whole.

Mental Tests and the Superior Child

Mental test surveys of large groups of intellectually superior children have revealed the *continuity* which exists between the average child and the highly gifted "prodigy." In order to include a sufficiently large number of cases in such studies, the standard of selection must be lowered. But by surveying a wider range of superior intellect, a more complete picture will be obtained. Since the rise of the mental testing movement, a number of studies on moderately large groups of superior children have appeared (cf. 29 for references). The most extensive investigations so far conducted by the mental test method are those of Terman and his associates, reported in Volume I of the *Genetic Studies of Genius* (31). Because of the more comprehensive nature of this study and its essential agreement with the findings of other investigations, it will be described in greater detail.

The major group employed in Terman's study consisted of 643 California schoolchildren between the ages of 2 and 14, whose Stanford-Binet I.Q.'s were *140 or above.* A special study was also conducted on 378 high school students. In the main study, the gifted children were compared in each of a series of tests or measures with equated control groups of intellectually normal children. For reasons of expediency, different control groups were employed for various comparisons, the number of cases in such groups ranging from about 600 to 800.

The *social and cultural level* of the gifted group was clearly superior. In regard to paternal occupation, 31.4% belonged to the professional class, 50% to the semi-professional or higher business class, 11.8% to the skilled labor class, and less than 7% to the semi-skilled or un-skilled labor class. The average cultural rating of the home [1] was 22.94 as compared to 20.78 for unselected homes. The average school grade reached by the parents of the gifted group was 11.8 and by the grandparents 10.0. These figures may be compared with the average amount of schooling of the native-born White draft of the United States army in the World War, which did not quite reach the seventh grade. It should be noted that the average age of the army draft was about 15 years lower than that of the parents of the gifted children and

---

[1] Obtained by the Whittier Scale, which takes into account necessities, neat-ness, size, parental condition, and parental supervision.

much lower than that of the grandparents. Since the amount of schooling has risen markedly in recent years, the showing made by the parents and grandparents of the gifted group is even better than it appears. In addition, over one-fourth of the children had at least one parent who was a college graduate. The number of eminent relatives and ancestors was also far in excess of that which would be expected through chance, and many of the families had highly distinguished geneologies.

We may next consider certain *vital statistics* as well as *medical* and *anthropometric data* obtained on the gifted and control groups. As in the studies on adult genius, a preponderance of first-born children was found in the gifted group. The frequency of insanity in the family was much lower than average. Only 0.4% of the parents and 0.3% of the grandparents and great-grandparents were reported to have had a record of insanity. The gifted children developed at a rapid rate from early infancy. They walked on the average one month earlier and talked $2\frac{1}{2}$ months earlier than the control groups. The onset of puberty was also somewhat earlier than normal. Physicians' examinations showed superior health and relative freedom from defects in the group as a whole. Similarly, such conditions as "nervousness," stuttering, headaches, general weakness, and poor nutrition were less common in the gifted than in the control groups. In height and weight, physical and muscular development, and strength, the overlapping of gifted and control groups was almost complete. Such differences as did occur, however, favored the gifted group.

The *educational accomplishments* of the gifted group were, of course, far in advance of the normal.[1] About

---

[1] This was partly the result of the method of selection. Teachers were asked to name the brightest children in each class, and from among these the gifted subjects were chosen by mental tests.

85% of the gifted children were accelerated and none were retarded. The administration of standardized achievement tests in school subjects revealed, however, that the majority of these children had already mastered the subject matter from one to three grades above that in which they were located. Thus in respect to actual abilities, the gifted child is often retarded and not accelerated in school status. The performance of the gifted children as a group was fairly uniform in different school subjects. One-sidedness was not characteristic of the group. The superiority of the gifted children was, however, greater in such subjects as language usage, reading, and "abstract" work, and least in manual training, painting, and similar abilities.

The gifted group displayed a wide range of *interests* outside of their school work, as well as an active *play life*. A two-months reading record kept by the children showed that the gifted subjects read more than the control at all ages. At 9, the number of books read by the gifted group was three times that of the control. The range of topics covered was also wider and the quality of the books superior in the gifted group. Similarly, the gifted children were more enthusiastic, had more intense interests in general, and reported more hobbies than the control group. Collections were also more common among the gifted. A questionnaire on play information showed that the typical gifted child of 10 knows more about plays and games than the average child of 13. Apart from the fact that the play interests of the gifted children were more mature than those of the control children of their own age, no conspicuous differences were found in their play activities.

In *character and personality development*, the gifted children were also found to be in advance of the normal.

istered to 150 subjects, the average score was practically identical with that obtained at the first testing. On tests of fairmindedness, social intelligence, and other similar traits, the group proved to be markedly superior to the norms. Leadership and ability to coöperate in social enterprises were manifested more frequently in the gifted group than among normal subjects. Terman reports that: "The gifted subjects take part in a wide variety of extra-curricular activities and are as likely to gain recognition in any one of several kinds of non-academic activity as they are in scholarship" (32, p. 132). Similarly 84% of the boys and 90% of the girls were reported by parents and teachers as possessing "good general health" and only 1% of each sex were said to be in "poor health."

From the evidence examined in this chapter, it is apparent that there is no basis in fact for many of the popular prejudices regarding genius. Insanity and pathological conditions, rather than being characteristic of genius, are somewhat *less common* among the intellectually ablest than among the normal. Nor are ill health, physical weakness, and narrow specialization common attributes of genius. Most men of genius display superior talent from an early age; and conversely, gifted children tend to develop into superior adults. The environmental conditions of early childhood have been found to exert a profound influence upon the development of genius. Such influences may operate either through direct intellectual stimulation or through the establishment of motivational tendencies and potent interests which will spur the individual on to overcome obstacles and to reach a difficult goal.

REFERENCES

1. Adler, A. *The Neurotic Constitution*. N. Y.: Moffat Yard, 1917. Pp. 456.

2. Brimhall, D. R. "Family Resemblances among American Men of Science," *Amer. Naturalist*, 1922, 56, 504–547; 1923, 57, 74–88, 137–152, 326–344.

3. Castle, C. S. "A Statistical Study of Eminent Women," *Arch. Psychol.*, No. 27, 1913. Pp. 90.

4. Cattell, J. McK. *A Statistical Study of American Men of Science:* III. *Science*, 1906, N. S. 24, 732–742.

5. ——. "Families of American Men of Science," I: *Pop. Sci. Mo.*, 1915, 86, 504–515; II: *Sci. Mo.*, 1917, 4, 248–262; III: *ibid.*, 1917, 5, 368–377.

6. Cattell, J. McK., and Cattell, J., ed. *American Men of Science*, Fifth edition. N. Y.: Science Press, 1933. Pp. 1278.

7. Clarke, E. L. "American Men of Letters," *Stud. in Hist., Econ., and Public Law*, Columbia Univ., Vol. 72, No. 168, 1916. Pp. 169.

8. Cox, C. M. *Genetic Studies of Genius:* Vol. II, *The Early Mental Traits of Three Hundred Geniuses*. Stanford Univ., Calif.: Stanford Univ. Press, 1926. Pp. 842.

9. de Candolle, A. *Histoire des sciences et des savants depuis deux siècles*. Genève: Georg, 1873. Pp. 482.

10. Dooley, L. "Psychoanalytic Studies of Genius," *Amer. J. Psychol.*, 1916, 27, 363–417.

11. Eells, W. C. "The Center of Population of Higher Education," *Sch. and Soc.*, 1926, 24, 339–344.

12. Ellis, H. *A Study of British Genius*. London: Hurst and Blackett, 1904. Pp. 300.

13. Galton, F. *Hereditary Genius*. N. Y.: Macmillan, 1914. Pp. 379 (original ed., London, 1869).

14. ——. *English Men of Science*. N. Y.: Appleton, 1875. Pp. 206.

15. Garrison, C. G., Burke, A., and Hollingworth, L. S. "The Psychology of a Prodigious Child," *J. Appl. Psychol.*, 1917, I, 101–110.

16. Hall, G. S. *Adolescence.* N. Y.: Appleton, 1905, Vol. I. Pp. 589.

17. Hirsch, N. D. M. *Genius and Creative Intelligence.* Cambridge, Mass.: Sci-Art, 1931. Pp. 339.

18. Hollingworth, L. S. *Gifted Children: Their Nature and Nurture.* N. Y.: Macmillan, 1926. Pp. 374.

19. ——. "Subsequent History of E—; Ten Years after the Initial Report," *J. Appl. Psychol.*, 1927, 11, 385–390.

20. Hollingworth, L. S., Garrison, C. G., and Burke, A. "Subsequent History of E—; Five Years after the Initial Report," *J. Appl. Psychol.*, 1922, 6, 205–210.

21. Jacoby, P. *Études sur la sélection chez l'homme.* Paris: Alcan, 1904 (original ed. 1881). Pp. 620.

22. Lombroso, C. *The Man of Genius.* N. Y.: Scribners, 1895. Pp. 370.

23. Moreau, J. *La psychologie morbide.* Paris: Masson, 1859. Pp. 576.

24. Nisbet, J. F. *The Insanity of Genius.* N. Y.: Scribners, 1912 (original ed., London, 1891). Pp. 341.

25. Odin, A. *Genèse des grands hommes, gens de lettres Français modernes.* Vol. I, Paris: Librarie Universitaire, H. Welter, ed., 1895. Pp. 640. Vol. II, Lausanne: H. Mignot, ed., 1895. Pp. 378.

26. Pintner, R. *Intelligence Testing: Methods and Results.* N. Y.: Holt, 1931. Pp. 555.

27. Redfield, C. L. *Great Men and How They Are Produced.* Chicago, 1915. Pp. 32.

28. Terman, L. M. "The Intelligence Quotient of Francis Galton in Childhood," *Amer. J. Psychol.*, 1917, 28, 209–215.

29. Terman, L. M., and Burks, B. S. "The Gifted Child." Ch. 19 in *Handbook of Child Psychology.* C. Murchison, ed. Worcester, Mass.: Clark Univ. Press, 1933. Pp. 956.

30. Terman, L. M., and Fenton, J. C. "Preliminary Report of a Gifted Juvenile Author," *J. Appl. Psychol.*, 1921, 5, 163–178.

31. Terman, L. M., *et al. Genetic Studies of Genius:* Vol. I.

Mental and Physical Traits of a Thousand Gifted Children. Stanford Univ., Calif.: Stanford Univ. Press, 1925. Pp. 648.

32. Terman, L. M., *et al. Genetic Studies of Genius:* Vol. III. *The Promise of Youth: Follow-Up Studies of a Thousand Gifted Children.* Stanford Univ., Calif.: Stanford Univ. Press, 1930. Pp. 508.

33. Witte, K. *The Education of Karl Witte* (tr. by L. Wiener). N. Y.: Crowell, 1914. Pp. 312.

34. Woods, F. A. *Mental and Moral Heredity in Royalty.* N. Y.: Holt, 1906. Pp. 312.

35. Yoder, A. H. "The Study of the Boyhood of Great Men," *Ped. Sem.*, 1894–96, 3, 134–156.

36. *Twenty-third Yearbook of the National Society for the Study of Education,* 1924.

CHAPTER XIV

SEX DIFFERENCES: MAJOR PROBLEMS

Specialization of function between the sexes has been a powerful social tradition in almost all cultural groups. The particular tasks assigned to each sex vary from group to group and are even occasionally reversed, but some differentiation of activity is practically universal. These distinctions are impressed upon the individual from early childhood, either by actual overt differences in training and play-activities, or by the more subtle but equally potent inculcation of traditional beliefs and ideals. It is apparent that in most societies the effectual environments of the two sexes are fundamentally diverse from an early age. Under such conditions, we should expect pronounced variation in the emotional and intellectual development of the two sexes. By a curious circular argument, however, these socially conditioned behavioral differences are attributed to innate factors.

The belief in hereditary sex differences in mental and emotional traits is an old and persistent one. It is only since the development of objective and quantitative testing methods that the notion of female inferiority has been dispelled among scientists. In the general public, this belief still prevails, as is manifested by the reluctance to open certain educational and professional opportunities to women and by the frequent discrimination against individuals on the basis of sex alone. The reasoning underlying such practices is that it would be futile to attempt to train men and women alike, since the existing differences in their behavior are so clearly apparent. This view, of course, fails to consider the possibility that the existing sex differences may themselves be the result of the diverse training and environment of the two sexes.

Sex Differences in Achievement

The relative intellectual achievements of men and women through the ages have frequently been cited as evidence of a sex difference in ability. An examination of any biographical directory or encyclopedia shows a far greater number of men than women to have achieved eminence. And of the few women listed in such compendiums, many acquired fame through special circumstances rather than through the possession of exceptional talent. In Ellis' study (9) of British genius, only 55 women were included in the total group of 1030 subjects. Nor did the standard of eminence seem to be higher for women than for men. On the contrary, Ellis claims that many of the women in his group had become famous "on the strength of achievements which would not have allowed a man to play a similarly large part" (9, p. 10).

Cattell, in a carefully drawn up list of the 1000 most eminent persons in the world, lists only 32 women. Of these, 11 were hereditary sovereigns and 8 became eminent through misfortune, beauty, or some other circumstance. This leaves an extremely small number who may be said to have distinguished themselves through their superior talents (5, p. 375).

Similar results were obtained by Castle (4) in her statistical study of eminent women. A total of 868 names of women were collected, representing 42 nations and covering a wide range of epochs from the seventh century B.C. to the nineteenth century. The *largest number* of women in the group achieved eminence through literary pursuits, 337 or 38.8% of the subjects being classified in this field. The *highest degree of eminence*, however, as indicated by the number of lines allotted to the individual in standard biographical directories, was obtained by women as sovereigns, political leaders, mothers of eminent men, and mistresses. Among the other non-intellectual factors through which women achieved fame in the past are listed marriage, religion, birth, philanthropy, tragic fate, beauty, and "immortalized in literature."

In interpreting these results, Castle seems to recognize certain environmental influences. Thus she states: "It is probable that woman has had more opportunity in literature than in any other line of work. Her actions have been restricted in various degrees at different times, and in different localities, and, to a certain extent, her thought has been regulated" (4, p. 41). In spite of this assertion, however, Castle suggests on the following page that, "the common concept of woman as a creature of feeling rather than a creature of reason may not be without foundation. If this conception is just, our classification tends to show that when woman has attained eminence, it has not been in spite of her femininity, but rather because of it" (4, p. 42). Since both the qualifications for "eminence" and the attributes of "femininity" are culturally determined, such a conclusion is rather redundant.

In more recent times, the discrepancy in number of men and women who have distinguished themselves in intellectual pursuits is still large, although constantly diminishing. In the 1927 edition of *American Men of Science* (cf. 6, p. 1264), there were listed 725 women out of a total of 9785 entries in the pure sciences. The percentage of women in the various fields ranged from 2.1% in physics to 22% in psychology. In the group of 250 scien-

.ists who were "starred" [1] in the 1933 edition, only 3 women vere included (6).

It is obviously impossible to draw any conclusions re-;arding the innate abilities of the two sexes from such :omparisons. The recorded differences in achievement :ould be fully accounted for in terms of the environmental :onditions which have prevailed. Many types of *occupa-ions* have been completely closed to women until recently. Thus, on the basis of their sex alone, women have been :ffectively barred from achieving eminence in a number)f fields. When women have eventually been admitted)fficially to such vocations, prejudice and discrimination igainst them have still been so prevalent that only a few :ould succeed. Even today, competition is not on an :qual basis for men and women in most occupational fields.

Educational opportunities [2] have likewise been very lissimilar for the two sexes, although at present the en-/ironments of the two sexes are more nearly equated in :his respect than in any other. Institutions of higher earning were slow to open their doors to women. Al-:hough America was in advance of most other countries n the education of women, until nearly the middle of the lineteenth century there was not a single institution of :ollegiate rank in this country which admitted women. Professional and post-graduate education was not avail-able until a much later date. Even in the elementary and secondary schools, the traditional curriculum of girls was different from that of boys, including much less science and more literature, art, and other "genteel" subjects.

Nor can *general home influences* be disregarded. Even

---

[1] The starred men of science represent approximately the 1000 most eminent scientists in the country. The original 1000 were selected in 1903; 250 additions were made in 1933, similar additions having been made at successive five-year intervals.

[2] Cf. Goodsell (11).

in the most enlightened and progressive homes, differences are introduced in the environments of boys and girls which may prove very important in determining subsequent development. In general, girls are considered weaker and more frail than boys; they are sheltered more and are taught to be neater and quieter than their brothers. Boys and girls are given different toys to play with and different books to read. All of these apparently minor environmental factors, operating constantly and from a very early age, may exert a lasting influence upon the development of the child's interests, emotional characteristics, and intellectual talents.

Finally, the relatively intangible but highly effective factor of *social expectancy* should be mentioned. This operates to perpetuate all group differences, once they have been established. What is expected of an individual is a powerful element in the determination of what he will do. When such expectation has the force of social tradition behind it and is corroborated at every instant by family attitudes, everyday contacts in work and play, and nearly all other encounters with one's fellow-beings, it is very difficult not to succumb to it. As a result, the individual himself usually becomes convinced that he is "superior" or "inferior," or that he possesses this or that talent, interest, or attitude, according to the dictates of his particular culture.

Sex Differences in Variability

During the last decade of the nineteenth century, the doctrine of sex differences in intellectual variability [1] became prominent. It was pointed out that, although the *average ability* of men and women might be equal, the

---

[1] The possibility of greater male variability in physical traits was originally alluded to by Darwin, although he does not seem to have considered the problem of great importance (cf. 20).

distribution of ability in one sex might cover a wider range than in the other. Thus it was suggested that the variability of intelligence among males is greater than among females, there being more men than women at either extreme of the distribution. These hypothetical distributions are illustrated in Figure 46. It will be noted

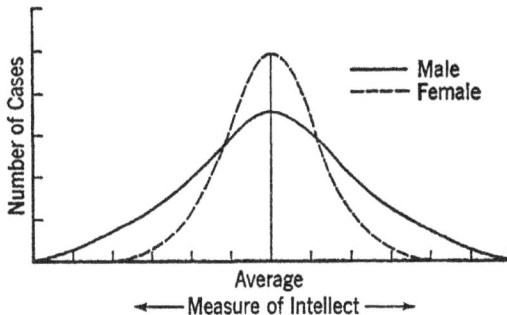

Fig. 46. Hypothetical Distribution of Intellect among Men and Women According to the Doctrine of Greater Male Variability.

that, theoretically, the averages of two groups can be identical while the ranges differ considerably.

The doctrine of greater male variability was regarded as a fundamental biological law and was believed to hold for all traits, physical as well as mental. Thus Havelock Ellis, one of its chief protagonists, wrote as follows:

> From an organic standpoint, therefore, women represent the more stable and conservative element in evolution (8, p. 421) . . . in men, as in males generally, there is an organic variational tendency to diverge from the average, in women, as in females generally, an organic tendency, notwithstanding all their facility for minor oscillations, to stability and conservatism, involving a diminished individualism and variability (8, p. 425).

This doctrine enjoyed a long popularity and was accepted by several psychologists in their analysis of sex differences (cf., e.g., 5, 24). The evidence offered in support of the greater intellectual variability of the male was two-fold. On the one hand, the statistics on eminence were cited as proof of the greater frequency of superior intellect as well as of the presence of more extreme positive deviations among the male sex. Similar data were introduced to establish the wider range of male intelligence at the lower end of the distribution. Surveys of institutions for the feebleminded in several countries revealed a consistent excess of males among the inmates. Thus it was argued that there were more idiots as well as more geniuses among men, and that women as a group tended to cluster more closely around the average or mediocre degrees of ability.

The cultural basis of sex differences in the attainment of eminence has already been discussed. No biological law need be invoked to account for the greater frequency of men in the biographical directories and encyclopedias. The greater incidence of males in institutions for mental defectives has likewise been found to result from cultural factors. This was especially demonstrated in a study by L. S. Hollingworth (14) on 1000 cases referred for examination to the Clearing House for Mental Defectives at the Post Graduate Hospital in New York City, as well as 1142 cases actually committed at the New York City Children's Hospital.[1] Analysis of intelligence test scores and other available data revealed the differential operation of a selective factor upon the two sexes.

In the first place, the males referred for examination, as well as those actually committed, were on the average much younger than the females. Secondly, the I.Q.'s of the females presented for examination were lower than those of the males. This difference in I.Q. was even greater when the cases actually committed were compared. A

[1] An institution for mental defectives, then located at Randall's Island, N. Y. C.

survey of the previous occupations and general case histories of the subjects suggested that the probable explanation of these findings lies in the uncompetitive nature of many occupations open to women. This makes the detection of feeblemindedness as well as the necessity of commitment less likely among women than among men. A woman of moron level can survive outside of an institution by turning to housework, prostitution, or marriage as a means of livelihood. The boy, on the other hand, is forced into industrial work at a relatively early age and will soon reveal his mental deficiency in the severe competition which he encounters. Thus, although there is an excess of males in institutions for mental defectives, it would seem that there are more feebleminded females outside of institutions.

Karl Pearson (20) was among the first to challenge the adequacy of studying sex differences in variability by a comparison of the extremes of the distribution. He called attention to the need for direct measurement of *variability around the average* in large groups of unselected subjects. Pearson himself computed coefficients of relative variability for several classes of data, consisting chiefly of physical and anatomical measurements on adults. He found no evidence of greater male variability, but rather a slight tendency to greater female variability. Similarly, Hollingworth and Montague (15) collected a large number of physical measurements on 1000 male and 1000 female infants at birth, thus ruling out any possible effects of differential environment. No consistent sex difference in variability was found.

A mass of data is now available on male and female variability in a wide variety of traits.[1] In such character-

---

[1] For summaries of a large portion of this material, cf. Henmon and Livingstone (13) and Lincoln (17).

istics as height, weight, physiological maturity, dentition, and anatomical development, the data are inconsistent. The relative variability of the two sexes differs with the specific trait under consideration, the age of the subjects, their social and economic level, and even the particular community in which the data are obtained. Intelligence test results exhibit a similar lack of consistency. On individual tests such as the Stanford-Binet, girls seem somewhat more variable, whereas boys show wider variability on many group tests. Age is also a factor in determining the relative variability of the sexes on these tests. The same is true of variability in school achievement. The findings differ with the specific situation, in one case the boys being more variable, in another the girls. In the large majority of cases, furthermore, the differences in variability in favor of either sex are too slight to be of much significance.

SELECTIVE FACTORS

In all group comparisons, selective factors may operate to vitiate the results. When a group is not a random or representative sample of the population from which it is drawn, it is said to be a select group. Such a sampling is unsuited for any type of investigation, since any results obtained with it could not be generalized but would apply only to the specific group employed. An additional complication in the comparison of two populations arises from the fact that selection may have operated differently in the two groups. Thus if a group of college girls were compared with trade school boys, the two samplings would be selected in different ways. Not only is neither group representative of men or women in general, but the one represents the upper end of the female distribution and the other a central or slightly inferior segment of the male distribution. In addition to being unrepresentative, these groups are not comparable.

Selective factors are often difficult to detect and usually difficult to control. An example of a selective factor whose presence was repeatedly overlooked is furnished by the data on the relative incidence of males and females in institutions for the feebleminded (cf. above). A similar selective influence has been demonstrated in high school enrollment. It would seem that groups of boys and girls attending the same high school constitute truly comparable samples for the study of sex differences. But investigations on elementary and high school students have demonstrated that this is not the case.

In two separate studies, the Pressey Group Test of intelligence was administered to 2544 elementary school-children between the ages of 8 and 16 (22) and to 5929 high school seniors ranging in age from 16 to 23 (3). The percentages of boys who reached or exceeded the *median score* of the girls, as well as the number of cases in each group, are shown below. In the elementary school study, the data are reported separately for each age group (cf. 22, p. 327). In the study on high school seniors, a single summary figure is given for the entire group (cf. 3, p. 61).

Elementary School Group	Number of Cases		Per Cent of Boys Reaching or Exceeding Girls' Median
Age	Boys	Girls	
8	57	92	40
9	132	154	34
10	176	177	42
11	179	167	41
12	182	180	44
13	174	174	39
14	138	162	43
15	102	139	41
16	62	97	49
High School Seniors	2422	3503	56.2

It will be noted that in the elementary school grades the girls excel at all ages, although the sex difference is negligible among the 16-year-olds. Among the high school seniors, however, this relationship is reversed, over 50% of the boys reaching or exceeding the girls' median score.

This reversal becomes intelligible if we examine the relative number of each sex in the elementary grades and in the senior year of high school. Throughout the high school period there is a much more rapid elimination of boys than girls. Boys whose academic work is not satisfactory are more likely to leave school and go to work, whereas girls tend to be kept in school longer. Girls also seem to adjust better to the school curriculum and school routine in general. The less intelligent girls will exert more effort and manage to pass sufficient subjects to stay in school, while boys in the same situation are more likely to rebel against school work. This explanation was borne out by an examination of the scholastic history of those students who had dropped out in the course of their high school work. Owing to the differential action of this selective influence upon the two sexes, differences between the intelligence test scores of high school boys and girls cannot be attributed to a true sex difference. In the evaluation of any study on group differences, selective factors are one of the most subtle forms of error to be guarded against.

Relative Maturity

A further complication in the analysis of sex differences arises from a difference in the developmental rate of boys and girls. It has been clearly established that in physical characteristics girls reach maturity earlier than boys. Moreover, at any one age during childhood, girls are usually farther advanced towards their ultimate adult status than boys.

Several investigators have compared the height and weight of boys and girls at successive ages. In order directly to compare the developmental status of the two sexes in these traits, each age average can be expressed as a percentage of the adult norm for that sex. In Table XVI will be found such percentages for boys and girls between the ages of 6 and 17. The figures are based upon data from several investigations. It will be noted that *at each age measured,* the girls have attained a greater percentage of their adult height and weight than the boys. Similar results were obtained in an extensive investigation by Baldwin (2), in which the *same subjects* were measured at successive ages. At certain ages the developmental acceleration of the girls is so great that they are actually taller and heavier than boys, in absolute measures. In Baldwin's data, the girls were found to be superior in height between the ages of 11 and 13, and in weight between 9 and 16.

TABLE XVI

Percentage of Final Growth Which Has Been Attained at Ages
Preceding Maturity

(After Lincoln, 17, p. 20)

Age	Height		Weight	
	Boys	Girls	Boys	Girls
17.5	100	100		
16.5	97.5	99.2	100	100
15.5	94.5	98.3	88.7	95.1
14.5	90.3	96.3	78.9	87.4
13.5	86.4	93.3	70.0	79.0
12.5	83.4	89.4	63.5	70.0
11.5	80.6	85.6	58.4	61.8
10.5	78.0	82.5	54.1	56.0
9.5	75.1	79.3	49.0	51.0
8.5	73.3	76.1	45.0	46.7
7.5	69.1	72.8	40.9	42.4
6.5	65.9	69.0	37.4	38.5

Other aspects of physical development show a similar acceleration of the female sex. It is a well known fact that girls reach the age of reproductive maturity earlier than boys. In two investigations (7, 1) on about 4800 boys and 1241 girls, respectively, the children were classified into pubescent and post-pubescent on the basis of several physiological observations. The average age at which the girls entered the post-pubescent stage was between 13 and 13½; the boys reached this stage approximately one year later. Except at age 16, the percentage of girls in each age group who were classified as post-pubescent exceeded the percentage of boys so classified by a substantial amount.

Anatomical development has been measured by the relative degree of ossification of the bones of the hand. In this also, girls have been found to be in advance of boys, the median anatomic indices of the girls being higher than those of the boys at every age from 6 to 16 (cf. 21). A similar difference has been found in dentition. In general, girls shed their deciduous teeth sooner and get their permanent teeth at an earlier age than boys. In the case of certain teeth, these differences amount to one year or over (cf. 12).

The significance of sex differences in the rate of physical growth has been emphasized by several writers (cf., e.g., 3, 17, 22). It has been suggested that girls might be accelerated in mental as well as physical development. Thus the fact that girls of elementary school age excel on most intelligence tests has been attributed to this factor. If this were the case, equated age groups of boys and girls would not be comparable. It would then be necessary to equate the sexes in regard to developmental stage or physical maturity rather than chronological age. But such a procedure would introduce an inequality in amount of training and general environmental stimulation. This problem only arises, of course, in the comparison of children, and does not apply to adults. Children, however, have been the most frequent subjects for surveys on sex differences, both because of their greater accessibility · in large numbers and because they have been exposed to a relatively more homogeneous environment.

It should be noted that mental acceleration of girls has not been directly demonstrated. Its possibility has only been inferred by analogy with physical development. It is doubtful, however, whether physical maturity can have much influence upon intellectual development. The data on the relationship of mental and physical traits are too consistently negative for such an assumption (cf. Ch. VIII). In emotional and other personality traits it is probable that the onset of puberty and the relative physiological maturity of the individual introduce a disturbing factor in sex comparisons at certain ages. But in regard to the child's intellectual status, the environmental stimulation to which he has been exposed is far more significant than slight differences in physical condition.

RELIABILITY OF A GROUP DIFFERENCE

In the evaluation of any obtained difference between two groups, it is necessary to determine the *statistical reliability* of such a difference. Reliability means, in this case, the degree of consistency among the results obtained on different samplings of the same population. The problem of reliability arises from the fact that in any investigation only a sample of the entire population is employed. For example, if the population under investigation is defined as public school children in American cities, data may be gathered on some 5000 or 6000 children in a dozen schools. From these results, the investigator generalizes to the entire population. If the sampling was carefully chosen to be representative of the given population, such conclusions will not be far in error. The figures thus obtained, however, will not be identical to those which would have been secured by testing the entire population of American city public school children. Nor will the results from successive samplings of the population coincide perfectly. Had a different sampling of 5000 city public school children been employed, slightly different results would have been obtained.

This variation in results from sampling to sampling within the same population is known as a *sampling error*. Statistical measures of reliability furnish a theoretical estimate of the probable limits within which such errors will fall. Formulæ are available for the computation of the sampling error of all statistical measures, such as averages, differences between averages, measures of variability, and correlation coefficients. It is thus possible to estimate the maximum amount of variation to be expected in any statistical measure if the experiment were repeated on another sampling of the same population.

The most common measures of reliability are the "probable error" (P.E.) and the "standard error" (S.E. or σ). The total estimated range within which a given measure will fall in successive samples is covered by $\pm$ 4 $\times$ P.E. and $\pm$ 3 $\times$ S.E. An hypothetical example will serve to illustrate the application of such measures. If the average score obtained by a group is 40 points and the P.E. of this average is found to be 2 points, then

$$4 \times \text{P.E.} = 8 \text{ and } \begin{matrix} 40 + 8 = 48 \\ 40 - 8 = 32. \end{matrix}$$

Therefore, in successive samples of the population from which this group was drawn, the average might fall between 32 and 48. These extreme values will, however, be rare, and in one-half of the samples the average will probably fall between 38 and 42, or ± 1 P.E. from the obtained value.

Similarly, let us suppose that a group of sixth grade public school boys and girls obtained the following average scores on an intelligence test:

Average Score

Girls	90
Boys	80
Difference	10

Let us assume further that the P.E. of this difference is 5. In different samples of sixth grade public school children, we should therefore expect the sex difference to vary from 30 points ($10 + [4 \times 5] = 30$) to -10 points ($10 - [4 \times 5] = -10$). In other words, the relative standing of the male and female groups would be *reversed* in certain samplings, and the boys' average might be as much as 10 points higher than that of the girls. This is what is meant by an *unreliable* difference. The same conclusion can be arrived at more directly by dividing the obtained difference by its P.E. If the difference is 4 or more times as large as its P.E., there will be no reversal of direction and the difference is said to be perfectly reliable. In the present example, it will be noted that the difference is only twice as large as its P.E. ($10 \div 5 = 2$). This value, called the *critical ratio*, is an index of the degree to which the obtained figures represent a reliable or consistent trend.

The probable error (and the standard error) of an obtained difference depends upon the *size* of the samplings employed as well as the amount of *variability* within the samplings. It is apparent that the larger the sampling, the more reliably will the results be established. If the sampling were infinitely large, the probable error would be zero, since the entire theoretical population would then have been included. In most of the earlier investigations on sex differences, the samples employed were so small as to yield extremely large probable errors, had the latter been computed. The sex differences reported in such studies may have been due entirely to chance errors of sampling.

Similarly, the wide variability existing within each sex in regard to any trait renders the differences between averages less reliable. If all women were of identical height, for example, and all men were likewise equal in height, then sex differences in height could be reliably established by comparing only one representative of each sex. All other samplings would yield the same difference, since variation within each sex would be zero. The greater the variability within either group, the larger will be the probable error of the obtained values. In the computation of P.E.'s and S.E.'s, both the number of cases and the variability of the group are taken into account.[1]

OVERLAPPING

The establishment of a perfectly reliable difference between two groups does not preclude the possibility of a large amount of overlapping between such groups. In Figure 47 will be found the distribution curves of a group of 189 boys and 206 girls in the third and fourth elementary school grades on a test of arithmetic reasoning. The average score of the boys is 40.39 and that of the girls 35.81. The difference between the averages is 4.58 points and the P.E. of this difference is only 0.58. The difference is thus nearly eight times as large as its P.E. and can be

[1] S.E. of an average $= \dfrac{\text{S.D. of the group}}{\sqrt{N}}$; P.E. of an average $= .6745$

$\times \dfrac{\text{S.D. of the group}}{\sqrt{N}}$. For a further discussion of the computation and use of these measures, see Garrett (10).

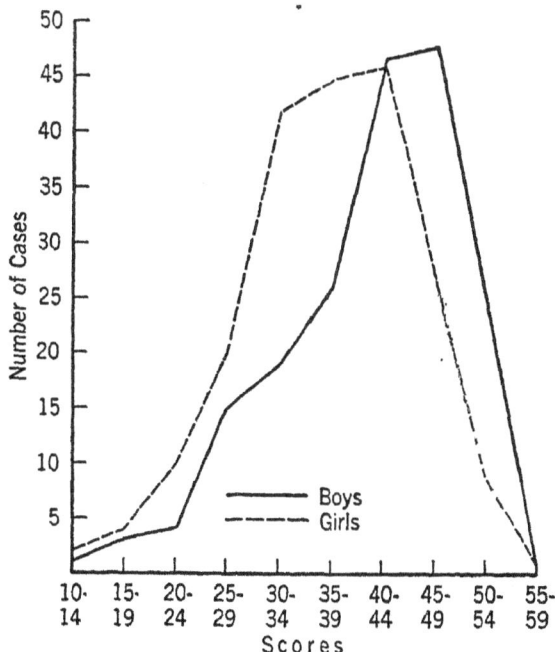

FIG. 47. DISTRIBUTION OF BOYS AND GIRLS ON A TEST OF ARITHMETIC REASONING. (Data from Schiller, 23, p. 67.)

regarded as perfectly reliable. An examination of the distribution curves, however, reveals a large amount of overlapping between the two groups. A very large percentage of boys and girls fall within the same range of scores. Furthermore, 38% of the girls obtained scores higher than the boys' average, and 24% of the boys scored below the girls' average.

Thus, on account of overlapping, any relationship established for the group averages will not necessarily hold for individual cases. Although one group may excel another by a large and significant amount, individuals can be found in the "inferior" group who will surpass certain individuals in the "superior" group. Owing to the large extent of individual differences within any one group as contrasted to the relatively small difference between group averages, an individual's membership in a given group furnishes little or no information about his status in any trait.

In the large majority of investigations on group differences, only averages are considered. For a complete picture of the relative standing of the two groups, however, some index of the degree of overlapping should be included. The best procedure would be to report the entire frequency distributions of the two groups. This is often impracticable, however. A simpler alternative, in the case of normally distributed samplings, is to state the percentage of subjects in one group who reach or exceed the median (or average) of the other. Complete overlapping would then be indicated if 50% of one group reached or exceeded the median of the other.[1] If more than 50% of group A reach or exceed the median of group B, then group A is superior to group B; if less than 50%, A is inferior to B. Occasionally, some other value is substituted for the median as the point of reference. Thus the investigator might report the percentage of group A which reaches or exceeds the highest score obtained in group B, or the percentage of group A which reaches or exceeds the upper quarter of group B.

Nature of the Measuring Instrument

It is a platitude to insist that, in order to obtain significant data on any question, an accurate measuring instrument must be employed. Yet the methods of measurement employed in the study of sex differences, as well as in other group comparisons, have frequently been crude and often wholly unsuited to the problem. Thus ratings by associates were used in many of the

---

[1] The curves will not coincide, of course, if the *ranges* are unequal. In such a case, complete overlapping is obtained only in the sense that one distribution is contained entirely within the other.

earlier investigations on sex differences, and especially in those concerned with personalty traits. Teachers' ratings of schoolchildren were especially common. It is obvious that such ratings do little more than reflect the systematic bias of the judges. In the comparison of such groups as the sexes or various "races" or nationalities about which definite beliefs are fostered within each culture, ratings cannot be regarded as an index of the subject's actual standing.

The reliability of the tests should also be considered. If a test is too short or if performance on it is affected by too many irrelevant factors, it will yield different results on repeated administrations. On such a test, the scores of the *same individuals* will vary widely from time to time. These discrepancies in test scores are known as *errors of measurement.* Group differences found with a short and poorly constructed test may be entirely spurious and may be expected to disappear upon a reëxamination of the same subjects.

Much confusion has also been introduced into discussions of group differences by the relatively loose designations assigned to most mental tests. If a test is labeled "analytic reasoning," there is a tendency to assume that it actually measures that trait, although such a trait may not even exist as a unitary function and may consist of a manifold of independent abilities. Similarly, if two tests are given the same name, they are commonly regarded as measuring the same function. An hypothetical example will show how this practice may affect group comparisons. Let us suppose that one investigator has constructed a sentence completion test, which he labels a measure of "logical thinking." In such a test, as in most verbal tests, girls will probably excel. If now another investigator also sets out to construct a test of "logical thinking" and decides to employ arithmetic problems as his material, he will find that boys excel in this trait. The results of the two studies will thus seem to be in direct contradiction, owing to the use of a common term to cover two discrete types of mental activity.

Many discrepancies in the data on sex differences may be attributed simply to such a confusion of terminology. Unless identical tests are administered in an identical manner, we cannot assume that the same mental processes were measured in every case. The use of a different time limit, for example, might change a power test into a speed test and thus yield entirely different results. A slight alteration in the directions might make it more difficult for the subjects to understand what is required of them and might thereby introduce a new element into the test, *viz.*, ability to follow verbal instructions. "Intelligence" scales are probably the best example of the use of general terms in describing widely diverse tests. Much controversy has been occasioned by the application of such scales. Owing to the employment of "intelligence" scales which sample different sets of abilities, some students of sex differences conclude that boys are more intelligent, others that girls are more intelligent.

A closely related problem pertains to the use of "lump scores" in group comparisons. Group differences in specific abilities may be completely obscured by the comparison of total or average scores on a battery of tests. If, for example, boys excel in numerical aptitude and girls in verbal aptitude, and a scale of so-called general intelligence is weighted equally with items from both fields, no significant sex difference in total score will be found. Should the scale be overweighted with items of one type, furthermore, it will favor the group excelling in that trait and indicate an apparent difference in general intelligence. In recent years, with the development of a more critical attitude towards mental testing, there has been a growing tendency to look for group differences in separate abilities rather than in "general level of performance." In the study of group differences, it is of the greatest importance to state results in highly specific terms and to limit conclusions to the particular materials, procedure, and other conditions of each investigation.[1]

SEX DIFFERENCES AND CULTURE

The most crucial problem in any analysis of group differences pertains to their origin. The theoretical and practical implications of behavioral characteristics which are innately fixed and of those which are socially conditioned are fundamentally different. The question of heredity and environment is always a difficult one to answer. It is especially elusive in the case of human development because of the practical impossibility of rearing children under rigidly controlled laboratory conditions. And as was shown above, we cannot otherwise assume that the environments of the two sexes have been equated, even in the case of fraternal twins.

There are, however, certain indirect sources of evidence which throw some light upon the origin of group differences. Thus a biological or hereditary determination of sex differences in psychological traits would imply the existence of *a universal pattern of male and female behavior.* If, on the other hand, such differences are environmentally conditioned, we should expect the traditional behavioral characteristics of each sex *to vary from one culture to another.* Data on this question are as yet relatively meagre. Psychologists have generally neglected the wealth of infor-

[1] For a further discussion of many of the difficulties involved in the study of sex differences, see Lehman and Witty (16).

mation offered by the comparative study of behavior phenomena in different cultural milieux. Certain facts collected by anthropologists, however, have a direct bearing upon this problem.

The play activities of boys and girls have been a subject of frequent speculation. Some would argue, for instance, that girls play with dolls because of a nascent "maternal drive" or some similar innate interest or emotional trait characteristic of their sex. The almost complete absence of this type of play activity among boys is regarded as an index of a fundamental biological diversification in emotional response. An observation made by Mead (18) in her studies on the island of Manus in New Guinea is of interest in this connection. Dolls are ordinarily unknown to the children on this island. But when they were presented for the first time with some wooden statuettes, it was the boys and not the girls who accepted them as dolls, crooning lullabies to them and displaying typical parental behavior. This reaction is to be understood in terms of the pattern of adult behavior in Manus. Owing to the traditional division of labor, the women are busy with their various duties throughout the day, while the men have much more leisure time between their activities of hunting and fishing. As a result the father rather than the mother attends to the children and plays with them. This socially established differentiation of behavior was reflected in the play responses of the boys and girls.

A vivid demonstration of the cultural determination of behavior is furnished by a more recent study of Mead (19) in which she observed the traditional emotional characteristics of men and women in three primitive societies in New Guinea. Each of these groups presented a different pattern of male and female personality. Among the

Arapesh both men and women displayed emotional characteristics which in our society would be labeled distinctly feminine. In this group both sexes are trained to be coöperative, unaggressive, gentle, non-competitive, and responsive to the needs of others. They are strongly imbued with a sense of obligation towards any who are weaker or younger than themselves. Even their typical response towards material objects is not one of possession but of solicitude.

The *Mundugumur*, a river-dwelling tribe of cannibals and head-hunters, present a sharply contrasting picture. In this society both men and women are violent, aggressive, ruthless, and competitive. They take great delight in action and in fighting. They are quick to perceive an insult and ever ready to avenge it. Because of an intricate system of family organization, the child is born into a hostile world, in which most members of his own sex are his enemies. This is particularly true of boys, but a child of either sex will be disliked and resented by some members of the family.

Perhaps the most interesting pattern is presented by the *Tchambuli*, among whom there is a genuine reversal of the sex-attitude of our culture. It is the women who have the position of power in Tchambuli. The group depends for its food supply upon the fishing of the women, the men rarely engaging in this activity. Fish is also the staple product of trade, in exchange for which several essential commodities are obtained. Similarly, it is the women who make mosquito bags, the most important article of Tchambuli manufacture and in great demand by outside purchasers. The men, on the other hand, engage predominantly in artistic and non-utilitarian pursuits. Most men are highly skilled in more than one art, including dancing, carving, painting, and others. It is the man in this society who is concerned with the beauty and elaboration of his costumes and the excellence of his artistic accomplishments. This type of life is reflected in pronounced personality differences between the sexes. The women are impersonal, practical, and efficient. Their attitude towards the men is one of kindly tolerance and appreciation. The men are graceful, artistic, emotionally subservient, timid, sensitive to the opinions of others, and throughout their lives dependent upon the security afforded to them by the women.

Each of these three cultures has its "deviants," its maladjusted individuals whose personality traits clash with the accepted standards, as in our society. But the deviant in one society often coincides with the traditional ideal of another. Thus the "masculine" woman among the Tchambuli is one who embodies the typically feminine characteristics of our society; the "effeminate" Tchambuli man displays behavior which we should characterize as typically masculine. These observations inevitably suggest an environmental interpretation. In a final evaluation of her findings, Mead writes:

> We are forced to conclude that human nature is almost unbelievably malleable, responding accurately and contrastingly to contrasting cultural conditions. The differences between individuals who are members of different cultures, like the differences between individuals within a culture, are almost entirely to be laid to differences in conditioning, especially during early childhood, and the form of this conditioning is culturally determined. Standardized personality differences between the sexes are of this order, cultural creations to which each generation, male and female, is trained to conform (19, pp. 280–281).

REFERENCES

1. Baldwin, B. T. "A Measuring Scale for Physical Growth and Physiological Age," *Nat. Soc. Stud. Educ., Fifteenth Yearbook*, 1916, Part I, 11–22.

2. ——. "The Physical Growth of Children from Birth to Maturity," *Univ. Iowa Stud. Child Welfare*, 1921, I. Pp. 411.

3. Book, W. F., and Meadows, J. L. "Sex Differences in 5925 High School Seniors in Ten Psychological Tests," *J. Appl. Psychol.*, 1928, 12, 56–81.

4. Castle, C. S. "A Statistical Study of Eminent Women," *Arch. Psychol.*, No. 27, 1913. Pp. 90.

5. Cattell, J. McK. "A Statistical Study of Eminent Men," *Pop. Sci. Mon.*, 1903, 62, 359–377.

6. Cattell, J. McK., and Cattell, J. *American Men of Science: a Biographical Directory.* (Fifth edition.) N. Y.: Science Press, 1933. Pp. 1278.

7. Crampton, C. W. "Anatomical or Physiological Age *versus* Chronological Age," *Ped. Sem.*, 1908, 15, 230–232.

8. Ellis, H. *Man and Woman: a Study of Human Secondary Sexual Characters.* N. Y.: Scribners, 1904. Pp. 488.

9. ——. *A Study of British Genius.* London: Hurst and Blackett, 1904. Pp. 300.

10. Garrett, H. E. *Statistics in Psychology and Education.* N. Y.: Longmans Green, 1932. Pp. 317.

11. Goodsell, W. *The Education of Women.* N. Y.: Macmillan, 1923. Pp. 378.

12. Hellman, M. "The Process of Dentition and Its Effect upon Occlusion," *Dental Cosmos*, 1923, 65, 1329–1344.

13. Henmon, V. A. C., and Livingstone, W. F. "Comparative Variability at Different Ages," *J. Educ. Psychol.*, 1922, 13, 17–29.

14. Hollingworth, L. S. "Differential Action upon the Sexes of Forces Which Tend to Segregate the Feebleminded," *J. Abn. Psychol.*, 1922, 17, 35–57.

15. Hollingworth, L. S., and Montague, H. "The Comparative Variability of the Sexes at Birth," *Amer. J. Sociol.*, 1914–15, 20, 335–370.

16. Lehman, H. C., and Witty, P. A. "Sex Differences: Some Sources of Confusion and Error," *Amer. J. Psychol.*, 1930, 42, 140–147.

17. Lincoln, E. A. *Sex Differences in the Growth of American Schoolchildren.* Baltimore: Warwick and York, 1927. Pp. 189.

18. Mead, M. *Growing up in New Guinea.* N. Y.: Morrow, 1930. Pp. 372.

19. ——. *Sex and Temperament in Three Primitive Societies.* N. Y.: Morrow, 1935. Pp. 335.

20. Pearson, K. *The Chances of Death and Other Studies in Evolution.* London: Arnold, 1897. Vol. I. Pp. 388. Ch. VIII: "Variation in Man and Woman."

21. Prescott, D. A. "The Determination of Anatomical Age in School Children and Its Relation to Mental Development," *Harvard Mon. in Educ.*, Series 1, No. 5, 1923. Pp. 59.

22. Pressey, L. W. "Sex Differences Shown by 2544 School Children on a Group Scale of Intelligence, with Special Reference to Variability," *J. Appl. Psychol.*, 1918, 2, 323–340.

23. Schiller, B. "Verbal, Numerical, and Spatial Abilities of Young Children," *Arch. Psychol.*, No. 161, 1934. Pp. 69.

24. Thorndike, E. L. *Educational Psychology.* N. Y.: Teachers College, Columbia Univ., 1914. Vol. III. Pp. 408.

CHAPTER XV

SEX DIFFERENCES: GENERAL RESULTS

Since the beginning of the mental testing movement, there has gradually accumulated a large body of data on sex differences. Every type of ability has been covered, from sensory and motor traits, through simple perceptual and associative tasks, to more complex intellectual processes and personality traits. Almost all tests, shortly after their construction, have been administered to members of the two sexes, and their scores compared. It was a relatively easy task to collect such data, especially after the advent of standardized group tests. But it was quite a different matter to determine what these data meant. It is now apparent that the sex differences found within any one cultural group reflect the social traditions of that group rather than the innate behavioral attributes of each sex.

The data which will be surveyed in the present chapter show *sex differences under existing conditions in our society.* Such data, although limited in their application, are not without value. Thus it is of considerable *practical* interest to ascertain the typical behavioral characteristics of men and women, whatever their origin. The number of situations in which such knowledge would prove useful is legion. In many fields of activity, definite assumptions are being made in regard to existing sex differences in interest, emotional appeal, and similar traits. This sex differentiation is noticeable in advertising and selling, political campaigning, the organization of newspapers and magazines, social work, crime prevention, and the treatment of offenders, to name only a few outstanding examples. Insofar as cultural conditioning may have produced certain clear-cut sex differences, these cannot be ignored in the practical adjustments of everyday life. In a descriptive account of any one cultural group, the question of sex differences in behavior can be legitimately raised.

It is also possible that a careful analysis of the material on sex differences, in conjunction with other available information, may throw further light upon the nature and genesis of such differences. Such an approach can never furnish a conclusive account of the origin of sex differences, but it may indirectly yield some corroborative evidence on this problem.

In surveying the vast array of studies on sex differences in each type of behavior, the general trend of the results will be reported. In addition, a few of the best illustrative studies in each field will be cited. No attempt has been made to present a complete survey of investigations on this topic, since such material has been frequently and extensively reviewed by various writers.[1]

In view of the problems discussed in the preceding chapter, such as selective factors, extensive overlapping of groups, errors of sampling, errors of measurement arising from inadequacy of the tests, and unwarranted generalizations regarding the functions measured, it would seem very difficult to formulate any summary statements regarding sex differences from the data of a number of independent investigations. This is especially true since such investigations differ widely in number and kind of subjects, specific tests or materials employed, and other important conditions. Similarly, all but the most recent

---

[1] Cf., e.g., Allen (1), Goodenough (12), L. S. Hollingworth (18, 19), Lincoln (26), Loutitt (27), Wellman (52), Woolley (57, 58), and the more recent and very comprehensive review by Miles (31).

and best controlled studies fail to report reliabilities of differences, degree of overlapping, and other essential facts, thus making it difficult to evaluate their findings. In the face of these conditions, the only available criterion for the acceptance of a conclusion is the *consistency of results of different investigators*. A survey of the experimental literature on sex differences reveals certain major findings which are so frequently reported by different investigators as to suggest a valid basis in fact. It is with these findings that we shall be primarily concerned.

Sensory Acuity and Motor Ability

Sex differences in sensory capacities are very slight, and consistent results are few. In color discrimination, most investigators find women slightly superior (49, 53), a fact which may be related to the more frequent practice which women have had in the use of color, as in dress, household decorating, and embroidery. Color blindness is also less common in the female, having been observed in about 4% of men and only 0.5% of women (53). In hearing, there seem to be no significant sex differences. Although several early investigators reported female superiority in pitch discrimination, more accurate experiments by Seashore (41) have demonstrated the absence of any such difference. In taste and smell, the data are too conflicting to allow any summary statement of sex differences.

In the discrimination of lifted weights, men have generally been found to excel slightly (53). This difference has sometimes been attributed to the better development of motor ability in general among men (cf. 49). On standard tests of sensitivity to pain, women obtain lower average thresholds. Thus in experiments in which pain was induced by a steadily increasing mechanical pressure on the skin, women report a sensation of pain on the average sooner than men. It is interesting to note that in one investigation (11) this difference was found to *increase with age*, until at the age of 18 or 19 it became over one kilogram. In experiments on college students (56), the average pressure at which pain was reported was 5.9 kg. for men and 2.4 kg. for women. It should be noted, of course, that such tests rely upon the subject's report of pain. The results are therefore open to the influence of social tradition and habits of endurance. In two-point threshold, i.e., the shortest perceptible distance between two points on the skin, women have also been found to have a finer discrimination (53). In the discrimination of temperature, degree of pressure on the skin, and other aspects of tactual sensitivity, no clear-cut sex difference has been demonstrated (53).

In regard to motor tasks, some reviewers (cf., e.g., 58) have ventured the conclusion that boys excel in speed and precision of movement in tasks in which the direction of attention remains fixed, whereas girls excel in tasks requiring rapid adaptations of response and shifts of attention. This generalization, although probably correct in most cases, is not without exception. In speed of tapping, most experimenters report male superiority. Thus Thompson (49) found 88% of the men reaching or exceeding the median tapping rate of the women. Burt and Moore (6) reported that 69.8% of the boys reached or exceeded the girls' median. But a few investigators have found a slightly faster tapping rate among women, probably owing to affective attitudes and motivational factors introduced by the conditions of the experiment (cf. 53, I, p. 140). Men have been found to have a shorter and somewhat more consistent reaction time than women. In coördination tests, such as aiming and tracing, boys generally excel. Two functions in which a very consistent female superiority is reported are mirror drawing and cancellation, both involving rapid shifts of attention and adaptation to a new mode of response (53).

The relation of these findings to the traditional play activities of the two sexes is apparent. Boys' games offer frequent opportunities for the development of rapid and well-coördinated movements. Finer adjustments of more restricted muscle groups, on the other hand, are more often involved in the activities of girls.

SPECIAL APTITUDES

A slight but highly consistent male superiority on tests of *mechanical or spatial aptitudes* has been established. In Thompson's pioneer investigation (49) on adult men and women, two mechanical problems were included in the series of tests. In both of these, the subject was to determine the method of operation of rather complex mechanical contrivances. The average amount of time required for the solution of each problem by the male subjects was considerably shorter than that required by the female subjects. Similar results have been obtained in practically all subsequent studies with spatial tests. In the solution of puzzle-boxes, as well as in a variety of form-board tests, in which the subject is to insert blocks of different shapes into the correct recesses, boys required less time on the average and had fewer failures within the allotted time limit than girls. In performance on a slot maze, boys were also found to excel markedly (cf. 12).

In a series of experiments with paper-and-pencil mazes, Porteus (38) found boys distinctly superior *when compared with girls of the same Stanford-Binet I.Q.* Porteus regards this finding as indicative of a sex difference in planning capacity, foresight, and similar personality traits which he believes to be measured by his maze tests. It seems more probable, however, that the obtained difference on the two tests is owing to the boys' superiority in spatial ability and the girls' superiority in verbal ability, the latter playing a large part in performance on the Stanford-Binet. Similar results were obtained by Goodenough (12) who administered the Wallin Peg Board test to 100 children between the ages of 2 and 4. In this test the subject is required to insert variously shaped pegs into the appropriate holes as rapidly as possible. A consistent sex difference was found in favor of the boys, although the same group yielded a reliable difference in favor of the girls in Kuhlman-Binet I.Q.

In a study (30) designed to measure "practical ability," a series of ten tests was administered to 172 boys and 184 girls between the ages of 10 and 11, all of whom were attending English schools. The tests included four construction tests—a wheelbarrow, a cradle, a girls' dress, and a boys' coat—as well as a puzzle box, a "painted cube" test which involved the ability to visualize spatial relations, and a "plunger" test measuring speed and coordination of movement. In all but the two garment tests, the boys obtained higher scores. It was also found that the boys' scores on the different spatial tests correlated more highly with each other and less highly with estimates of "general intelligence" than did the girls' scores. From this it was suggested that performance on such tests depends largely upon a special aptitude among boys, while among girls it is influenced to a greater extent by those processes which are included under the heading of "general intelligence." The method of arriving at a solution of the same problem might thus have differed for the two sexes.

In another investigation (10) on English schoolchildren, 52 boys and 48 girls were given a series of tests selected from various current performance and non-language scales.[1] When scores on all the tests were lumped into a single measure and I.Q.'s computed from it, no significant sex difference was found, the average I.Q. of the boys being 96 and that of the girls 93. Analysis of performance on separate tests, however, revealed several marked sex differences. In general it was concluded that girls excel in tests of memory, learning, and non-geometrical form relationships, and boys excel in tests of geometrical form relationships and reasoning.

Stenquist (43) reports that on his mechanical aptitude tests, elementary school girls obtained only about 65% as many correct items as boys, and that women in graduate school obtained about 80% as many correct items as unselected adult men. In an extensive investigation conducted with the Minnesota Mechanical Aptitude Tests (37), similar differences were found. Seventh grade boys and girls, as well as male and female college sophomores, were employed in the sex comparisons. In Table XVII are shown the *critical ratios* $\left(\frac{\text{difference}}{\text{S.E. of difference}}\right)$ of the differences between male and female averages in each of these two populations. Sex differences were found in single tests as well as in Batteries A, B, C, and D. These batteries were composites of several tests, each test being weighted so as to yield the best possible estimate of mechanical aptitude.

Those tests in which male superiority was most marked involved the use of mechanical materials which would be more common in the environment of boys. In block packing and card sorting, female superiority is usually

[1] Including Pintner-Paterson, Army Performance Scale, and Porteus maze tests.

TABLE XVII

Critical Ratios of the Differences between Male and Female Averages

(After Paterson, *et al.*, 37, p. 274)

Test	Critical Ratios *	
	Seventh Grade Pupils	College Sophomores
Minnesota Assembly	12.1	10.4
Battery B	6.1	6.8
Battery A	5.9	7.9
Battery C	3.9	5.8
Paper Form Board	2.0	2.4
Battery D	1.6	2.2
Minnesota Spatial Relations	−3.2	2.4
Packing Blocks	−5.0	1.4
Card Sorting	−8.9	−0.6

* In this table a minus sign indicates a difference in favor of the girls.

found. These tests involve chiefly visuo-motor coördination with rapid shifts of attention, in which women generally excel (cf. above).

In *numerical aptitude* a tendency towards male superiority has likewise been found, although the data are not so consistent as in the case of mechanical aptitude. This also is to be expected from social tradition and environmental conditions, since the sex differentiation in regard to mathematical work is not so pronounced as it is for mechanical pursuits. Girls are afforded relatively more opportunity for the development of mathematical abilities than for the exercise of mechanical functions. In the elementary school, for example, girls are taught arithmetic in the same classes as boys, but the latter are still segregated for "shop courses."

A few studies on the development of number concepts in pre-school children yield conflicting data (cf. 12). These studies are difficult to interpret on account of the relatively crude techniques employed, and also because of the close linkage between number concepts and language development in the young child. Test results on older subjects indicate a slight but fairly general male superiority in both the mechanics of computation and mathematical reasoning.

An analysis of the data employed in the standardization of the Stanford-Binet showed that the average percentage of boys who succeeded on the numerical tests was greater than that of girls. The difference in favor of the boys was 33% on the arithmetic reasoning test, 15% on the test of making change, and 10% on the "induction" test in which a generalized numerical rule must be discovered (46, p. 82). In an investigation on German schoolchildren (8), a continuous addition test was administered to 1214 boys and girls in grades 1 to 8. In almost every grade, the boys completed more additions within the time allowed and made fewer errors than the girls. An extensive investigation on various aspects of mathematical aptitude was conducted on 500 boys and girls in English secondary schools. The tests covered the following fields: arithmetic computation, arithmetic reasoning, mechanical algebraic processes, the use of algebraic symbols in problem solving, the manipulation of geometric constructs and spatial relationships, and geometric reasoning. It will be noted that both mechanical and numerical abilities are involved in such tests. A small but consistent difference in favor of the boys was found on the series as a whole, larger and more significant differences being obtained on certain specific tests.

Since 1930 a mathematical section has been added to the Scholastic Aptitude Tests administered by the College Entrance Examination Board to prospective college students (35). A large and significant sex difference in performance on this part of the test has been found, as is illustrated by the 1930 results reported below.

	Boys	Girls	Critical Ratio of Difference
Number of cases	4394	3318	
Average score in mathematical section of Scholastic Aptitude Test	510.22	484.37	11.59

It will be seen that the difference between the male and female averages is 11.59 times as large as its standard error, which is far in excess of the minimum critical ratio of 3 required for perfect reliability. Similar results have been obtained in subsequent years. It is interesting to note that this large and highly reliable difference was found among subjects who had been exposed to the differentiating effects of environment over a considerable period of time, and that the corresponding differences among younger subjects were far less pronounced.

In *verbal* or *linguistic aptitude* there is a fairly consistent difference in favor of the female sex. These differences are manifested from a very early age.[1] Observations on normal as well as gifted and feebleminded children have shown that on the average girls begin to talk earlier than boys. Similarly, girls of pre-school age have a larger vocabulary than boys. In one investigation on 51 children at the age of 18 months, the average number of words employed by the girls was found to be 78.6 and by the boys only 59. In another study the *percentage* of comprehensible verbal responses was determined for each child. The average percentages proved to be 14 and 49 for boys at 18 and 24 months, respectively, as compared to 37 and 78 for girls at the same ages. Speech defects and reading

[1] Cf. McCarthy (29) for a survey of sex differences in early language development.

disabilities are also less common among girls than among boys. Similar results have been obtained with all other indices of linguistic development (cf. 29, 52).

Female superiority on linguistic tests persists through the successive academic levels. It is equally apparent among elementary schoolchildren and college students. Female superiority has been consistently reported in speed of reading, naming opposites, and in all verbal association tests (53). Girls excel on sentence completion tests (12, 53), and a similar difference has been found in tests of story completion (53). On the verbal part of the Scholastic Aptitude Test, a large and highly reliable sex difference has been obtained in the reverse direction from that found in the numerical part (35). The average scores of the two sexes, as well as the number of cases in each group and the reliability of the difference, are shown below.

	Boys	Girls	Critical Ratio of Difference
Number of cases	4394	3318	
Average score in verbal section of Scholastic Aptitude Test	486.98	517.54	13.52

It is particularly significant that this reversal in the relative standing of the two sexes was obtained *within the same group of subjects*. It cannot therefore be attributed to selective factors or other spurious influences.

Finally we may consider the results obtained in a large number of studies on *memory*. On practically all tests of memory, a sex difference in favor of the female has been found. As in the case of verbal ability, these differences have been observed very early in life and persist at all ages. There is considerable evidence to show female superiority in memory among pre-school children. Terman (45), in a study on 112 kindergarten children with the

Stanford-Binet, found the girls superior on the tests of digit span and memory for sentences. Among the results obtained with the Stanford-Binet on older children, Terman reports girls superior in memory for digits and reproduction of drawings from memory (46).

In a number of studies (cf., e.g., 34, 40), girls have been found to excel more markedly in logical than in rote memory. This is doubtlessly owing to the greater dependence of logical memory tests upon verbal comprehension. In a few cases in which the specific material of the test was more familiar or more interesting to boys, the relative standing of the two sexes was reversed. But these instances are very infrequent, and on the large majority of memory tests female superiority is found. This superiority has been established for a wide range of materials, for recall as well as recognition, and direct as well as incidental memory. In this connection mention may also be made of the fact that women have more vivid mental imagery than men in every sense modality. This finding, first suggested by Galton on the basis of his famous "breakfast table" questionnaire, has been subsequently corroborated by several investigators.

Further data on sex differences in these various aptitudes will be discussed in the following sections, in connection with intelligence test performance and records of scholastic achievement. The material on verbal and numerical aptitudes, in particular, needs to be largely supplemented from intelligence test results. Since these abilities have not been generally recognized as distinct from "general intelligence," there are relatively few studies on sex differences in verbal or numerical abilities as such.

In reference to the possible origin of sex differences in special aptitudes, a comment offered by Burt several years ago is of interest. He states:

Sheltered, supervised, detained at home, girls . . . incline to sedentary lives and engage in literary pursuits; and . . . they consequently excel in linguistic work and conversational activities. Boys . . . have more to do with practical, perceptual, out-of-door pursuits. They are sent to shops with money. They are allowed to play and wander in the streets. They are encouraged to handle tools—to construct toys for amusement and articles for use. No wonder that . . . boys grow more ready with hand and eye than with tongue or pen (5, p. 196).

General Intelligence

On the Binet test and its revisions, sex differences are slight but usually favor the girls up to the age of about 14. Terman (44) reports results obtained with the Stanford-Binet on 457 boys and 448 girls between the ages of 5 and 14. The average I.Q. of the girls was found to be higher than that of the boys at every age except 10, at which they were equal, and at 14, at which the boys excelled. The specific data for each age group are reproduced below.

Age	Boys	Girls
5	100	104
6	99	105
7	101	103
8	100	102
9	98	102
10	103	103
11	96	101
12	97	99
13	96	97
14	100	96

These differences, although slight, are consistent with the findings of other investigators. Burt (5) tested 3500 London schoolchildren, ranging in age from 3 to 14, with his own revision of the Binet tests. With the exception of a single age group, the girls obtained higher average mental ages than the boys. In general this difference amounted to about ⅓ of a year. Goodenough (13) administered the Kuhlman-Binet to 50 boys and 50 girls at each of the ages 2, 3, and 4. The average I.Q. of the girls was again higher than that of the boys, this difference persisting when the children were retested after a lapse of six weeks. Thus the obtained difference could not be attributed to chance fluctuations or a response to novel situations.

With most group tests, a similar female superiority up to the age of 14 has been found. Thus in several extensive school surveys with the National Intelligence Test, girls have obtained consistently higher scores than boys (cf., e.g., 54). On the Dearborn group scale, which is *less dependent on verbal ability than most group scales*, however, no consistent sex difference was found in a group of 3400 children between the ages of 7 and 17 (cf. 25).

Among high school students, on the other hand, boys generally excel on intelligence tests. Thorndike (50), using a group intelligence scale especially constructed for the high school level, with about 2500 high school students between the ages of 13 and 18, found the boys to be superior on the average. Similarly, in an investigation on 1453 high school students with the South Dakota Group Intelligence Test,[1] boys were found to excel, *their superiority increasing from the first to the last year of high school* (3). In a number of studies employing the Army Alpha with both high school and college groups, consistent male superiority was also found (cf., e.g., 55).

These sex differences in total scores on intelligence tests can be explained in terms of certain previously reported findings. The superiority of girls of elementary school age on the Binet tests, as well as on most of the group tests,

---

[1] Including tests of directions, analogies, synonym-antonym, reading comprehension, information, and arithmetic.

is to be expected on the basis of the large *verbal content* of such scales and their frequent use of *memory* tests. It will be recalled that girls excel in both of these aptitudes. This interpretation of female superiority in general intelligence tests is supported by the fact that the sex difference disappears or becomes reversed when tests like the Dearborn, which lay less emphasis upon verbal ability, are employed. The consistent male superiority on Army Alpha has likewise been attributed to the fact that this scale was originally standardized on men and thus may contain an excess of items which favor men. Finally, the reversal of the relative status of the two sexes in high school groups has already been explained in terms of selective factors (cf. Ch. XIV). Even when predominantly verbal tests are employed, male superiority is found among high school students. The fact that this superiority of the boys tends to *increase* throughout the four years of high school further corroborates the proposed explanation.

That sex differences on tests of so-called general intelligence are attributable to differences in special aptitudes is also indicated by an analysis of scores on the separate subtests of intelligence scales. Thus an examination of the scores obtained by 834 high school students on Army Alpha showed male superiority only on the arithmetic reasoning, number series completion, and information tests (55). The differences on these tests were sufficient to pull up the total scores and produce a sex difference in favor of the boys on the scale as a whole.

In a previously mentioned investigation with the Pressey Group Test (cf. Ch. XIV), the scores of 880 children between the ages of 9 and 14 were examined with reference to performance on each of the ten subtests of the scale. It will be recalled that at these ages the girls excelled in total score. On the separate tests, however, the boys excelled in arithmetic at all ages and in practical information from age 11 on. The girls excelled in rote memory for words, naming opposites, word completion, dissected sentences, analogies, and moral classification, the last depending largely upon verbal comprehension. In the remaining two tests, no significant sex difference was exhibited (39).

It will be recalled that among high school seniors, owing to a differential elimination of male and female students, boys excelled in *total scores* on the Pressey test (4). Performance on the separate tests, however, showed the same hierarchy as in the younger groups. Thus the boys excelled markedly in the arithmetic and information tests. The girls obtained higher average scores in word completion, dissected sentences, and logical memory. On the remaining tests there was either no difference or a slight superiority of the boys. The reversal in total score from the elementary to the high school groups results from the fact that the high school senior boys excelled *by a much larger amount* in those same tests in which elementary school boys excelled. Similarly, the high school senior girls excelled *by a smaller amount* in the tests in which the elementary school girls had excelled markedly.

Scholastic Achievement

On the whole girls excel in *general scholastic achievement*, as revealed both by achievement test records and by school grades. Performance on the separate parts of standardized *achievement tests*, however, shows a hierarchy of abilities in different school subjects, which corresponds closely to that found with tests of intelligence and special aptitudes. In an investigation (8) on 300 schoolchildren with the Stanford Achievement test, no sex difference was found in total achievement quotient. But an analysis of the scores indicated a definite superiority of the girls in reading, language usage, and dictation, and of the boys in arithmetic, nature study, and history. In another investigation (51) a standard geometry test was administered to 410 high school boys and 349 high school girls, all of whom had previously been given the Terman Group Test of Intelligence. The boys as a group were found to excel in geometric ability *when compared with girls of equal "intelligence,"* as indicated by the Terman scores.

Numerous other extensive school surveys have yielded the same general results.[1] In general girls obtain higher achievement test scores in subjects requiring verbal ability or memory. Boys excel in those subjects which call into play numerical or spatial aptitudes, as well as in certain "information" subjects such as history, geography, and general science. This is in agreement with the common superiority of boys on tests of general information, and probably results from the less restricted and more heterogeneous environment to which boys are exposed as well as from their wider range of reading interests. Thus Terman (47), in his survey of the reading habits of gifted children, reports that the girls read imaginative and emotional fiction as well as stories of school and home life far more often than the boys, while the latter showed a predominant interest in books on science, history, biography, travel, and informational fiction and adventure tales.

In regard to *school progress,* girls are consistently more successful than boys. The differences, although small, appear irrespective of the particular criterion of school progress employed. Girls are less frequently retarded, more frequently accelerated, and promoted in larger numbers than boys. Typical results from a survey conducted in the schools of 318 cities are shown in Table XVIII. Since girls make more rapid progress than boys in school

[1] Cf. Lincoln (26), Ch. IV, for a survey of this material previous to 1927.

promotions and since most comparisons of achievement are made on the basis of school grade, it follows that age comparisons would show an even greater superiority of girls.

In *school grades* girls excel consistently *even in those subjects which favor boys.* Thus a comparison of grades in arithmetic, or history, or any other subject in which boys obtain higher achievement test scores, shows a sex difference in favor of girls. The advantage enjoyed by girls in school grades was made particularly vivid in an investigation (25) on 202 boys and 188 girls in grades 2 to 6, all of whom were given the Stanford Achievement test. The girls were found to excel consistently in school grades, *when compared with their achievement test scores.* Thus the grades showed a far greater female superiority than seemed to be warranted by performance on objective achievement tests.

TABLE XVIII

Median Percentage of Boys and Girls in Normal Age-Grade Location, as Well as Those over Age and under Age

(After Lincoln, 26, p. 100)

School Status	Cities of over 25,000		Cities of less than 25,000	
	Boys	Girls	Boys	Girls
Normal	56	60	54	58
1 year over age	20	18	20	18
2 years over age	10	9	11	8
3 years over age	5	3	4	3
4 years over age	2	1	2	1
Total over age	38	32	38	36
Total under age	4	4	4	5

Similarly, high school girls generally obtain better grades than high school boys, even though the latter are a more select group and make a better showing on intelligence tests (cf. 36). This is illustrated by a survey of the grades given to students in each of the four years of a single high school, the results of which are shown in Table XIX. It will be noted that in each year, without a single exception, the percentage of A's and B's is larger and the percentage of D's and F's is smaller among the girls than among the boys. The larger percentage of boys than girls who left school further suggests the better adjustment of girls to the school situation.

TABLE XIX

THE PERCENTAGE OF EACH LETTER GRADE RECEIVED BY BOYS AND
GIRLS IN A SINGLE HIGH SCHOOL

(After Lincoln, 26, p. 93)

Grades	First Year		Second Year		Third Year		Fourth Year	
	Boys	Girls	Boys	Girls	Boys	Girls	Boys	Girls
A	3.2	8.7	3.5	7.6	4.0	10.9	11.6	15.5
B	10.3	18.4	12.9	20.9	13.0	25.6	16.3	31.9
C	20.8	20.0	16.9	22.3	22.8	27.5	31.0	29.7
D	23.8	21.1	27.0	20.3	31.3	21.3	29.4	16.5
F	25.7	18.3	22.7	15.3	17.2	5.7	7.9	1.6
Left school	16.1	13.5	16.9	13.6	11.7	9.0	3.9	4.6

Various explanations have been offered for the greater scholastic success of girls. Among the major factors may be mentioned girls' demonstrated superiority in *linguistic aptitude*, which probably plays an important part in nearly all school subjects. Current methods of instruction, as well as methods of testing, are predominantly verbal. The child who expresses himself well, furthermore, will impress the teacher as being relatively brighter than one who is linguistically backward, and this may in turn affect their respective grades. A second possible factor in the higher scholastic ratings of girls is the neatness and general superiority of their *handwriting*. In most investigations on both elementary and high school groups, girls have been found to excel markedly in the quality of their handwriting, as judged by standardized product scales (cf. 26, pp. 72–77).

Finally owing to the obvious presence of a subjective element in school grades, *personality differences* between boys and girls may influence the allotment of such grades. Girls are generally more docile, quieter, less resistant to school discipline, and are less often "behavior problems" than boys. This difference in the child's attitude towards school affects his grades both through the amount of material actually learned and, more directly, through the general impression created on the teacher.

INTERESTS, PREFERENCES, AND ATTITUDES

That definite personality differences exist between adult men and women in our society is clearly apparent from everyday observation. In many emotional and social characteristics, this differentiation is noticeable from an early age. An important aspect of personality development in which traditional sex differences are manifested includes interests, preferences, ideals, attitudes, and personal sense of values. These characteristics, because of their relatively subtle and persistent nature, often exert an unsuspected influence, not only upon the development of emotional and character traits, but also upon the individual's achievements and effective abilities. An interesting observation recorded by Thompson (49) illustrates this effect. In discussing the superior performance of a group of men as contrasted to a group of women on a problem of mechanical ingenuity, she wrote:

It is very difficult to evaluate this difference because of the indefinite nature of the problem. Most of the women expressed a great distaste for all such problems, because they were uninteresting. Many of them were so uninterested that they did not really work at it. Whether the men found it equally uninteresting, but forced themselves to work in spite of lack of interest, or whether the problem appealed to them as more interesting, it is difficult to say. From the voluntary comments of the subjects the latter hypothesis seems more probable (49, p. 116).

It has proved quite difficult to obtain objective or quantitative measures of these characteristics. A number of early studies (cf. 53, II) on sex differences employed the free association technique, whereby the subject is presented with a list of stimulus-words and is required to respond by giving the first word suggested to him by each stimulus-word. Although admittedly crude, these early experiments yielded fairly consistent results which were also in general agreement with common observation.[1] In general women's associations seemed to indicate an interest in the immediate surroundings, finished products, the ornamental, the individual, and the concrete, whereas men's associations suggested an interest in the more remote, constructive, useful, general, and abstract. Dynamic concepts were more common among the men's responses, static among those of the women. Time was more prominent in the men's associations, space in the women's. The free association responses of women also tended to be more subjective, personal or particular, social, and emotionally toned than those of men.

Equally characteristic and traditional differences were revealed in a large number of subsequent studies on children. Sex differences were investigated through an analysis of literary and reading preferences, spontaneous constructions and drawing choices, æsthetic preferences,

[1] For a survey of these studies, see Miles and Terman (32).

vocational choices, and choice of ideals. Thus in one typical investigation (21), 200 schoolchildren were required to rank nine pictures, each representing a specific type of appeal, in order of merit. The chief sex difference noted was the relatively high position assigned by girls to pictures dealing with children, and by boys to those whose main theme was action and the heroic.

A series of more recent studies have approached the same problem through an analysis of *conversations*. In the first of these investigations (33), a record was made of conversations heard in the evening along a busy thoroughfare in the heart of New York City's theatre district. When the participants were classified according to sex, it was found that the most frequent topics of conversation among women were clothes and social affairs, and among men, money and business affairs. In conversations between men and women, there was a predominance of men's conversational topics, which suggested a tendency for women to adapt themselves to the interests of their male companions.

In a subsequent study (24), conversations were collected in a wider variety of situations in a mid-western city. Observations were made on a college campus, in barber shops, churches, hotel lobbies, street cars, and other public or semi-public places. Although typical conversational differences were noted from one locale to another, the general results corroborated those of the New York study. The two major topics in order of their frequency were, among women, (1) men and (2) clothes; and among men, (1) business and money, and (2) sports and amusements. It is also interesting to note that "people" of either sex played a larger part in the conversations of women than in those of men, having been observed in 37% of the former and only 16% of the latter. A similar series of observations was made in two London streets (23). The results resembled closely those of the American studies, with two major exceptions. First, in all conversations business and money were less prominent, and secondly, in conversations between men and women there seemed to be a greater tendency for the men to adapt to women's interests than in the American groups.

Consistent sex differences have also been reported in the individual's conception of *values*. The application of

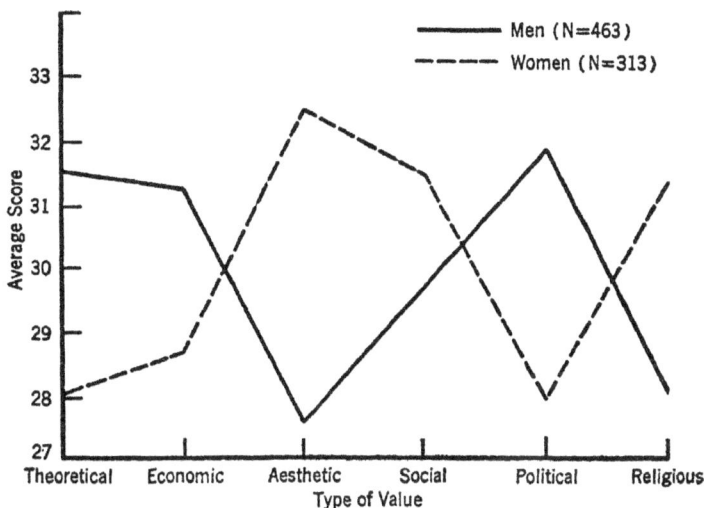

FIG. 48. COMPOSITE PSYCHOGRAPHS OF ADULT MEN AND WOMEN ON THE ALLPORT-VERNON STUDY OF VALUES. (Data from Allport and Vernon, 2, p. 246.)

the Allport-Vernon "*Study of Values*" (2) has furnished some information on these differences. This is a test of the questionnaire type, in which each response is given a numerical weight in one of six sets of values, *viz.*, theoretical, economic, æsthetic, social, political, and religious. The relative standing of the subject in each set is then determined by totaling scores on separate items, and a psychograph is constructed from these six measures. Psychographs showing the average scores of 463 men and 313 women will be found in Figure 48. It will be noted

that among the women the highest average values fall
in the *æsthetic, social,* and *religious* groups, in the order
given, while among the men they fall in the *theoretical,
economic,* and *political.*

In connection with the higher rating of social values
among women, mention may be made of the widely quoted
female superiority in *social perception.* Relatively little
information is available on this point, but a comparison
of the performance of men and women on the George
Washington Social Intelligence Test may prove relevant.
In a group of 430 college students of both sexes who took
this test, a small difference in total score was found in
favor of the women (20). The average scores obtained by
freshmen and upperclassmen of each sex were as follows:

	Freshmen	*Upperclassmen*
Men	101	109
Women	108	115

Upon analysis, this difference was found to be owing almost entirely to the higher scores of the women students
on two subtests. One of these was designed to measure
the ability to decide the "best thing to do" in a difficult
social situation. The other involved a knowledge of common facts of human behavior which could be acquired
through the everyday observation of people. In view
of the larger part played by women in social situations
and the more frequent concern of women with the reactions of others, such differences are easily understand-
able.

CHARACTER TRAITS

Those aspects of personality commonly designated as
moral or character traits also present typical differences
between the sexes. In an investigation (42) on moral

judgment, a list of 100 acts, including commendable as well as reprehensible activities all of which might be carried out by a young man of 18, were to be rated on a scale ranging from −10 to +10. The subjects were college students, 39 men and 39 women. Analysis of responses showed that the *relative ratings* given to each act by men and women were very similar, i.e., the same acts were chosen as best and worst by both sexes. There was, however, a tendency for women to assign *more extreme ratings* both to good and to bad acts. The men gave more mediocre or indifferent ratings, while the women employed more frequently the values towards the −10 and +10 ends of the scale. Although the procedure was crude and the number of cases small, these findings are suggestive. The tendency of the female group to be more critical, both favorably and unfavorably, is in line with the traditional belief that women are the custodians of the social mores, as well as with the common practice of attaching a greater ethical or moral significance to the activities of women than to those of men.

In an extensive series of tests by Hartshorne, May, and Shuttleworth (16) on approximately 850 elementary schoolchildren in three cities, reliable differences in favor of the girls were found in moral knowledge and social attitudes. Several tests of each of these aspects of character development were employed. In order to keep as close as possible to the children's own opinion, the tests were worked up in the form of ballots and the children were asked to "vote" on each item. In the so-called "duties test," for example, several propositions were given with the request that the subject indicate whether it is his duty to do these things, by underlining *Yes, No,* or *S* (sometimes yes and sometimes no). Some of the items in this test were as follows (16, pp. 46–47):

1. To help a slow or dull child with his lessons	Yes	S	No
2. To call your teacher's attention to the fact if you received a higher grade than you deserved	Yes	S	No
3. To smile when things go wrong	Yes	S	No
4. To report another pupil if you see him cheating	Yes	S	No

In total scores on both the moral judgment and social attitudes tests, the differences in favor of the girls were 4.31 times as large as their standard errors and can therefore be regarded as perfectly reliable. The investigators conclude that: "It appears on the surface at least that girls are more sensitive to both conventional and ideal social standards than boys" (16, p. 119).

Certain significant sex differences have also been discovered in objective behavioral tests of character. In a series of investigations by Hartshorne and May (14, 15), tests were devised for the measurement of "*deceit*," including cheating, lying, and stealing, "*service*," including coöperative and charitable behavior, and "*self-control*," including persistence and inhibition. Among the special advantages of these tests may be mentioned the fact that the subjects did not realize that they were being tested or that their actions could be detected. All observations, furthermore, were made in the course of ordinary every-day activities of the children, including school work, homework assignments, athletics, and party games. Data on deceit were collected on some 10,865 elementary school pupils in several parts of the country. For the main studies on service and self-control, about 900 children were employed.

No consistent sex difference in deceptive behavior was discovered. Analysis of separate tests showed that: "On some tests the girls are more dishonest, whereas on others the boys show the greater tendency to deceive" (14, p. 168). In the analysis of service and self-control, comparisons were made both in test scores and in "reputation" among classmates and teachers. The final summary data on sex differences in these traits are shown below (cf. 15, pp. 156, 380, 382):

	$\dfrac{Difference}{S.E.\ of\ Difference}$	Direction of Difference
Total service scores	1.9	Girls more coöperative
Reputation for service	7.9	Girls more coöperative
Total persistence scores	1.7	Girls more persistent
Reputation for persistence	7.6	Girls more persistent
Total inhibition score	5.5	Girls better inhibited
Reputation for inhibition	5.0	Girls better inhibited

It will be noted that all of the above differences are in favor of the girls. In service and persistence, however, the differences in total score are not reliable. The relative standing of the two sexes also varied from test to test. In inhibition, on the other hand, the girls were reliably superior in total score and consistently superior on each individual test. The more successful adjustment of girls to the school situation may be owing partly to these personality differences. It is also interesting to note in this connection that in *reputation* the girls excel the boys markedly *in all traits.* This too may influence their school success.

The discrepancy between reputation and performance is also of interest in relation to social pressure. It may be that with increasing age the cumulative force of social expectancy becomes more effective and the discrepancy between behavior and traditional belief is lessened. With this would come an increasing differentiation between the sexes. Until similar behavior tests are made on adult subjects, these questions cannot be answered.

EMOTIONAL ADJUSTMENT

In general emotional adjustment and nature of emotional response, our cultural tradition has taught us to expect pronounced differences between man and woman. The recent development of standardized personality tests and their application to college groups have revealed a number of significant sex differences. The belief in the greater emotional instability of the female has been reflected in test scores. Thus the responses of about 600 male and 400 female college students on one of the Colgate Mental Hygiene Tests (22) indicated an average of 20% more psychasthenic symptoms among women.

In an investigation on introversion (17), 100 college men and 100 college women rated themselves and were also rated individually by two associates on 54 typical introvert traits. No significant sex difference was found in introversion-extroversion, the average scores of men and women being 11.41 and 11.12, respectively. But further analysis of responses showed a sex difference in another trait which cut across introversion-extroversion and seemed to bear no relation to it. This trait is concerned predominantly with social relations. The introvert traits marked most often by men were those which would interfere with social adjustments. Those marked most often by women, on the other hand, were such as to interfere with efficient work. A few examples will illustrate this difference.

Typical "masculine" symptoms of introversion:
  1. Outspoken
  2. Works things out on own hook; hesitates to accept help
  3. Keeps in background on social occasions
  4. Conservative and painstaking in dress
  5. Introspective

Typical "feminine" symptoms of introversion:
  1. Shrinks when facing a crisis
  2. Works by fits and starts
  3. Has ups and downs in mood without apparent cause
  4. Feels hurt readily
  5. Hesitates in making decisions on ordinary matters

Comparisons of male and female college students have also been made on the Bernreuter Personality Inventory. This test, consisting of 125 questions, can be scored with six different keys for as many different traits.[1] The average scores obtained by male and female college groups, as well as the critical ratios [2] of the differences, are shown below. The number of cases in these groups varied from 144 to 658.

Scale	Average Score		$\dfrac{Difference}{S.E.\ of\ Difference}$	Direction of Difference
	Male	Female		
B_1N: Neuroticism	−57.3	−42.8	3.15	Women more neurotic, or unstable
B_2S: Self-sufficiency	27.0	6.8	5.89	Men more self-sufficient
B_3I: Introversion	−25.6	−14.7	3.50	Women more introverted
B_4D: Dominance	45.9	30.6	3.77	Men more dominant
F_1C: Confidence	−51.5	8.7	9.62	Men more self-confident
F_2S: Sociability	−25.9	−31.1	0.88	Women more gregarious and socially dependent

In all but the sociability scale, the sex differences are perfectly reliable. This trait may include more than one

[1] The fact that some of these traits have recently been shown to be mutually interdependent introduces unnecessary duplication in the scores but in no way vitiates the comparisons made. All six scores are reported here for the sake of completeness.

[2] Computed by the writer from Bernreuter's published data—see manual of directions and norms, October, 1934.

counteracting factor in which the sexes might differ significantly. In introversion, it will be noted that women obtain significantly higher average scores. This seems to conflict with the findings reported above. The explanation of this discrepancy may lie in the particular choice of items in the two tests. Thus Bernreuter's test may be overweighted with the more "feminine" type of introvert items. In all studies on personality, it is difficult to generalize regarding trait differences because of the specificity of responses. The sex differences in confidence and self-sufficiency on the Bernreuter test are particularly large. The differences in dominance and neuroticism are clearly reliable, but smaller. It should be kept in mind, of course, that these data apply only to college students. A different picture might be presented by other adult groups. It is unlikely, however, that the sex differences in non-college groups should be smaller, since the environment of college students is probably more uniform than that of other male and female adults in our society.

Interesting comparative data on the emotional differences between boys and girls at successive ages have been obtained with the Woodworth-Mathews questionnaire (28). This is an adaptation of the Woodworth psychoneurotic inventory for use on children. It consists of 100 questions dealing with the following classes of symptoms:

1. Fears, worries, perseverations
2. Physical symptoms, such as muscular twitchings
3. Unhappiness, anti-social moods
4. Dreams, phantasies, sleep disturbances

This test was administered to 575 boys and 558 girls between the ages of 9 and 19. The median number of neurotic symptoms reported by the boys was 20, and by the girls 25.5. This sex difference is in agreement with the findings on adults. But an analysis of scores in different age groups brought out certain rather suggestive facts. The changes in score with age among boys and girls are shown graphically in Figure 49.

It will be seen that at age 10 the median number of symptoms reported by the boys is *greater* than that re-

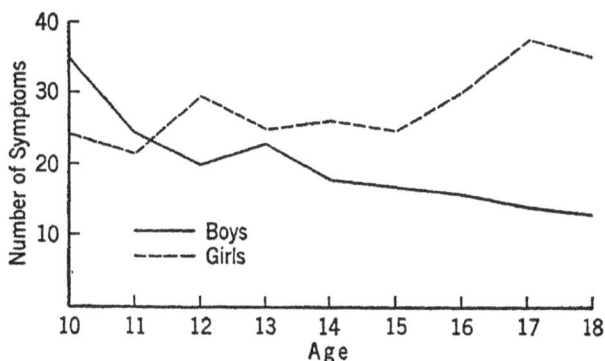

FIG. 49. MEDIAN NUMBER OF SYMPTOMS REPORTED BY BOYS AND GIRLS ON THE WOODWORTH-MATHEWS TEST OF EMOTIONAL INSTABILITY. (After Mathews, 28, p. 21.)

ported by the girls. At 11 there is no appreciable sex difference, and beyond this the girls show an *increase* in emotional instability and the boys a *decrease*. This, to be sure, is what would be expected from an analysis of the environments of the two sexes. The emotional problems and affective milieux of boys and girls are quite similar in early childhood. Gradually, however, the environmental differentiation becomes pronounced and this is reflected in the increasing divergence of the sexes in emotional instability.

A "MASCULINITY-FEMININITY" INDEX OF PERSONALITY TRAITS

A very comprehensive approach to the problem of sex differences in personality traits has recently been made by Terman and Miles (46). The aim of this investigation was to devise a scale which would differentiate clearly between the characteristic male and female patterns of response. After an exhaustive survey of the literature and prolonged research, items were selected which revealed the most pronounced differences between representative samplings of the two sexes in our society. Data were collected on many hundreds of subjects, including elementary, high school, college, and graduate students, unselected adults, members of several occupations, and specially selected groups such as athletes, juvenile delinquents, and adult homosexuals.

Seven tests were included in the final scale. The first is a *word association* test and the second an *ink-blot association* test. In both tests the response is of the multiple choice form, the alternatives under each item including distinctly masculine as well as distinctly feminine responses. An *information* test, drawing upon a wide variety of fields, is likewise of the multiple choice variety. In a test of *emotional* and *ethical response*, the subject is required to check the degree to which a given situation provokes in him emotions of anger, fear, disgust, or pity; in the second part of this test, the degree of moral seriousness of each given type of behavior is to be indicated by checking 3, 2, 1, or 0. An *interest* test follows, in which the subject expresses his liking, disliking, or indifference towards a wide range of items, including occupations, people, games and amusements, movies, magazines, school studies, books and literary characters, travel and sightseeing preferences, and special interests. The sixth is a test of *opinions*, in which a series of common beliefs and superstitions are to be marked true or false. The last is a test of *introvertive response*, the items having been selected from several current scales of introversion-extroversion. A composite weighted score on all seven tests can be obtained for each subject.

This scale proved very successful in differentiating between the responses of male and female groups. All sex differences in average score were statistically reliable, the smallest being 3.4 times as large as its standard error. An intensive analysis of the characteristic male and female responses on each test revealed a distinct picture of the "temperaments" of the two sexes in our culture. Terman and Miles summarize these differences as follows:

> From whatever angle we have examined them the males included in the standardization groups evinced a distinctive interest in exploit and adventure, in outdoor and physically strenuous occupations, in machinery and tools, in science, physical phenomena, and inventions; and, from rather occasional evidence, in business and commerce. On the other hand, the females of our groups have evinced a distinctive interest in domestic affairs and in æsthetic objects and occupations; they have distinctly preferred more sedentary and indoor occupations, and occupations more directly ministrative, particularly to the young, the helpless, the distressed. Supporting and supplementing these are the more subjective differences—those in emotional disposition and direction. The males directly or indirectly manifest the greater self-assertion and aggressiveness; they express more hardihood and fearlessness, and more roughness of manners, language, and sentiments. The females express themselves as more compassionate and sympathetic, more timid, more fastidious, and æsthetically sensitive, more emotional in general (or at least more expressive of the four emotions considered), severer moralists, yet admit in themselves weaknesses in emotional control and (less noticeably) in physique (46, pp. 447–448).

In regard to the origin of such differences, the authors offer only tentative hypotheses. The rôle of cultural factors is, however, constantly admitted throughout their discussion. Several lines of evidence are cited which suggest the importance of nurture in the development of what in our society is regarded as a typically "masculine" or "feminine" personality. Thus the *masculinity-femininity index* was found to be associated with amount of education, occupation, and domestic milieu. Such factors as the death of one parent, excessive or exclusive association with one or another parent, and predominance of brothers or sisters among the siblings, were much more closely linked with masculinity-femininity scores than were physical traits. Highly intelligent and well-educated women tended to score more "masculine" than their sex norms. Similarly, "cultured" men, i.e., men who had cultivated avocational interests of an artistic or intellectual sort, tended to test more "feminine." Thus the equalizing influence of specific training or experience in the two cases seemed to bring about a convergence of the temperamental qualities of the two sexes.

REFERENCES

1. Allen, C. N. "Studies in Sex Differences," *Psychol. Bull.*, 1927, 24, 294–304.
2. Allport, G. W., and Vernon, P. E. "A Test for Personal Values," *J. Abn. and Soc. Psychol.*, 1931, 26, 231–248.
3. Batson, W. H. "The South Dakota Group Intelligence Test for High School," *Sch. and Soc.*, 1920, 15, 311–315.
4. Book, W. F., and Meadows, J. L. "Sex Differences in 5929 High School Seniors in Ten Psychological Tests," *J. Appl. Psychol.*, 1928, 12, 56–81.
5. Burt, C. *Mental and Scholastic Tests.* London: King, 1922. Pp. 432.
6. Burt, C., and Moore, R. C. "The Mental Differences between the Sexes," *J. Exper. Ped.*, 1912, 1, 273–284; 355–388.
7. Cameron, A. E. "Comparative Study of the Mathematical

Ability of Boys and Girls in the Secondary Schools," *Brit. J. Psychol.*, 1925, 16, 29–49.

8. Commins, W. D. "More about Sex Differences," *Sch. and Soc.*, 1928, 28, 599–600.

9. Fauth, E. "Testuntersuchungen an Schulkindern nach Methode des fortlaufenden Addierens," *Arch. f.d. ges. Psychol.*, 1925, 51, 1–20.

10. Gaw, F. "A Study of Performance Tests," *Brit. J. Psychol.*, 1925, 15, 374–392.

11. Gilbert, J. A. "Researches upon School Children and College Students," *Univ. Iowa Stud. in Psychol.*, 1897, 1. Pp. 39.

12. Goodenough, F. L. "The Consistency of Sex Differences in Mental Traits at Various Ages," *Psychol. Rev.*, 1927, 34, 440–462.

13. ——. "The Kuhlman-Binet Tests for Children of Preschool Age: a Critical Study and Evaluation," *Univ. Minn. Inst. Child Welfare, Mon. Series*, No. 2, 1927.

14. Hartshorne, H., and May, M. A. *Studies in the Nature of Character.* Vol. I: *Studies in Deceit.* N. Y.: Macmillan, 1928. Pp. 414 + 306.

15. Hartshorne, H., May, M. A., and Maller, J. B. *Studies in the Nature of Character.* Vol. II: *Studies in Service and Self-Control.* N. Y.: Macmillan, 1929. Pp. 559.

16. Hartshorne, H., May, M. A., and Shuttleworth, F. K. *Studies in the Nature of Character.* Vol. III: *Studies in the Organization of Character.* N. Y.: Macmillan, 1930. Pp. 503.

17. Heidbreder, E. "Introversion and Extroversion in Men and Women," *J. Abn. and Soc. Psychol.*, 1927, 22, 52–61.

18. Hollingworth, L. S. "Sex Differences in Mental Traits," *Psychol. Bull.*, 1916, 13, 377–384.

19. ——. "Comparison of the Sexes in Mental Traits," *Psychol. Bull.*, 1918, 15, 427–432.

20. Hunt, T. "The Measurement of Social Intelligence," *J. Appl. Psychol.*, 1928, 12, 317–334.

21. Kuper, G. M. "Group Differences in the Interests of Children," *J. Phil., Psychol., and Scient. Method*, 1912, 9, 376–379.

22. Laird, D. A., and McClumpha, T. "Sex Differences in Emotional Outlets," *Science*, 1925, 62, 292.

23. Landis, C. "National Differences in Conversations," *J. Abn. and Soc. Psychol.*, 1927, 21, 354–357.

24. Landis, H. M., and Burtt, H. E. "A Study of Conversations," *J. Comp. Psychol.*, 1924, 4, 81–89.

25. Lentz, T. F. "Sex Differences in School Marks with Achievement Test Scores Constant," *Sch. and Soc.*, 1929, 29, 65–68.

26. Lincoln, E. A. *Sex Differences in the Growth of American School Children*. Baltimore: Warwick and York, 1927. Pp. 189.

27. Loutitt, C. M. "A Bibliography of Sex Differences in Mental Traits," *Tr. Sch. Bull.*, 1925, 22, 129–138.

28. Mathews, E. "A Study of Emotional Stability in Children," *J. Delinq.*, 1923, 8, 1–40.

29. McCarthy, D. "Language Development." Ch. 8 in *Handbook of Child Psychology*. C. Murchison, ed. Worcester, Mass.: Clark Univ. Press, 1933. Pp. 956.

30. McFarlane, M. "A Study of Practical Ability," *Brit. J. Psychol., Mon. Suppl.*, 1925, 3. Pp. 75.

31. Miles, C. C. "Sex in Social Psychology." Ch. 16 in *Handbook of Social Psychology*. C. Murchison, ed. Worcester, Mass.: Clark Univ. Press, 1935. Pp. 1195.

32. Miles, C. C., and Terman, L. M. "Sex Differences in the Association of Ideas," *Amer. J. Psychol.*, 1929, 41, 165–206.

33. Moore, H. T. "Further Data concerning Sex Differences," *J. Abn. and Soc. Psychol.*, 1922, 17, 210–214.

34. Mulhall, E. F. "Tests of the Memories of School Children," *J. Educ. Psychol.*, 1917, 8, 295–302.

35. *N. Y. College Entrance Examination Board: Reports of the Commission on Scholastic Aptitude Tests*, 1930.

36. Paterson, D. G., and Langlie, T. A. "The Influence of Sex on Scholarship Ratings," *Educ. Admin. and Super.*, 1926, 12, 458–468.

37. Paterson, D. G., *et al. Minnesota Mechanical Ability Tests*. Minneapolis: Univ. Minn. Press, 1930. Pp. 586.

38. Porteus, S. D. "The Measurement of Intelligence: 643 Children Examined by the Binet and Porteus Tests," *J. Educ. Psychol.*, 1918, 9, 13–31.

39. Pressey, L. W. "Sex Differences Shown by 2544 School Children on a Group Scale of Intelligence, with Special Reference to Variability," *J. Appl. Psychol.*, 1918, 2, 323–340.

40. Pyle, W. H. *The Examination of School Children: a Manual of Directions and Norms.* N. Y.: Macmillan, 1913. Pp. 70.

41. Seashore, C. E. "The Measurement of Pitch Discrimination," *Psychol. Mon.*, 1910, 13, No. 1, 21–59.

42. Snyder, A., and Dunlap, K. "A Study of Moral Evaluation by Male and Female Students," *J. Comp. Psychol.*, 1924, 4, 289–324.

43. Stenquist, J. "Measurements of Mechanical Ability," Teachers College, Columbia Univ., *Contrib. to Educ.*, No. 130, 1923. Pp. 101.

44. Terman, L. M. *The Measurement of Intelligence.* N. Y.: Houghton Mifflin, 1916. Pp. 362.

45. Terman, L. M., and Cuneo, I. "Stanford-Binet Tests of 112 Kindergarten Children and 77 Repeated Retests," *Ped. Sem.*, 1918, 25, 414–428.

46. Terman, L. M., and Miles, C. C. *Sex and Personality: Studies in Masculinity and Femininity.* N. Y.: McGraw-Hill, 1936. Pp. 600.

47. Terman, L. M., *et al. The Stanford Revision and Extension of the Binet-Simon Scale for Measuring Intelligence.* Baltimore: Warwick and York, 1917. Pp. 179.

48. Terman, L. M., *et al. Genetic Studies of Genius.* Vol. I. Stanford Univ., Calif.: Stanford Univ. Press, 1925. Pp. 648.

49. Thompson, H. B. *The Mental Traits of Sex.* Chicago: Univ. Chicago Press, 1903. Pp. 188.

50. Thorndike, E. L., *et al.* "Sex Differences in Status and Gain in Intelligence Test Scores from 13–18," *Ped. Sem.*, 1926; 33, 167–181.

51. Webb, P. E. "A Study of Geometric Abilities among Boys and Girls of Equal Mental Abilities," *J. Educ. Res.*, 1927, 15, 256–262.

52. Wellman, B. L. "Sex Differences." Ch. 15 in *Handbook of Child Psychology*. C. Murchison, ed. Worcester, Mass.: Clark Univ. Press, 1933. Pp. 956.

53. Whipple, G. M. *Manual of Physical and Mental Tests*. Baltimore: Warwick and York, 1921. Parts I and II.

54. ———. "Sex Differences in Intelligence Test Scores in the Elementary School," *J. Educ. Res.*, 1927, 15, 111–117.

55. ———. "Sex Differences in Army Alpha Scores in the Secondary School," *J. Educ. Res.*, 1927, 15, 269–275.

56. Wissler, C. "The Correlation of Mental and Physical Tests," *Psychol. Mon.*, 1901, 3. Pp. 62.

57. Woolley, H. T. "Psychology of Sex," *Psychol. Bull.*, 1910, 7, 335–342.

58. ———. "Psychology of Sex," *Psychol. Bull.*, 1914, 11, 353–379.

CHAPTER XVI

RACIAL COMPARISONS: PROBLEMS OF GROUPING

The comparative evaluation of the races of man has long been a subject of keen interest and lively controversy. It is an interesting commentary upon human thought that nearly all theories of racial inequality proclaim the superiority of the particular race of their respective exponents. Thus Aristotle (cf. 1, pp. 318–320) endeavored to demonstrate that the intellectual leadership of the Greeks must of necessity follow from their favorable geographical location. He argued that the peoples inhabiting the colder regions of northern Europe, although outstanding for bravery and physical prowess, were intellectually incapable of a high degree of political organization or leadership. Similarly, the Asiatics, although intellectually keen and inventive, lacked spirit. The Greeks alone, being geographically intermediate, were endowed with the proper balance of these traits and were thus by nature fitted to rule the earth. Similar claims have been made for such groups as the Arabians, the Romans, the French, the Anglo-Saxon, the "White" race as distinguished from those having a different skin pigmentation, the Nordics, the Alpines, the Mediterraneans, and various others.

Outstanding among such theories, because of its widespread popularization, is that proposed by de Gobineau (10) in the nineteenth century and subsequently expanded by Chamberlain (7). This doctrine had numerous followers who reformulated it and developed it along various lines.

Its basic contention, however, is the superiority of the Nordic or "Aryan" race, a loosely and ambiguously defined group whose descendants are now supposed to inhabit for the most part the countries of northern Europe. The array of evidence cited in support of this theory is incomplete and one-sided at its best and fantastic and mythical at its worst. The concepts involved in such a theory will be critically examined in the course of the subsequent discussion.

At present, race problems are a particularly lively issue. Outworn and forgotten theories are being revived in the attempt to rationalize political actions and policies. Under the stress of emotional appeal, it is especially difficult to carry on unbiased and objective analysis of facts. It is one of the earmarks of prejudice to draw logically unwarranted inferences from the data at hand. In a current test (34) for the measurement of the prejudice-fairmindedness variable, for example, one of the subtests is based on just such behavior. The subject is given certain facts bearing upon controversial issues, with the instructions to check any of the proposed conclusions which seem to him to follow *directly* from the given data, regardless of their truth or falsity in general. The individual who is biased or who responds emotionally to any of the issues involved will ignore the limitations of the facts actually presented and will generalize far beyond them. The procedure in this test presents a close parallel to what probably occurs all too often in the interpretation of data on such emotionally toned issues as race differences.

Under such conditions it is essential to emphasize and to bear clearly in mind the possible vitiating factors and sources of error in the data. As in all group comparisons, studies on race differences must take into account selective factors and adequacy of sampling, overlapping of distributions, reliability of an obtained difference, inaccuracy or ambiguity of the measuring instrument, and other similar factors which have already been discussed and illustrated (cf. Ch. XIV). It is probably not an exaggeration to state that failure to consider such factors has invalidated the large majority of investigations which purport to have established a racial difference in one or another behavioral trait.

Racial comparisons are an extremely difficult problem of differential psychology. In addition to the above-mentioned sources of error which they share with all group comparisons, studies on race differences are handicapped by special difficulties inherent in every phase of the problem. Thus it has proved a difficult matter in such studies to decide *whom* to measure, *what* to measure, and *how* to measure it. These difficulties will be analyzed in the present and subsequent chapter. The first of these two chapters will be concerned with questions of *whom* to measure, or the selection and classification of subjects in racial studies. In the second chapter will be discussed some of the major problems which arise in the efforts to *measure* and *compare* widely diverse groups.

The data of investigations on race differences have been grouped about these methodological questions. No general summary of findings or intellectual hierarchy of racial groups is presented because, although apparently useful as a mnemonic device, such a tabulation would be highly misleading and of very dubious value. Isolated facts are particularly misleading in racial comparisons and should at all times be evaluated in terms of the conditions under which they were collected. Conclusions on race differences will therefore be drawn only in the light of a critical analysis of the entire problem and will not be divorced from their limiting conditions. No attempt has been made, furthermore, to survey the vast array of investigations on psychological differences among racial groups. For summaries and more extensive discussions of this problem, the reader is referred to a review (14) and book (16) by Garth and to the more recent and very stimulating book by Klineberg (24). For an orientation into the general problem of race, books on anthropology, such as those of Boas (4) and Kroeber (26), may be consulted.

What Is a Race?

Tradition, prejudice, and the snap judgments of everyday observation have contributed to the development of a concept of race as a clearly differentiated and easily identifiable group, possessing distinctive physical, mental, and temperamental characteristics. The observations of biologists, anthropologists, and psychologists, however, fail to support such a view.[1] The classification into racial groups is essentially a biological one and corresponds to such divisions as breed, stock, and strain in infrahuman organisms. In its simplest terms, any definition of race implies a certain *community of physical characteristics based primarily upon a common heredity.*

The task of race classification is far more complex than would appear from the glibness with which individuals are commonly assigned to one group or another. The five-fold classification of races memorized by every schoolchild is of historical interest only. This division can be traced to Linnæus (27), the great classifier, who recognized four races of men—*Europæus albus* (white), *Americanus rubescens* (red), *Asiaticus fuscus* (yellow), and *Africanus niger* (black). A fifth group, the brown race, was subsequently added by Blumenbach (2), who also

[1] For a very readable account of many of the difficulties of race classification, see Huxley and Haddon (21).

altered the terminology, proposing the now familiar classification into Caucasian, Mongolian, American, Ethiopian,
and Malayan. This classification is crude and superficial,
as will shortly become apparent.

The essential problem in the classification of racial
groups consists in the identification of inheritable physical
characteristics which differ clearly from one group to
another and which may thus serve as *criteria* of race. A
wide variety of such criteria have been proposed and
applied (cf. e.g., 24, 26). *Skin color* is popularly employed
as one of the most obvious means of racial identification.
In spite of its widespread use, however, it has proved
to be one of the least satisfactory of the possible criteria.
It is a well-established fact that the same pigments are
present in all human skins and that different skin colors
result from varying relative amounts of each pigment.
For this reason, there is found a complete series of transition shades, making exact classification very difficult.
Such a classification is also rendered somewhat unstable
by the fact that environmental conditions, such as exposure to the sun's rays, have a marked effect upon skin
color.

Pigmentation of the eyes has proved a somewhat more
fruitful index, insofar as it is unquestionably an hereditary
trait. In the same connection may be mentioned *hair
color*. These traits, however, are also difficult to describe
quantitatively because of continuous gradations. A
further difficulty in the use of such criteria is their relatively narrow distribution, black hair and eyes being the
universal rule outside of a single stock.

In addition to coloring, other characteristics of the
hair have been employed as differentiating signs. The
texture of the hair is generally regarded as a valuable
criterion of race classification. Fullness of the beard and

degree of development of the downy hair which covers the body as a whole are also coming to be recognized as useful indices.

Racial groups have been differentiated on the basis of *gross bodily dimensions*, chief among which is stature. Group differences in this respect are, however, surprisingly small and consequently of doubtful value in racial identification. *Facial* and *cranial measurements* have been employed to somewhat better advantage. Among the former, the most common are nasal index, which expresses the relative length and breadth of nose, and various indices of prognathism, or the degree of protrusion of the jaws. Cranial capacity, or volume of the skull, yields rather ambiguous results because of its dependence on general body size and because of the wide variation *within* groups with consequent overlapping *between* groups. Cephalic index,[1] on the other hand, has proved to be one of the most satisfactory criteria of classification and is now widely employed.

In view of the relative paucity of satisfactory anatomical criteria, attempts have been made to evolve physiological or biochemical schemas of classification. It has been suggested, for example, that races might be classified on the basis of the *blood groups* which have become familiar in connection with blood transfusions (cf. 19). These blood groupings refer to the agglutinative reactions of the red blood corpuscles, i.e., the tendency of such corpuscles to clump together when the blood of certain individuals is mixed with that of certain other individuals. It is now well known that there exist so-called "universal donors" whose blood can be safely added to that of any individual, as well as "universal recipients" who can

---

[1] Cephalic index $= \dfrac{100 \times \text{head width}}{\text{head length}}$. For fuller description, see Ch. VIII.

safely receive the blood of any other person. There are, in addition, classes of persons who can receive blood from certain specific groups only, and who can likewise donate only to certain groups. Some data on the relative incidence of the various blood groups in different racial stocks suggest a possible relationship between the two, although the differentiation is by no means clear. A serious objection to such a classification is that it cuts across and conflicts with the usual anthropological divisions obtained with other criteria. On the basis of blood groupings, very diverse groups would be lumped together indiscriminately.

The *endocrine glands* have also played their part in race classification. Likenesses have been noted, for instance, between the physical and alleged mental characteristics of certain groups and those of pathological conditions associated with glandular dysfunction (cf. e.g., 22). Thus a parallel has been drawn between the cretin and the African pygmy. Pituitary enlargement has been attributed to the Hottentots and adrenal deficiency to the Negro. The "childlike" appearance of the Chinese has been ascribed to an over-active thymus. Such methods of classification are especially questionable for two reasons: they take a superficial and partial resemblance as their point of departure; and they reason from pathological conditions existing within a single group to the normal characteristics of entire groups.

Finally, mention should be made of the efforts to deal with race in terms of constitutional type (cf. Ch. IX). Kretschmer (25), for example, believes the ratio of leptosomes and pyknics to differ in various racial groups and offers this as a possible explanation of the psychological differences between such groups. Others, both prior and subsequent to Kretschmer, have attempted similar classifications. The reader should recall in this connection the difficulty of finding "pure types" and the absence of valid evidence for a correlation between the physical characteristics of such types and any of their alleged mental differentia.

EVALUATION OF THE CRITERIA OF RACE

In addition to the special deficiencies of individual methods of classification discussed in the preceding section, certain major difficulties are encountered in the application of all, or nearly all, criteria of race. In the first place, a wide *variability* exists within any one group in respect to any trait. Closely related to this is the marked *overlapping* between different groups in any of the criteria mentioned. Thus, although two groups may differ significantly in average height, individuals can readily be found in the "shorter group" who are taller than certain individuals in the "taller group." This obviously makes group delineations indistinct and relatively arbitrary.

A third difficulty is the *inconsistency* frequently found when more than one criterion is employed. An individual might have the coloring of a Nordic, the cephalic index of an Alpine, and the stature of a Mediterranean. Or very dark skin pigmentation and woolly hair might be found in association with Caucasian features. Such instances are frequent and cannot be dismissed as exceptions.

Finally, it should be noted that many of the alleged racial characteristics which were formerly believed to be stable and innate are being found susceptible to *environmental influences*. Even such apparently "hereditary" traits as body height, skull shape, and facial conformation have proved to be dependent in part upon stimulating conditions in early childhood. This was clearly demonstrated in the investigations of Boas (3) on the American-born children of immigrants from several European countries. These children were compared with foreign-born children from the same countries, who were also living in America. Differences were found in stature, weight, and length and width of head.

The most striking indication of environmental influence, however, was furnished by an examination of the cephalic indices of two immigrant groups which differ markedly in head shape (3). American-born and foreign-born boys were compared within the east European Hebrew and the Sicilian groups living in New York City. The former are characteristically round-headed, having a high cephalic index; the latter are characteristically long-headed. As will be seen in Table XX, residence in the new environment tends to make the Jewish group more long-headed and the Sicilian more round-headed, both groups converging toward the American norm. It will also be noted that those boys born after a relatively long period of American residence of the mother exhibit a greater change than those born after a shorter residence period. This was also found to be the case in the data on other immigrant groups.

That these physical changes were the result of changing environmental conditions rather than selective factors was clearly demonstrated. A comparison of foreign-born persons who had immigrated at different periods showed no significant differences in the traits under consideration. The measurement of American-born and foreign-born children *of the same parents*, furthermore, revealed differences in the expected direction.

The results of Boas have subsequently been corroborated by Guthe (17), who compared the cephalic indices of 187 Russian-born Jewish children and 127 American-born Jewish children in Boston. The cephalic indices found by Hirsch (18) on American-born children of

TABLE XX

Change in Cephalic Index of Two Immigrant Groups

(After Boas, 3, p. 10)

Group	N	Average Age	Average Cephalic Index
Foreign-born Sicilian boys	241	9.6	79.5
American-born Sicilian boys:			
Born less than 10 years after arrival of mother	375	10.0	80.0
Born 10 or more years after arrival of mother	127	9.5	81.8
Foreign-born Hebrew boys	179	9.1	84.6
American-born Hebrew boys:			
Born less than 10 years after arrival of mother	257	9.2	82.4
Born 10 or more years after arrival of mother	290	9.2	82.3

South Italian, Russian-Jewish, and Swedish parentage were also in general agreement with the corresponding figures reported by Boas.

More recently, similar investigations have been conducted on Oriental groups. Spier (33) obtained a series of anthropological measures on 320 American-born Japanese schoolchildren in Seattle, Washington, and its vicinity. The same measurements were repeated on 521 schoolchildren living in those sections of Japan from which most of the Seattle group was believed to have come. In general, the American-born children were larger, taller, more round-headed, and had wider faces than those born in Japan. Many of the individual comparisons of corresponding age and sex groups yielded statistically reliable differences between the American-born and native subjects. As in the case of the European immigrants, the differences tended to become more marked the longer the mother had lived in this country.

A variety of factors have been proposed to account for the changes in physical type found in immigrant groups. Differences in bedding and cradling, as well as the gradual abandonment of swathing customs practiced in the mother country, have been cited as possible explanations of the changes in head shape. Nutrition and type of diet are doubtlessly important factors in all of the physical changes noted. Alteration in the activities of the endocrine glands under the stress of adjusting to a new culture has also been suggested as a possible factor (cf. 18). Most of these explanations are, to be sure, highly speculative. Whatever the specific influence or influences at work, however, it is quite definitely established that they are of an environmental nature.

A Tentative Classification of Racial Groups

It is apparent that no one criterion of race can yield a satisfactory classification. Nor can clear-cut group distinctions be made with a combination of such criteria. It should be borne in mind that at best any racial classification is approximate. No sharp line of demarcation can be established between groups, nor can every individual be unequivocally assigned to one particular group. The classification which is most widely accepted at present is one based upon a combination of criteria, chief among which are cephalic index, hair quality, hairiness on the body, facial conformation, and bodily proportions. An outline of this classification (cf. 26, p. 41) is shown below:

I. Caucasian or "white"
   1. Nordic
   2. Alpine
   3. Mediterranean
   4. Hindu

II. Mongoloid or "yellow"
  1. Mongolian
  2. Malaysian
  3. American Indian

III. Negroid or "black"
  1. Negro
  2. Melanesian
  3. Dwarf Black

IV. Of doubtful classification
  1. Australian
  2. Polynesian
  3. Ainu
  4. Small, scattered Indo-Australian groups

Within the Caucasian or white race, four subdivisions are generally recognized. Three of these groups are the Nordic, Alpine, and Mediterranean classes into which the population of Europe is divided; the fourth consists of the Hindus. The Nordics are described as tall, blond, blue-eyed, fair-skinned, and dolichocephalic, or long-headed. They occupy a horizontal belt around the Baltic and North Seas, covering most of England, northern France, the Scandinavian peninsula, Holland, and northern Germany. The Alpines, located chiefly in central Europe, are of medium stature and intermediate coloring, but definitely brachycephalic, or broad-headed. In the Mediterranean group, we again find a pronounced dolichocephaly, accompanied by black or brown hair and eyes, relatively dark skin, and short stature. As its name implies, this group is found on the shores of the Mediterranean, comprising most of the population of Spain and Portugal, southern France, southern Italy, Greece, and certain parts of northern Africa. The Hindu, although darker skinned, bears a very close resemblance to the

Mediterranean and is sometimes included within this group.

The Mongoloid race is characterized by straight hair, very little hair on the face and body, thin lips, and frequently the epicanthic fold which produces the appearance of "oblique" eyes. Short limbs are usually the rule in this group. Skin color may be yellow, brown, or reddish. This race comprises the Oriental Mongolian, as well as the American Indian and the Malaysian. All three are believed to have evolved by differentiation of the same primary stock. Close and extensive observation shows the physical differences between these groups to be much less significant than is popularly supposed.

The Negroid race has relatively long arms and legs, woolly hair, relatively little hair on the face and body, full lips, and a flat nose. In coloring, it is black or dark brown. This stock has been subdivided into the African Negro proper, the Oceanic Melanesian, and the Dwarf Blacks or "pygmies" found in equatorial Africa and other scattered locations. The Bushmen and Hottentots are also occasionally included under the Dwarf Blacks.

There still remain certain groups of people of doubtful classification. These cannot be assigned definitely to any one of the three major human stocks. These peoples exhibit the characteristics of more than one group and would thus be classified inconsistently with different sets of racial criteria. They include such groups as the Australian and Indo-Australian, the Polynesian, and the Ainu, a people of very low cultural status inhabiting an island off the coast of Japan. The Ainu have both Caucasian and Mongoloid traits, but are characterized by a thick hair-covering on the entire body. The impossibility of classifying these groups is not a serious deficiency of the present schema, however, since they comprise only a very small segment of the human species. It has been estimated that about 99% of all mankind can be assigned to one or another of the three major races.

NATIONAL AND LINGUISTIC GROUPINGS

Racial affiliation should not be confused with nationality. A race is a biological group; it implies a certain community of hereditary background and is identified by physical criteria. A nation, on the other hand, is a cultural, political, and geographic grouping. It has been a common practice, especially in the popular literature on the subject, to regard all the individuals of a given nation as members of a single race. This is far from the truth and can only yield very misleading results. Thus in France can be found representatives of all three European racial groups, depending upon the particular section of the country surveyed: in the extreme north the population is predominantly Nordic, in the large central portion Alpine, and in the southern part Mediterranean. Similarly, northern Germany is chiefly Nordic, but the southern portions are Alpine. In northern Italy the Alpine type predominates and in southern Italy the Mediterranean. It is apparent that racial classifications must be made on an individual and not a national basis.

Another common source of confusion is that between racial and linguistic or philological categories. Thus the terms Latin, Aryan, Semitic, and Anglo-Saxon are frequently employed in popular discussion to signify races. But the groups which now speak languages of Latin origin, including French, Italian, Spanish, Portuguese, Roumanian, and others, present an extremely varied racial composition and are not a unit in any but the philological sense. The term Aryan is likewise a very broad one applied by students of linguistics to all those peoples using a derivative of the original Indo-European language. Similarly, the terms Semitic and Anglo-Saxon refer to groups of languages and not to any biologically distinct groups of people. The loose use of national and linguistic nomenclature interchangeably with racial designations has further complicated an already difficult problem of classification. It is well to bear in mind the distinction between these various types of categories.

RACE MIXTURE

An additional difficulty in the way of racial classification is introduced by the extensive amount of race mixture which has been going on for countless generations. Such mixture is particularly common among the subgroups of the White race, so that as a result it is difficult to find many "pure" Nordics, Alpines, or Mediterraneans even in those regions which are supposed to be characteristically populated by these groups. Similar interbreeding has occurred to a greater or lesser extent among nearly all racial groups. There exist at present only a very small number of isolated primitive groups which may be regarded as racially "pure."

When the racial mixture has occurred in violation of social dictum or group mores, as in the case of Whites and Negroes in the United States, the problem of racial identification is further confused by the arbitrary classification imposed by society. Thus a "Negro" in many parts of the United States means an individual with any discoverable traces of Negro ancestry. Biologically such an individual may be much more closely affiliated with the Caucasian than with the Negroid race, but culturally he is a member of the Negro group and shares the social heritage of the latter.

Race mixture, or miscegenation, is a problem which

has aroused much discussion in its own right. Its advantages and disadvantages have been argued at great length; enthusiastic exponents can be found for both sides of the question. Among those who consider miscegenation biologically injurious may be cited Davenport (9) who argues that race mixture produces physical as well as mental "disharmony," the mixed group being a "badly put-together people." Negroes, for example, have relatively long limbs, Whites relatively short limbs. Interbreeding between these two groups might, according to Davenport, result in individuals with long legs and short arms, or vice versa. Similarly, the mixture between a race with large teeth and large jaws and one with small teeth and small jaws might produce individuals with disproportionate combinations of jaws and teeth. This is, in fact, offered by Davenport as a possible explanation for the frequency of tooth decay in the United States.

The fallacy in this argument lies in its assumption that specific organs are inherited as unit characters. The relation between an individual's bodily and mental traits and his gene constitution is, of course, much more complicated than that. In the process of growth, furthermore, all parts of the organism interact and influence each other's development, thus producing a balanced and harmonious relationship of parts.[1] Observations on hybrids, both in the human and infrahuman species, reveal no significant disharmonies. The success of many animal breeding experiments certainly testifies to the beneficial results which may be obtained with race crossing. Physical measures of hybrid races have likewise shown either an increased physical vigor in the hybrid generation or a physical status which is midway between that of the parent groups. In no case has a consistent

[1] For a fuller discussion of these criticisms, cf. 5, 6.

physical inferiority of a hybrid group been reliably established.

The effects of race mixture have also been discussed from the standpoint of the historical achievements of various groups (cf. 31). Two opposed theories have been proposed regarding the influence of race mixture upon the rise and fall of civilizations. On the one hand are cited ancient Egypt, classical Greece, and the Roman Empire, whose decline was coincident with the widespread intermixture with culturally inferior immigrant or servile groups. Similarly, the relative backwardness of certain present-day groups, such as are found in Mexico and South America, has been attributed to the fact that they are of hybrid stock.

An equally strong case can be made, however, in support of the opposite theory. Racial purity is often associated with a very low level of cultural development. Thus among the most racially pure human groups may be mentioned the hill folk of India, the Andaman Islanders, and certain Eskimo groups. In our own country, the closest approximation to purity of racial stock is probably to be found among the southern mountaineers, a group notoriously backward in social and intellectual development. Conversely, the achievements of the modern world can be shown to be the cultural expression of hybrid stocks. All of the great European nations present a complexity of racial composition. The history of the United States furnishes a particularly striking example of the achievements of a highly mixed group. It can also be shown that many great men were the product of much interbreeding of diverse stocks.

The apparent inconsistencies in such data arise from the attempt to establish a *causal relationship* between race mixture and cultural level. There is, in fact, no reason to expect a direct relation between the two. Both are in turn dependent upon a third factor, the degree of social contact or social isolation of a group. Cultural development is promoted by contacts between groups, with the resulting interchange of diverse material and intellectual products. At the same time, such contacts are conducive to race mixture. Hence a heightened cultural development is often found in association with race mixture.[1]

In certain situations, social factors may cause the reverse relationship to hold between degree of racial purity and cultural development. Thus in a period of degeneration, miscegenation with a despised group may be tolerated as social barriers are lowered. In such a case, as in ancient empires in their decadent periods, the race mixture is but another symptom of a disruption of traditional behavior and may temporarily coincide with a period of low intellectual achievement and cultural deterioration. In either case, the association is a superficial one, and cannot be employed to prove a biological basis of cultural development.

Psychological Studies of Hybrid Groups

It is apparent that the effects of race mixture cannot be determined by comparing the achievements of different groups or periods of history. Nor can an understanding of the problem be furthered by speculation on hypothetical biological influences. The direct examination of hybrid individuals is more relevant to the problem. A few scattered groups of mixed racial origin have been tested or observed in Hawaii (30), Jamaica (9), Africa (12), and elsewhere. The most extensive data, however, have been collected on the American Indian and the American Negro, owing to the relative accessibility of these groups in large numbers.

Hunter and Sommermier (20) administered the Otis Group Intelligence Test to 711 American Indians attending the Haskell Indian Institute at Lawrence, Kansas. The subjects ranged from fourteen years of age upwards. A wide variety of tribes was represented. It was possible to determine the degree of racial mixture directly by an examination of records of ancestry. No evidence was found of mixture with any race other than the White. The full-blood Indians formed the largest group, numbering 265. Only seven members of the entire sampling tested had less than ¼ Indian blood. Individuals with such a small percentage of White blood would tend to become assimilated to the White population and attend the regular school rather than go to a special institute for Indian students. This may have introduced a selective factor in the data, since the mixed-bloods who attend Haskell are probably a poorer sampling of their group than the full-bloods. Such a selective factor, as the authors point out, would give an advantage to the full-bloods.

The average Otis score of the Haskell group as a whole was found to be much lower than the White norms, age by age. Within the Indian group, a correlation of +.41 was obtained between Otis score and degree of White blood, as determined from the ancestry records. Analysis of performance on the separate parts of the test showed the Indian groups to be most markedly inferior in the more highly verbal tests such as analogies, opposites, matching proverbs, and narrative completion.

In a subsequent study, Garth (16) analyzed the National Intelligence Test scores of 609 mixed-blood and 89 full-blood Indians attending Indian Reservation schools in South Dakota, Oklahoma, New Mexico, and Colorado. A group of 67 White children was also tested for comparative purposes. The intelligence test scores again showed a

steady rise with decrease of Indian blood, the averages for
¾-bloods, ½-bloods, and ¼-bloods being 74, 75, and 77.5,
respectively. The correlation between degree of White
blood and test score proved to be +.42. The data were
further analyzed in respect to separate school grades. In
Table XXI will be found the number of cases in each
grade as well as the correlation between National Intelligence Test score and degree of White blood within that
grade. It should be noted that the distribution of White
blood was similar in all grades and could not therefore
account for the differences obtained.

TABLE XXI

CORRELATION BETWEEN DEGREE OF WHITE BLOOD AND NATIONAL
INTELLIGENCE TEST SCORES WITHIN SINGLE SCHOOL GRADES
(After Garth et al., 16, p. 274)

Grade	Number of Cases	Correlation
Fourth	134	.70
Fifth	169	.76
Sixth	180	.22
Seventh	112	.23
Eighth	75	.24

These data suggest rather strongly an environmental
interpretation of the correlation between degree of White
blood and intelligence test performance. In the lower
grades, those children with a larger percentage of White
blood clearly excelled their fellows. In the three upper
grades, however, the relationship is very low and barely
significant. Thus continued education in a common
school seems to reduce and even wipe out the apparent
effects of degree of Indian blood.

Klineberg (23) reports an absence of linear relation
between degree of Indian blood and test performance in a
group of 100 Yakima Indians in the state of Washington.

The tests were taken from the Pintner-Paterson Performance Scale and were largely dependent upon speed. The Indians as a whole obtained lower scores than a group of 100 White boys who had been similarly tested. Comparison of full-blood and mixed-blood groups, however, gave conflicting results, the poorest scores having been obtained by those subjects with the most and those with the least Indian blood.

The same general results have been obtained with the American Negro. In an early study, Ferguson (11) administered four simple psychological tests [1] to 907 Negro schoolchildren in three cities in Virginia. As is usually the case, the Negroes as a group were most deficient in the two verbal tests; in the remaining two tests, the differences were slight and inconsistent. The subjects were divided into four groups on the basis of skin color, hair color, and shape of the head and face. This classification was made by inspection only, no anthropometric measurements having been made. On this basis, Ferguson estimated that there is a steady rise in general intellectual performance with increase of White blood. In view of the crude method of classification employed, little weight can be attached to such results.

More recently, Peterson and Lanier (29) administered a number of "ingenuity" tests as well as intelligence scales to 12-year-old Negro schoolchildren in Nashville, Chicago, and New York City. Several of the tests were non-language, an important consideration in the comparison of racial groups with diverse educational opportunities. Ratings of skin color on a seven point scale were obtained on the Nashville and Chicago groups. In Table XXII are shown the correlations between lightness of skin and scores on the five tests employed.

---

[1] Analogies, sentence completion, A-cancellation test, and stylus maze.

TABLE XXII

CORRELATIONS BETWEEN LIGHTNESS OF SKIN AND MENTAL TEST
SCORES IN GROUPS OF 12-YEAR-OLD CHILDREN
(After Peterson and Lanier, 29, p. 86)

Test	Number of Cases	Correlation
Binet group test	83	.18
Myers mental measure	75	.30
Rational learning, time score	117	.05
Mental maze, time score	113	.14
Disc transfer, time score	119	.39

In view of the inadequacy of skin color as a criterion
of race, more extensive measures were obtained on the
group of 75 New York City subjects. Correlations were
computed between score on the Yerkes revision of the
Binet Intelligence Scale and the four physical traits which
were found to differentiate most clearly between White
and Negro subjects. These correlations are shown in
Table XXIII below. As will be seen, the correlations are
all too low to indicate a reliable degree of relationship.

TABLE XXIII

CORRELATIONS BETWEEN INTELLIGENCE TEST SCORE AND
ANTHROPOMETRIC MEASURES ON 75 NEGRO SCHOOLBOYS
(After Peterson and Lanier, 29, p. 90)

Trait	Correlation
Nose width	−.11
Lip thickness	.07
Ear height	−.15
Interpupillary span	.01
Composite of these four traits	−.13

Klineberg (23), in the previously described investigation with the Pintner-Paterson Scale, also tested 139 Negro boys between the ages of 7 and 16 in rural sections of

West Virginia. The correlation [1] between intelligence test score and three anthropometric measures indicative of degree of Negro blood are given below:

Nose width	—.083
Lip thickness	—.068
Black pigmentation	—.12

As in the study of Peterson and Lanier, the relationship between test performance and index of Negro blood is negligible when accurate measures are employed.

The fact that a few investigators have found a positive relationship between degree of White blood and intelligence test performance is considered very significant by those who attribute a biological basis to race differences in intelligence. Thus it is argued that just such a relationship would result from the mixture of a superior and an inferior stock, the mixed group being intermediate between the better and the poorer parent races. Similarly, the greater the contribution of the superior race to the individual's hereditary background, the higher should be his intellectual status.

Such an interpretation fails to take into account those cases in which negative results have been obtained under carefully controlled conditions. There are, furthermore, other possible explanations of the intermediate position of certain hybrid groups. In the first place, race mixture is often *selective*. This is especially true of those mixtures which are discouraged or frowned upon by society. In such cases, miscegenation may be confined largely to the socially and educationally inferior members of both groups. More often, perhaps, the selection occurs only in the group which is held to be "superior," there being no prejudice against such a mixture among members of the

---

[1] The influence of age was ruled out by the partial correlation technique.

supposedly "inferior" race. This was doubtlessly the case when an "advanced" and a "primitive" group first came into contact. It has also been suggested (cf. 31) that a certain amount of selection may occur in the reverse direction, the superior individuals of the "lower" race being chosen more often for such unions. It is doubtful, however, whether such a selection is made on an intellectual basis. It is apparent that the problem of selection in race mixture is a very complicated one which can only be settled by an analysis of actual historical and social developments in individual groups. The relative status of the hybrid and parent groups, therefore, will vary with the specific circumstances.

In any discussion of race mixture, the *social and cultural conditions* imposed upon the hybrid group cannot be ignored. On the one hand, such groups are frequently stigmatized and may be despised by both parent groups. The hybrid individual is often made to feel that he belongs to neither group and that he stands apart from his fellow-beings. Such a situation may produce serious personality disorders, maladjustments, and anti-social behavior. As Reuter expresses it: "The hybrids tend to be distinct in social position, culture status, and personality organization: sociologically, as well as racially, they are hybrid" (31, p. vi). On the other hand, the hybrid individual often assimilates more readily than the full-blood to the culture of the "superior" race. Because of the prevailing beliefs on the relative status of the two races, he is usually considered to be more capable than his full-blooded cousins. As a result, he is given better educational opportunities, admitted to more responsible positions, and afforded better facilities for advancement in every way.

It should also be noted that *the mixed-bloods have been exposed more directly to the influence of the manners and*

customs of the "superior" group than have the full-bloods.
Whether the miscegenation occurs through legal marriages
or illicit unions, the presence of the White parent will on
the whole tend to bring about a closer contact with the
White culture than is the case in families where no such
mixture has occurred. As a result, the economic and
social level of the home, as well as the degree to which
English is spoken at home, frequently differentiate hybrid
from full-blood groups. This is particularly true of the
American Indian. And it will be recalled that in this
group a significant positive correlation between degree of
White blood and intelligence test performance was found
more often than in the Negro group.

Immigrant Groups

Many alleged "racial" comparisons have been made
on immigrant groups in the United States. The subjects
are usually classified according to country of birth; if
American-born children of immigrants are employed, they
are classified on the basis of parents' birthplace. Such
investigations cannot yield any information on the problem of *race differences.* As has already been pointed out,
national groups cannot be assigned *as a whole* to one or
another racial stock. But even for the study of *national
differences* such data are inadequate and misleading. Immigrants cannot be assumed to be representative samplings of their home population. They are not drawn
proportionately from all educational, economic, and social
levels but usually represent a select group.

A more serious difficulty is that such selective factors
may operate differently in each country. As a result,
immigrant groups from different nations are *neither fair
samplings of their home populations nor comparable among
themselves.* If it could be shown, for instance, that immi-

grants from all nations were drawn consistently from the lower levels of society, then such groups would at least be comparable with each other. But it is well known that, through purely historical reasons, the immigrants from some nations may represent a relatively inferior sampling of their population, from others a more nearly random or average sampling, and from still others a relatively superior sampling.

It has been frequently suggested, for example, that the superior performance of Chinese and Japanese children in America on our intelligence tests may be the result of selective factors, only the more progressive families emigrating from these countries (cf., e.g., 8, 32). Many of the immigrants from southern Europe, on the other hand, are probably an inferior sampling of their own national population. In a recent study (13), Danish and Italian girls both in the United States and in Europe were examined with the International Group Mental Test. Although the Danish samplings in this country excelled the Italian, no reliable difference was found between the groups tested in Copenhagen and in Rome.

It is apparent that the testing of immigrants can throw little or no light upon the relative status of the national groups from which they are drawn. It might be argued, however, that the determination of the abilities and personality traits of the immigrants themselves is of direct practical value for restriction of admittance, assimilation, and similar purposes. Such an argument fails to take into account two important aspects of the problem. In the first place, the behavior of immigrants may simply reflect their former environmental background. We cannot assume that the emotional and intellectual traits of such persons are innately determined just because they persist under the new environment. The influence of early conditioning is too strong to be readily wiped out. Similar traits would also be noticeable to a slighter extent in the offspring of immigrant parents, as long as family traditions and the practices of the home country endure.

A further point to note in the study of immigrant groups is that the immigration itself, with its resulting necessity of adjusting to a new culture, is an important environmental influence. This factor cannot be ignored in analyzing the mental and emotional make-up of the immigrant. The confusion of standards and shifting reference points contingent upon such an adjustment cannot fail to have an effect upon the subject's behavioral development. The point has frequently been made that the maladjustment is greatest not in the case of the immigrating generation who retain their customs to a large extent, nor in the case of the third and succeeding generations where adaptation and assimilation is virtually complete, but in the case of the offspring of the immigrants—or second generation—who are caught in the maelstrom occasioned by two different frames of reference.

In an extensive survey with a revision of the Woodworth Personal Data Sheet, Mathews (28) found a much greater number of neurotic symptoms on the average among the children of immigrants than among those of native parentage. The children tested ranged in age from 9 to 19 and in school grade from the fourth to the twelfth. Both sexes were included in the study. The median number of neurotic symptoms reported by each of the three major groups selected for comparison was as follows:

"Mixed" group: largely of north European
   ancestry; resident in America for several
   generations (N = 87)   16
Jewish group (N = 199)   20
Italian group (N = 188)   36

Data such as these do not constitute an adequate basis for the conclusion that Jewish or Italian groups in this country are by nature emotionally unbalanced. In a similar situation, the "normal" individual upon whom the test was standardized might have reacted similarly.

REFERENCES

1. Aristotle. *The Politics of Aristotle*, ed. by W. L. Newman. Oxford: Clarendon Press, 1887. Vol. I. Pp. 580.

2. Blumenbach, J. F. *Anthropological Treatises* (transl. by T. Bendyshe). London: Longman, Green, Roberts, 1865. Pp. 406.

3. Boas, F. *Abstract of the Report on Changes in Bodily Form of Descendants of Immigrants*. Washington: Gov't. Printing Office, 1911. Pp. 58.

4. ——. *Anthropology and Modern Life*. N. Y.: Norton, 1928. Pp. 246.

5. Castle, W. E. "Biological and Social Consequences of Race Crossing," *Amer. J. Phys. Anthrop.*, 1926, 9, 145–156.

6. ——. "Race Mixture and Physical Disharmonies," *Science*, 1930, 71, 603–606.

7. Chamberlain, H. S. *Die Grundlagen des neunzehnten Jahrhunderts*. München: Bruckman, 1901. Pp. 531.

8. Darsie, M. L. "Mental Capacity of American-Born Japanese Children," *Comp. Psychol. Mon.*, 1926, 15, No. 3. Pp. 89.

9. Davenport, C. B., and Steggerda, M. *Race Crossing in Jamaica*. Washington: Carnegie Inst. of Wash., 1929. Pp. 516.

10. de Gobineau, A. J. *Essai sur l'inégalité des races humaines*. Paris: Firmin-Didot, 1853. Vol. I, pp. 492; Vol. II, pp. 512.

11. Ferguson, G. O. "The Psychology of the Negro," *Arch. Psychol.*, No. 36, 1916. Pp. 138.

12. Fischer, Eugen. *Die Rehobother Bastards und das Bastardierungsproblem beim Menschen*. Jena: G. Fischer, 1913. Pp. 327.

13. Franzblau, R. N. "Race Differences in Mental and Physical Traits Studied in Different Environments," *Arch. Psychol.*, No. 177, 1935. Pp. 44.

14. Garth, T. R. "A Review of Racial Psychology," *Psychol. Bull.*, 1925, 22, 343–364.

15. ——. *Race Psychology: a Study of Racial Mental Differences.* N. Y.: McGraw-Hill, Whittlesey House, 1931. Pp. 260.

16. Garth, T. R., Schuelke, N., and Abell, W. "The Intelligence of Mixed-Blood Indians," *J. Appl. Psychol.*, 1927, 11, 268–275.

17. Guthe, C. E. "Notes on the Cephalic Index of Russian Jews in Boston," *Amer. J. Phys. Anthrop.*, 1918, 1, 213–223.

18. Hirsch, N. D. M. "Cephalic Index of American-Born Children of Three Foreign Groups," *Amer. J. Phys. Anthrop.*, 1927, 10, 79–90.

19. Hirszfeld, L., and Hirszfeld, H. "Seralogic Differences between the Blood of Different Races," *Lancet*, 1919, 197, No. 5016, 675–679.

20. Hunter, W. S., and Sommermier, E. "The Relation of Degree of Indian Blood to Score on the Otis Intelligence Test," *J. Comp. Psychol.*, 1922, 2, 257–277.

21. Huxley, J. S., and Haddon, A. C. *We Europeans: A Survey of "Racial" Problems.* London: Jonathan Cape, 1935. Pp. 299.

22. Keith, A. "On the Differentiation of Mankind into Racial Types," *Lancet*, 1919, 197, No. 5013, 553–556.

23. Klineberg, O. "An Experimental Study of Speed and Other Factors in 'Racial' Differences," *Arch. Psychol.*, No. 93, 1928. Pp. 111.

24. ——. *Race Differences.* N. Y.: Harper, 1935. Pp. 367.

25. Kretschmer, E. *The Psychology of Men of Genius* (transl. by R. B. Cattell). N. Y.: Harcourt, Brace, 1931. Pp. 256.

26. Kroeber, A. L. *Anthropology.* N. Y.: Harcourt, Brace, 1923. Pp. 523.

27. Linnæus, C. v. *Systema Naturæ.* Stockholm: Kiesewetter, 1740 (Second edition). Pp. 87.

28. Mathews, E. "A Study of Emotional Instability in Children," *J. Delinq.*, 1923, 8, 1–40.

29. Peterson, J., and Lanier, L. H. "Studies in the Comparative Abilities of Whites and Negroes," *Ment. Meas. Mon.*, No. 5, 1929. Pp. 156.

30. Porteus, S. D., and Babcock, M. E. *Temperament and Race.* Boston: Badger, 1926. Pp. 364.

31. Reuter, E. B. *Race Mixture: Studies in Intermarriage and Miscegenation.* N. Y.: McGraw-Hill, Whittlesey House, 1931. Pp. 224.

32. Sandiford, P., and Kerr, R. "Intelligence of Chinese and Japanese Children," *J. Educ. Psychol.*, 1926, 17, 361–367.

33. Spier, L. "Growth of Japanese Children Born in America and in Japan," *Wash. State Univ. Publ. in Anthrop.*, 1929, 3, No. 1, 1–30.

34. Watson, G. B. *A Survey of Public Opinion on Some Religious and Economic Issues.* N. Y.: Teachers College, Columbia Univ., Bur. Pub., 1927 (test blank and manual).

CHAPTER XVII

RACIAL COMPARISONS: PROBLEMS OF MEASUREMENT [1]

In the preceding chapter it was shown that the classification of individuals into distinct races, as well as the choice of groups suitable for comparison, presents many difficulties. Even when a satisfactory selection of subjects has been made, however, additional problems remain to be solved. It is not sufficient to determine whom to measure. The questions what to measure and how to measure it are equally important. Thus it is necessary to decide which are the most significant traits for comparison and what materials and techniques are applicable to the testing of culturally dissimilar groups. The interpretation of the obtained differences also raises important questions. Is it possible to establish a universal criterion of "intellect" so that we may speak of one group as being intellectually "superior" and another "inferior"? What shall we use as norms or standards for the evaluation of widely diverse peoples? The latter is a very fundamental issue in differential psychology.

Individuals who differ in racial affiliation also differ in many other respects. It is therefore very difficult to *isolate* the factor of race so as to determine its direct influence upon the subject's behavioral development. Members of different racial groups frequently speak different lan-

---

[1] For the sake of brevity, the term "race" will be employed without quotation marks or other qualifications to refer to groups so designated in the particular investigation under consideration. It is not to be assumed, therefore, that such groups constitute races in the sense in which this term was defined in the preceding chapter. In each case, the nature of the groups will be apparent from the context.

guages, a fact which greatly restricts the range of traits in which inter-group comparisons can validly be made. The differences in general educational opportunities and specific type of training available to each group have an undoubted influence upon mental test performance. Such groups may likewise differ in their general social and economic level and in the facilities for intellectual advancement offered in their own homes. The background of tradition and culture against which the individual develops is also fundamentally diverse from group to group. The emotional attitudes, interests, ideals, and preferences fostered by such surroundings will not be the same. To this may be added the many difficulties arising when an examiner from one racial or national group administers psychological tests to subjects in another group. This situation is not comparable to the testing of subjects within one's own group.

A considerable body of evidence is available which demonstrates the influence of the above factors upon mental test performance. Frequently such data were gathered incidentally in studies whose major purpose was the establishment of race differences in ability. A few investigations, on the other hand, have been conducted with the explicit aim of analyzing the pitfalls in racial comparisons. In either case, the data seem clear in their implication that factors other than race are operative in alleged racial differences. It should be noted that the question of race *versus* culture in the production of group differences is one phase of the general problem of heredity and environment. Race, it will be recalled, is a biological unit based upon hereditary community. Culture, on the other hand, refers to the environmental conditions and behavior shared by the members of a single group.

Language Handicap

It is obvious that in the comparison of groups speaking different languages, verbal tests cannot be employed. Non-language and performance tests have been devised for this purpose. It is not to be concluded, however, that the same traits are being measured by all of these tests. As was shown in Chapter XI, many tests included under the heading of "intelligence scales" call into play widely different abilities. Thus when unfamiliarity with the language makes the application of verbal tests impossible in a given group, the range of processes which can be measured in that group is thereby narrowed. There is no substitute for verbal tests. It is a psychological impossibility to eliminate the verbal content of a test without altering the mental processes involved.

The effect of language handicap upon test performance is most serious, however, when it is present *in a mild degree*. If the individual has a moderate understanding of English, it is usually deemed unnecessary to give him a non-verbal test. But such an individual may lack the facility in the use of English or the range of vocabulary required to compete fairly on a verbal test. This situation is often encountered in immigrants who have lived in America for many years, or in the children of immigrants. The latter are frequently bilingual, speaking their own language at home and English at school.

That such relatively mild language handicaps may have a pronounced effect upon intelligence test scores has been frequently demonstrated. Pintner and Keller (24) conducted a special investigation of this problem with children of immigrants from several European countries. All of the children tested were in the kindergarten or the first two grades of elementary school. In order to determine the effect of bilingualism upon test performance, the subjects were divided into two groups. The first group comprised all those from homes in which English was presumably spoken; in this group were included all children of American parentage, both White and Negro, as well as those of English, Canadian, Scotch, Irish, and Welsh parentage. In the second group were placed those who probably spoke a language other than English at home; these included chiefly children of Italian or Slavish immigrants, as well as a few whose parents had come from Germany, Greece, Hungary, Poland, and other European countries. Both groups were given a revision of the Binet test. The average I.Q.'s obtained by each group, as well as the number of cases, are shown below:

	Number of Cases	Average I.Q.
English-speaking homes	367	92
Foreign-speaking homes	674	84

In one of the schools, these investigators were able also to administer the Pintner Non-Language tests to the second grade children. A comparison of the subjects from English-speaking and foreign-speaking homes on the two tests showed the latter group to be *less inferior* on the Non-Language test. The relevant data are given below:

	Number of Cases	Average Binet I.Q.	Average Pintner I.Q.
English-speaking homes	49	99	109
Foreign-speaking homes	56	89	103

As a final check on the influence of language handicap, the same authors compared the Stanford-Binet and performance test [1] scores of children referred to a psychological clinic for examination. The subjects were again

[1] Each child was given three or more of the following tests: Pintner Cube Test, Form Board, Witmer Cylinder Test, Healy Construction Puzzle A, and Mare and Foal Test.

classified into those from English-speaking and those from foreign-speaking homes. This analysis corroborated the findings on the other groups. Among the foreign-speaking children, 75% obtained higher mental ages on the performance tests than on the Stanford-Binet. In the English-speaking group, on the other hand, only 52% scored higher on the performance tests, i.e., there was no tendency for the group as a whole to excel in either test. Similarly, the average difference between performance scale and Stanford-Binet mental age was 16 months in the foreign-speaking group, as compared to an average difference of only 6 months in the English-speaking group.

In a later study, Pintner (23) analyzed the scores of third and fourth grade schoolchildren on the National Intelligence Test and the Pintner Non-Language Scale. The subjects were classified into an "American" group, mostly of Irish descent, and a foreign group composed of children of Italian, German, or Polish parents. The percentages of "foreign" children who reached or exceeded the median of the 121 "American" children in each of the two tests are shown in Table XXIV.

TABLE XXIV

PERCENTAGE OF "FOREIGN" CHILDREN REACHING OR EXCEEDING
THE MEDIAN OF "AMERICAN" CHILDREN
(After Pintner, 23)

Nationality of Parents	Number of Cases	Pintner Non-Language Scale	National Intelligence Test
Italian	102	43	36
German	45	61	41
Polish	18	62	36
Total "foreign"	165	50	37

It will be noted that in the total "foreign" group, as well as in each of the three national groups, the percentage reaching or exceeding the median of the American children is greater for the Non-Language than for the National Intelligence Test. On the Non-Language test, the "foreign" group as a whole equals the performance of the American group, although it falls definitely below the latter on the National Intelligence Test.

In an analysis of data secured independently by different investigators, Goodenough (12) found a correlation of —.75 between the average I.Q. of children in various immigrant groups and the tendency of such groups to retain their own language for use in the home. An index of the latter was obtained by finding the ratio of the number of parents in each national group who had been in this country for a period of 20 years or over and had not adopted English, to the total number of parents in that group who had adopted it. The high negative correlation between these two factors indicates a strong tendency for children in those immigrant groups in which English is not readily adopted to obtain lower scores on our intelligence tests. Goodenough points out that there are two possible explanations of such a finding. On the one hand, the lower intelligence test scores of some groups may result directly from their greater language handicap. On the other hand, those national groups in which English is not commonly adopted may be less intelligent and less progressive from the outset. Their failure to learn English would thus be the result of lower intelligence and poorer adaptability.

Neither interpretation can be selected solely on the basis of the correlation between the two factors. Other data, however, suggest that the former is the more probable hypothesis. Thus, the inferiority of the immigrant groups is greatly diminished and may disappear entirely when non-language tests are employed. In tests such as the Stanford-Binet, on the other hand, it is well known that verbal facility plays a major part. The vocabulary test in the Stanford-Binet, for example, has been found to correlate so highly with performance on the entire scale that it has been proposed as a short substitute for the latter. In one investigation (14), this vocabulary test was administered to 562 public school children in a small industrial community in Pennsylvania, 90% of whom were of foreign parentage. The percentage of "foreign" children who scored at or above their age norms on the vocabulary test proved to be only 10, as contrasted to 53.5 for the "American" group. It is apparent that such a group would suffer a severe handicap when tested with the Stanford-Binet or similar scales.

The fact that immigrants from English-speaking countries obtain relatively high average scores on intelligence tests, while those whose language is most unlike our own make a relatively poor showing, seems also to support the explanation in terms of language handicap. Further corroboration of this hypothesis is furnished by a study with the Otis Group Test on Italian children in New Jersey (20). When the subjects were divided into four language groups—those who spoke only Italian at home, those who spoke Italian and some English, those who spoke English and some Italian, and those who spoke exclusively English—a consistent rise in score was found with increase in amount of English spoken at home.

The data on language handicap are not limited to immigrant groups from European nations. In investigations on American Indians, the influence of language deficiency upon intelligence test performance has been vividly demonstrated. Jamieson and Sandiford (13) administered a series of standard tests to 717 pupils attending Indian schools in Ontario, Canada. All of the children

could speak English, but their ability to do so was below
that of the average American child. The median I.Q.'s
obtained by the Indian children on each test are shown
in Table XXV.

TABLE XXV

MEDIAN I.Q.'s OF INDIAN SCHOOLCHILDREN
(After Jamieson and Sandiford, 13)

Test	Number of Cases	Median I.Q.
National Intelligence Test	275	79.8
Pintner Non-Language Test	280	96.9
Pintner-Paterson Performance Tests	115	96.4
Pintner-Cunningham Primary Test	59	77.9

A comparison of the median I.Q. on the verbal and non-
verbal tests reveals the influence of language handicap.
On the National Intelligence Test, a predominantly verbal
test, the Indian children are clearly below the American
norms. On the Pintner Non-Language and Pintner-
Paterson Performance Scales, on the other hand, their
performance is practically up to the norms. The Pintner-
Cunningham Test was administered to the younger children. In this test, the median I.Q. again proved to be
low. It should be noted, however, that although this
test does not involve the use of written English, rather
detailed directions are given orally, a fact which would
handicap the Indian child.

A more conclusive demonstration of the importance of
language handicap was furnished by a comparison of the
scores of a group of "monoglots," who spoke only English,
with those of "bilinguals," who spoke an Indian language
at home all or part of the time. The median I.Q.'s of
these two groups on each test are shown in Table XXVI.
It will be noted that *on the performance scale the bilingual
children obtain a higher median I.Q. than the monoglots,*

TABLE XXVI

MEDIAN I.Q.'s OF MONOGLOT AND BILINGUAL INDIAN SCHOOL-
CHILDREN

(After Jamieson and Sandiford, 13)

Test	Number of Cases		Median I.Q.	
	Monoglot	Bilingual	Monoglot	Bilingual
National Intelligence Test	153	115	82.4	76.6
Pintner Non-Language Test	152	121	100.0	93.6
Pintner-Paterson Performance Tests	80	30	80.8	87.5
Pintner-Cunningham Test	33	23	80.5	68.1

whereas the reverse is true on the other three tests. This suggests that the poorer showing of the bilinguals is not due to their inferior mental status but to the verbal nature of the test. In the case of the Pintner Non-Language Test, it is possible that the use of paper-and-pencil materials gave a disadvantage to the children from the less highly assimilated homes. Those children who were relatively unfamiliar with such materials would also tend more often to come from Indian-speaking homes.

Similar results have been obtained with Oriental groups in America. Darsie (7) tested 570 American-born Japanese children between the ages of 10 and 15. Only those children who reported that English was the language most familiar to them were included in this group. The linguistic difficulties were therefore not very pronounced, but were just such as might be commonly found among the children of immigrants. On the Army Beta, a non-language test, there was no consistent difference in score between Japanese and American children. The direction of the difference varied from one subtest to another; the total scores showed no significant difference at ages 10 and 11 and Japanese superiority beyond this.

The Stanford-Binet, however, yielded clear-cut differences. The median I.Q. of the Japanese group was 89.5 as contrasted to 99.5 for White children of the same districts. That this difference was attributable to the verbal nature of the test was definitely demonstrated by a special analysis conducted by Darsie. Each individual test on the Stanford-Binet scale was ranked for degree of Japanese inferiority. The tests were then rated independently by seven psychologists on the basis of the degree to which success on each depends upon verbal ability. A final ranking of the tests was obtained by taking the average of the ratings by the seven judges. When these two sets of ranks—the one for Japanese inferiority and the other for "verbality"—were compared, they were found to correlate +.87. Further corroboration of this relationship was furnished by a comparison of the performance of Japanese and Whites on the separate tests. Thus the superiority of the American children was found to consist chiefly in their greater success on the linguistic tests. The Japanese surpassed the Whites, on the other hand, in certain non-verbal tests of the Stanford-Binet scale involving sustained attention and visual perception.[1]

DIFFICULTIES OF TEST ADMINISTRATION

In addition to language handicap, other special difficulties are encountered in the attempt to administer tests to widely differing groups. The use of *pantomime* and gesture in non-language tests is often confusing to the subject since it is not his normal mode of communication. This is illustrated in certain observations regarding the administration of the Army Beta to the Negro draft in the United States army. Several examiners called

[1] The Japanese children were reliably superior in the Induction, Paper Cutting, Code Learning, and Enclosed Boxes tests.

attention to the fact that it was difficult to keep up their subjects' interest in the test. In the report from one camp, it was stated that, "it took all the energy and enthusiasm the examiner could muster to maintain the necessary attention, as there was a decided disposition for the Negroes to lapse into inattention and almost into sleep" (27, p. 705). One of the reasons offered in explanation of this reaction was the artificiality of the situation produced by the elimination of language. It is also difficult to standardize directions given in pantomime and to insure that they shall always be repeated in identical fashion.

The use of *pictures* as test materials is also somewhat questionable, especially among certain groups who have had no experience with pictorial representation in their everyday life. A two-dimensional reproduction of an object is not a perfect replica of the original; it simply presents certain cues which, through the influence of past experience, lead to the perception of the object. If the cues are highly reduced, as in a simplified or schematic drawing, or if the necessary past experience is absent, the correct perception may not follow. It might be added that pictures of objects which are themselves unfamiliar in the cultural group to be examined are obviously unsuitable as test materials. They have, nevertheless, been included in certain non-language scales [1] which have been employed in racial comparisons.

A further problem arises in connection with *rapport*. Test manuals repeatedly urge that the examiner must

---

[1] Such as the Army Beta and the Pintner Non-Language Scales. It might be mentioned that the International Group Mental Test is at present the most satisfactory scale for the comparison of widely varying cultural groups. In it a definite attempt has been made to include only items which are universally familiar, although possibly not to the same degree in every group (cf. Dodd, 8, Blackwood, 5).

establish the proper rapport with his subjects. By this is meant, in general, that the testees should be put at their ease, their interest and coöperation should be secured, and they should be made calm and comfortable before the test is begun. In other words, it is assumed that each subject will be in a condition to do his best. In an individual test a definite effort is usually made to establish rapport with the subject. With group tests, however, this is much more difficult. The examiner in such a case must limit himself to a few reassuring introductory remarks and to the elimination of any obvious handicaps under which individual members of the group may be laboring. For this reason, group tests are frequently considered less accurate than individual tests.

When an examiner from one cultural or racial group administers a test to subjects in a different group, rapport is even poorer, the situation being much more strained and unnatural for the subjects than when they are tested by a member of their own group. This is particularly noticeable in the testing of American Indians and Negroes by a White examiner. In addition to the racial disparity, the presence of a stranger will in itself occasion more emotional disturbance among the members of certain cultures than it would among American city schoolchildren who are accustomed to sudden visits from a succession of supervisors, research workers, psychologists, and others. Furthermore, the suspicion and hostility manifested by many "primitive" peoples towards strangers will necessarily affect the individual's attitude and responsiveness towards a foreign examiner.

EDUCATIONAL DIFFERENCES

It is well known that the educational facilities available to the individual vary widely from one racial or national group to another. This is apparent even if we consider only the *total duration* of school training.[1] The *irregularity of school attendance* prevalent in certain groups, such as the American Indian, reduces still further the effective length of time devoted to instruction. Finally, the *quality* of the available training and the conditions under which it is obtained cannot be ignored. In general, it is just in those groups which receive the least schooling that the quality of instruction is poorest. The type of education offered in rural Negro schools of the South, for example, is far inferior to that in the average White public school.

Contrary to a rather prevalent belief, intelligence tests are not independent of educational background. Thus in one investigation (15), several common intelligence tests were found to correlate as highly with standardized tests of school achievement as they did with each other. Similarly, an analysis of the army data showed a close correspondence between median Army Alpha score and academic level attained. These data are summarized in Table XXVII. Within any one group, there is a consistent rise in median Alpha score with increase in amount of education. That differences still exist when comparisons are made vertically, within a single educational class, is attributable to a number of factors. Chief among these are differences in the quality of education, a factor which is ignored in the system of classification here employed. Differences in the social and economic level of the home as well as other more general conditions may also be mentioned in this connection.

The reverse explanation has occasionally been proposed to account for the relationship between educational level and intelligence. Thus it is argued that the more intelli-

---

[1] In rural sections of the United States, for example, the school year is often drastically shortened, sometimes to as little as six months.

TABLE XXVII

MEDIAN ARMY ALPHA SCORE OF MEN IN DIFFERENT
EDUCATIONAL GROUPS

(After Yerkes, 27, Part III, Ch. 10)

Group	Elementary School		High School	College	Beyond College
	0–4 Years	5–8 Years			
White officers	112.5	107.0	131.1	143.2	143.5
White native-born draft	22.0	51.1	92.1	117.8	145.9
White foreign-born draft	21.4	47.2	72.4	91.9	92.5
Northern Negroes	17.0	37.2	71.2	90.5	
Southern Negroes	7.2	16.3	45.7	63.8	

gent individual will be more successful in his school work
and will pursue his education further than the less intelligent. Intellectual differences are regarded as the cause
rather than the effect of educational differences. Persons
in the higher educational groupings would thus represent
a more highly selected sampling from the outset. This
explanation seems unnecessary in view of the obvious
lack of adequate educational facilities among the supposedly less intelligent groups. *When opportunities for
continued education or for satisfactory instruction at any
level are so unlike from one group to another, failure to obtain such education cannot be attributed to inferior intelligence.*

The effect of educational handicap upon intelligence
test performance is especially apparent in the American
Negro. Since his native language is English, the Negro is
frequently tested with the common verbal type of intelligence test. Because of his pronounced educational deficiency, however, the Negro has a very limited command
of the language, as well as serious gaps in other fields of
knowledge. A comparison of the median Alpha and Beta

scores obtained by the Negro and White draft in the United States army is of some interest in this connection (cf. 27, p. 764). These medians were as follows:

	Alpha	*Beta*
White	58.9	43.4
Northern Negro	38.6	32.5
Southern Negro	12.4	19.8

Although the relative standing of the three groups remains the same on the two tests, the actual differences among them are greatly reduced on the Beta. This test is not only non-language, but it is much less dependent upon educational background in general than is the Alpha.

SOCIAL AND ECONOMIC STATUS

As was demonstrated in Chapter III, the type of home in which the individual is reared exerts a pronounced effect upon his intellectual development. It is apparent that the economic, social, and cultural level of the homes of such groups as immigrants, Negroes, or American Indians is far below the general American average. Arlitt (2) conducted a special investigation to determine the influence of social or occupational status upon racial differences in intelligence test performance. The Stanford-Binet was administered to 191 American children of native-born White parents, 87 children of Italian immigrants, and 71 Negro children. All of the subjects were taken from a single school district and all spoke English with no apparent difficulty. Each child was classified on Taussig's five-point scale on the basis of father's occupation; this was taken as an approximate index of the social and economic level of the home.

When the three racial groups were compared as a whole, the following median I.Q.'s were obtained:

Native White	106.5
Italian	85.0
Negro	83.4

The differences in occupational level among these three groups were, however, very large. Over 90% of the Italians and Negroes fell into the "inferior" or "very inferior" classes on the Taussig scale. When only the children in these two occupational levels are included, the median I.Q. of the native White group drops to 92.0. Thus the intellectual differences among the three racial groups are reduced to a very small quantity when comparisons are restricted to children of the same social or economic level.

It might again be objected that we cannot determine which is cause and which is effect in the relationship between intellectual and occupational level. Since, however, the opportunities for employment in higher positions are far from equal for native Americans and immigrants, and this difference is still greater when Negroes are considered, it seems unwarranted to attribute the lower occupational status of the latter groups to inferior intelligence.

In investigations on American Indians, the relatively low socio-economic level of the home is an important factor to be considered in the evaluation of their test performance. Opportunities for intellectual development, as well as the general level of material comfort, are far below the average for American homes. Thus in the study by Jamieson and Sandiford (13), the homes of the Indian children received an average rating of only 13 points on the Chapman Socio-Economic Scale, as compared to the White norm of 56 points. A close correspondence between the social status of various Indian groups and their relative standing on the National Intelligence Test was found by Garth (11).

GENERAL CULTURAL MILIEU

A further factor in the behavioral development of the individual is the particular locale in which he lives, the tempo of the life about him, and other conditions characteristic of his general surroundings. This represents a broader environmental background than that furnished by his own home. The first striking demonstration of the wide variations in intelligence existing within the native White population from different parts of our own country was furnished by the army data (27, Part III, Ch. 5). When the distributions of Alpha and Beta scores were tabulated separately for each state, distinct regional differences appeared.

In a subsequent analysis (1) of the army data, median Alpha scores were computed for each of 41 states. Seven states were omitted from these calculations because of insufficient data; only those states were included from which records of at least 500 men were available. The states obtaining the ten highest medians and those obtaining the ten lowest are shown below. It might be added that, owing to changing economic and educational conditions, this rank-order probably does not hold at present.

State	Median Alpha Score	State	Median Alpha Score
1. Oregon	79.9	32. New Jersey	48.7
2. Washington	79.2	33. South Carolina	47.4
3. California	78.1	34. Tennessee	47.2
4. Connecticut	73.6	35. Alabama	46.3
5. Idaho	73.5	36. Louisiana	45.2
6. Utah	72.2	37. North Carolina	43.2
7. Massachusetts	71.6	38. Georgia	42.2
8. Colorado	69.7	39. Arkansas	41.6
9. Montana	68.5	40. Kentucky	41.5
10. Vermont	67.5	41. Mississippi	41.2

Since only the distribution of the White draft was considered, the percentage of Negro population in the various states does not enter into these results. Similarly, the differences cannot be attributed to an influx of foreign immigration into certain states, since a correlation of —.61 was found between Alpha medians and percentage of native-born population in each state. It was therefore the states with a greater proportion of native Americans, rather than those with a large foreign population, which tended to have the lower Alpha medians.

Several interesting correspondences were noted between the rank-order of the 41 states for intelligence and a number of other factors. Thus high positive correlations were found between indices of the economic level of each state and their median Alpha scores. The educational facilities within each state also corresponded closely with the Alpha ranks. The states were ranked for the efficiency of their educational systems on the basis of such information as percentage of daily school attendance, percentage of children attending high school, average per capita expenditure for education, teachers' salaries, etc.[1] The educational ranking for the year 1900 was employed in this analysis, since 1900 was approximately the time when the average man in the draft had been of school age. The two sets of ranks, those for Alpha score and those for educational efficiency, correlated .72 with each other.

The relative influence of race and environment upon intelligence test performance is rather vividly illustrated by a comparison of the median Alpha scores of the White draft from the less "progressive" states with the scores of the Negro draft from the more "progressive" states (cf. 27). A few of these medians are shown below:

---

[1] The Ayres rank-order of educational efficiency for each state was employed for this purpose.

Whites		*Negroes*	
Mississippi	41.25	Pennsylvania	42.00
Kentucky	41.50	New York	45.02
Arkansas	41.55	Illinois	47.35
Georgia	42.14	Ohio	49.50

These figures suggest the degree to which environmental stimulation may overrule alleged racial differences in intellectual capacity. They also indicate the extensive overlapping in intelligence test performance which exists between the Negro and White groups in the United States.

A consistent difference has also been found between the intellectual level of northern and southern Negroes. This was again shown by the army data (27). The median Alpha scores of northern and southern Negroes were 38.6 and 12.4, respectively. On the Beta, the median scores of these two groups were 32.5 and 19.8. Similar results have been obtained in studies on Negro schoolchildren in northern and southern states (cf., e.g., 6, 22). In certain localities, the Negro child's performance shows no inferiority to that of the White child; in others, the difference between the two groups is very striking. Two explanations have been offered to account for the intellectual differences between northern and southern Negroes. One hypothesis attributes the differences to *selective migration*. Thus the more intelligent Negroes, who have more initiative and are more progressive and capable of adjusting to a new environment, would be more likely to migrate to the North. The second hypothesis explains the superiority of the northern Negro in terms of *environmental factors*, such as better educational facilities and other opportunities for advancement.

A series of recent investigations by Klineberg and his associates (17) have thrown considerable light upon the relative validity of these two hypotheses. The problem was approached in two ways. In the first place, the relative intellectual status of Negro children whose families migrated to the North was investigated by comparing their former grades in southern schools with the norms for those schools. In this part of the study, the records of 562 Negro children who had moved to the North from three southern cities [1] were examined. Since all grades were transmuted into a percentile scale, 50 points represents the average status and this figure may be employed as a standard of comparison. The average percentile rating of those children who had moved to the North proved to be 49.3, which is not significantly different from the general average. It is thus apparent that, at least in these groups, there was no tendency for the initially more intelligent children to migrate.

A second approach to the problem was the comparison of intelligence test scores obtained by groups of Negro schoolchildren who had lived in New York City for different periods of time. The subjects were examined with a variety of standard tests, including the Stanford-Binet, performance scales, and several common group tests. Over 3000 Negro children in the Harlem district of New York City were employed. The subjects in the different residence groups were equated for age and sex; they all attended the same schools and were approximately equal in social and economic background, the only important difference between them being the number of years spent in New York City. A group of Negro schoolchildren born in New York City was also included for comparison.

In Table XXVIII will be found the average scores of each residence group on the National Intelligence Test, the Stanford-Binet, the Pintner-Paterson Performance Scale, and a paper-and-pencil form board test. In both the

[1] Nashville, Tenn., Birmingham, Ala., and Charleston, S. C.

TABLE XXVIII

RELATION BETWEEN LENGTH OF RESIDENCE IN NEW YORK CITY
AND INTELLIGENCE TEST SCORES OF NEGRO SCHOOLCHILDREN
(After Klineberg, 17)

National Intelligence Test			Stanford-Binet		
Length of Residence	Number of Cases	Average Score	Length of Residence	Number of Cases	Average I.Q.
1–2 years	150	72	Less than one year	42	81.4
3–4 years	125	76	1–2 years	40	84.2
5–6 years	136	84	2–3 years	40	84.5
7–8 years	112	90	3–4 years	46	85.5 *
Over 8 years	157	94	Over 4 years	47	87.4
Northern-born	1017	92	New York-born	99	87.3

Paper Form Board			Pintner-Paterson		
Length of Residence	Number of Cases	Median Score	Length of Residence	Number of Cases	Average Point Score
1–2 years	27	39.00	Less than 2 years	20	142.5
3–4 years	25 ·	26.67	2–5 years	20	139.8
5–6 years	30	31.88	Over 5 years	20	152.1
7–8 years	23	37.50			
9–10 years	25	37.50			
Over 10 years	41	37.50			
New York-born	223	41.61	Northern-born	50	164.5

* This figure is misprinted as 88.5 in the Klineberg monograph (17, p. 46).

National Intelligence Test and the Stanford-Binet, there
is a progressive rise in average score with increasing
length of residence in New York City. It is interesting to
note that the groups born in the North or in New York
City are not superior to those who were born in the South
but had lived in New York for a long period. This fact,
as well as the consistent increase in score with length of
New York City residence, tends to support the environ-

mental rather than the selective factor hypothesis. Further corroboration of this explanation is furnished by the fact that the differences between successive residence groups are greater on the National Intelligence Test than on the Stanford-Binet, the former being also more closely dependent upon environmental stimulation and schooling. Finally, it will be noted that on the two performance tests, the paper form board and the Pintner-Paterson, the results are less consistent than on the linguistic tests. Although the groups having the longer New York City residence tend in each case to be superior, the position of individual groups is ambiguous. This is to be expected from the fact that the existing environmental differences have less effect upon performance tests than upon tests of a more verbal nature.

It might be argued that the Negroes migrating to the North at different times may not be directly comparable. Thus the quality of the migrants might be deteriorating and this would account for the lower averages obtained by the later groups. This question was investigated directly by testing two groups of twelve-year-old boys on two successive years. At the time of testing, each group had spent an equal length of time in New York, although they had migrated in different years. No evidence was found for a decline in the quality of immigration within this two-year period, the later migrants being, in fact, superior in nearly every comparison. Anthropometric measurements of different residence groups were also taken. These showed no difference among the groups in the possession of negroid traits. Race mixture could not therefore have been a factor in producing the intellectual differences among such groups.

That length of residence in a favorable environment is directly related to intelligence test performance had been previously suggested in several other studies on Negro schoolchildren (cf., e.g., 19, 21). The series of investigations directed by Klineberg established this fact more conclusively. These findings, together with the data on the school achievement of Negro children before migration to the North, furnish definite evidence that the regional differences in the intelligence of Negroes are to be understood in terms of environment and not selective migration.

TRADITIONS, CUSTOMS, AND INTERESTS

The particular culture in which the individual is reared may influence his behavioral development in many ways. The operation of environmental forces is not limited to the extent and quality of educational opportunities available in the school, the home, and the neighborhood. The question is not only one of amount, but of kind. The experiences of people living in different cultures may vary in such a way as to lend a different meaning to their actions, stimulate the development of totally different interests, and furnish diverse ideals and standards of behavior.

The importance of motivation and interest in intelligence test performance has been repeatedly emphasized. Yet it is apparent that many of the tests in current use cannot arouse the same emotional reaction in other cultures as they do in our own. Thus for an American schoolchild, the average intelligence test bears a close resemblance to his everyday school work, which is probably the most serious business of his life at the time. He is therefore easily spurred on to exert his best efforts and try to excel his fellows. For an Indian child, on the other hand, the same test cannot have such a significance. This type of activity has no place in the traditional behavior of his family or tribe. Similarly, many investigators have noted that among Negro children interest in intelligence tests is not as keen as among White children, and that the former seem not to be as strongly motivated as the latter.

In addition to emotional and motivational factors, special customs and traditions peculiar to one group may influence the subject's behavior in a test situation. Several curious examples of such traditional behavior have been reported. Thus Porteus (25), in administering performance tests to Australian aborigines, found it difficult to convince his subjects that they were to solve the problems individually and without assistance. In explanation of this behavior, he writes:

> . . . the aborigine is used to concerted thinking. Not only is every problem in tribal life debated and settled by the council of elders, but it is always discussed until a unanimous decision is reached. On many occasions the subject of a test was evidently extremely puzzled by the fact that I would render him no assistance, especially when, as happened in the centre, I was testing some men who were reputedly my tribal brothers. This was a matter which caused considerable delay as, again and again, the subject would pause for approval or assistance in the task (25, p. 308).

Similarly, Klineberg (18) reports that among the Dakota Indians it is considered bad form to answer a question in the presence of someone else who does not know the answer. This creates a particularly difficult situation in school, where the teachers find it difficult to induce the children to recite in class. In the same group, custom forbids one to answer a question unless he is absolutely sure of the answer. The effect which this would have upon intelligence tests in which the subject is advised to "guess" when not sure and is urged to "try his best" on a difficult problem, can readily be foreseen. The child who refuses to give any answer unless he is certain of its correctness will lose many points which he might have earned through partial credits and chance successes.

Another medium through which the cultural background may influence mental test performance is the special associations and meanings which have been built up by social conditioning. In one of the subtests of the National Intelligence Test, the child is required to underline the two words which tell what the given item always has. One of the examples in this test reads:

Crowd (closeness, danger, dust, excitement, number).[1]

Although "closeness" and "number" are given in the key as the correct answers, it was found that, among Plains Indians, "danger" and "dust," or even "excitement," were frequently underscored. The experience which these children had had with crowds on the prairie had taught them that these were necessary attributes of a crowd (cf. 9).

Many similar instances can easily be found (cf., e.g., 18). In one of the tests of the Army Alpha, Form 6, occurs the question, "Why should all parents be made to send their children to school?" Of the several alternative answers given, the "correct" one is that "school prepares the child for his later life." But this is not true for the Indian child, whose schooling often unfits him for life on the Reservation. In a sentence completion test of the National Intelligence Scale is found the statement," —— should prevail in churches and libraries." The word to be inserted in this case is "silence." Among Negro children, however, this problem would be complicated by the fact that their own churches are seldom silent. Noise is not only common in their houses of worship but is frequently an integral and essential part of the ritual.

A further example of the inapplicability of a mental

[1] Scale A, Form I, Test 3, Exercise 17.

test to groups differing from the one upon which it was constructed is furnished by an incident which occurred in the testing of children in the Kentucky mountains.[1] The following is one of the problems in the Binet Scale: "If you went to the store and bought 6 cents worth of candy and gave the clerk 10 cents, what change would you receive?" One alert young boy, upon being asked this question, replied, "I never had 10 cents, and if I had I wouldn't spend it for candy, and anyway candy is what your mother makes." Still wishing to find out if the child could subtract 6 from 10, the examiner reformulated the problem as follows: "If you had taken 10 cows to pasture for your father and 6 of them strayed away, how many would you have left to drive home?" The child now replied promptly, "We don't have 10 cows, but if we did and I lost 6, I wouldn't dare to go home." The examiner tried once more with the following inquiry: "If there were 10 children in a school and 6 of them were out with the measles, how many would there be in school?" This answer came even more promptly: "None, because the rest would be afraid of catching it too."

Finally, mention should be made of the important rôle of speed in nearly all intelligence tests and of the widely varying emphasis placed upon speed in different cultures. An investigation by Klineberg (16) on Indian, Negro, and White schoolboys illustrates the operation of this factor. Several of the tests in the Pintner-Paterson Performance Scale were administered to the following groups:

107 Whites in Toppenish, Washington [2]
120 Indians at the Yakima Reservation, Washington
136 Indians attending Haskell Institute in Kansas
139 Negroes in a rural district of West Virginia

[1] This incident is reported in Pressey, S. L., *Psychology and the New Education.* N. Y.: Harper, 1933. Pp. 237–238.
[2] In the heart of the Indian Reservation.

25 Whites in the same district of West Virginia
200 Negroes in New York City
100 Whites in New York City

In *accuracy* of performance, as measured by the number of errors on each test, the Indians excelled the Whites, and the Negroes were either equal or slightly superior to the Whites. All measures of *speed*, on the other hand, favored the Whites. A comparison of groups *of the same race but living in different environments* suggested that these differences in speed were cultural rather than biological. Thus the New York City Negroes clearly excelled the West Virginia Negroes in every comparison. Similarly, the Haskell Institute Indians were consistently faster than those tested on the Yakima Reservation. A further division of the Haskell group into those who had previously lived on a Reservation and those who had lived among Whites in a town or city showed the latter to excel in speed.

In explanation of these results, Klineberg calls attention to the relatively insignificant part which speed plays in the life of the Reservation Indian or the rural southern Negro. Most observers are impressed with the Indian's almost complete lack of concern with speed. Time means nothing in the daily activities of the Indian. He can see no reason for hurrying through a task, especially if he finds it congenial and interesting. Thus insofar as the examiner arouses the child's interest in the test, he makes the necessity of speeding appear even more absurd. At Haskell Institute, on the other hand, time is much more important than on the Reservation. The students are constantly kept busy with a variety of tasks and the entire day is carefully scheduled. The White teachers, too, foster the attitude that it is desirable to finish things as quickly as possible. Similarly, the New York City

Negroes have been exposed to the hustle of life in a big metropolis, whereas the rural Negroes are adapted to a much slower tempo of activity.

The Criterion of Intellectual Superiority

In all group comparisons, there is a tendency to go beyond the actually observed *differences* in behavior and to evaluate the *relative status* of each group in terms of some presumably universal criterion. Linear comparisons are made in terms of better or worse. Thus we frequently find national or racial groups arranged in a rank-order for "intelligence." One group is said to be "superior," another "inferior" in its mentality. Such a point of view implies either that one group is consistently poorer than another in *all* mental traits, or that certain behavioral processes are universally more significant, more valuable, or even more "mental" than others.

In regard to the first of these assumptions, it can easily be shown that racial or national groups vary in the relative inferiority or superiority which they manifest in different traits. Thus Japanese children have been found to excel White children significantly in tests involving sustained attention, visual perception, or spatial orientation, while falling behind on verbal or arithmetic tests. This was demonstrated in Darsie's study (7) by the relatively superior performance of the Japanese children on four of the Stanford-Binet tests, viz., Induction, Paper Cutting, Enclosed Boxes, and Code Learning, as well as on the Digit-Symbol Learning and the Number Comparisons tests of the Army Beta. A slight superiority was also shown by these children in the Cube Analysis and Geometric Construction tests of the Beta Scale.

Similarly, differences in specific traits have been found when comparing European immigrants in this country (cf., e.g., 4). Italian children in general do relatively well on performance tests and relatively poorly when examined with abstract or linguistic materials. Jewish children, on the other hand, excel on verbal tests and fall behind in problems dealing with concrete objects and spatial relations. This difference may be accounted for on the basis of the cultural traditions of the two groups. Among Jewish families there is a marked emphasis upon the formal aspects of education and "abstract" intelligence, to the almost total neglect of "mechanical" intelligence and manual dexterity. Italians, on the other hand, have a traditional and age-old admiration for manipulative arts and crafts. The skill exhibited in the production of a beautiful object, a complex object, or an object well adapted to its practical use, is held in high esteem and encouraged from early childhood. Relatively little emphasis, however, is placed upon the more abstract types of talent.

Even in groups which rank very low on the basis of our "intelligence" tests and our cultural standards, specific abilities can be found in which they excel markedly. That these differences have not frequently appeared in test results is attributable to the fact that the current intelligence tests are a characteristic American development and that the testing of racial groups has been conducted largely by American psychologists. It is not a very difficult matter, however, to construct tests in which an apparently "inferior" group makes an excellent showing. Thus in the course of an investigation by Klineberg (cf. 18) among the Dakota Indians, a "beadwork test" was devised in which a small sample of beadwork was shown to the subjects for four minutes; the sample was then removed and the subjects asked to reproduce it from memory on a loom. The test was applied to both White and Indian girls, all of whom were first taught how to do beadwork on a loom. As would be expected from their greater familiarity with this type of material, the Indian girls clearly surpassed the Whites.

Porteus (25) tried a similar experiment while working among the Australian aborigines. Having been impressed with the remarkable tracking skill of these people, he constructed a test with photographs of footprints, the task being to match the two prints made by the same foot. On this test, the Australians did practically as well as a group of 120 White high school students in Hawaii who were tested for comparison. In commenting upon these results, Porteus remarks:

> Allowing for their unfamiliarity with photographs we may say, then, that with test material with which they are familiar the aborigines' ability to discriminate form and spatial relationships is at least equal to that of whites of high school standards of education and of better than average social standing (25, p. 401).

The point is frequently made that racial or national groups can be arranged in a consistent hierarchy if we consider only the "higher mental processes." Tests of abstract abilities, for example, are considered more diagnostic of "intelligence" than those dealing with the manipulation of concrete objects or with the perception of spatial relationships. The aptitude for dealing with symbolical materials, especially of a verbal or numerical nature, is regarded as the acme of intellectual attainment. The "primitive" man's skill in responding to very slight sensory cues, his talents in the construction of objects, or the powers of sustained attention and muscular control which he may display in his hunting behavior, are regarded as interesting anthropological curios which have, however, little or no intellectual worth. As a result, such activities have not usually been incorporated in intelligence scales but have been relegated to a relatively minor position in mental testing.

Upon closer analysis it will become apparent that this conception of intellect is itself culturally conditioned. By "higher mental processes" is usually meant those aspects or segments of behavior which are at a premium in our society. Intelligence tests would be very different if they had been constructed among American Indians or Australian aborigines rather than in American cities. The criterion employed in validating intelligence tests has nearly always been success in our social system. Scores on the test are correlated with school achievement or perhaps with some more general measure of success in our society. If such correlations are high, it is concluded that the test is a good measure of "intelligence." The age criterion is based on the same principle. If scores on a given test show a progressive increase with age, it may simply mean that the test is measuring those traits which our culture imparts to the individual. The older the subject, the more opportunity he will have had, in general, to acquire such aptitudes.

Thus it would seem that intelligence tests measure only the ability to succeed in our particular culture. Each culture, partly through the physical conditions of its environment and partly through social tradition, "selects" certain activities as the most significant. These it encourages and stimulates; others it neglects or definitely suppresses. The relative standing of different cultural groups in "intelligence" is a function of the traits included under the concept of intelligence, or, to state the same point differently, it is a function of the particular culture in which the test was constructed.

The Comparative Achievements of Different Races

The point is sometimes made that the vast differences in the achievements of various races testify to their dissimilar innate mental equipment. Thus it is argued that the differences in cultural achievement among racial groups might be a result rather than a cause of such mental differences. The cultural milieu in which the individual is reared, with its special opportunities and limitations for intellectual and emotional development, might itself be a reflection of the capacities of each race. The individual of a given race might thus be handicapped by poor facilities for intellectual development just because his predecessors lacked the capacity to produce a more "favorable" environment.

As evidence of the wide inter-racial variations in achievement are cited contributions to the development of industry and invention, accomplishments in the realm of science, literature, and other artistic productions, complexity of social and political organization, and many other aspects of cultural status. Comparisons have also been made in terms of the "eminent" men produced by each race. Thus Galton (10, pp. 325–337) at one time proposed a 16-point scale for estimating the "comparative worth of different races" by comparing the relative merits of men in each group who had achieved eminence. On this basis he suggested, for example, that the Negro is two grades lower than the Englishman, and the modern Englishman two grades below the Athenian of Greece's golden era.

It should be noted that any argument based upon the relationship between the cultural level and the capacity of races is reversible. On the basis solely of the association between these two factors, it is impossible to determine which is cause and which is effect. There is therefore no reason for concluding *ipso facto* that racial differences in cultural achievement indicate or result from a racial difference in capacity. There is considerable evidence, on the other hand, which suggests that the cultural differences may be responsible for the group differences in "capacity."

In the first place, achievement and cultural level are frequently found to vary not with race but with environmental factors. Thus a group which is characterized by a given achievement level may be racially very heterogeneous and may constitute a unit only in terms of a common experiential background.[1] Secondly, the relative achievements of a given group are influenced by a number of factors which cannot themselves be attributed to racial capacity without stretching the point unduly. The characteristics of the physical environment, the degree of contact with other groups, the discovery of new routes of travel and communication, and historical events within *other* groups—and thus not within the control of the group under consideration—have played an important part in the cultural development of many societies.

Thirdly, mention may be made of certain broad shifts in the relative cultural status of different racial groups from time to time. This is particularly well illustrated by some of the ancient African civilizations, such as the kingdom of Benin, whose achievements in many fields far outstripped the European cultures of the same period. A number of "lost arts" of these civilizations represent, in fact, abilities which have never been attained in any other group. In several cases, the shifts in relative cultural level occurred in the absence of any known change in the nature of the stock, as might occur through race mixture.

[1] Data bearing on this point will be found in the following chapter.

Concomitant historical developments can, however, be found which might account for the change in cultural level. Finally, the reader may consider in this connection the weight of the evidence from other sources, discussed throughout the present book, which indicates the extent to which behavioral development depends upon environmental factors.

REFERENCES

1. Alexander, H. B. "A Comparison of the Ranks of American States in Army Alpha and in Social-Economic Status," *Sch. and Soc.*, 1922, 16, 388–392.

2. Arlitt, A. H. "On the Need for Caution in Establishing Race Norms," *J. Appl. Psychol.*, 1921, 5, 179–183.

3. Bagley, W. C. *Determinism in Education*. Baltimore: Warwick and York, 1925. Pp. 194.

4. Bere, M. A. "Comparative Study of Mental Capacity of Children of Foreign Parentage. Teachers College, Columbia Univ., *Contrib. to Educ.*, No. 154, 1924. Pp. 105.

5. Blackwood, B. "A Study of Mental Testing in Relation to Anthropology," *Ment. Meas. Mon.*, No. 4, 1927. Pp. 120.

6. Clark, W. W. "Los Angeles Negro Children," *Educ. Res. Bull.*, Los Angeles City Schools, 1923, 3, No. 2, 1–2.

7. Darsie, M. L. "Mental Capacity of American-Born Japanese Children," *Comp. Psychol. Mon.*, 1926, 15, No. 3, 1–89.

8. Dodd, S. C. *International Group Mental Tests*. Princeton Univ. Ph.D. Dissertation, 1926. Pp. 101.

9. Fitzgerald, J. A., and Ludeman, W. W. "The Intelligence of Indian Children," *J. Comp. Psychol.*, 1926, 6, 319–328.

10. Galton, F. *Hereditary Genius: An Inquiry into Its Laws and Consequences*. London: Macmillan, 1914 (1st ed. 1869). Pp. 379.

11. Garth, T. R. "A Comparison of the Intelligence of Mexican and Mixed and Full Blood Indian Children," *Psychol. Rev.*, 1923, 30, 388–401.

12. Goodenough, F. L. "Racial Differences in Intelligence of School Children," *J. Exp. Psychol.*, 1926, 9, 388–397.

13. Jamieson, E., and Sandiford, P. "The Mental Capacity of Southern Ontario Indians," *J. Educ. Psychol.*, 1928, 19, 536–551.

14. Jones, A. M. "Vocabulary Study of Children in a Foreign Industrial Community," *Psychol. Clinic*, 1928, 17, 13–21.

15. Kelley, T. L. *Interpretation of Educational Measurements.* Yonkers, N. Y.: World Book Co., 1927. Pp. 363.

16. Klineberg, O. "An Experimental Study of Speed and Other Factors in 'Racial' Differences," *Arch. Psychol.*, No. 93, 1928. Pp. 111.

17. ——. *Negro Intelligence and Selective Migration.* N. Y.: Columbia Univ. Press, 1935. Pp. 66.

18. ——. *Race Differences.* N. Y.: Harper, 1935. Pp. 367.

19. Long, H. H. "The Intelligence of Colored Elementary Pupils in Washington, D. C.," *J. Negro Educ.*, 1934, 3, 205–222.

20. Mead, M. "Group Intelligence Tests and Linguistic Disability among Italian Children," *Sch. and Soc.*, 1927, 25, 465–468.

21. McAlpin, A. S. "Changes in Intelligence Quotient of Negro Children," *J. Negro Educ.*, 1932, 1, 44–48.

22. Peterson, J., and Lanier, L. H. "Studies in the Comparative Abilities of Whites and Negroes," *Ment. Meas. Mon.*, No. 5, 1929. Pp. 156.

23. Pintner, R. "Comparison of American and Foreign Children on Intelligence Tests," *J. Educ. Psychol.*, 1923, 14, 292–295.

24. Pintner, R., and Keller, R. "Intelligence Tests for Foreign Children," *J. Educ. Psychol.*, 1922, 13, 214–222.

25. Porteus, S. D. *The Psychology of a Primitive People.* N. Y.: Longmans, Green, 1931. Pp. 438.

26. Strong, A. C. "Three Hundred Fifty White and Colored Children," *Ped. Sem.*, 1913, 20, 485–515.

27. Yerkes, R. M., ed. "Psychological Examining in the United States Army," *Mem. Nat. Acad. Sci.*, 1921, 15.

CHAPTER XVIII

RACIAL VERSUS CULTURAL DIFFERENCES

The comparison of racial and cultural groups within the same population may help to clarify the relative contribution of innate and environmental factors in the development of group differences. If members of the *same race* can be found living under varying cultural conditions, and members of *different races* living within a single and more or less homogeneous cultural group, fruitful cross-comparisons can be made. Such a situation is furnished by many European nations whose members are drawn from more than one of the subdivisions of the Caucasian race. Thus it will be recalled that in France may be found Nordic, Alpine, and Mediterranean groups, in Germany Nordic and Alpine, in Italy Alpine and Mediterranean. A similar racial heterogeneity is to be found in several other European countries.

The representatives of these racial groups living within a single nation are exposed to relatively uniform cultural conditions. To a greater or less extent, they share the social traditions and customs of their country. Since all belong to the "White" race, social distinctions and discriminations are far less prevalent than is the case with Negroid or Mongoloid groups living among Caucasians. To be sure the members of each racial group often cluster in a certain section of the country. In France, for example, the Nordics are found chiefly in northern provinces, the Alpines in the central part, and the Mediterraneans in the south. Specific differences in economic level, nature of occupations, educational opportunities, and other conditions may and often do exist among the regions inhabited by each racial group. Such environmental variations are not so large, however, as those found from one nation to another, or those which set off the American Negro from his White compatriots. In general the environments of Nordics, Alpines, and Mediterraneans living within a single nation are far more similar than the environments of members of the same race living in different countries.

In certain cases comparisons have been made between narrower and more clearly defined cultural groups, characterized by common traditions, beliefs, or social and educational background. Thus students attending one educational institution may be compared with those in another, while at the same time racial comparisons may be made within each institution. The unit of comparison may be a single neighborhood, consisting of a few city blocks. This division is particularly well-adapted to a large metropolis, such as New York City, in which are to be found a number of special national districts, clearly differentiated by customs, traditions, and even language. The residents of such districts may be compared to "assimilated" groups of the same racial or national origin but living in a more typically "American" environment.

Investigations of this nature cannot, of course, offer a conclusive analysis of the relative contribution of cultural and biological factors. Many uncontrolled conditions still remain. Perfect control of conditions, however, cannot be obtained outside of an experimental set-up. The study of groups in which racial and cultural classifications cut across each other at least brings us a step closer to an unraveling of the complex of factors which produce group differences.

THE ARMY DATA

The testing of the United States army draft during the World War furnished the first extensive body of data on "intellectual" differences among ·immigrant groups in this country. In the original report prepared by the army psychologists are to be found the distributions of scores on Alpha, Beta, and individual intelligence scales for 12,492 foreign-born men, classified according to country of birth (26, Part III, Ch. 6). These data were subsequently submitted to a special analysis by Brigham and the results published in a book entitled *A Study of American Intelligence* (4).

TABLE XXIX

AVERAGE COMBINED SCALE SCORES OF WHITE FOREIGN-BORN
DRAFT CLASSIFIED ACCORDING TO COUNTRY OF BIRTH

(After Brigham, 4, pp. 120–121)

Country of Birth	Number of Cases	Combined Scale	
		Average	Range
England	411	14.87	4–23
Scotland	146	14.34	5–22
Holland	140	14.32	6–22
Germany	308	13.88	5–22
Denmark	325	13.69	5–21
Canada	972	13.66	2–22
Sweden	691	13.30	4–21
Norway	611	12.98	4–21
Belgium	129	12.79	4–19
Ireland	658	12.32	2–22
Austria	301	12.27	2–21
Turkey	423	12.02	2–21
Greece	572	11.90	2–20
Russia	2,340	11.34	1–22
Italy	4,009	11.01	1–22
Poland	382	10.74	2–19
Total foreign-born	12,492	12.05	1–23
Native born	81,465	13.77	1–24

In order to make direct comparisons among individuals who had taken different intelligence scales, all scores were transmuted into a "combined scale" rating which ranged from zero to 25 points. The average and range of the combined scale scores of each national group, as well as the number of cases, are shown in Table XXIX. The reliabilities of the differences between each group and every other were computed and showed the majority of such differences to be statistically significant. It should be noted, however, that the differences are very small and the overlapping of groups large.

TABLE XXX

AVERAGE COMBINED SCALE SCORES OF WHITE FOREIGN-BORN DRAFT CLASSIFIED ACCORDING TO LENGTH OF RESIDENCE IN THE UNITED STATES

(After Brigham, 4, p. 90)

Years of Residence	Number of Cases	Average Score on Combined Scale
0– 5	3576	11.41
6–10	4287	11.74
11–15	1897	12.47
16–20	771	13.55
Over 20	764	13.82

These data were further analyzed in respect to length of residence in the United States. Average combined scale scores were computed for men in each residence group. All foreign-born men, regardless of country of birth, were combined in this tabulation. The number of men in each group and their average scores will be found in Table XXX. All but one of the differences between the residence groups are statistically reliable. After examining several alternative explanations, Brigham concluded that the steady decrease in average intelligence test score from the earliest to the most recent immigrant groups indicates a progressive deterioration in the quality of immigrants entering the United States.

Finally an attempt was made to classify the subjects into "racial" categories. Tentative estimates were made of the proportion of Nordic, Alpine, and Mediterranean blood in each country. France, for example, is estimated as 30% Nordic, 55% Alpine, and 15% Mediterranean; Sweden is listed as 100% Nordic; Roumania 100% Alpine; Germany 40% Nordic and 60% Alpine. The distributions of intelligence test scores for each national group were then cut according to these proportions and recombined into Nordic, Alpine, and Mediterranean groups. Thus, for example, all of the Swedish scores were classified under Nordic, all of the Roumanian under Alpine. In those cases in which more than one racial group is represented within a single nation, the average score of that national group was allotted proportionately to each racial group. Thus 40% of the German sampling was entered under Nordic and 60% under Alpine. Since there was no way of determining in which portion of the national distribution of scores the Alpine and Nordic individuals fell, all subjects were given the *average score* of their respective national group.[1] When the scores were combined in this fashion, the averages for the three "racial" groups proved to be as follows:

Group	Number of Cases	Average Score on Combined Scale
Nordic	3456	13.28
Alpine	4766	11.67
Mediterranean	4196	11.43

[1] It is apparent that this procedure involves a logical fallacy insofar as it assumes the absence of differences in score between racial groups within a single nationality, and at the same time it undertakes to prove the existence of just such a difference among racial groups.

The difference between these averages are all statistically significant, being many times larger than is required for perfect reliability.

In a final evaluation of all of these data, Brigham concluded that the differences in intelligence test performance found among immigrant groups were racial in character. He also suggested that the decline in score in successive residence groups was due to a decreasing immigration from the predominantly Nordic countries and an influx of Alpine and Mediterranean immigrants. These conclusions have been widely criticized from several angles. The representativeness of the immigrant groups as samplings of their home population has been challenged. The adequacy of the tests as instruments for measuring the "intelligence" of groups with widely differing educational and cultural backgrounds has likewise been questioned. The progressive rise in average score with increasing length of residence in the United States may itself be due in large measure to the influence of environment. Language handicap, furthermore, was not ruled out. In fact a comparison of English-speaking and non-English-speaking "Nordics" revealed a reliable difference in favor of the former, although the non-English-speaking Nordics still surpassed the Alpine and Mediterranean groups. Finally the allocation of a certain proportion of each national group to one or another "race" can but serve to confuse the issues. Since no differentiation was made among members of different races within a single national group but the subjects were chosen indiscriminately from the entire distribution of national scores, nothing was gained by the reclassification.

It might be added that in a subsequent publication (5) Brigham himself has withdrawn completely from his earlier position. On the basis of recent findings on mental organization and their bearing upon the interpretation of test results, he concludes:

> If the Army Alpha test has thus been shown to be internally inconsistent to such a degree, then it is absurd to go beyond this point and combine alpha, beta, the Stanford-Binet and the individual performance tests in the so-called "combined scale," or to regard a combined scale derived from one test or complex of tests as equivalent to that derived from another test or another complex of tests. As this method was used by the writer in his earlier analysis of the army tests as applied to samples of the foreign-born in the draft, that study with its entire superstructure of racial differences collapses completely (5, p. 164).

In spite of its criticism by psychologists and anthropologists, however, Brigham's book has been widely quoted and has proved very influential in determining popular opinion on questions of race and immigration. It is chiefly for this reason that an analysis of the main conclusions put forth in this book has been included in the present discussion.

The most direct interpretation which can be put upon the army data themselves is that they indicate the relative standing of contemporary immigrant groups in the United States on certain specific tests. These tests were so constructed as to be more or less valid indices of success in our particular society, calling into play those characteristics or segments of behavior which are valued in our culture. At the same time the subjects approached the tests with a background of early training and environment which may have varied widely from one national group to another and which was probably reflected in their responses. Envisaged in these terms, the army data have been amply corroborated by subsequent studies. The testing of American-born schoolchildren of immigrant parents has in general yielded the same rank order of national groups as was found in the army draft. Several studies employing a wide variety of tests report about the same relative standing for the different national groups in this country, although the actual amount of difference varies with the nature of the test and other factors.[1]

"NATIO-RACIAL" DIFFERENCES AMONG CHILDREN OF IMMIGRANT GROUPS

An attempt to classify individuals more empirically into racial groups was made by Hirsch (14) in an investigation of children of immigrants in the United States. The main group of subjects consisted of 4983 Massachusetts public school children ranging in age from 5½ to 18 and in school grade from the first to the ninth. In social and occupational level the group was quite homogeneous, all of the subjects living in small manufacturing communities. There was no segregation of national groups into districts and all of the children attended the same schools.

The Pintner-Cunningham Primary Scale was given to all first grade children. This is a non-verbal picture test in which the directions are, however, given in oral English. The children in grades 2 and 3 were examined with the Dearborn Test A and those from grade 4 upwards with the Dearborn Test C. The former test is largely non-verbal in its content, the latter about half non-verbal. Thus an effort was made to minimize the influence of language handicap by the selection of these tests. The rôle of speed was also reduced by allowing a longer time limit on all tests than is specified in the standard directions. The children were first classified into national

---

[1] For a good summary of such studies prior to 1926, the reader is referred to Kirkpatrick (16). Cf. also Berry (2), Brown (6), Feingold (10), Goodenough (13), Hirsch (14), Murdock (22), Young (27).

groups on the basis of parents' birthplace. An "American" group of native parentage was also included for comparative purposes.

The results of this analysis are shown in Table XXXI. Most of the differences between the average I.Q.'s of these national groups were statistically reliable. The same rank order of nationalities was obtained when the groups were compared in the percentage of "very superior intelligence" and of "borderline deficiency." The relative status of the national groups also agreed in general with that reported by previous investigators.

TABLE XXXI

Average I.Q.'s of Children of Immigrant Groups

(After Hirsch, 14, p. 287)

Nationality	Number of Cases	Average I.Q.	Nationality	Number of Cases	Average I.Q.
Polish Jews	75	102.8	British Canadians	115	93.8
Swedes	232	102.1	Russians	90	90.0
English	213	100.7	Poles	227	89.6
Russian Jews	627	99.5	Greeks	270	87.8
Germans	190	98.5	Italians	350	85.8
Americans	1030	98.3	French Canadians	243	85.3
Lithuanians	468	97.4	Portuguese	671	82.7
Irish	214	95.9			

Taking the national groups as a whole, Hirsch found no evidence in support of the so-called "Nordic myth." There seemed to be no very close connection between high I.Q. and the possession of "Nordic blood." Thus among the eight highest entries in Table XXXI are to be found two predominantly Nordic groups (English and Swedes), two which are largely Alpine (Germans and Lithuanians), one Mediterranean (Irish), two Jewish (Polish and Russian Jews), and one composite group (American).

In order to arrive at a somewhat more accurate determination of "race," Hirsch classified each individual into a racial type on the basis of eye and hair color. All subjects, irrespective of their national descent, were divided into three major categories: the "*blond type*" with light hair and blue, gray, or hazel eyes; the "*brunette type*" with black hair and gray, hazel, brown, or black eyes; and the "*mixed type*" exhibiting all other combinations of hair and eye color. The blond type was taken to correspond roughly to the Nordic and the brunette to the Mediterranean race. The mixed type would of course include Alpines as well as mixtures of any of the three racial stocks. This method of classification is, to be sure, crude. Hair and eye color are not generally considered to be very reliable criteria of race. The analysis is, however, suggestive as a first attempt in the direct classification of individuals into racial categories.

In Table XXXII will be found the number of cases and the average I.Q. of blond, mixed, and brunette types within each national group.[1] These data lend no support to a racial interpretation of group differences. No one of the three physical types is *consistently* superior or inferior within all national groups. Thus among the representatives of one nation the blonds stand first; among those of another nation the brunettes lead. The differences *among* physical types, furthermore, are much smaller than those *within* a single type. The differences in I.Q. between any two types within a single nation range from 0.1 for French Canadians to 6.7 for Poles. The differences between the lowest and highest national averages within any one physical type, on the other hand, are all larger. For each of the three types, these differences are as follows:

[1] One national group, the Scotch, has been omitted because of the small number of cases tested, although Hirsch includes it in his "racial" analysis.

Physical Type	Largest I.Q. Difference within Physical Type among National Groups	National Groups
Blond	14.8	English and Poles
Mixed	21.3	Polish Jews and Portuguese
Brunette	18.1	English and Portuguese

These cross-comparisons between national and "racial" categories suggest that the obtained differences are more closely linked with nationality than with racial background.

TABLE XXXII

COMPARISON OF THE I.Q.'S OF THE BLOND, MIXED, AND BRUNETTE TYPES WITHIN AND AMONG NATIONAL GROUPS

(After Hirsch, 14, p. 333)

National Group	Blond Type		Mixed Type		Brunette Type	
	N	Aver. I.Q.	N	Aver. I.Q.	N	Aver. I.Q.
Americans	73	98.9	377	98.4	158	95.6
English	15	106.2	68	101.9	20	100.3
British Canadians	6	96.0	54	97.5	34	91.6
French Canadians	3	86.0	31	86.1	24	85.5
Germans	9	101.1	16	99.6	3	92.0
Greeks	3	81.0	56	88.3	152	86.2
Irish	4	112.5	51	93.3	79	83.8
Italians	3	84.6	70	85.1	184	84.1
Lithuanians	93	99.0	102	101.1	11	95.6
Poles	43	91.4	91	89.2	25	95.9
Polish Jews	2	95.0	15	103.6	18	97.5
Portuguese	0	....	29	82.3	74	82.2
Russians	7	91.0	31	93.8	12	95.3
Russian Jews	11	100.6	170	97.9	198	98.8
Swedes	73	102.4	53	101.8	4	95.0

Curiously enough Hirsch's own interpretation of these findings is strongly hereditarian, the differences among national groups being regarded by him as innate. In this connection he proposes a "Natio-Racial Hypothesis" which is essentially a suggestion for the reclassification of subgroups within the Caucasian race. The division into Nordic, Alpine, and Mediterranean he considers outworn. Hirsch's contention is that although these may have represented the original stocks, new racial units have been built up through such influences as migration, interbreeding, and natural selection. These units correspond to many of our modern nations, such as England, France, Germany, Italy, Spain.[1] According to Hirsch "each distinct nation may be regarded as a psycho-biological species which constitutes and fabricates a social milieu that is congenial to and is an expression of its innate psychic structure" (14, p. 374).

It might be noted that if present-day national groups have become crystallized into distinct "natio-races" or biological groups, we should expect the members of such groups to manifest distinctive physical as well as mental characteristics. But all physical criteria reveal a wide range of variation within any one nation with marked overlapping between nations. The members of a given nation cannot be identified on the basis of physical differentia and do not therefore constitute a "race" in the biological sense. There is, furthermore, no need to hypostatize "natio-races" in order to explain the behavioral similarity of members of a single nation. The cultural bonds which tie such individuals together supply ample evidence to account for their community of behavior as well as for their differences from other national groups.

Cross-Comparisons among Racial and National Groups in Europe

Regardless of the particular interpretation which may be put upon Hirsch's study, the data themselves are clear

---

[1] This correspondence is not considered to be perfect, however, since some nations which are at present political units are composed of distinct "racial" and cultural groups. Several of the Balkan countries are examples of this.

in showing that group differences tend to be larger when individuals are classified according to *nationality* than when they are classified according to *physical resemblance*. This conclusion, however, is subject to two limitations. In the first place, the data were obtained exclusively on the children of immigrant groups in the United States. Thus the samplings employed may not have been representative of their national populations. Secondly, the physical criteria employed to classify the subjects into "racial" groups are open to criticism and the resulting categories are very crude approximations of the three racial subgroups of Europe.

Both of these limitations were avoided in a study by Klineberg (17), in which the attempt was made to obtain as pure samples as possible of the three European races *in Europe*. In order to permit cross-comparisons of national and racial groups, the investigation was conducted in three countries which are heterogeneous in racial composition. The subjects were 10- to 12-year-old schoolboys in rural sections of Germany, France, and Italy.[1] The samples were taken from those geographical areas in which, according to maps of the distribution of various physical traits, pure types of each race were most likely to be found. Only children who had themselves, as well as their parents, been born in each particular area were included in the study. The subjects were further selected on the basis of three physical criteria: eye color, hair color, and cephalic index. No subject was employed unless he fell within the specified limits for his race in all three criteria. The groups were comparable in economic, social, and occupational level, the differences among them in these respects being relatively slight.

[1] Rural groups were chosen since too much intermixture had occurred in urban districts to yield a sufficient number of "pure types." Three city groups in Hamburg, Paris, and Rome were also tested for comparative purposes. The results of this testing will be reported in the following chapter.

Each subject was examined individually with a short performance scale consisting of six of the Pintner-Paterson tests.[1] These tests are all non-verbal and involve the manipulation of objects. Brief oral directions were given in the subject's native language. Performance was scored in terms of speed as well as accuracy. In Table XXXIII will be found the average, median, and range of scores within each group. The geographical location of the group and the number of villages covered are also given. The number of cases is exactly 100 in each of the seven groups.

TABLE XXXIII

COMPARISON OF NATIONAL AND RACIAL GROUPS ON A
PERFORMANCE SCALE

(After Klineberg, 17, p. 27)

Group	Province	Number of Villages Covered	Performance Scale Scores		
			Average	Median	Range
1. German Nordic	Hanover	17	198.2	197.6	69–289
2. French Mediterranean	Eastern Pyrenees	12	197.4	204.4	71–271
3. German Alpine	Baden	10	193.6	199.0	80–211
4. Italian Alpine	Piedmont	10	188.8	186.3	69–306
5. French Alpine	Auvergne and Velay	19	180.2	185.3	72–296
6. French Nordic	Flanders	13	178.8	183.3	63–314
7. Italian Mediterranean	Sicily	9	173.0	172.7	69–308

These results show marked variations among different samples of the same racial group. The alleged Nordic-Alpine-Mediterranean hierarchy is not maintained. Although the highest average score is obtained by a Nordic group, the highest median is found in a Mediterranean group. Similarly, the rank-order of the racial groups

[1] The Knox Cube, as well as the Triangle, Healy A, Two-Figure, Five-Figure and Casuist form boards.

within any one nation is inconsistent. Thus in France
the Mediterranean group is best, the Alpine intermediate,
and the Nordic poorest; whereas in Germany the Nordic
is superior to the Alpine sampling, and in Italy the Alpine
is superior to the Mediterranean. The marked overlapping
of groups, as indicated by the range, should also be noted.
When all Nordics, Alpines, and Mediterraneans are compared, regardless of nationality, the following average
scores are obtained:

Nordic	188.5
Alpine	187.5
Mediterranean	185.2

None of these differences is statistically reliable. The
variation from one Nordic sample to another, on the
other hand, is large and reliable. The same is true of the
other two racial groups. Thus there is a difference of
24.4 points between French and Italian Mediterraneans;
one of 19.4 points between German and French Nordics;
and one of 13.4 between German and French Alpines.

These results clearly show that the differences among
national groups cannot be attributed to their "racial"
composition, or the percentage of Nordic, Alpine, and
Mediterranean "blood" in each country. Because of the
variations found among different samples of the same
nation, Klineberg proposes that the differences may not
even be national in scope but should be envisaged in
terms of smaller cultural units. That the differences are
the result of environmental rather than hereditary factors
is suggested by two considerations. In the first place, the
predominance of a single inbred family strain in any one
of the samplings tested is very unlikely because of the
wide area covered. It will be recalled that from 9 to 19 villages were canvassed for each single sampling. In the
second place, very interesting parallelisms were found

between the cultural, economic, and educational conditions in any one region and the intelligence test performance of its inhabitants.

RACE VERSUS CULTURE IN THE DEVELOPMENT OF PERSONALITY TRAITS

Owing to the relatively recent advent of personality tests in the field of mental measurement and to the complexity and elusiveness of personality traits, very little objective information is available on racial and national differences in these traits. Popular opinion, on the other hand, has consistently attributed characteristic temperamental qualities to each race or nationality. Group differences in personality are considered to be even greater than in intelligence, and the belief in such emotional differences persists even when intellectual equality is granted. It is relatively difficult to challenge the existence of racial differences in personality because of the frequency with which such differences are apparently demonstrated in everyday observation. The Irish wit, the excitability of the South European, the easy-going nature of the Negro, the stolidity of the American Indian, the composure of the Englishman, and a host of similar characterizations have all become a part of our daily vocabulary.

Statements have frequently been made in regard to the predisposition of various racial groups to *crime* (cf., e.g., 1). Thus the large percentage of crime in the United States has been attributed by some to the influx of certain classes of immigrants into our country. Statistics have been cited to show the greater frequency of crime among Negroes and among immigrants from eastern and southern Europe than among the native-born White population.

Figures often lie, and in the interpretation of crime statistics it is particularly difficult to disentangle the

many uncontrolled factors which confuse the issue. Among
such factors may be mentioned the inequality in arrests
and convictions among various groups; Negroes and "foreigners," for example, are more readily arrested "on
suspicion" and on less grounds than is in general required
for native-born Whites. The fact that most foreigners are
adults would also give them a disproportionate percentage
of crime if they are compared with the figures for native-
born persons of *all* ages. Similarly, foreigners are more
often city-dwellers and live in poorer social and economic
conditions than native-born Americans, all of which is
conducive to crime. The foreigner, furthermore, may
have brought with him traditions which happen to conflict
with the accepted standards in our country. Finally,
the maladjustment which ensues from adaptation to a
new culture will have its effect upon first and second
generation immigrants, although the nature of this effect
probably differs in the two generations. In spite of the
many factors which load the dice against the foreign-
born in crime statistics, recent careful analyses of the
data on native and foreign-born persons *over 18 years of
age* have failed to reveal a higher rate of arrests, convictions, or commitments among the foreign-born (cf. 25).

The same may be said in regard to statistics on *insanity*
among different racial or national groups (cf., e.g., 20).
Most of the conditions which render the evaluation of
crime statistics difficult also affect the data on insanity.
In addition may be mentioned the factor of hospitalization. Institutional subjects may not be a representative
sampling of the actual cases of mental disorder in different groups. Thus the opportunities for hospital care
are not equal for such groups as Whites and Negroes in
certain parts of the country. On the other hand, because
of economic conditions, certain groups are better able to

care for the mentally disordered persons at home, thus eliminating the necessity for hospitalization. In regard to the predisposition of certain racial groups to a particular *form* of insanity, the results have been entirely negative.[1]

The application of *personality tests* to various groups has yielded results which are almost equally difficult to interpret. Most of these studies have been conducted on the American Negro (cf. 3, 7, 15, 23, 24), although some data on Oriental (8), American Indian (12) and European immigrant groups (11, 21) are also available. The doubtful reliability and validity of many personality tests reduce the significance of the results which have been obtained. Some investigators have found no reliable difference among the racial or national groups compared. Others have obtained slight differences in the direction expected from tradition and popular belief. In this connection environmental conditions and especially the force of "social expectancy" in determining the development of personality traits cannot be ignored. What is expected of an individual frequently determines what he will do, especially if such expectation is manifested early and consistently.

In a more recent investigation (19), the problem of race and personality was analyzed more directly by: (1) the use of more reliable and carefully standardized personality tests; (2) the classification of racial groups on the basis of accepted physical criteria; and (3) cross-comparisons among certain cultural divisions within the groups employed. Over 400 male and female students attending eight different institutions of collegiate rank in New York City and its environs were examined with a series of personality tests. The tests included the Bernreuter Personality Inventory scored for six "traits," the Allport-

[1] Cf Klineberg (18), Ch. XIII for a summary and discussion of this material.

Vernon Study of Values, an honesty test (Maller Test of Sports and Hobbies), and two tests specially devised for use in this investigation, one to measure suggestibility and the other persistence.[1] The subjects were classified into Nordic, Alpine, and Mediterranean groups on the basis of cephalic index, eye color, hair color, and skin color. In general if all but one of these criteria pointed to a certain group, the subject was placed in that group. If, however, one measure was far out of keeping with the limits set for each group, or if more than one measure fell even slightly beyond such limits, the subject was omitted from the classification. By this method it was possible to obtain approximately 50 men and 50 women in each of the three racial groups.

The average scores of Nordic, Alpine, and Mediterranean groups on each test are given in Table XXXIV. The data for the two sexes have been reported separately. On the Allport-Vernon Study of Values, only one of the differences is significant in each of the sex groups. Among the women there is a reliable difference between Mediterraneans and Alpines in the score for "æsthetic value." This difference is 3.26 times as large as its standard error, the higher average occurring in the Mediterranean group. Among the male students a reliable difference was found between Nordic and Alpine groups in the score for "religious value." This difference was in favor of the Nordics, the critical ratio being 4.64. Upon further analysis, both of these differences seemed to be rather closely linked up with institutional groupings. Thus the highest average score for "religious value" was obtained in a Catholic college for men in which were found only three Alpines. This would tend to pull down the average of the

---

[1] For a fuller discussion of these tests, the reader is referred to Chapter IX, in which another part of the same investigation was reported.

TABLE XXXIV

AVERAGE SCORES OF NORDICS, ALPINES, AND MEDITERRANEANS
ON PERSONALITY TESTS

(After Klineberg, Fjeld, and Foley, 19) [1]

Test	Male			Female		
	Nordic	Alpine	Mediterranean	Nordic	Alpine	Mediterranean
	(N=47)	(N=49)	(N=54)	(N=64)	(N=43)	(N=45)
Allport-Vernon Study of Values:						
1. Theoretical	29.20	32.19	32.74	28.84	29.14	28.59
2. Economic	27.80	29.32	28.87	27.48	26.66	25.50
3. Æsthetic	27.95	29.35	27.34	33.27	32.14	37.39
4. Social	31.32	34.75	31.80	31.98	32.45	31.13
5. Political	29.96	30.33	30.87	30.20	30.24	30.54
6. Religious	33.86	24.07	28.35	28.08	29.36	26.84
Bernreuter:						
1. B_1N: Neuroticism	−54.11	−35.37	−56.17	−52.44	−44.79	−20.29
2. B_2S: Self-sufficiency	43.13	37.55	29.59	14.48	13.91	2.62
3. B_3I: Introversion	−25.11	−14.76	−27.13	−28.05	−22.00	− 7.91
4. B_4D: Dominance	46.72	36.73	48.91	46.05	31.91	23.91
5. F_1C: Self-confidence	−28.17	− 2.14	−24.43	−15.67	− 7.37	23.16
6. F_2S: Sociability	7.85	− 2.76	−18.13	−19.31	−16.44	−21.78
Suggestibility	11.77	11.67	11.59	12.53	10.93	11.04
Persistence *	8.13	11.37	8.82	9.40	9.60	8.39
Honesty. *	95.48	96.84	96.70	99.40	97.94	99.00

*Not all subjects were given these tests.

Alpine group in relation to those of the other two "racial" classes. Similarly, among the female subjects, the highest scores in "æsthetic value" were obtained in an institution which encourages the æsthetic attitude, as is evidenced by a large and popular art department. This institution furnished a relatively large number of Mediterraneans, thus raising the average "æsthetic value" score of the latter group. None of the other Allport-Vernon scores yielded reliable differences between racial groups.

[1] The writer is indebted to Drs. Klineberg, Fjeld, and Foley for making available to her the unpublished data of this investigation.

None of the differences on the six Bernreuter scores proved to be statistically reliable in either male or female group. All of these critical ratios are less than three. Likewise, in the three remaining tests, i.e., suggestibility, honesty, and persistence, no significant group differences were found.

It is apparent that in the personality traits measured in this study, the differences among Nordics, Alpines, and Mediterraneans within college samplings are very slight. Nor can it be argued that the lack of differentiation among these groups was due to the homogeneity of college students in the characteristics under investigation. Although relatively homogeneous in intellectual traits, college students exhibit large individual differences in personality development. This is borne out by the very wide ranges and S.D.'s found within each group. It may also be mentioned that as a result of the wide range covered by each group, a large and almost complete overlapping of the distributions of Nordics, Alpines, and Mediterraneans was obtained on each test.

Since the academic institutions included in this survey differed from each other in a number of important respects, a comparison of subjects from each institution was believed to be of some interest. Although all of these institutions offer courses of collegiate level, they vary widely in the social and economic status of their student body as well as in the specific attitudes which they traditionally foster. Thus two institutions draw their students very largely from wealthy and socially prominent families. In several the student body comes from the upper middle class, thus being more nearly typical of the general college population. In one school the majority of the students fall into the "laboring" and lower middle classes, and are definitely of a lower social and economic level than the other groups. One institution is a Catholic college with a strongly religious tone in all of its academic work. At least two of the academic groups, on the other hand, are notoriously agnostic and foster a very critical attitude towards all religions. Equally pronounced differences are to be found in radicalism and conservatism, in the relative emphasis placed upon the scientific and the æsthetic approach, and in other attitudes characteristic of each institution.

In sharp contrast to the generally insignificant differences found between racial groups, large and reliable differences in average score were frequently obtained between institutions. Several of these differences were many times larger than is required for complete statistical reliability. In both male and female samplings, the Allport-Vernon scores showed the largest differences. These differences tallied closely with well-known characteristics of the institutions under consideration. Thus in "religious value," the Catholic college obtained the highest average score and a traditionally radical, agnostic group of low economic status obtained the lowest, the difference being 14.49 times as large as its standard error. It is interesting to note that another very large difference was obtained between these same two groups in "theoretical value." In this case, however, the difference was in favor of the latter group, the critical ratio being 7.18. On the Bernreuter scales the differences were not so marked, although many were statistically reliable. The tests of suggestibility, honesty, and persistence yielded relatively small and unreliable differences.

In summary, it will be noted that differences among the three racial groups tended to be small and unreliable, whereas those among institutional groups were much larger and very frequently reliable. Whatever the cause of these institutional differences, it cannot be "race" in the biological sense, since the differences disappear when individuals are classified according to the physical criteria of race. The explanation of these personality differences from one institution to another is not difficult to find. In the first place, *selection* obviously operates in the students' enrollment in any particular institution. Individuals with certain attitudes and emotional characteristics will be more readily attracted to those institutions which are by tradition congenial to such traits. The evidence indicates, however, that such selection operates on the basis of the economic and cultural group in which the individual was reared rather than in terms of race. In the second place, *attendance in a particular institution* will itself foster the development of certain personality traits through the resulting social contacts and other direct stimulating circumstances.

Gesture: An Example of Culturally Conditioned Behavior

It has frequently been proposed that racial groups manifest characteristic *bodily attitudes* and *movements*. Thus the habitual postures, the peculiar walk, and other traditional motor habits of various groups have been described at great length. Attention has also been called to the large group differences in the speed and tempo of movement. Special interest, however, has always been attached to the *gestural behavior* of different peoples. The frequent emotional connotations of gestures, their peculiar relationship to language, and the easily observable differences in the traditional gesture patterns of various groups have made their study a particularly fascinating one. A voluminous literature has accumulated on this subject, most of the writings being either purely descriptive or speculative in nature. Artists, historians, philosophers, anthropologists, and many others have contributed their observations or theories to this topic. The layman, depending upon his mood and disposition, is amused, estranged, or repelled by the spectacle of a gestural pattern too unlike his own. In popular thought, gesture has been linked with underlying personality differences among racial groups. As a result, this phase of motor behavior has acquired a special significance in discussions of race differences.

A suggestive approach to the problem of characteristic "racial" gestures has been made in a recent investigation (9).[1] The groups employed were: (1) "traditional" Italians living in "Little Italy," one of the Italian districts in New York City; (2) "traditional" Jews living in the East Side Ghetto, New York City; and (3) "assimilated" Italians and Jews, both living in similar "Americanized" environments. In view of the wide diversification in behavior patterns among different samplings of Italian and Jewish subjects, the authors point out that the Jews included in this investigation were predominantly of Lithuanian or Polish extraction, and the Italians were from Southern Italy, chiefly from the vicinity of Naples, and from Sicily. The findings are thus restricted to these particular groups. Similarly, the results are to be qualified by the fact that only immigrant groups in America were employed.

The gestural behavior of these subjects was investigated by the following methods: (1) direct observation of gestures in natural situations; (2) sketches made by an artist under the same conditions; (3) motion pictures. In all three methods, the subjects were unaware of the

[1] The writer is indebted to Drs. Efron and Foley for making available to her the unpublished manuscript of this article which is to appear shortly.

fact that they were being observed. The motion picture material was subjected to two types of analysis. In the first place, the films were shown to naïve observers who were asked to judge various characteristics of the movements. The second method was more quantitative. The film, taken with a constant speed moving picture camera, was projected frame by frame upon coördinate paper. The position of motile parts, such as fingers, wrist, elbow, etc., was marked in successive frame projections. When these points were joined, a precise representation of the gestural behavior pattern was obtained. Figure 50 illustrates this graphic technique in the case of a traditional Italian. It will be noted that there are four distinct lines of motion portrayed, the continuous lines representing the paths of movement of the right and left wrists and the broken lines depicting the accompanying motions of the respective elbows. The numbers indicate the direction of movement, representing the position of the given part in each successive frame projection. A study

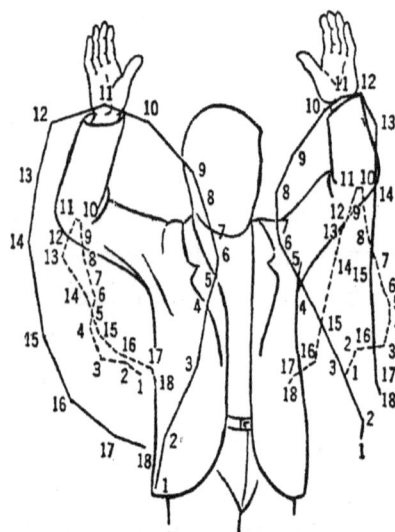

Fig. 50. Graphic Technique Employed in the Analysis of Gestural Behavior. (After Efron and Foley, 9.)

of the curves constructed by this technique, as well as a consideration of the data collected by the other more qualitative methods, led to certain tentative conclusions.

Clearly distinguishable and characteristic gestural patterns were exhibited by the traditional Italian and Jewish groups. Some of the major differences between these patterns will be summarized briefly. In regard to the *parts of the body used in gesticulating*, it was found that whereas the Italian tends to use preferably his arms, the Jew frequently employs his head as well as his arms, hands, and fingers in a functionally differentiated way. The head and finger gestures are rather typical of the Jewish expressive movement.

The *form of the movement* also showed marked contrast in the two groups. In the Jew, the movements are often sinuous and change direction frequently; whereas the Italian is more inclined to continue in the same direction until completion of the entire gesture segment. In regard to *laterality* (i.e., unilateral or bilateral) as well as *symmetry* of movement, pronounced differences were noted. The Jewish gesture is predominantly asymmetrical, with frequent crossings and intertwinings. Gesticulation is usually executed with one hand and arm, and if two are used they are employed in a sequential rather than a simultaneous fashion. The Italian, on the other hand, frequently uses two arms simultaneously, and the movements are highly symmetrical in character.

The *radius* of the movement also differs in the two groups, the Jew employing a relatively confined area, while the Italian sweep is characteristically large, with movements involving the entire arm. The two groups also differ in the *area in which gesticulation usually occurs*, the Jewish group seldom deviating from the medial plane of the body, whereas the Italian is more likely to perform his movements within a lateral area. Within each of these general areas, a difference was found in the *direction* of the gestural movements themselves, the Jewish movements being more frequently towards and the Italian away from the body of the gesturer. Significant differences were likewise noted in *rhythm* or *tempo*, the Jewish movements being characteristically jerky, sporadic, and variable, while those of the Italians were more even and less variable.

In addition to the above spatio-temporal characteristics of the traditional gestural movements themselves, certain major differences were observed in regard to the *meaningful* or *linguistic* function of such gestures. The Jewish gestures are characteristically of the *discursive* or *logical* types, being, as it were, a gestural portrayal not of the object of reference or thought, but of the process of ideation itself. This discursive or logical type is absent among the traditional Italians, whose gestures are frequently *pictorial* and *pantomimic*, the latter being a sort of reënactment or imitation of the actions verbally described. Purely symbolic gestures are also common among the traditional Italian and convey definite meaningful associations. These may be used to accompany verbal intercourse or may even function as the exclusive means of communication.

All of the above characteristics of the traditional Italian and Jewish groups seemed to disappear in the "assimilated" groups. In general, the more assimilated the individual, the less Jewish or Italian gestural characteristics he was found to portray. The traditional differences between Italian and Jewish gestures were absent in the fully assimilated groups, and both resembled the particular "American" group with which they had become associated. On the whole, gesticulation was much *less frequent* in such assimilated groups. The differences in gestural behavior between traditional groups and the lack of such differences between assimilated groups could not, furthermore, be explained on the basis of "generation." It was found, for example, that the American-born students at an orthodox Jewish school in New York City exhibited the gestural behavior of the traditional groups in the Ghetto, while the American-born Jewish subjects obtained at an exclusive Fifth Avenue club showed no such traditional gestures. In summary, a marked disparity was found between the patterns characteristic of most of the gestures of the traditional Jewish and Italian groups investigated and a lack of such contrasting patterns in assimilated groups of the same "racial" extraction. Thus cultural stimulation or habituation rather than so-called "racial" descent seems to be operative in the development of gesture.

GENERAL EVALUATION

We have seen in the two preceding chapters the many difficulties which beset the study of race differences in psychological traits. Race, defined as a biologically distinct group differentiated by common innate physical characteristics, is a difficult category to apply to contemporary man. In the attempt to arrive at a classification of human races, one proposed criterion after another has proved inadequate. An analysis of the major alleged physical differentia of race reveals wide variation within a single group, overlapping of groups, inconsistency with other criteria, and susceptibility to environmental influences. One or more of these criticisms can be leveled against each of the proposed criteria. Thus even the best possible classification of races is to be regarded as tentative and approximate. In fact the very concept of race itself could be questioned on both theoretical and empirical grounds.

Race mixture, which has been going on for many generations, also adds to the complexity of the problem. The issue is further confused by the testing of immigrant groups which may not be representative samplings of their national populations. Immigrants are also undergoing a period of intense readjustment and conflict arising from their contacts with the new culture, and this cannot fail to affect their behavior in many ways.

The problem of testing and comparing racial groups also presents serious difficulties. Members of different races usually differ in many other respects as well. These differences often make direct comparison of behavior impossible. Thus language handicap has been shown to have a marked influence upon mental test performance. The subject's reaction to an examiner of a different race, the establishment of "rapport," the use of pantomime or of pictures which may not be equally familiar to all groups, all make the administration of tests a difficult task. The racial groups to be compared, furthermore, may not be equated in educational opportunities and facilities, social and economic status, and the general cultural milieu in which they live. The special traditions, customs, and interests characteristic of each group may further "interfere" with test responses. Finally, it is impossible to establish a hierarchy of groups in terms of *absolute* intellectual superiority or inferiority. "Intelligence" tests measure the ability to succeed in the particular culture in which they were developed. Cultures differ in the specific activities which they encourage, stimulate, and value. The "higher mental processes" of one culture may be the relatively useless "stunts" of another.

Insofar as the members of different races live under varied cultural conditions, it is extremely difficult to compare them directly and impossible to determine the relative contribution of hereditary and environmental factors in producing any behavioral differences among them. In a few recent investigations, which have been reported in the present chapter, it was found possible to make cross-comparisons among racial and cultural groupings. Insofar as these two categories, race and culture, cut across each other, it is possible to tease out the relative influence of biological and environmental factors. The results of such investigations are highly suggestive. It would be extremely premature, of course, to hazard any conclusive statements on so complex a problem, although the bulk of the evidence is definitely against the existence of behavioral differences among "races" in the biological sense.

REFERENCES

1. Bauer, E., Fischer, E., and Lenz, F. *Human Heredity* (transl. by E. and C. Paul). N. Y.: Macmillan, 1931. Pp. 734.
2. Berry, C. S. "The Classification by Tests of Intelligence of Ten Thousand First Grade Pupils," *J. Educ. Res.*, 1922, 6, 185–203.
3. Bond, H. M. "An Investigation of the Non-Intellectual Traits of a Group of Negro Adults," *J. Abn. and Soc. Psychol.*, 1926, 21, 267–276.
4. Brigham, C. C. *A Study of American Intelligence*. Princeton, N. J.: Princeton Univ. Press, 1923. Pp. 210.
5. ——. "Intelligence Tests of Immigrant Groups," *Psychol. Rev.*, 1930, 37, 158–165.
6. Brown, G. L. "Intelligence as Related to Nationality," *J. Educ. Res.*, 1922, 5, 324–327.
7. Crane, A. L. "Race Differences in Inhibition," *Arch. Psychol.*, No. 63, 1923. Pp. 84.
8. Darsie, M. L. "Mental Capacity of American-Born Japanese Children," *Comp. Psychol. Mon.*, 1926, 15, No. 3, 1–89.
9. Efron, D., and Foley, J. P., Jr. "A Comparative Investigation of Gestural Behavior Patterns in Italian and Jewish Groups Living under Different as Well as Similar Environmental Conditions," *Zscht. f. Sozialforschung*, 1937, 6, 151–159.
10. Feingold, G. A. "Intelligence of the First Generation of Immigrant Groups," *J. Educ. Psychol.*, 1924, 15, 65–82.

11. Garrett, H. E. "Jews and Others: Some Group Differences in Personality, Intelligence, and College Achievement," *Pers. J.*, 1929, 7, 341–348.

12. Garth, T. R., and Barnard, M. A. "The Will-Temperament of Indians," *J. Appl. Psychol.*, 1927, 11, 512–518.

13. Goodenough, F. L. "Racial Differences in the Intelligence of School Children," *J. Exper. Psychol.*, 1926, 9, 388–397.

14. Hirsch, N. D. M. "A Study of Natio-Racial Mental Differences," *Genet. Psychol. Mon.*, 1926, 1, 231–406.

15. Hurlock, E. B. "Will-Temperament of White and Negro Children," *J. Genet. Psychol.*, 1930, 38, 91–100.

16. Kirkpatrick, C. "Intelligence and Immigration," *Ment. Meas. Mon.*, No. 2, 1926. Pp. 127.

17. Klineberg, O. "A Study of Psychological Differences between 'Racial' and National Groups in Europe," *Arch. Psychol.*, No. 132, 1931. Pp. 58.

18. ——. *Race Differences*. N. Y.: Harper, 1935. Pp. 367.

19. Klineberg, O., Fjeld, H., and Foley, J. P., Jr. "An Experimental Study of Personality Differences among Constitutional, 'Racial,' and Cultural Groups." (To appear.)

20. Laughlin, H. H. *An Analysis of America's Modern Melting Pot. Hearings before the Comm. on Immigration and Naturalization*. Washington: U. S. Gov't Printing Office, 1923. Pp. 725–831.

21. Mathews, E. "A Study of Emotional Instability in Children," *J. Delinq.*, 1923, 8, 1–40.

22. Murdock, K. "Race Differences in New York City," *Sch. and Soc.*, 1920, 11, 147–150.

23. Peterson, J., and Lanier, L. H. "Studies in the Comparative Abilities of Whites and Negroes," *Ment. Meas. Mon.*, No. 5, 1929. Pp. 156.

24. Sumner, F. C., and Sumner, F. H. "Mental Health of White and Negro College Students," *J. Abn. and Soc. Psychol.*, 1931, 26, 28–36.

25. Wickersham, G. W., *et al. Report on Crime and the Foreign*

Born. U. S. National Commission on Law Observance and Enforcement, Report No. 10. Washington: U. S. Gov't Printing Office, 1933. Pp. 416.

26. Yerkes, R. M., ed. "Psychological Examining in the United States Army," *Mem. Nat. Acad. Sci.*, 1921, 15. Pp. 890.

27. Young, K. "Mental Differences in Certain Immigrant Groups," *Oregon Univ. Stud. in Psychol.*, 1922, 1, 11. Pp. 103.

CHAPTER XIX

URBAN AND RURAL POPULATIONS

Within any single racial or national group, wide differences are frequently found from one region to another. An illustration of such regional differences is the large variation in median Army Alpha scores existing among different states in our country (cf. Ch. XVII). The comparison of northern and southern Negroes in the United States is a further example of regional variation. In Klineberg's study (16) of racial groups in Europe, marked dissimilarities in intelligence test performance were likewise found among the individual provinces examined. An analysis of such regional variations in "intelligence" in relation to other factors which differentiate each area should yield suggestive data on the origin of intellectual differences.

One of the most fundamental and widespread types of regional division is that between city and country. The dichotomy between urban and rural populations is one which is frequently made for practical purposes. The layman recognizes marked differences, not only in abilities but also in interests, emotional qualities, and general outlook, between the urban and the rural dweller. Actually the division is not a two-fold one, but includes a series of groups, each differing from the others in distinct ways. From the large metropolis, through the moderately large city, the small town, the village with its one general store and post office, to the open country and the isolated mountain community, there are to be found all degrees and types of variation. The extremes of this series present definitely contrasting pictures of intellectual development. Among the intermediate and more nearly adjacent members, there may not be a very pronounced intellectual variation, but in such cases well known personality differences are often found. Thus the attitudes and emotional traits of the isolated mountain dweller and of the inhabitants of a small village may be fundamentally diverse. Similarly, between the resident of a large city and the member of a small town community there exist differences in outlook which have been repeatedly described and dramatized in literature.

The general environment and stimulational milieu in which the individual develops are clearly dissimilar in urban and rural centers. City and country groups also differ markedly in occupational status and general economic background. Similarly, educational opportunities are notoriously poor in many rural districts of our country, in sharp contrast to the excellent facilities available in most towns and cities. The length of the school term is usually shortened in rural communities because of the impassable condition of the roads at certain times of the year, or because the children are needed to help with farm duties in busy seasons, or for other reasons of a local nature. In some cases the school term lasts only six months. Similarly, the difference in type and amount of instruction received in the "consolidated" and the "one-room" school is a very real one. In the latter type of school, in which pupils of all ages and grades are taught by a single teacher and in a single classroom, progress must necessarily be very halting. Differences in the provision of books and other supplies, as well as in teacher training, are too obvious to mention.

The general cultural milieu of different localities likewise presents striking contrasts. Libraries, museums, and other facilities for the intellectual or artistic stimulation of the community are far more accessible and better developed in urban than in rural districts. The extent and variety of social contacts also differentiates city and country groups. From the cosmopolitan associations of the large urban center with its kaleidoscopic array of diverse customs, manners, and peoples, through the relatively homogeneous population of the small town or farm community, to the isolated mountain dwelling cut off from all outside contacts during a large part of the year, there exists a wide range of social stimulation.

Certain historical factors should also be considered in any analysis of regional variations. Migrations between city and country are constantly occurring for a variety of reasons. During a period of settlement and development, migration occurs predominantly from the urban to the rural districts. The westward expansion of the United States is an example of such a movement. The tide of migration soon turns, however, and the farm dweller is attracted to the city with its promise of wider vocational opportunities and other facilities. At any time, however, such economic events as the opening of mines, the discovery of oil or gold, and to a lesser extent, the construction of roads or the establishment of railway connections will bring about a sudden influx into a previously isolated area. These movements of population, either *en masse* or by single individuals, depend upon a complex manifold of economic, political, social, and psychological factors. No single generalization can be applied to all migrations. In spite of this, attempts have been made to treat the phenomenon of migration as the key to the explanation of urban-rural differences in psychological traits.

Theories of Urban-Rural Differences in Intelligence

It has been repeatedly argued that the intellectual inferiority of rural groups is the direct result of *selective migration*. According to this theory, the more intelligent, progressive, and energetic families or individuals are attracted to urban centers, while the duller and less ambitious remain in the country. The operation of such a selective process for several generations would eventually lead to an inferior rural stock. Urban-rural differences in intelligence would thus be attributed primarily to an hereditary basis.

There have been many exponents of this view. Estabrook, in an article entitled *Blood Seeks Environment* (7), writes, "energetic individuals will not in general remain in areas that do not afford opportunity for development" (p. 112). Similarly, Pintner (23), after a survey of test results on urban and rural children, concludes that: "In general, therefore, it would appear as if the urban districts rate higher in intelligence than rural districts and that this is due to the migration of superior intelligence to the cities" (p. 253). Pintner admits the greater familiarity of city children with tests as a possible factor in their superior performance, but regards this as a relatively minor factor. In an investigation on east Kentucky mountain children, Hirsch (10) likewise proposes selective migration to account for the intellectual backwardness of his subjects.

The hypothesis of selective migration has been carried even further by some writers. In an investigation on rural children by S. L. Pressey and Thomas (21), the subjects were divided into those living in "poor" farming districts where the land is hilly and the soil inferior and those living on "good" farming land. These two groups were found to differ significantly in intelligence test performance. Among the children in the "good" farming districts, 36% reached or exceeded the median score of city children, as contrasted to only 20% in the "poor" districts. In explanation of these findings, the authors suggest that a constant selective process goes on in country districts, the inferior, less intelligent stock being pushed back more and more into the hill country where the soil is poorest. Thus they propose that within an agricultural community there should be some relationship between intelligence and land value.[1]

In a further check on this hypothesis, L. W. Pressey (20) tested 183 rural children between the ages of six and eight with the Pressey Primer Scale. These subjects were taken from the "poorer" of the two farming areas covered in the earlier study. It was argued that since the Primer Scale is non-verbal the effects of the educational deficiency of the rural children would be minimized. The use of younger subjects should also reduce the extent of environmental influences. In spite of these conditions, only 22% of the rural children reached or exceeded the corresponding age medians of city children. Pressey regards this as cogent evidence for an hereditary view of urban-rural differences. She points out, however, that even among these relatively young children, environmental handicaps were not completely eliminated. Thus the early home environment, including, for instance, play activities and nursery games, will affect a child's score on a non-verbal test. Country children, furthermore, are less adept in the use of paper-and-pencil material and are more shy with strangers than city children. All of these

[1] It might be added that in the "poor" farming area of this investigation, educational facilities were notoriously deficient.

factors must be taken into account in evaluating the rural child's test performance.

Another modification of the selective migration hypothesis was suggested by Thomson (28), on the basis of test results obtained on English schoolchildren. In this study, although city children again surpassed country children as a group, a relatively large percentage of high scores was also found in remote rural districts which were far removed from the urban centers. In discussing these data, Thomson offers the following comment:

> The distribution of intelligence suggested by the tests is such that the highest ability appears to be found *close to the* cities and *far away* from the cities, the intermediate areas having fewer cases of high ability, as though they were drained by selection (p. 222).

A similar view has been expressed by L. S. Hollingworth. In a book on *Gifted Children*, she writes:

> As regards the comparative frequency of gifted children in urban and rural environments, we have not much information at present. Such data as bear on the subject indicate that we shall probably find a greater proportion of gifted in the cities except in districts so remote from means of transportation as to have precluded migration of intellectual deviates to the city (p. 58).

It might be added that subsequent investigations on remote and relatively isolated rural districts have failed to confirm these suggestions. It has been generally found that the intellectual status of the inhabitants becomes progressively *poorer* as the degree of remoteness of the area increases.[1]

In contrast to the above efforts to account for urban-rural differences in terms of heredity, there is now an

[1] Cf., e.g., the studies on mountain children reported below.

increasing tendency to look to the *environment* for an explanation. Migration may have drained the country of its best families in certain localities, but this cannot be offered as a universally applicable conclusion. The opposite argument could just as readily be put forth, i.e., that it is the shiftless and the dull who migrate because they have been unable to succeed at home. The forces of selection are too difficult to disentangle, unless the specific history and conditions of the district under consideration are known. An examination of environmental conditions, on the other hand, offers ample evidence for the differentiation of urban and rural groups. Thus Lehman and Witty (19), for example, in a survey of play activities found the recreations of rural children to be very different from those of urban children, and suggested that these differences were "directly traceable to environmental opportunities." They concluded that

> the rural and the city children do not have the same social contacts . . . the environments of the town and country children are quite different and these environmental differences *may have* an influence upon the mental age ratings of the two groups of children (pp. 124–125).

This was among the first investigations explicitly to emphasize environmental factors in the interpretation of urban-rural differences.

MENTAL TEST SURVEYS OF RURAL SCHOOLCHILDREN

The fact that country children fall distinctly below the city norms on current intelligence tests has been quite generally established. Numerous investigations, some employing several thousand children, have consistently revealed the inferior performance of rural groups. In a survey on 1165 children in grades three to eight of several schools, Book (4) classified the results in respect to city and country. The median scores of the two groups at each age were as follows:

Age	City	Country
8	67	50
9	74	58
10	93	62
11	105	89
12	116	97
13	125	107
14	122	110
15	115	117

With the exception of age 15, the city children surpassed the country children at each age. Between the ages of 8 and 13, only 24% of the country children fell above the medians of the city groups. The highest age groups may not have been comparable because of a possible differential effect of selection among urban and rural schoolchildren. The older children in country schools tend to be a more highly select group than those in city schools.

Pintner (22) tested the pupils in four city schools, a village school, and a rural school. The median percentiles of the four city schools were 58.5, 58.5, 47, and 44.5, the first two schools being slightly above and the latter two slightly below the test norms. In the village school, however, the median percentile was 30, and in the rural school 17. In the investigation by Pressey and Thomas (21) cited above, the country children as a group fell clearly below the norms for city children. The percentages of rural children in a group of 321 who tested at or above the city medians at each age were as follows:

Age	10	11	12	13
Per Cent	29	33	21	25

Pyle and Collings (24) report the results obtained in a survey of the entire population of schoolchildren between the ages of 8 and 18 in a Missouri county with the Pyle tests. The median scores of the rural boys were only 72.7% as high as those of the urban boys; those of the rural girls were 77.5% as high as the urban girls' scores. The differences between city and country groups were smaller, however, on the non-linguistic tests. Kempf and Collins (14), in a comprehensive testing program conducted in two counties of Illinois, report the following median I.Q.'s for urban and rural samplings.

	Northern County	*Southern County*
Urban	103.5	91
Rural	95.0	84

Irion and Fisher (12) found that 361 rural children between the ages of 11 and 16 scored on the average 10 points below the urban norm on the National Intelligence Test.

Hinds (9) administered the Otis Group Test to 581 Texas high school students in cities, in large and small towns, and in the open country. The median "Index of Brightness" [1] of the students in each type of locale is shown below.

	Number of Cases	*Median*
City schools	164	100.5
Affiliated town schools	290	98.0
Unaffiliated small town schools	59	84.4
Rural schools	68	77.0

Hinds points out that these differences cannot be attributed to the presence of a foreign element, since foreigners were about equally distributed in the different types of schools, with a slight predominance in city schools. The consistent decrease in median score from the best to the poorest and most outlying schools is very suggestive.

[1] The Otis "Index of Brightness" can be interpreted in a similar way to the I.Q.

Mention should also be made of the comprehensive *rural surveys* which have been conducted in several states (cf. 27). These include an analysis of both intelligence test performance and educational achievement. On such intelligence scales as the National Intelligence Test, the Terman Group Scale, the Otis Classification Test, and the Pintner-Cunningham Primary Scale, country children made a consistently poorer showing than city children. The comparison of pupils in one-room with those in union or consolidated schools showed the former to be inferior. In educational achievement as measured by standard achievement tests in school subjects, the rural child is found to be even farther behind than in intelligence test score.[1]

In summary, numerous investigations by psychologists, as well as state educational surveys, have consistently shown the rural schoolchild to be inferior in performance on current tests of general intelligence. This inferiority tends to be greater in those districts with the poorest school facilities. On linguistic tests, the country child tends to make a relatively poorer showing than on non-verbal tests. Rural inferiority is also more marked on group than on individual scales. It has been suggested that the country child's performance on a group scale may be handicapped by his greater shyness with strangers (20). This difficulty would be overcome in part by the examiner's efforts to establish "rapport" in the administration of an individual scale.

CITY AND COUNTRY DIFFERENCES IN EUROPE

It is not to be supposed that regional differences are a special characteristic of our own country. They cannot be regarded as a result of the peculiarly heterogeneous

[1] Cf., e.g., Frost (8).

nature of our population or the relatively large geographical expanse of our nation. Ample evidence for equally large inter-regional and urban-rural variations in intellectual traits can be found in European countries. Several English studies reveal the same general inferiority of rural schoolchildren which has been reported by the American investigators. Thus on a battery of tests administered in the county of Northumberland, the rural children obtained scores which placed them on the average more than one year behind the norms for large cities (6).

Bickersteth (3) examined 1200 English schoolchildren with a series of verbal tests. The subjects were drawn from the Yorkshire Dales, an extremely isolated rural district, and from Leeds, an urban settlement. On the whole, the rural group excelled on the memory tests, the urban children on tests of "reasoning." This discrepancy may be due to the relatively greater dependence of the latter type of test upon specific information and experiential background. Thus one of the "reasoning" tests was the Burt Analogies Test, in which occur items such as the following:

policeman : burglar : : cat : _____
writing : typewriting : : voice : _____

It is apparent that such a test would place the rural child at a disadvantage; whereas memory tests would be relatively uninfluenced by his environmental handicap.

A particularly vivid demonstration of urban-rural differences is to be found in the investigation by Klineberg (16) reported in the preceding chapter. Among the subjects tested in this study were three city groups from Paris, Hamburg, and Rome, respectively. The rural groups, it will be recalled, were selected from several provinces in France, Germany, and Italy. Each of the city groups, as well as each of the individual rural groups, was composed of 100 10- to 12-year-old schoolboys. All subjects were given an abbreviated series of performance tests from the Pintner-Paterson Scale. The scores obtained by each of the city groups, as well as by all city and all country groups combined, will be found in Table XXXV.

TABLE XXXV

PERFORMANCE TEST SCORES OF URBAN AND RURAL
GROUPS IN EUROPE

(After Klineberg, 16)

Group	Number of Cases	Average	Median	Range
Paris	100	219.0	218.9	100–302
Hamburg	100	216.4	218.3	105–322
Rome	100	211.8	213.6	109–313
Total city	300	215.7	216.9	100–322
Total country	700	187.1	187.0	63–314

The difference between the average scores of the composite city and country groups is much greater than any other difference, racial or national, which was obtained in this investigation. This difference is over eight times as large as its standard error, and is thus many times larger than would be required for complete statistical reliability. In terms of overlapping, only 30.12% of the rural children reached or exceeded the median of the urban children. It is also interesting to note that the three city groups differ little *among themselves*. None of the differences among these three averages is statistically reliable. The rural groups, it will be recalled, revealed larger and fairly reliable national differences. It would seem that the equalizing effect of life in a large cosmopolitan city tends to obliterate many of the differences arising from the specific national culture.

The Intelligence of Mountain Children

An unusually good opportunity for the study of isolated communities is offered by the Highlanders of our southern mountains. Owing to poor roads and general inaccessibility, many of these groups live in complete isolation during the larger part of the year. In certain districts, the cultural level is extremely low, little more than the bare necessities of life being available. Families are frequently found living in the original crude huts built by their ancestors several generations ago. Racially these groups are relatively homogeneous, being predominantly of British descent. They are highly inbred, and in certain communities only two or three different surnames are to be found. The peculiar customs and manners [1] of the southern mountaineer have long stirred the imagination of author and playwright. As a result these highland people have achieved a certain amount of glamor in the mind of the public which overshadows the squalor of their lives. To the psychologist, these groups offer a challenging opportunity to unravel the forces of heredity and environment.

In a study of east Kentucky mountaineers, Hirsch (10) examined 1945 schoolchildren in five private, one town, and 29 county schools. All of the subjects lived in three fairly isolated mountain counties. Private agencies had, however, coöperated in the establishment and maintenance of relatively good schools in this area, so that the children did not suffer from as great an educational handicap as is usually the case in mountain communities. All first grade pupils were tested with the Pintner-Cunningham Primary Scale. Those in grades II, III, and IV were

---

[1] For descriptive material regarding these people and their surroundings, the reader may examine the accounts of Campbell (5), Kephart (15), and Raine (25).

given the Dearborn Test A, and those in grades V to XII, inclusive, the Dearborn Test C.[1] The average I.Q.'s of the entire group at successive age levels are shown below.

Age	5–6	7	8	9	10	11	12	13	14	15 up
I.Q.	86.6	85.1	81.1	79.2	78.6	77.2	75.4	73.1	74.6	81.1

The successive age groups may not be strictly comparable, owing to differential selection. Thus among the older subjects were included high school students who are definitely a select group in such a community. This might account for the rise in score at the upper age levels. In general, however, there is a tendency for I.Q.'s to drop with age, as is usually found among subjects living within a restricted environment. Hirsch bases most of his conclusions upon a more intensive analysis of children in a single school. This was a relatively superior school and the children attending it represented a select group. Within this sampling, a correlation of −.23 was found between I.Q. and age. Since this correlation is so low, and the correlation of age with an index of educational achievement was still lower (−.10), Hirsch concluded that the intellectual backwardness of these children was not the result of poor education. Other similar evidence was cited in support of this conclusion. Thus a comparison of successive age averages showed very little drop. Within 44 families having from 3 to 6 siblings in the school, no consistent drop was noted from the youngest to the oldest child. Hirsch places a rather strongly hereditarian interpretation upon these findings, suggesting that the "better stock" has gradually left the mountainous regions in successive migrations.

The data of this study are complicated by a number of

---

[1] In addition to Form C, Dearborn D was administered to 175 of these subjects.

conditions. In the first place, the fact that educational facilities were relatively good tends to reduce the effect of a restricted home environment and low cultural status. Selective factors in school enrollment and attendance, especially at the upper ages, also confuse the issue. It is therefore not surprising that the results are somewhat ambiguous and interpretation is difficult.

In a later study by Sherman and Key (26), the groups chosen for investigation were much more effectively isolated. The subjects included 102 mountain children living in four "hollows" in the Blue Ridge Mountains, approximately 100 miles from Washington, D. C. In addition, a fifth group of 81 children was tested at Briarsville, a small village situated at the base of the Blue Ridge. These subjects represented over one-half of all children living in the five centers. Each of the five communities differed in length of school term, quality of schooling, and general level of material culture. Racially, however, they were quite homogeneous, all being descended from a common ancestral stock. It was thus possible to make intercomparisons among the groups, in addition to an evaluation of scores in terms of urban norms.

The tests employed in this survey were the Stanford-Binet, the National Intelligence Test, the Pintner-Cunningham Primary Scale, and a series of performance tests, including five from the Pintner-Paterson Scale [1] and the Goodenough test of drawing a man. The average I.Q.'s of the composite mountain group and the Briarsville group are given in Table XXXVI. The I.Q.'s obtained on each test, as well as the number of children taking the test, have been tabulated for the two groups. The scores on the Pintner-Paterson tests have been expressed in two ways.

[1] Manikin, Seguin Form Board, Mare and Foal, Healy A, and Knox Cube.

TABLE XXXVI

AVERAGE I.Q.'S OF CHILDREN LIVING IN FOUR MOUNTAIN
HOLLOWS AND IN A SMALL VILLAGE
(After Sherman and Key, 26, p. 283)

Test	Mountain		Village	
	Number of Cases	Average I.Q.	Number of Cases	Average I.Q.
Stanford-Binet	32	61.5	....	....
National Intelligence Test	24	61.2	50	96.1
Pintner-Cunningham Performance Tests:	42	75.9	31	87.6
Year Scale	54	83.9	10	118.6
Median M.A.	54	79.1	10	95.6
Goodenough Test	63	72.3	67	76.3

It will be noted that both groups are inferior in terms of the "normal" I.Q. of 100, although the village group is very close to the norms on most tests. In every comparison, the village children clearly excel the mountain group. It should also be noted that in both groups, the highest I.Q. is obtained on the performance tests, which are least dependent upon environment. Among the country children, with their pronounced deficiency in linguistic training, the lowest I.Q.'s are obtained on the Stanford-Binet and the National Intelligence Test, the two most predominantly verbal tests in the series. The village children, on the other hand, do relatively well on the National Intelligence Test, probably because of their better educational facilities. The mountain children are reported to have been handicapped on the speed tests, as is generally the case with groups whose environment is not conducive to haste.

All tests showed a consistent drop in score with age, in both mountain and village children. The average

I.Q.'s of each age group are shown in Table XXXVII. In the entire table, there are only two very minor and probably negligible exceptions to the general trend. The authors interpret the age decrement as follows:

> An intelligence test is an indirect measure. An estimate of intelligence is based on the information the child has been able to obtain. In the mountain environment increments of information become less large with increases in age, and the seven-year-old has relatively more chance to gather information than the 12-year-old in the same environment (p. 287).

A comparison of the four hollows showed that the percentage of children who tested below average intelligence increased as the cultural level of the community decreased.

TABLE XXXVII

AVERAGE I.Q. IN RELATION TO CHRONOLOGICAL AGE

(After Sherman and Key, 26, p. 287)

| Age | Pintner-Cunningham | | National Intelligence Test | | Drawing of a Man | | Performance Scale | | | |
| | | | | | | | Year Scale | | Median M.A. | |
	Mt.	Vill.	Mt.	Vill.	Mt.	Vill.	Mt.	Vill.	Mt.	Vill.
6–8	84	94	..	...	80	93	91	...	89	..
8–10	70	91	..	117	66	82	84	119	76	93
10–12	53	76	66	101	71	69	86	108	70	87
12–14	..	..	67	91	69	73	83	...	83	..
14–16	..	..	52	87	49	70	75	...	73	..

Very recently, Asher (1) has conducted a similar investigation in a mountain county of southeastern Kentucky. The Myers Mental Measure was administered in 15 rural schools to 363 children between the ages of 7 and 16. In 11 of these schools, all children above the second grade were also given the National Intelligence Test; this group included 234 cases. An additional group of 56 children who were absent at the time of testing were subsequently examined with either the Herring or the Stanford Revision of the Binet Scale. The median I.Q.'s on each of these tests were as follows:

National Intelligence Test	71.5
Myers Mental Measure	67.7
Binet Revisions	72.85

A steady age decrement was found,[1] the median I.Q.'s dropping from 83.5 at age 7 to 60.6 at age 15.

Asher calls attention to the serious deficiency in material environment which characterizes these mountain communities. In a final evaluation of his findings, he offers the following comment:

> Of course such comparisons can be made, and one can conclude that mountaineers do not know what other children know or cannot do what other children can do, but it is just about as likely that the city children do not know some of the things that the mountain children know, things that may require as much ability to learn as the things which they do not know (1, p. 485).

The Specificity of Intellectual Differences

There is a growing tendency to envisage group differences in terms of specific abilities rather than in terms of general intellectual inferiority or superiority. The application of this concept to racial and national comparisons has already been discussed (cf. Ch. XVII). In this connection, it was pointed out that each culture "selects" and stimulates certain abilities, skills, and fields of knowledge as the most significant. Through the fostering of certain talents, specific patterns of mental development may be produced within each culture. Under such conditions, any

---

[1] The age analysis was only carried out with scores on the Myers test.

attempts to evaluate the mentality of one culture in terms of another would be misleading and would tend to give a decided advantage to the group within which the measuring instrument was standardized. The same may be true of urban-rural comparisons. Intelligence tests have been standardized almost exclusively on city children, because of the greater accessibility of the latter in large numbers. As a result such tests may be overweighted with items which favor the city child, and may fail to sample adequately those abilities in which the rural child excels.

A direct attack upon this question was made by Shimberg (27). The basic plan of this investigation was to standardize one test on city children and a second parallel test on country children. Both tests were then administered to urban and rural groups, and the relative status of the two groups on *each* test was determined. The particular test selected for this purpose was an *information test*. This choice can be justified on the grounds that, in the first place, such tests are frequently included in intelligence scales.[1] Secondly, even in scales which do not contain a separate information test, specific items of information are called into play in nearly all other tests. Thus a picture completion test, for example, implies the possession of information regarding the characteristic appearance and function of presumably familiar objects.

Each form of the information test consisted of 25 questions. The tests were "scaled," i.e., the questions were arranged in order of difficulty and represented approximately equal increments of difficulty from the easiest to the hardest. This was accomplished by giving a large number of questions to the standardization group and tabulating the percentage of children who answered each correctly. From these percentages, the difficulty value of

[1] Cf., e.g., the Army Alpha.

each question can be computed.[1] In the final step, the 25 questions which are most evenly spaced in difficulty value are selected for inclusion in the *scaled test*. This procedure was followed with 764 urban children for Information Test A and with 416 rural children for Information Test B. It should be noted that no question dealing with items of purely local knowledge was included in either form. Both forms were "fair" to city and country children in the sense that the subjects in either group had some opportunity to acquire the requisite information. There were, in fact, a number of items common to the two forms. In the original series from which the scaled items were selected, 37 questions were identical in forms A and B.

Both scaled information tests were administered to two new groups of urban and rural children.

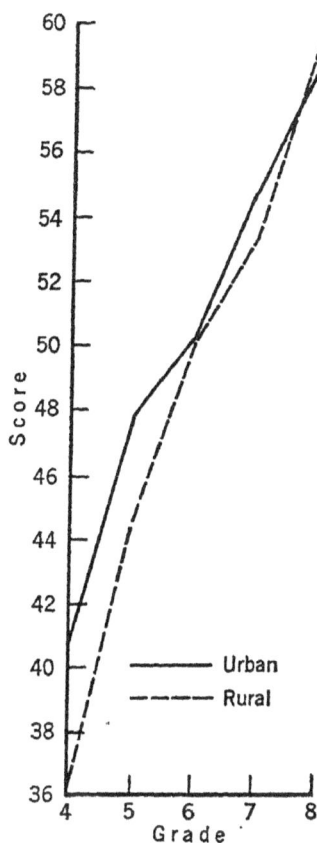

FIG. 51. AVERAGE SCORES OF URBAN AND RURAL CHILDREN ON INFORMATION TEST A; SCALED ON URBAN GROUPS. (Data from Shimberg, 27, p. 45.)

The number of subjects in each category was as follows:

	Urban	Rural
Form A	6477	610
Form B	962	4875

In Table XXXVIII will be found the average scores obtained by urban and rural groups on each form of the test.

[1] For a discussion of these scaling techniques, the reader may consult Garrett, H. E., *Statistics in Psychology and Education*. N. Y.: Longmans, Green, 1937, and McCall, W. A., *How to Measure in Education*. N. Y.: Macmillan, 1923.

The results have been tabulated separately for each school grade. The same data are shown in graphic form in Figures 51 and 52.

It will be noted that on Test A, which was constructed and scaled on city children, the urban groups excel (Figure 51). At grade IV, this difference is 6.5 times as large as its standard error, and at grade V, 4.5 times as large. In the upper grades, the critical ratios are under 3, and at grade VIII the difference is reversed, indicating a very slight and unreliable superiority of the rural group. This reversal is attributed by Shimberg to the more rigid

TABLE XXXVIII

AVERAGE SCORES OF URBAN AND RURAL SCHOOLCHILDREN ON
INFORMATION TESTS A AND B
(After Shimberg, 27, pp. 45, 50)

Grade	Urban		Rural	
	N	Average *	N	Average *
Information Test A †				
4	970	40.7	127	36.3
5	988	47.8	125	44.6
6	955	50.2	116	50.1
7	932	54.7	96	53.3
8	822	58.6	89	59.3
Information Test B †				
4	297	8.31	884	10.67
5	233	9.94	841	13.82
6	276	12.67	804	15.87
7	156	13.61	745	17.60

* The scores on Forms A and B are not expressed in the same terms. The former are transmuted "T" scores (cf. McCall, *op. cit.*); the latter represent the actual number of correct items out of 25.

† Information Test A was also administered to children below the fourth grade, but these were not included in the grade comparisons because of the relatively small number of cases. In this test, therefore, the number of cases given in the table does not cover all subjects tested. Similarly, it was not possible to include all of the subjects who took Information Test B in the grade comparisons reported in this table.

selection operative in the rural groups at the upper school grades. Rural children as a whole, and one-room school pupils in particular, tend to be more retarded than urban groups. As a result, a large percentage of the duller children have left school before reaching the upper grades, and those who remain are a relatively select group. It might be added in confirmation of this explanation that *age comparisons*, from 9 to 16, revealed a consistent superiority of the urban groups on Test A. In terms of age, the rural children were approximately one year retarded on this test.

On Information Test B, the situation is entirely reversed (Figure 52). The rural group is now consistently superior, the differences in its favor being completely reliable at each grade. The critical ratios of these differences are all over 3, ranging from 5.56 to

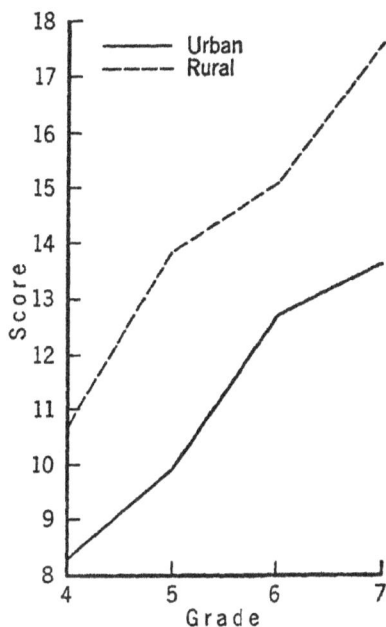

FIG. 52. AVERAGE SCORES OF URBAN AND RURAL CHILDREN ON INFORMATION TEST B; SCALED ON RURAL GROUPS. (Data from Shimberg, 27, p. 50.)

9.33. Thus the hypothesis which this investigation undertook to test seems to have been completely verified. The urban group excelled on the test constructed on city children, the rural group on that constructed on country children. Either group might be ranked "superior" depending upon the specific test employed.

The specificity of urban-rural differences was likewise brought out in a study by Jones, Conrad, and Blanchard (13). The subjects of this investigation were 351 children between the ages of 4 and 13, all of whom lived in rural communities of Massachusetts and Vermont. The Stanford-Binet I.Q.'s of these children were found to be consistently inferior to the test norms established by Terman. It should be noted that Terman's standardization group was drawn chiefly from urban centers.

The performance of the rural children on the Stanford-Binet was analyzed from several angles. In the first place, the "difficulty value" of each individual test was computed from the percentage of children passing it. These difficulty values revealed marked irregularities in the scaling of the Stanford-Binet *when applied to rural samplings*. Thus the tests placed within a single year level were often of uneven difficulty; and the range of difficulty within a single year level was occasionally greater than the difference between successive year levels. This discrepancy between the difficulty values of items for urban and rural children is in line with the findings of Shimberg.

A survey of the performance of the rural group on each test also showed that these children were significantly inferior on only six tests. Their inferiority on other tests, although consistent from age to age, was statistically unreliable. The tests which yielded the largest degree of rural inferiority were: those involving the use of paper and pencil, as in copying a square; those implying specific experiences more common in an urban environment, such as familiarity with coins, street-cars, etc.; and distinctly verbal tests, such as vocabulary and the definition of abstract terms. In all of these cases, the *specific environmental handicap* of the rural child is apparent.

As a further check upon the influence of cultural factors, each of the 50 tests between age levels 4 and 12 of the Stanford-Binet was rated by 10 clinical psychologists for the degree of specific rural handicap involved in it. The averages of these 10 ratings yielded a correlation of .46 with the actual degree of rural inferiority found on each test. That this correlation is not higher is attributed by the authors to the inadequacy of the ratings, since the judges based their decisions upon *a priori* considerations rather than upon actual experience with rural children. The influence of environmental handicap is further attested by the subjects' performance on the four Pintner-Paterson tests which were selected for use in this study. On the Mare and Foal, a picture completion test employing a rural scene, the country children excelled the norms, their average I.Q. being 110. On the Five Figure Form Board and the Knox Cube, involving more abstract materials, they were slightly inferior; and in Digit-Symbol Substitution, a paper-and-pencil test, they were very inferior.

A comparison of the I.Q.'s of successive age groups also proved illuminating. In Figure 53 will be found curves showing the age changes in I.Q. in urban and rural samplings. The urban averages are based on the data collected by Terman in the course of the standardization of the Stanford-Binet. The rural curve shows two clear-cut drops and one rise not to be found in the urban curve. The first drop, occurring between the ages of 4 and 6, may re-

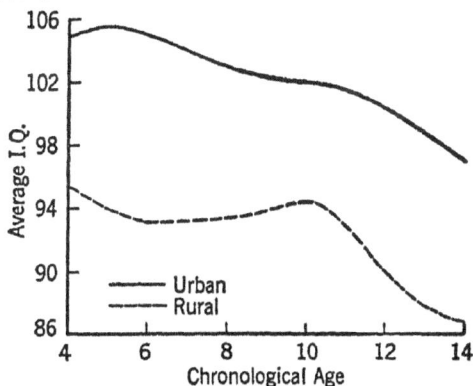

FIG. 53. AGE CHANGES IN AVERAGE STANFORD-BINET I.Q. IN URBAN AND RURAL GROUPS. (After Jones, Conrad, and Blanchard, 13, p. 65.)

flect the general inferiority of home environment. This environmental handicap becomes progressively more effective as the child grows older and his intellectual life becomes more complex. The rise at about age 10, on the other hand, may be attributed to the cumulative effect of schooling which has been gradually counteracting the deficiencies of the home environment. Beyond a certain grade, however, the inadequacies of the schooling too become apparent, in contrast to urban educational facilities. The final drop beyond age 10 may be due in part to inferior schooling in the upper grades and in part to the accumulation, at the upper Stanford-Binet year levels, of verbal items and other tests which are relatively more difficult for the rural child.

An analysis of age curves for *each individual test* supports the latter interpretation. The greatest divergence with age between urban and rural curves is to be found in such tests as vocabulary, dissected sentences, naming 60 words, and word definitions. A diminishing urban-rural difference with age, on the other hand, was found in such tests as ball and field, giving the number of fingers on the two hands, counting 13 pennies, and other predominantly non-verbal tests.

The Mental Development of Farm Children

A very thorough and comprehensive investigation of the mental development of children in farming communities has been conducted by Baldwin, Fillmore, and Hadley (2). The principal data were collected in four rural communities in Iowa. For comparison with urban groups, the test norms were usually employed; data were also obtained for this purpose on a group of children in Iowa City. The youngest subjects, 123 infants between the ages of 4 and 40 months, were examined with the Iowa Baby Tests. The Detroit Kindergarten Test was administered to 163 preschool children between the ages of 3 and 6. A group of 871 schoolchildren was tested with the Stanford-Binet, the Otis Intelligence Test, and some of the Pintner-Paterson performance tests.[1]

The results of this investigation lend strong support to an environmental interpretation of urban-rural differences. Among the rural *infants*, there was no noticeable inferiority on the baby tests. Nor can this lack of differentiation be attributed to a deficiency in the discriminative power of the tests, since wide individual differences were obtained. In the *preschool* group, a rural inferiority appears in the 5- and 6-year-old groups, no significant differences having been found at the younger ages. The rural *schoolchildren*, however, showed a definite mental retardation which became increasingly large as they progressed through school.

This deficiency, furthermore, was more pronounced in the one-room than in the consolidated schools. In the latter type of school, the mentally retarded children were found chiefly at the upper ages; whereas in the one-room schools, the median mental age was always lower than the median chronological age. The median mental age deficit in the one-room schools ranged from 1 to 6 months up to the age of 9; between the ages of 9 and 12 it increased from 7 to 14 months; and at ages 13 and 14 it amounted to 16 and 39 months, respectively. In the consolidated schools, on the other hand, the median mental age exceeded the median chronological age up to the age of 13, the excess for each age ranging from 1 to 8 months. From 13 to 18 years, the median mental age was lower than the median chronological age, the deficit in successive years being 2, 6, 19, 10, 11, and 10 months, respectively. The drop in amount of retardation beyond age 14 may be due to the more select nature of the older groups in rural schools.

---

[1] Mare and Foal, Seguin Form Board, Healy Puzzle A, Ship, and Picture Completion.

An analysis of the rural child's performance on different tests or parts of tests again revealed his handicap with verbal materials. Comparison of the separate tests in the Stanford-Binet Scale yielded results quite similar to those of Jones, Conrad, and Blanchard reported above. Among the performance tests, it is interesting to note that the farm children again excelled on the Mare and Foal. On all other performance tests which involved *speed*, the rural subjects were deficient, their movements tending to be slow and deliberate. The need for speeding alone seemed to provide insufficient motivation. The rate of movement could, however, be increased if other appeals were added, or if the materials came within the subject's range of experience, as in the case of the Mare and Foal test. The authors suggest that:

> The children's apparent lack of comprehension of the meaning of hurry is to be expected as a consequence of some of the influences that surround them (2, p. 254).

Some Data on Selective Migration versus Environmental Handicap

The data on *specificity* of rural inferiority, as well as those on *age changes* in the relative intellectual status of urban and rural children, are especially suggestive of an environmental interpretation of the differences between these groups. Other data in support of such an interpretation have also been cited in the course of the present chapter. A more direct test of the two proposed hypotheses, *viz.*, selective migration and environmental handicap, would be the direct study of migrating groups. Are the individuals who move from a rural to an urban community intellectually superior? How do they compare, as a whole, with those who remain in the country? Is there a rise in mental test score with increasing length of residence in an urban center?

This problem has recently been attacked by Klineberg (17) in a series of very suggestive studies. In one of these investigations, rural Negro children who had migrated to three large southern cities were examined with the National Intelligence Test. All of the subjects were 12-year-old schoolboys, and the majority had been born in the country. A city-born group was also included for comparative purposes. This investigation was part of the general study of selective migration among Negroes which was reported in Chapter XVII. In the data now under consideration, however, the problem of northern and southern Negroes does not enter, since all of the migrations occurred from rural to urban areas *within* the southern states.

The average National Intelligence Test scores of the different residence groups, as well as the number of cases, are shown in Table XXXIX. A definite improvement in test score is to be found with increasing length of residence in an urban environment. The difference is particularly striking if we compare those who had lived in the city for only one year with those who had lived in it for seven years or more. The superiority of the city-born children may be due to their longer residence in the city, all of these subjects having been exposed to an urban environment for 12 years. The intellectual differences among the residence groups may be attributed not only to the varying length of time which the subject had spent in a more favorable environment, but also to the age at which such environmental influences operated. Thus since all subjects were 12 years of age, those in the one year residence group had not been exposed to the urban environment until the age of 11, when they were relatively more immune to the effects of environmental changes. The group with the longest urban residence, on the other hand, had moved to the city at the age of 5 or younger.

TABLE XXXIX

AVERAGE NATIONAL INTELLIGENCE TEST SCORES AND LENGTH OF CITY RESIDENCE

(After Klineberg, 18, p. 197)

Years of Residence	Number of Cases	Average Score
One	39	38.3
Two	25	43.2
Three	36	44.7
Four	47	62.5
Five	52	56.2
Six	53	62.2
Seven and more	165	68.7
City-born	359	74.6

The same general problem was approached from a different angle by a study of the school records of White rural children in New York, New Jersey, and Connecticut who had subsequently migrated to large cities (cf. 18). An analysis of the age-grade location of these children revealed no superiority of the migrating population. The children who had subsequently moved to cities were no more often accelerated and just as often retarded in rural schools as those who stayed behind. In a number of rural counties in these states, intelligence test scores were available for most of the schoolchildren. An examination of these scores showed the same results, viz., no tendency for those who migrated to the city to be initially superior in intelligence test performance.

Thus from several converging lines of evidence, it would seem that the inferiority of rural children on the current tests of intelligence results from environmental handicap rather than from a process of selective migration which might drain the rural areas of their "better stock." To be sure, selective migration may operate in specific areas, or at certain periods, but it cannot be applied as a general rule without a direct analysis of the historical and social factors at work in each particular case. A comparison of rural and urban environments, on the other hand, has always revealed adequate evidence to account for the observed intellectual differences. Finally, the *specificity* and *relativity* of such urban-rural differences must be borne clearly in mind in any attempt to evaluate the intellectual merits of the two groups.

REFERENCES

1. Asher, E. J. "The Inadequacy of Current Intelligence Tests for Testing Kentucky Mountain Children," *J. Genet. Psychol.*, 1935, 46, 480–486.

2. Baldwin, B. T., Fillmore, E. A., and Hadley, L. *Farm Children*. N. Y.: Appleton, 1930. Pp. 337.

3. Bickersteth, M. E. "Application of Mental Tests to Children of Various Ages," *Brit. J. Psychol.*, 1917, 9, 23–73.

4. Book, W. F. "Variations in Mental Ability and Its Distribution among the School Population of an Indiana County." *Bull., Ext. Div., Indiana Univ.*, 1918, 4, No. 4, 100–131.

5. Campbell, J. C. *The Southern Highlander and His Homeland*. N. Y.: Russell Sage Foundation, 1921. Pp. 405.

6. Duff, J. F., and Thomson, G. H. "The Social and Geographical Distribution of Intelligence in Northumberland," *Brit. J. Psychol.*, 1923, 14, 192–198.

7. Estabrook, A. H. "Blood Seeks Environment," *Eugenical News*, 1926, 11, 106–114.

8. Frost, N. "A Comparative Study of Achievement in Country and Town Schools." Teachers College, Columbia Univ., *Contrib. to Educ.*, No. 11, 1921. Pp. 70.

9. Hinds, J. H. "Comparison of Brightness of Country and City High School Children," *J. Educ. Res.*, 1922, 5, 120–124.

10. Hirsch, N. D. M. "An Experimental Study of the East Kentucky Mountaineers," *Genet. Psychol. Mon.*, 1928, 3, 183–244.

11. Hollingworth, L. S. *Gifted Children.* N. Y.: Macmillan, 1926. Pp. 374.

12. Irion, T., and Fisher, F. C. "Testing the Intelligence of Rural School Children," *Amer. Schoolmaster*, 1921, 14, 221–223.

13. Jones, H. E., Conrad, H. S., and Blanchard, M. B. "Environmental Handicap in Mental Test Performance," *Univ. Calif. Publ. in Psychol.*, 1932, 5, No. 3, 63–99.

14. Kempf, G. A., and Collins, S. D. "A Study of the Relation between Mental and Physical Status of Children in Two Counties in Illinois," *U. S. Public Health Rep.*, 1929, 44, 1743–1784.

15. Kephart, H. *Our Southern Highlanders.* N. Y.: Outing Pub. Co., 1913. Pp. 395.

16. Klineberg, O. "A Study of Psychological Differences between 'Racial' and National Groups in Europe," *Arch. Psychol.*, No. 132, 1931. Pp. 58.

17. ——. *Negro Intelligence and Selective Migration.* N. Y.: Columbia Univ. Press, 1935. Pp. 66.

18. ——. *Race Differences.* N. Y.: Harper, 1935. Pp. 367.

19. Lehman, H. C., and Witty, P. A. *The Psychology of Play Activities.* N. Y.: Barnes, 1927. Pp. 242.

20. Pressey, L. W. "The Influence of Inadequate Schooling and Poor Environment upon Results with Tests of Intelligence," *J. Appl. Psychol.*, 1920, 4, 91–96.

21. Pressey, S. L., and Thomas, J. B. "A Study of Country Children in a Good and a Poor Farming District by Means of a Group Scale of Intelligence," *J. Appl. Psychol.*, 1919, 3, 283–286.

22. Pintner, R. *The Mental Survey.* N. Y.: Appleton, 1918. Pp. 116.

23. ——. *Intelligence Testing: Methods and Results.* N. Y.: Holt, 1931. Pp. 555.

24. Pyle, W. H., and Collings, P. E. "Mental and Physical

Development of Rural Children," *Sch. and Soc.*, 1918, 8, 534-539.

25. Raine, J. W. *The Land of Saddle Bags: a Study of the Mountain People of Appalachia.* N. Y.: Pub. Jointly by Council of Women for Home Missions and Missionary Educ. Mov. of the U. S. and Canada, 1924. Pp. 260.

26. Sherman, M., and Key, C. B. "The Intelligence of Isolated Mountain Children," *Child Dev.*, 1932, 3, 279-290.

27. Shimberg, M. E. "An Investigation into the Validity of Norms with Special Reference to Urban and Rural Groups," *Arch. Psychol.*, No. 104, 1929. Pp. 84.

28. Thomson, G. H. "The Northumberland Mental Tests," *Brit. J. Psychol.*, 1921, 12, 201-222.

CHAPTER XX

THE INDIVIDUAL AS A MEMBER OF MULTIPLE GROUPS

Differential psychology, in its broadest sense, is concerned with all variations in behavior phenomena among individuals and among groups. The observation and measurement of such differences have led to the accumulation of a vast body of descriptive material which has proved scientifically interesting and practically useful. Examples of such material have been given throughout the present book. The fundamental aim of differential psychology is not, however, the collection of descriptive material. Its aim is similar to that of all psychology, *viz.*, the understanding of behavior. Differential psychology approaches this problem through a comparative analysis of behavior under varying environmental and biological conditions. By relating the observed differences in behavior to other known concomitant phenomena, it may be possible to tease out the relative contribution of different factors to behavioral development. If we can determine why one person reacts differently from another, we shall know what makes people react as they do.[1]

The unit of differential psychology is the individual, conceived as a reacting organism. Our interest in groups is only secondary. Traditional groupings, furthermore, have proved to be arbitrary and ill-defined. From the standpoint of behavioral development, the effective groupings

---

[1] For a further discussion of this general point of view in reference to other fields of psychology, the reader is referred to Foley (3, 5).

are stimulational and not biological. It is not the race, or sex, or physical "type" to which the individual belongs by heredity that determines his psychological make-up, but the cultural group in which he was reared, the tradi-tions, attitudes, and points of view impressed upon him, and the type of abilities fostered and encouraged.

In the present chapter, some of the major conclusions of differential psychology will be brought together. These conclusions have been suggested by the analysis of both individual and group differences presented throughout the book. An attempt will be made to interpret and integrate the scattered pieces of evidence offered by different in-vestigations. The information furnished by the study of groups will also be reformulated in terms of the individual, and the implications of such data for the behavioral development of the individual will be examined.

STRUCTURE AND FUNCTION

The fundamental question of heredity and environment runs through all of the problems covered by differential psychology. Heredity is the prime factor in the develop-ment of structural characteristics, although a "normal" physical environment is presupposed in every case. Especially important in this connection is the prenatal environment. Physical or chemical variations in the stimulation of the developing embryo have been shown to produce drastic departures from the "normal" course of growth. The experimental production of one-eyed, two-headed, and other forms of monsters will be recalled by the reader (cf. Ch. III). On the whole, however, the wide range of structural variation which we see about us in the organic world can be traced to specific hereditary con-stitution. Whether a given germ cell will develop into a chicken, or a monkey, or a man is a matter of heredity.

Similarly, certain major structural differences among members of a given species can be traced to innate properties. Even this generalization, however, must be applied with a certain measure of caution, as is illustrated by the structural modifications noted in second generation immigrants (cf. Ch. XVI).

The proper domain of psychology is the behavior of individuals. Structure is to be considered only insofar as it sets certain limitations to the development of behavior. An individual cannot learn to fly if he has no wings; he cannot play certain musical combinations if his fingers are too short. If he is born with a defective thyroid, his movements will very probably be slow and sluggish and his general behavior dull and stupid.

We cannot, however, overgeneralize from such facts. In the first place, the presence of a given structure will not necessarily lead to the development of any specific function. If a child who is in every way structurally normal, with normal vocal organs, nervous system, auditory mechanism, etc., be confined in a room by himself from early infancy, he will be unable to speak. If we gave such a child an intelligence test, knowing nothing of his environmental background, we should probably classify him as an idiot. Secondly, and conversely, the absence or deficiency of a given type of behavior does not *imply* any structural deficiency as its cause. The absence of language in the above example is a case in point.

Within the limits set by the individual's structural characteristics, there are almost infinite possibilities for varied behavioral development. The tremendous scope of these possibilities is gradually being recognized by students of behavior. Nor is it correct in this connection to speak of realizing one's potentialities or of falling short of such a realization. One type of development is not necessarily better or higher than another, but just different.[1] The individual's potentialities of behavioral development, furthermore, are not something definitely or specifically predetermined. To use a crude analogy, it is as though one had some flour with which could be prepared a wide variety of cakes. We cannot say that any one cake is the realization of the potentialities of the flour, any more than any other cake. They are just different results which can be achieved with the available materials. In fact, there is no intrinsic characteristic of the flour which would necessitate cake-making of any sort.

Experiential Determination of Behavior

That the previous experience of the individual affects his present behavior is a well-established fact. Even the simplest *perceptual responses* are influenced by the subject's preceding reactions.[2] Whether we judge a stimulus as light or heavy, long or short, hot or cold, pleasant or unpleasant, depends in part upon the immediately preceding stimuli. What we observe, as well as what we remember within a given situation is determined largely by our mental set. This mental set was in turn established by some previous experience. Our very conception of the world about us thus seems to be influenced by our own specific reactional history. A purely "impartial" or "objective" observer is a psychological impossibility. Each individual's observation and description of any fact is conditioned by his special past experiences as well as by the more general traditions and customs inculcated by his group.

The effect of experiential background upon *intelligence test performance* has been repeatedly demonstrated. The decrease in I.Q. with age among children reared in a

---

[1] Cf. especially the discussions of this point in Chs. XVII and XIX.

[2] For several interesting examples, see Sherif (22), Ch. III.

restricted environment is evidence of this fact. It will be recalled that in investigations on canal-boat and gypsy children in England (Ch. III) as well as those on mountain children in the Kentucky highlands (Ch. XIX), little or no inferiority was noted in the youngest age groups. As the child grows older and his intellectual demands increase, however, the environmental handicap becomes increasingly apparent in his test score. The case studies of identical twins reared apart also illustrate the degree of intellectual differentiation which may result from environmental variation (Ch. V). Recent studies on migrating groups likewise furnish clear-cut evidence of the effect of a change to a better environment upon the child's "intelligence." The migrating individuals, not initially superior to their group average, showed a steady rise in intelligence test score with increasing length of residence in a more "favorable" environment (Chs. XVII and XIX). Cross comparisons among racial and national groups also suggested that intellectual differences are predominantly cultural and not biological (Ch. XVIII).

In the development of *emotional responses*, the rôle of experiential factors is being rapidly recognized. This was demonstrated in many of the findings on sex differences (cf. Ch. XV). Thus the divergence of boys' and girls' scores with age on a test of emotional instability suggests the increasing differentiation of the sexes under the demands of their social milieu. It will be recalled that, whereas no appreciable sex difference in the number of neurotic symptoms was found at the youngest age levels, the girls' average became progressively higher than that of the boys in the older groups. The recent researches of Terman and Miles (23) revealed many lines of evidence pointing to the rôle of environment. The degree to which the individual displayed the characteristic masculine or feminine personality of our society could in many instances be traced to his education, occupation, domestic milieu, and general experiential background. Similarly, the observations of Mead (17) in three primitive societies suggested a cultural determination of the conventional male and female patterns of emotional response. In connection with personality development, mention may also be made of the cross-comparisons of racial and institutional groups among college students (Ch. XVIII). It will be recalled that an analysis of the subjects' responses on a series of personality tests showed large differences from one educational institution to another, but only negligible differences among the Nordic, Alpine, and Mediterranean groups.

A particularly interesting illustration of the effect of experience upon behavior is furnished by *æsthetic preferences* and artistic "taste." The evolution of styles in music, painting, sculpture, architecture, and the other fine arts testifies to the shifting demands of "taste." The styles which are derided as harsh, barbaric, and uncouth by one generation have often been accepted as masterpieces by the next. Any artistic innovation which clashes too vigorously with the familiar and the traditional forms of artistic expression requires a period of gradual habituation. It is an unfortunate but perhaps psychologically indispensable fact that the great art leaders who are subsequently hailed as the initiators of new movements suffer the greatest ridicule and derision during their lifetime. This follows necessarily from the fact that they come at a time when the adequate experiential background for the enjoyment of their products is lacking.

The question of the sophisticated and the naïve observer is also relevant to this point. The trained critic or the sophisticated observer has had certain specific experiences which enable him to enjoy artistic products that may appear meaningless, indifferent, or even unpleasant to others. Psychologically, there is no "naïve critic"; such an individual is naïve only from the standpoint of a specific class of experiences. His judgments are, however, directly influenced by other experiences which he has had. His artistic reactions will be largely dictated by common everyday observations and popular fashions. Thus the observer may enjoy realistic art because he is more familiar with photographic reproductions of objects; or he may reflect some traditional artistic conception which has been inculcated in him from early childhood. But in no case is his judgment made independently of experience. The essential difference between the sophisticated and the naïve observer is in the *kind* of past experience which they have had.

A very suggestive experimental approach to the question of æsthetic preference was made by Moore (18). The specific problem under investigation was the experience of consonance and dissonance in music. In surveying the history of Occidental music, Moore finds a progressive change in the point of separation between consonance and dissonance. Intervals which were considered dissonant at one period were accepted as consonant in the next. The transition occurred from those intervals in which fusion of the notes is easily obtained to those in which fusion is more difficult. As the newer intervals came into use, the intervals which fused more readily declined in popularity. The preferred intervals at any one period seem to have been those which were "just consonant," i.e., those in which fusion was neither too easy nor too difficult. The former were regarded as relatively uninteresting, the latter as dissonant.

As an experimental check upon this "genetic" theory of

consonance, Moore analyzed the judgments of nine subjects on four musical intervals. Two of these intervals were considered dissonances (major and minor 7th) and two consonances (3rd and 5th) at the beginning of the experiment. The subjects underwent a period of habituation in which all four intervals were repeatedly experienced in musical passages. The judgments obtained at the end of this period showed certain unmistakable changes in the relative preference for each interval. Of the two initially consonant intervals, the 3rd lost rapidly in affective value, while the 5th maintained a fairly constant level. The dissonances, on the other hand, showed a gain in preference, the minor 7th gaining more rapidly than the major 7th. According to Moore's theory, the region of highest affective value for an interval is the "barely consonant" region. The greatest changes with repetition were therefore to be expected in the intervals nearest this region, viz., the 3rd on the one hand and the minor 7th on the other. This experiment furnishes a vivid demonstration of the dependence of artistic "taste" and æsthetic judgments upon experiential factors.

Even in the realm of science, where "objective truth" presumably reigns supreme, the effect of the individual's past experience cannot be eliminated. The data of science admit of various interpretations. One or another of such interpretations may seem to follow inevitably from the given facts, depending upon the observer's experiential background. This is exemplified by the various approaches of different sciences to the same phenomenon, as well as by the presence of distinct "schools" within a single science. There are "fashions" in science as in art. The general cultural milieu of the period is reflected in the nature of its scientific products and theories as in other phases of human activity. It is not a coincidence that certain basic similarities can be found in such diverse phenomena as the science, art, social structure, and economic policies of any given period. The setting for all such developments is the common experiential background of the people of that age.

SPECIFICITY OF BEHAVIORAL DEVELOPMENT

Since all types of behavior are influenced by the subject's stimulational background, it follows that psychological data obtained within any one cultural group cannot be generalized to cover all human behavior. Many statements offered under the heading of general psychology are not general at all, but are based upon human behavior as it develops within a single culture.[1]

Theories of developmental *stages* furnish a good illustration of the tendency to overgeneralize from observations within a single group. Child psychology is replete with such theories. Much interesting material has been gathered, for example, on the formation of *concepts* in childhood. The child's ideas about the physical world, his consciousness of self, his interpretation of dreams, and similar conceptions have been analyzed into definite developmental sequences. Outstanding in this field are the theories of the Swiss psychologist, Piaget (19, 20).

In an extensive series of investigations, Piaget arrived at the conclusion that the thinking of the child is *animistic* and that the transition from this initial animism to the adult's conception of the world is made through four major stages. For children between the ages of 4 and 6, everything active is alive. Since children of this age are also anthropocentric, "activity" is regarded as synonymous with usefulness to man. Thus the sun is active

---

[1] For a fuller discussion of such limitations, see Foley (3), Klineberg (9), and Sherif (22).

because it gives warmth, stones are active because you can throw them. At this first stage, therefore, all objects are considered to be alive and conscious. In the next stage (6–7 years), only movable objects are believed to be alive. In the third stage (8–10 years), life is attributed only to things which can move spontaneously. Thus the sun and a river are alive, but an automobile is not. In the final stage (11 years on), life is restricted to animals and plants, or sometimes to animals only.

Such stages have been commonly accepted as an inevitable or natural development through which the child must pass. There are, however, numerous factors within the experience of a child in our society which might account for such animistic tendencies. The language which the child is taught encourages him to form an animistic conception of the world. Thus he hears the sun referred to as he, and the moon or a ship as she. Figurative expressions, such as the rising and setting of celestial bodies, the running brook, and the howling wind, are not conducive to an impersonal conception of natural phenomena. If to this are added the fancies of poetry, fairy tales, and other imaginative literature, it is apparent that the child's experience has a strongly animistic flavor. It is not until he has had the opportunity to accumulate a certain amount of information from direct observation of cause and effect in everyday situations, that such a child can arrive at a realistic notion of the world.

Some corroborative data on this interpretation are to be found in the investigations of anthropologists on children in different cultures. Thus Mead (15, 16) found no evidence of animism among children of the Manus tribe in New Guinea. Both the spontaneous remarks of these children and their replies to questioning revealed a very realistic conception of natural objects and events. The drifting away of a canoe, for example, was not attributed to supernatural causes but to the fact that it was not fastened. Mead attributes this realistic attitude of thought to the type of training which such children receive. From early childhood they are forced to make a correct adjustment to the physical demands of their environment. The responsibility for a mishap is never shifted to an inanimate object, as in blaming the log if the child trips over it. If the child hurts himself, he is told that it is the result of his own clumsiness. It is interesting to note that in certain respects in this culture the adults are more animistic than the children, since they explain sickness, death, and other misfortunes as the activity of "spirits."

Emotional development and personality adjustments have also been analyzed from the point of view of "stages." The most widely discussed of such stages is probably the period of "storm and stress" characteristic of the adolescent. Almost all writers on child psychology ascribe emotional upheavals, personality changes, conflicts, and maladjustments to this age. There is evidence, however, to show that this is not a universal phenomenon. In certain societies (cf., e.g., 14, 16), the adolescent assumes his altered status, both physical and social, without emotional disturbance. His tasks are cut out for him by tradition; there are no momentous choices and decisions to be made; no mystery attaches to his position; and no trace of embarrassment is encountered.

There is much in our society, on the other hand, which fosters adolescent maladjustments. Thus the individual is placed in an ambiguous and ill-defined position, being treated neither as a child nor as an adult. Restrictions upon his actions are frequently increased, while at the same time he is expected to be more self-reliant than heretofore. Embarrassment and a general atmosphere of mystery are often directly induced by adults through their attitudes, remarks, and actions. In view of the many experiential factors in our society which might lead to adolescent maladjustments, there seems to be no need to posit an innate or physiological basis to the storm and stress of this period, nor to regard it as a necessary developmental stage.

Another phase of child behavior in which the concept of developmental stages has been widely applied is *drawing*. Children's drawings have been collected in large numbers and submitted to detailed analyses, in the hope that they might furnish a cue to the child's mentality. Thus, for example, a scale for measuring general intelligence has been elaborately constructed and standardized from drawing behavior. In this scale, the child is directed to draw a picture of a man; his mental level is then determined by allotting specific points of credit for each detail or characteristic of the drawing (cf. 6). The extensive literature on children's drawings reveals a widespread belief among psychologists in the existence of definite developmental sequences in drawing behavior. These stages are generally regarded as products of maturational factors and are assumed to be independent of specific environmental stimulation. The drawings characteristic of each age level are believed to be distinguishable in subject-matter as well as in many aspects of technique and execution.

Such generalizations in regard to the drawing behavior of children are, however, limited to certain specific groups with a common experiential background. Spontaneous drawings by children of different national and cultural groups have been gathered and described by several investigators.[1] These data bring out very clearly the part

[1] For a survey of this literature, see Anastasi and Foley (1).

played by the child's environment in determining every phase of his drawing behavior. Thus the type of object most frequently drawn at each age showed a wide variation from one group to another. In the studies on American children (cf., e.g., 10, 11, 13), drawings of the human figure predominate at the younger age levels. That this is not a universal tendency among young children has, however, been repeatedly demonstrated. In a study on Swiss children, for example, the human figure occupied a relatively insignificant position, miscellaneous objects and houses heading the list (8). Representations of people are likewise infrequent or almost completely absent in the drawings by children from several other countries (cf. 1). In general, the subject-matter of children's drawings varies so widely from group to group as to make any attempted universal classification quite meaningless.

Similar differences are apparent in all other aspects of the drawings (cf. 1). Whether the child draws broad panoramic views or scenes at close range, isolated objects or organized pictures, imaginative themes or realistic portrayals seems to depend in large measure upon his specific environmental milieu. In certain groups, the drawings are full of action (cf., e.g., 12), in others stationary objects and figures predominate. The organization of the picture likewise differs from one group to another. In some a single unified scene is presented, in others a sequence of events, in still others isolated objects. The degree to which color is employed, as well as the choice of specific hues, usually reflects the influence of both physical environment and social traditions.

The representation of detail brings out some interesting facts. In certain groups, detail is relatively poor, total impressions and broad vistas being emphasized. In others, the minutest details are painstakingly drawn into the picture. An even more significant point, however, is the specificity of the details which are represented. Thus among a group of children belonging to a hunting tribe in Siberia, remarkably accurate and naturalistic drawings of reindeer and elk were obtained (21). These drawings were clearly superior to those of the human form or of any other subject executed by the same children. It should be noted that none of these children had had previous experience in drawing. The investigator points out that the sharpened visual perception, manual dexterity, and keen observation fostered in such a hunting tribe probably influenced the accuracy of the drawings, especially when the objects represented were the animals commonly hunted by the tribe.

This tendency to elaborate those details which are specifically observed and which play an important part in the individual's everyday activities, while ignoring other details, is very commonly found in children's drawings. Examples can easily be multiplied (1). Thus in drawings by European children, vegetation is portrayed only in a general way, with no attempt to show specific type or variety. The children from many tropical and semi-tropical countries, on the other hand, often feature fruit trees and dense forests as a major part of the drawing and include sufficient detail to indicate the particular type of plant pictured. One group of drawings by Hungarian and Czecho-Slovakian children, although crude in other respects, showed minute and carefully executed details in the peasants' gowns. In drawings by American Indian and Balinese children, elaborate details occurred in the ceremonial masks and head-dress, in contrast to the paucity of detail in other objects. In the light of such findings, it is impossible to regard the richness of detail, general technique, or any other feature of the child's drawing as an index of his developmental stage.

Theories of *mental organization* are a further example of the specificity of many psychological facts. Little is known about the relationship of mental traits in different cultural groups. Results obtained with various educational and occupational groups within our society would, however, lead us to suspect that widely dissimilar patterns of mental organization may exist. If we limited ourselves to descriptive analyses of trait relationships within our own culture, we might propose developmental stages in mental organization as in other aspects of behavior. Thus it will be recalled (cf. Ch. XI) that investigations on schoolchildren usually reveal a large and significant general factor which might correspond roughly to the common conception of general intelligence. As the child grows older, an increasing differentiation of abilities is manifested, with the appearance of more numerous and broader group factors. Investigations at the college level show the general factor to be relatively insignificant, the subject's abilities now being organized into a number of independent group factors.

That this sequence of development is not fixed by innate constitution is suggested by the experimental alteration of trait relationships through the interpolation of specific experiences (Ch. XI). It also follows that the pattern of trait relationship established within any one cultural group is not necessarily universal for the age under consideration. By stimulating the development of certain abilities and ignoring others, by specialization of education and vocations along certain clearly defined lines, and by many social traditions and other factors, each culture may determine the pattern of mental organization among its members, as well as the progressive changes in such a pattern.

"Normal" and "Natural" Behavior

The influence of cultural factors is also reflected in the varied conceptions of "normality" which are found in different groups. Psychologically, all behavior follows normally from its antecedent conditions—there is no essential distinction between the mechanism of normal and abnormal behavior. Abnormality can have meaning only in a statistical sense, as a more or less pronounced deviation from a norm. This norm is socially determined by the specific demands and traditions of life within any given group. Thus it follows that behavior which is considered normal in one group may be looked upon as distinctly abnormal in another.

Examples of intercultural variations in the definition of normality can readily be found.[1] The *line of demarcation* between normal and abnormal behavior is drawn at different points from one group to another. Thus a violent display of emotion may be regarded as normal in one group and classified as definitely neurotic in another. Similarly, the *direction* of deviation from the norm is evaluated in terms of specific cultural standards. The inferior or subnormal deviate of one society may be acclaimed as a genius or leader in another. Those personality traits which may lead to the greatest maladjustment in one culture often make for the most satisfactory and successful adjustment in another. Nor should this be construed to mean solely that the misfits of "civilization" may be well-adjusted in a "primitive" society. The reverse may just as often be the case. The misfit in a "primitive" group would as a rule be more likely to make a satisfactory adjustment in a different culture than would the individual who is well-adjusted and "normal" in his own group.

[1] See Ch. XII for references.

Another popular concept which needs to be revised in the light of recent findings is that of "natural" behavior. Certain ways of acting have long been regarded as "natural." This designation usually implies that the behavior in question is "normal" as well as innate and biologically predetermined. Closely related to this concept are those of "perversion" and "reversion." The former refers to behavior which is considered unnatural; the latter implies a revival or reënstatement of a more "primitive" and less "artificial" type of behavior. Thus if one type of behavior is assumed to be *natural*, then any environmentally produced variation of such behavior is considered a *perversion*. Similarly, if a "civilized" person be put in a "primitive" environment, the behavioral changes which may ensue are regarded as a *reversion* to a natural state. The latter is implicitly assumed to have existed all along, but to have been held in abeyance, so to speak, by conditions in a civilized community. It is apparent that the concepts of perversion and reversion have meaning only as long as one specific way of behaving is assumed to be the "natural" way.

It has been repeatedly demonstrated, however, that no one form of behavior is any more natural than another in the sense of being predetermined by innate constitution. The data on this question are derived chiefly from two sources. The first is the *experimental production* of behavioral variations. A number of such experiments on infrahuman organisms have been reported in Chapter III. The import of their results was to show that different types of behavior will follow as a natural result of varying environmental conditions. Much so-called instinctive behavior has been shown to be natural only under given environmental conditions.

The same point has been demonstrated by *intercultural*

comparisons. Many forms of behavior which have been labeled "instincts" and "fundamental drives" are found to differ significantly from one cultural group to another.[1] Thus the rôle of cultural factors in the expression of the *maternal drive* is illustrated by the widespread custom of adopting children, which is practiced among several Melanesian, South African, and American Indian groups. In certain tribes, children are so infrequently reared by their own parents that it is very difficult to obtain genealogies. *Aggressiveness* and *fighting*, popularly considered to be among primitive man's natural impulses, are unknown among several groups. In certain tribes, no weapons or implements of warfare are to be found. That men should attack each other seems inconceivable to individuals reared in certain cultural groups. Similarly, *acquisitiveness* and the desire for personal property are not a universal phenomenon.[2] The manifestations of the *sex drive*, with its attendant feelings such as love and jealousy, likewise exhibit wide intercultural variations. The diverse customs and conventions associated with mating behavior in different groups have been extensively described by anthropologists and many are undoubtedly familiar to the reader. Finally, mention may be made of the sets of rules and restrictions imposed by different societies upon many forms of behavior, including aggressiveness and physical violence, reaction to personal property, sex activities, and others. The wide variations in such restrictions show them to have little or no basis in "human nature" as such. The moral code of one society often appears as a quaint set of taboos to another.

The traditional sex differences in intelligence and in

---

[1] For many illustrations of this point, see Klineberg (9) Ch. XIV, and Sherif (22) Ch. VIII.

[2] See Beaglehole (2) for a comprehensive treatment of this question.

personality traits are another case in point. It was long considered "natural" for the sexes to differ in general mentality and especially in aptitude for scientific pursuits and similar branches of learning. Men, too, were regarded as naturally more stoical, less given to emotional displays, more competitive, less sympathetic. If a given individual displayed the intellectual or personality traits of the opposite sex, this was considered "unnatural." An understanding of the experiential basis of such behavioral characteristics shows the artificiality of such a distinction between natural and unnatural behavior.

NATURE AND VARIETY OF PSYCHOLOGICAL GROUPS

Psychologically the individual belongs to every group with which he shares behavior.[1] From this point of view, group membership is to be defined in terms of stimulational value rather than biological categories. The effective grouping is not based upon the individual's race or sex or physical characteristics, but upon his experiential background. Thus if the individual is reared as a member of a certain national group with its own traditions and cultural background and its own peculiar complex of stimulating conditions, he will display the behavioral characteristics of that group regardless of his racial origin. It should be understood, of course, that mere physical presence does not constitute group membership in a psychological sense. Thus if a Negro child were brought up in a community composed exclusively of Whites, he would not necessarily receive the same social stimulation as a White child. Similarly, a boy who is brought up exclusively by female relatives will not develop the per-

---

[1] This criterion of a psychological group is essentially that formulated by Kantor (7) who seems to have been the first to discuss social behavior in terms of *shared responses* to objects having common stimulus functions.

sonality traits of a girl. An experiential group is based solely upon shared behavior and not upon geographical proximity or biological resemblance.

It follows from such a concept of group that any one individual is effectively a member of a large and varied set of groups. A multiplicity of behavioral groups, large and small, cut across each other in the individual's experiential background. Some of the most important of these groups have already been discussed in Part II of the present book. The individual is born into a broad cultural division such as, for example, "western civilization" with its characteristic sources of stimulation. He will develop certain intellectual aptitudes, emotional traits, attitudes, and beliefs as a result of his affiliation with this group. He is also a member of a given national group with its more specific traditional ways of acting.

If the individual displays certain physical characteristics, such as a particular skin color, facial conformation, body build, etc., he may be classified as a member of a given "racial " group which occupies a distinct position within the broader national division. Insofar as his racial background leads to certain social distinctions and culturally imposed differentiations of behavior, it will operate as an effective grouping. The same may be said of sex. If, within a given society, traditional beliefs in regard to sex differences exist so that the sexes are exposed to dissimilar psychological stimulation, then the individual's sex will in part determine his behavioral characteristics.

There are a number of other behavioral groupings which, although less frequently recognized and less clearly defined, may be equally effective in the individual's development. Thus it will be recalled that important psychological differences are usually found between the city-bred and country-bred child (cf. Ch. XIX). Similarly, the particular state, province, or other major division of a nation in which the individual is reared, and even the specific neighborhood in which he lives, will exert a significant influence upon his intellectual and emotional development (cf. Ch. XVII). Other groups with which an individual identifies himself behaviorally are his occupational class, his religious sect, his political party, his club, his educational institution. That such groupings represent true cultural distinctions is readily illustrated by the associations which have become attached to each. To people within our society, a distinct picture will be suggested by the mention of such designations as country doctor, business man, Roman Catholic, Orthodox Jew, Republican, Rotarian, Harvard man. These groups influence the individual's behavior in two ways. First, they directly stimulate and foster certain ways of acting. Secondly, the reactions of other people to the individual are influenced by his group affiliation. The social attitudes and "social expectancy" which the individual encounters will in turn affect his behavior.

Family background and traditions frequently constitute an important part of the individual's psychological environment. The famous Herreshof family of boat-designers and builders, the degenerate Kallikaks, eminent families such as the Huxley's and the Darwin's, and many other striking examples testify to the cultural influence of family membership. Cutting across such family groupings are age distinctions. "Stages" are socially imposed upon the continuous life activities of the individual and he is treated more or less differently at each period. The individual may also look upon himself as belonging to a particular generation—he may be a member of the "younger set," the "present generation," the "older generation," and so forth. Even such apparently minor factors as one's hobbies and recreations will in turn react upon the individual and alter his subsequent behavior. Effective membership in many new experiential groups may result from a sudden interest in stamp collecting or early American glass. The number of behavioral groupings could easily be multiplied. These examples will suffice to illustrate the nature of such groupings and their effect upon the individual.

The Meaning of Individuality

The individual may be regarded partly as a resultant of his multiple group memberships. To be sure, each individual also undergoes experiences which are absolutely unique to himself. Such experiences are probably less significant, however, in shaping the more basic aspects of his personality than is his shared behavior. The experiences which are common to a group of individuals have a certain degree of permanence in the sense that they will tend to be repeated more often and to be corroborated or reënforced by other similar experiences. In general, the more highly organized the group, the more consistent and systematic will be the experiences which its members undergo. This will tend to make the shared experiences on the whole more effective than the purely individual.

In view of the pronounced effect of such shared or common behavior upon the individual's development, it may appear surprising that individuals are no more alike in their behavior repertoire than we ordinarily find them to be. The extent of individual differences within any one group is extremely large. In fact, the variations among individuals have always proved to be more marked than the differences from one group to another. How can the complete "individuality" of each person be explained in terms of his shared experiential background?

The key to this problem seems to lie in the *multiplicity* of overlapping groups with which the individual may be behaviorally identified. The number of such groups is so great that the *specific combination* is unique for each individual. Not only will this furnish an experiential basis for the existence of wide individual differences, but it also suggests a mechanism whereby the individual may "rise above" his group. There are many examples of individuals who have broken away from the customs and traditional ways of acting of their group. Through such situations, the modification of the group itself may also be effected.

In these cases the individual is not reacting contrary to his past experience, as might at first appear. This would be psychologically impossible. His behavior is the result of psychological membership in various *conflicting* groups. Many group memberships can exist side by side in a composite behavioral adjustment. But in certain cases two or more groups may foster different ways of reacting to the same situation. This enables the individual to become aware of the arbitrariness of the restrictions and traditions of each group, to become critical of them, and to regard them more "objectively." Membership in many unlike groups frees the individual from the intellectual and other limitations of each group and makes possible the fullest development of "individuality."

REFERENCES

1. Anastasi, A., and Foley, J. P., Jr. "An Analysis of Spontaneous Drawings by Children in Different Cultures," *J. Appl. Psychol.*, 1936, 20, 689–726.

2. Beaglehole, E. *Property: A Study in Social Psychology.* N. Y.: Macmillan, 1932. Pp. 327.

3. Foley, J. P., Jr. "The Comparative Approach to Psychological Phenomena," *Psychol. Rev.*, 1935, 42, 480–490.

4. ———. "The Criterion of Abnormality," *J. Abn. Soc. Psychol.*, 1935, 30, 279–291.

5. ———. "Psychological 'Ultimates': a Note on Psychological 'Fact' versus Psychological 'Law,'" *J. Gen. Psychol.*, 1936, 15, 455–458.

6. Goodenough, F. L. *Measurement of Intelligence by Drawings.* Yonkers, N. Y.: World Book Co., 1926. Pp. 177.

7. Kantor, J. R. *An Outline of Social Psychology.* Chicago: Follett, 1929. Pp. 420.

8. Katzaroff, M. D. "Qu'est-ce que les enfants dessinent?" *Arch. de psychol.*, 1909–10, 9, 125–133.

9. Klineberg, O. *Race Differences.* N. Y.: Harper, 1935. Pp. 367.

10. Lukens, H. J. "A Study of Children's Drawings in the Early Years," *Ped. Sem.*, 1896, 4, 79–110.

11. Maitland, L. "What Children Draw to Please Themselves," *Inland Educ.*, 1895, 1, 77–81.

12. ———. "Notes on Eskimo Drawings," *Northwestern Monthly*, 1899, 9, 443–450.

13. McCarty, S. A. *Children's Drawings.* Baltimore: Williams and Wilkins, 1924. Pp. 32.

14. Mead, M. *Coming of Age in Samoa.* N. Y.: Morrow, 1928. Pp. 297.

15. ———. *Growing Up in New Guinea.* N. Y.: Morrow, 1930. Pp. 372.

16. ———. "The Primitive Child." Chapter 24 in *Handbook of Child Psychology*, C. Murchison, ed. Worcester, Mass.: Clark Univ. Press, 1933. Pp. 956.

17. ———. *Sex and Temperament in Three Primitive Societies.* N. Y.: Morrow, 1935. Pp. 335.

18. Moore, H. T. "The Genetic Aspect of Consonance and Dissonance," *Psychol. Mon.*, 1914, 17, No. 73. Pp. 68.

19. Piaget, J. *The Child's Conception of the World* (transl. by J. and A. Tomlinson). N. Y.: Harcourt, Brace, 1929. Pp. 397.

20. ———. "Children's Philosophies." Chapter 12 in *Handbook of*

Child Psychology, C. Murchison, ed.   Worcester, Mass.: Clark Univ. Press, 1933. Pp. 956.

21. Schubert, A. "Drawings of Orotchen Children and Young People," *J. Genet. Psychol.*, 1930, 37, 232–244.

22. Sherif, M. *The Psychology of Social Norms.* N. Y.: Harper, 1936. Pp. 209.

23. Terman, L. M., and Miles, C. C.   *Sex and Personality: Studies in Masculinity and Femininity.* N. Y.: McGraw-Hill, 1936. Pp. 600.

AUTHOR INDEX

SUBJECT INDEX

.

www.ingramcontent.com/pod-product-compliance
Lightning Source LLC
Chambersburg PA
CBHW030632270326
41929CB00007B/42